CONFUCIANISM AND SACRED SPACE

Confucianism and Sacred Space

THE CONFUCIUS TEMPLE FROM
IMPERIAL CHINA TO TODAY

Chin-shing Huang

TRANSLATED BY
Jonathan Chin with Chin-shing Huang

Columbia University Press
New York

Columbia University Press wishes to express its appreciation for assistance given by the Chiang Ching-kuo Foundation for International Scholarly Exchange and Council for Cultural Affairs in the publication of this book.

Columbia University Press
Publishers Since 1893
New York   Chichester, West Sussex
cup.columbia.edu
Copyright © 2021 Columbia University Press
All rights reserved

Library of Congress Cataloging-in-Publication Data
Names: Huang, Jinxing, author. | Chin, Jonathan (Translator), translator.
Title: Confucianism and sacred space : the Confucius temple from imperial China to today / Chin-shing Huang ; translated by Jonathan Chin with Chin-shing Huang.
Description: New York : Columbia University Press, 2021. | Includes bibliographical references and index.
Identifiers: LCCN 2020014408 (print) | LCCN 2020014409 (ebook) | ISBN 9780231198967 (hardback) | ISBN 9780231198974 (trade paperback) | ISBN 9780231552899 (ebook)
Subjects: LCSH: Temples, Confucian—China. | Confucianism—China.
Classification: LCC BL1882.C6 H8313 2021 (print) | LCC BL1882.C6 (ebook) | DDC 299.5/1235—dc23
LC record available at https://lccn.loc.gov/2020014408
LC ebook record available at https://lccn.loc.gov/2020014409

Cover image: Confucian temple at Qufu, the ancestral temple in Confucius's hometown and the "original" temple. Rebuilt in 1724. Courtesy of Cultural Relics Publishing House, Beijing, 2010
Cover design: Chang Jae Lee

Contents

Preface vii

Introduction: The Confucius Temple as a Ritual System: Manifestations of Power, Belief, and Legitimacy in Traditional China 1

I Expanding the Symbolic Meaning and Function of the Rites: The Evolution of Confucius Temples in Imperial China 21

II Confucianism as a Religion: A Comparative Study of Traditional Chinese Religions 58

III Sages and Saints: A Comparative Study of Canonization in Confucianism and Christianity 88

IV The Cultural Politics of Autocracy: The Confucius Temple and Ming Despotism, 1368–1530 125

V Xunzi: The Confucius Temple's Absentee 149

VI The Disenchantment with Confucianism in Modern China 171

VII The Lonely Confucius Temples Across the Taiwan Straits:
The Difficult Transformation of Modern China's
Traditional Culture   198

Conclusion: Reflections on My Study of Confucianism
as a Religion   212

Notes   229
Bibliography   299
Index   323

Preface

The Holy Grounds of Confucian Religion

In his analysis of religions, famous theologian and historian of religion Mircea Eliade (1907–1986) highlighted sacred space, sacred time, and myths as essential attributes of religion—a thesis that led to much academic discussion.[1] Although Confucius temples are obviously the holy grounds of Confucianism, fortuitous factors unrelated to Eliade's work inspired my research of the temples. Many years ago, by sheer chance, I visited the Confucius temple in Taipei with a friend, an excursion that initiated an intellectual pilgrimage into the world of these temples. Historically, Confucius temples dotted the entire East Asian landscape, spreading far and wide, from China to Korea, Japan, Ryukyu, and Taiwan, with Vietnam at the southernmost reach of their limit. Although each region's temples were marked by certain local characteristics, they represent a supraregional cultural phenomenon that deserves attention. Confucius temples are magnificent sanctuaries invested with deep cultural and political significance.

That Confucius temples are the holy grounds of Confucianism is an irrefutable fact, easily proven by perusing historical texts. For example, Feng Menglong 馮夢龍 (1574–1646) of the Ming dynasty included a statement in his compiled *Tales Old and New* (*Gujin xiaoshuo* 古今小說) that reads:

> Since the ending of the primordial chaos, there were the Three Religions: Taishang Laojun 太上老君 founded Daoism, the Buddha founded Buddhism, and Confucius founded Confucianism. Confucianism yields sages, Buddhism yields bodhisattvas, and Daoism yields immortals. Among the three, Confucianism is the most commonplace and Buddhism is the most austere; however, Daoist teachings promise immortality and infinite transformative powers, which makes it the most liberating.[2]

Though the author obviously had a bias favoring Daoism, it is important that he acknowledged that Confucian sages were directly comparable to bodhisattvas and immortals as virtuous exemplars of a religion. Furthermore, as the holy grounds of Confucianism, Confucius temples performed the same roles that shrines and temples played for other religions. *Record of the Rebuilding of a Qingzhen Temple*, dating to the year 1489, during the Ming dynasty, proclaimed:

> In my humble opinion, each of the Three Religions glorifies its founding master by establishing halls and shrines. Confucians have Dacheng halls 大成殿 to glorify Master Confucius, Buddhists have Shengrong halls 聖容殿 to glorify Sakyamuni Buddha, and Daoists have Yuhuang halls 玉皇殿 to glorify their Three Pure Ones 三清. In Qingzhen 清真 temples, Yicileye halls 一賜樂業殿 are erected to honor God.[3]

The fact that the Dacheng hall—the main structure of the Confucius temple—was directly commensurate to the temples of Buddhism, Daoism, and Judaism showed that Confucius temples were sacred spaces fully invested with religious meaning and symbolism. My project, then, is to excavate the religious nature and character of Confucianism through the history of its temples.

Over the past thirty years, I have dedicated myself to the study of Confucius temples. Certainly it has been a long and exciting intellectual journey, with very rewarding results. Conceptualizing temples as the holy ground of Confucianism is a perspective that could shed light on many aspects of traditional society, including the intellectual, political, social, and religious dimensions of imperial China.

Conventionally, the problem of whether Confucianism is a religion is tackled via philosophical, theological, or textual analysis of the classics, such as *The Analects* and *The Doctrine of the Mean*. I consider these methodologies to be reductionist, essentialist, and unfruitful. Instead, my analysis of Confucianism as religion is inspired conceptually by Ludwig Wittgenstein's (1889–1951) "family resemblance," which takes into account the diverse and variegated nature of religions. Furthermore, I treat Confucius temples as the sacred sites of Confucianism. Beyond the addition of historical and anthropological analysis, I approach these places with the viewpoint of historical subjects in mind. In brief, I argue that deciding whether Confucianism is a religion is a question of history, not of philosophy or theology. A historical question can be answered only by evaluating Confucianism in its original context. To consider Confucius temples as arrangements of scared space is to ground the study of Confucianism on practices that are tangible and accessible to analysis.

With this understanding in mind, I will briefly introduce the arrangement of this book. Chapter 1 is a relatively recently written and published essay, "Expanding the Symbolic Meaning and Function of the Rites: The Evolution of Confucius Temples in Imperial China," which sums up much of my work exploring Confucius temples as a cultural phenomenon. Taking a broad overview, this essay traces the historical process through which Confucius temple rites were integrated with the system of imperial rites, and thus approaches both from a broad cultural perspective. Formerly, my studies focused on the origins of Confucius temple rites, with particular attention to the interactions between the literati and imperial rulers. This chapter shifts the focus to an institutional level, especially the dynamics of structural changes within Confucius temple rites throughout history.

Although particular aspects of the rites varied in time and place, they generally conformed to operations of imperial ritual systems. As an institution, Confucius temple rites were either a "Symbol," with an uppercase S, or "symbols" in the plural. Confucian temple rites existed in China for more than two thousand years, and over time they acquired new meaning and functions through the process of generation and accretion. Compared to my earlier studies of Confucius temples, this essay has two distinctly new findings. First, the central court and local governments, particularly in late imperial China, continued to expand the scope and elevate the status of

Confucius temple rites. Second, as the sacred space of a state religion, Confucius temples embodied the exclusive and monopolistic tendencies of the official state.

Chapter 2, "Confucianism as a Religion: A Comparative Study of Traditional Chinese Religions," addresses why and how Chinese-speaking people have questioned Confucianism's religiosity since the founding of the republic in 1911. Using internal comparisons, this chapter shows that traditional Chinese society had always thought of Confucianism, Buddhism, and Daoism as its three religions. I raise the question: Why is it that modern Chinese society only places Buddhism and Daoism in the taxonomical category of religion, whereas traditional Chinese society included all three?

Chapter 3, "Sages and Saints: A Comparative Study of Canonization in Confucianism and Christianity," takes a cross-cultural approach to compare Confucianism's institution of enshrinement with Christianity's institution of canonization, in order to emphasize Confucian religiosity and its political and social implications.

Chapter 4, "The Cultural Politics of Autocracy: The Confucius Temple and Ming Despotism, 1368–1530," focuses on the reform of the Confucius temple system by Emperor Shizong 世宗 (r. 1521–1566) of the Ming dynasty. It demonstrates how China's rulers were able to weaken and transform the temples' cultural symbolism to strengthen autocratic rule. I will show that Confucius temple rites were contested and fought over by imperial rulers and scholar-officials.

Chapter 5, "Xunzi: The Confucius Temple's Absentee," addresses the practice of Confucius temple enshrinement through the example of Xunzi, the great pre-Qin scholar and philosopher. It aims to show the intertwined political and intellectual factors that effected great changes in Xunzi's enshrinement throughout history.

Chapter 6, "The Disenchantment of Confucianism in Modern China," addresses an issue that arises if the preceding analysis is correct; that is, modern Chinese largely refuse to think of Confucianism as a religion, a phenomenon that begs explanation. This chapter narrates the process of Confucianism's decline from imperial China's state religion to a mere collection of "nonreligious" teachings in the late Qing and the early republic. The narrative illustrates that the controversy over Confucianism's religious taxonomy was a conflict rooted in a highly specific historical context rather than in a philosophical inquiry.

Chapter 7, "The Lonely Confucius Temples Across the Taiwan Straits: The Difficult Transformation of Modern China's Traditional Culture," speaks to the predicament of Confucianism in modern Chinese societies. Moreover, it suggests that the depoliticization of Confucianism is perhaps the only hope for reviving the temples' system of rites in today's Chinese-speaking societies.

The book's final chapter, "Reflections on My Study of Confucianism as a Religion," is a retrospective examination of my basic theoretical perspective and methodological approach in researching the cultural phenomenon of Confucius temples. This could be considered a companion piece to chapter 6, and it also aptly serves as the conclusion to the whole volume.

Although scholarly attention to the Confucius temple has perhaps not been phenomenal in recent years, it is certainly quite strong, and theses and monographs continue to be published internationally. Although my research on Confucius temples began many years ago, I am immensely pleased to see works by other scholars who break new ground or bring new understanding to the field.[4] In the past three decades, my work has focused exclusively on the Chinese Confucius temples as a whole system, whereas my understanding of local Confucius temples is somewhat lacking in granular detail. In particular, I have not conducted research of the temples on a cross-regional or cross-cultural basis and thus must leave that task to others, in the hope that they will bring their own sympathetic understanding to traditional culture.

I dedicate this book to the memory of Professor Li Yi-yuan 李亦園 (1931–2017) and Professor Anthony C. Yu 余國藩 (1938–2015), in gratitude for their steadfast support for my study of Confucius temples. Professor Li was a renowned Taiwanese anthropologist who made vital contributions to the development of an indigenous approach to Taiwanese anthropology. In college, I took his Introduction to Anthropology course, and later many of his other classes; I remember his course on primitive religions particularly vividly. Those lessons Li taught were to have an abiding influence on my approach to studying the religiosity of Confucius temples.

For many years, Professor Anthony C. Yu taught at the University of Chicago, where he was widely respected as the rarest type of humanist, who demonstrated mastery over the study of both China and the West. The history of religions was one of the fields of his topical concern. Although I met him in person just once, in Taipei, and in spite of our age difference, we became fast friends and frequently exchanged views online.

In recent years, he persistently urged me to write a monograph in English that would summarize my research on Confucius temples, in order to facilitate dialogue with Western historians of religions. Professor Yu believed that the focus of my writing on religious sacred space was distinctive and that Western scholars in the field of comparative religions should consult my work.

Although these mentors repeatedly urged me to publish in English to encourage international academic exchange, it is to my great regret that I threw myself into this project only after their passing. Ultimately, I selected eight essays for translation, out of a total of sixteen that I authored over the three decades I researched the topic, because these are most suited for an English-speaking audience.

Mr. Jonathan Chin 金振玄 was responsible for translating most of the main texts; Dr. Lin Yicheng 林易澄 was responsible for translating the scholarly apparatus, Ms. Chen Ching-fen 陳靜芬 proofed and organized the texts, Professor Hoyt Tillman copyedited, and I was the overall editor in chief. In putting together the final manuscript, Ms. Linda Chu did the final proofread and indexing. I sincerely thank them for their tireless efforts, which were indispensable for completing this difficult and laborious project. Any errors in the book are ultimately my responsibility as the author. I hope the publication of my book will contribute to a meeting of minds as learned friends around the world discuss and contribute to our continuing efforts to improve our understanding of Confucianism and East Asian culture.

Finally, a generous research grant by Taipei Medical University, from 2016 to 2018, made this translation project possible. I am honored that this book is among those for which Professor David Wang of Harvard University has secured support from the Chiang Ching-Kuo Foundation for International Scholarly Exchange.

Chin-shing Huang
Institute of History and Philology
Academia Sinica
Taipei, Taiwan

CONFUCIANISM AND SACRED SPACE

Introduction

The Confucius Temple as a Ritual System: Manifestations of Power, Belief, and Legitimacy in Traditional China

Before proceeding with our analysis, it is necessary to give a general account of Confucius temples, including the particular characteristics that defined them and the formative historical processes that produced them. Specifically, a Confucius temple was defined by three things: the involvement of the sage's descendants in the conduct of its rites, being invested with political legitimacy, and being invested with cultural legitimacy in the form of Confucian enshrinement.

The spirit of the May Fourth Movement in 1919 is most clearly captured by the slogan "Down with the Confucian shop." That year, Chen Duxiu 陳獨秀 (1879–1942) called for the abolition of all Confucius temples and their ritual practices.[1] During the proletarian Cultural Revolution in the 1960s, his wish achieved its greatest fulfillment, as Red Guards desecrated and ransacked Confucius temples. Although the Confucius temple at Qufu 曲阜 was restored in the 1980s and is sometimes used to stage Confucian rites before international audiences, the anti-Confucian spirit of the May Fourth Movement still largely prevails, almost a century after the original movement began, and it continues to cloud contemporary understanding of Confucian rituals and spirituality.

My research culminated in one Chinese-language book situating the Confucius temple in Chinese history and another Chinese book comparing the enshrinement of Confucian sages and Catholic saints. The

Figure 0.1 Tomb of Confucius.
Photo by Chin-shing Huang

present English-language volume includes some chapters from those two books, along with other related articles; this introduction seeks only to provide a context for or overview of the significance in traditional China of worship in the Confucius temple. Whereas my Chinese publications give very detailed historical analysis and presentation of the institutional and ritual changes in the temple's function at numerous points in history, this introduction will focus on structural issues instead.

The phrase *"you ru shengyu"* 優入聖域, which I render as "entering the master's sanctuary," has two meanings: to appreciate the spirituality of Confucius's teaching and/or to physically to enter the sacred ground of the Confucius temple (Kongzi miao 孔子廟).[2] Even though the temple was, by definition, dedicated to the worship of Confucius (Kongzi 孔子, 551–479 BCE), the sacrifices performed there were, over the centuries, extended to his most prominent followers as well. While they were worshipped within the Confucius temple, some distinguished Confucians also had their own temples. Among these, temples to Yanzi 顏子 (c. 521–481 BCE), Mencius

Figure 0.2 Confucian temple at Qufu, the ancestral temple in Confucius's hometown and the "original" temple. Rebuilt in 1724.
Cultural Relics Publishing House, Beijing, 2010

孟子 (c. 372–c. 289 BCE), and Zhu Xi 朱熹 (1130–1200 CE) stand out as the most important, but these should be viewed as the derivative subsystem of the Confucius temple. Although the Confucius temple as an institution and ritual system spread beyond China proper to other East Asian countries, such as Japan, Korea, Taiwan, and Vietnam, I confine my exploration here to the Confucius temple in traditional China, and particularly to its ritual performances.

Institutionally speaking, there are at least three elements vital to the practice of the Confucius temple as a ritual system: Confucius's descendants, the spread of Confucius temple worship beyond the place of its origin, and finally Confucian enshrinement (*congsizhi* 從祀制). Each of these has made its own historical impact on the formation of the Confucius temple as the locus of a state cult, and I will discuss them in turn.

Figure 0.3 Ritually equal in importance with the one in Qufu, the Confucian temple at Beijing was politically at the center of academic instruction for the whole empire. Photo by Chin-shing Huang

Sage's Descendants

The term "sage's descendants" (*shengyi* 聖裔) refers to the official branch of the Kong family that takes charge of making sacrifice to their ancestor, Confucius. The "official" branch is the so-called legitimate heir to Confucius in terms of both direct bloodline and approval from political rulers.

The Confucius temple in its initial form was a private ancestral shrine. When Confucius passed away in 479 BCE, he was buried by his disciples, because his only son, Kong Li 孔鯉 (532–483 BCE), had predeceased him, and his grandson, Kong Ji 孔伋 (483–402 BCE), was simply too young. According to the rite to which a deceased nobleman of low rank (*shi* 士) was entitled, a shrine was set up to worship Confucius.[3] He had enjoyed a positive reputation as a great scholar and educator in his lifetime; therefore, both tomb and shrine soon attracted large numbers of admirers, either to pay respect or to perform rituals there. To revere the memory of Confucius, some of his students and compatriots (people of the state of Lu) even moved and settled in the area around his tomb.

Figure 0.4 Dismounting stele in front of the Confucius temple. Chinese inscription reads, "Officials and citizens, dismount from your horses here."
Photo by Chin-shing Huang

These households, it was reported, numbered more than one hundred, and thus the place was named Kong village (Kongli 孔里).⁴

Because it was immovable and could not be duplicated, the tomb had limitations as a ritual center. In view of subsequent developments, Confucius's shrine, rather than his tomb, has played the much more important role as the paradigm for worshipping Confucius. His personal belongings—including clothes, lute, chariot, and books—were stored in his shrine, and these cultural treasures undoubtedly enhanced the shrine's fame as a cultural resource. It became a sacred place and attracted pilgrims, a fact that was afterward witnessed and recorded by the grand historian, Sima Qian 司馬遷 (c. 145–86 BCE), in the middle of the Western Han.⁵

In short, after the death of Confucius, his image became increasingly prominent through the dissemination of his doctrine by his disciples. Together with those of Mozi 墨子 (c. 480–389 BCE), his teachings stood out as the most "prominent learning" (*xianxue* 顯學) in China of the late classical period, and each continued to attract considerable numbers of followers long after their masters had passed away.⁶ The influence of the Confucian school was further attested to by Fu Su's 扶蘇 (242–210 BCE) worries. The crown prince, Fu Su, advised Qin emperor Shihuang 秦始皇 (r. 221–210 BCE) not to provoke unrest in the state by persecuting students who admired and followed Confucius.⁷

Fu Su's concern suggests the popularity of the Confucian school in the late third century BCE. Even though Liu Bang 劉邦 (256–195 BCE), the founding Han emperor Gaozu 漢高祖 (r. 202–195 BCE), was notorious for his contempt for Confucian scholars and publicly humiliated them, he did not refrain, when passing through the state of Lu, from paying his respects at the temple and offering full sacrifice (*tailao* 太牢) of an ox, a sheep, and a pig to Confucius. Soon thereafter, a convention became established in the early Han that local officials in that area paid respect to Confucius's shrine before undertaking their other duties.⁸

Moreover, from the early Han onward, the nature of Confucius's shrine gradually underwent a great transformation. It was the Han emperor Liu Bang who first bestowed an official title (*fengsi jun* 奉嗣君) on a descendant of Confucius. However, the title was limited to Kong Teng 孔騰 (fl. 195 BCE), from the ninth generation of Confucius's descendants, and was thenceforth discontinued.⁹ In the year 8 BCE, the court adopted Mei Fu's 梅福 petition that created a ritual category for worshipping Shang dynasty ancestors and designated Confucius as a descendant of the Shang clan to receive sacrifices. Thus, Han emperor Chengdi 漢成帝 (r. 32–7 BCE) conferred the noble title Marquis of Yinshaojia 殷紹嘉侯 on Kong Ji 孔吉, a descendant of the major lineage (*dazong* 大宗) of Confucius, and put him in charge of the sacrificial offerings.[10] Mei Fu's justification for state sacrifices for Confucius deserves attention, for he complained:

> Until now [worship in] the Confucius temple has not gone beyond Queli 闕里 [its original clan location]. His descendants are treated as commoners. It is not the will of heaven for a sage to receive sacrifice merely as a commoner does. If Your Majesty ennobles Confucius's descendants on account of his great cultural achievements, the state will receive blessing and the honor of Your Majesty will endure as long as heaven![11]

Moreover, by virtue of the fact that Mei Fu confessed that, in reality, Confucius was not a legitimate heir to the Shang house, it seems that Mei Fu and other scholars were concerned with enhancing the worship of Confucius rather than with preserving the Shang lineage. Their proposal should be regarded as only the first move to implement the glorification of Confucius.

In the year 1 CE, the Han imperial court adopted two additional measures. Confucius for the first time received an official posthumous title, Duke Baocheng Xuanni 襃成宣尼公.[12] A descendant of Confucius in the sixteenth generation of minor lineage (*xiaozong* 小宗) also received a title, Marquis Baocheng 襃成侯, and thus was given sole and full responsibility for offering sacrifice to Confucius. This title and assigned task became fixed and inherited.[13]

Both of these measures were decreed by the Han emperor Ping 漢平帝 (r. 1 BCE–6 CE) but were actually initiated by the usurper, Wang Mang 王莽 (r. 9–23). Because the state had already extended sacrificial privileges to Confucius as a prominent descendant of the Shang house, the newly added status for his descendant—even if selected from one of his minor lineages—conveyed much more meaning than ancestral worship alone. Implicitly, the descendants of Confucius henceforth performed sacrificial duty not only for their clan but also for the government. The Confucius temple had thus undergone a major transformation, from a mere private family temple (*jiamiao* 家廟) to an official ceremonial institution.

During the reign of the Eastern Han emperor Huan 東漢桓帝 (r. 146–167), the Confucius temple became so impersonal that the local official of the state of Lu discovered, in the year 153, that the Kong families did not take care of temple affairs on a daily basis but rather came only on prescribed sacrificial occasions of the four seasons. Hence, he requested that the court follow the precedent set at Biyong 辟雍 (the Royal Academy), where sacrifices to Confucius were completely sponsored by the government and certain Kong families were officially assigned the duty of making them.[14] This reveals that previously the government had taken the worship of Confucius at the Royal Academy more seriously than the worship at the Confucius temple in Queli; moreover, such state action further politicized the rite of worshipping Confucius.

Even though the dynastic state transformed the Confucius temple into an official institution, it preserved a certain character of ancestral shrine. This was particularly true for the Confucius temple in Queli. As evident in extant maps, even into the Song, Ming, and Qing periods, the Confucius temple there still contained a tiny shrine for the Kong family within its boundary (see figure 0.5).[15]

The situation at the original Confucius temple location was in sharp contrast to Confucius temples in other localities, where the Kong family shrine was not continued. Although the support and preservation of Confucius's lineage were obviously required to legitimize the political rulers' claims regarding the worship of Confucius, the example of the presence or absence of a Kong family shrine on the grounds of the temple suggests some of the complexity of the relations between the rulers and the sage's descendants. The underlying or potential tension found concrete expression in Ming Taizu's 明太祖 (r. 1368–1398) personal letter to Kong Kejian 孔克堅 (1316–1370). When the Kong descendant excused himself from an audience with the emperor, Ming Taizu responded angrily:

> I am told that you have been sick for a long time, but I wonder if this is true. Your Kong family is a distinguished house known for your ancestor's teachings, which generation after generation of rulers have followed. Your family has served different dynasties over time and should surely make no exception to this rule when it comes to my regime. I have received the mandate of heaven to lead the Chinese people and drive away the barbarians in order to bring peace to China.

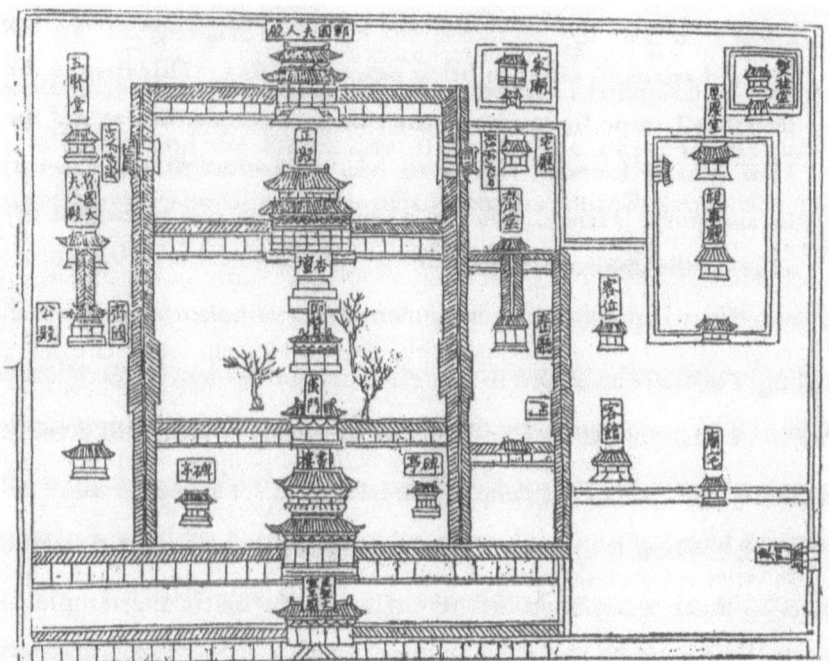

Figure 0.5 The Confucius temple of Que-li in the Song period.
From Kong Yuan-cuo 孔元措, *Kongshi zuting guangji* 孔氏祖庭廣記, in *Congshu jicheng chubian* 叢書集成初編, vol. 3316–3317 (Shanghai: Commercial Press, 1939), 8.

This despite the fact that I arose from among the common people, but so did the Han dynasty founder, Gaozong [*sic*; Gaozu] in antiquity. Hence, it is not permissible for you to neglect my state on the pretext of illness!¹⁶

Ming Taizu was aware that it was essential for Confucius's descendants to recognize his newly established regime if it was to achieve legitimacy in the eyes of the people. He later even set a rule for all of his successors: when they ascended the throne, they should dispatch officials to make a sacrifice and report to Confucius in the temple of Queli.¹⁷

Regarding all the honors the Ming founder bestowed upon the Kong family, Ming emperor Wuzong 明武宗 (r. 1505–1521) simply remarked, "It is the high glory of my state, but not your clan's honor alone!"¹⁸ This concise statement explains the stance of Ming and other rulers toward the Kong family over the centuries. In fact, because of the wars at the end of the

Han dynasty, the fief of the Kong family was eradicated and the direct line of Confucius's descendants was terminated.[19]

Later rulers resorted to many means in their search for a suitable Kong family to serve as the sage's official descendant. Whenever the lineage was interrupted, rulers did not hesitate to construct an artificial one out of expediency. Furthermore, as often happened during the period of division called the Northern and Southern dynasties, rulers of rival states set up contending lineages to support their competing claims for cultural legitimacy. When China was reunited, the newly established dynasty sometimes designated a minor lineage of the Kong clan as the legitimate line of the sage's descendants—all at the expense of what had been the major lineage.[20] This was seen in the case of the Yuan dynasty. Thus, politically designated succession within the Kong clan obviously overrode the standard Chinese rule of blood ties and further politicized the Kong family as the sage's descendants.

In other words, although the Kong family was itself a cultural symbol, it was manipulated by rulers as a political tool in power struggles over the centuries. As a result, a number of inconsistencies between official history (*zhengshi* 正史) and family pedigree records (*jiapu* 家譜) were inevitably created in descriptions of Confucian genealogy.[21] In spite of these inconsistencies, the Kong family was still given the privilege of claiming "one lineage through ten thousand generations" (*wanshi yixi* 萬世一系).

The Proliferation of the Confucius Temples Through Political Struggles for Legitimacy

The worship of Confucius spread only gradually through the period from after the Han to the mid-Tang. As early as the year 59, the Eastern Han emperor Ming 東漢明帝 (r. 57–75) and the state required everyone attending schools in China to worship two sagely teachers: the Duke of Zhou 周公 (c. 1100–1032 BCE), and Confucius.[22] The Duke of Zhou fell into oblivion shortly after the fall of the Han Empire and lost his status as a patron of scholars. In contrast, the cult of Confucius retained its importance as long as interest endured in the classics he edited. Rulers, after having received the teaching of classics, were also accustomed to making a ritual offering to Confucius. For example, King Qi of Wei 魏齊王 (r. 239–253) finished reading the *Analects* 論語 in 241, the *Book of Documents* 尚書 in 244, and the

Book of Rites 禮記 in 246. On each of these occasions, he sent an official on his behalf to make full offering to Confucius in the Royal Academy.[23] Some Eastern Jin rulers, such as Cheng 東晉成帝 (r. 325–342), Mu 穆帝 (r. 344–361), and Xiaowu 孝武帝 (r. 372–396), performed the ritual worship to Confucius personally.[24]

Even on such occasions when the ruler was personally involved, though, the rite of venerating Confucius still was only performed in the Royal Academy. During the Jin period, no place other than Queli was ever specified as having a Confucius temple. However, by the mid-Tang period, there were seven hundred to one thousand Confucius temples in the areas directly controlled by the government. Such figures did not even include the Confucius temples in "loose-rein" prefectures (*jimi zhou* 羈縻州) beyond Tang state control.[25] Thus, what happened from the fourth century to the seventh century is crucial to our understanding of the proliferation of Confucius temples.

When, why, and how was a second Confucius temple set up? The second Confucius temple demands scrutiny because in terms of symbolism it signified a clear departure from the original model of having only one temple. It set an institutional precedent for later Confucius temples, erected at places other than Queli. Such proliferation was possible only after the Confucius temple was ritually viewed as no longer merely an ancestral shrine but primarily a state temple for official rites.

With the breakdown of the Han Empire, the legitimate line of the sage's descendants ended, and the Confucius temple in Queli fell into ruin as well. Thirty years later, in 221, the new ruler of northern China, Wei emperor Wen 魏文帝 (r. 220–226), ordered a search for the sage's possible descendants. As a result, Kong Xian 孔羨 was set as the twenty-first-generation descendant of Confucius, and a temple on the old base was built to worship Confucius.[26] In addition, dormitories surrounding the temple were added to accommodate students, an educational undertaking that could be taken as the harbinger of the temple school system in later dynasties.

However, from the middle of the third century to the early seventh century, Qufu, where the Confucius temple was located, was repeatedly ravaged by war due to nomadic invasions from Central Asia. As a battleground, the area became desolate, and the Confucius temple was destroyed and lay in ruins for as long as an entire century at a time.[27] During this period, the worship of Confucius scarcely continued. Those retreating from northern China established the Eastern Jin regime in the South, and in the year 385, a court official from the Eastern Jin passed through Qufu. Seeing the ruins of the Confucius temple and lamenting over the misfortunes of Confucius, the official petitioned the court to rehabilitate the worship of Confucius.[28] capital

Thus it was Emperor Xiaowu of the defeated royal house of Jin who reinstated, in 386, the whole system of Confucius worship in the southern Jiankang 建康. He designated a certain Kong family as the sage's legitimate descendants and built the first Confucius temple outside of Queli.[29] Court officials debated vigorously in trying to determine the proper rites for the Confucius temple in the capital, and thus we can ascertain that this reestablishment of worship of Confucius was culturally very significant to people in South China.[30]

Inspired by Emperor Xiaowu's precedent, later rulers established a Confucius temple in their own capitals, and this triggered a series of competitions between different states. For instance, both Southern Qi emperor Wu 南齊武帝 (r. 482–493) and Northern Wei emperor Xiaowen 北魏孝文帝 (r. 471–499) set up a Confucius temple in their capitals in the same year (489).[31] For rulers such as Emperor Xiaowen of the Northern Wei, in 489; Northern Zhou emperor Xuan 北周宣帝 (r. 578–579), in 580; and Tang Gaozu 唐高祖 (r. 618–626), in 619, the construction of a new Confucius temple in the capital was given even higher priority than the rehabilitation of the old Confucius temple in Queli.[32] These rulers' dependence on the Confucius temple for political legitimacy was pressing and direct.

Confucius temples further spread down to the local level. Northern Qi emperor Wenxuan 北齊文宣帝 (r. 550–559) decreed in 550 that every prefectural school (*zhouxue* 州學) ought to include a Confucius temple.[33] In 630, Tang Taizong 唐太宗 (r. 626–649) ordered that a Confucius temple be erected in every county school (*xianxue* 縣學), the lowest unit of state-sponsored education.[34] Confucius temples thus combined state ideology with education, and thereafter, the preservation or the establishment of a Confucius temple became the duty of the local official. In contrast to Emperor Wen of Wei's practice, the Confucius temples in the early Tang were attached to schools, rather than vice versa. The Tang merger marked the completion of the temple school system. In time, Confucius temples outnumbered state schools, because the temple's operation was clearly stipulated as a ritual duty for local officials; moreover, it was less demanding to maintain a temple than to manage a school.[35] In Ming-era China, it was estimated that there were more than 1,560 Confucius temples.[36]

The ranks of rituals were divided into two separate categories. The Confucius temple of Queli and the Confucius temple in the dynasty's capital belonged to the same ritual level. Both stood out as the exemplars for others, but each possessed a unique symbolic function. While culturally the Confucius temple in Queli was regarded as the symbol of the tradition of the Way and served as the primordial model to imitate,[37] the Confucius temple in the dynasty's capital was politically the center of academic instruction for the whole empire. Moreover, the ritual worship at the capital was conducted either by the ruler in person or by high officials on his behalf. The remaining Confucius temples belonged to a second ritual level, and the highest local officials performed the worship there on special occasions during the spring and autumn. The prescribed rituals were one rank below the former two temples.[38] These Confucius temples served as local agents of state ideology, exemplifying cultural correctness for the empire.

Confucian Enshrinement

In ancient China, there was no precedent for disciples or followers to be worshipped along with their master (*shi* 師), but the cult of Confucius developed a code of enshrinement for Confucian scholars.[39] In Confucian context, enshrinement meant to be enshrined posthumously with Confucius in the Confucius temple, a supreme honor for which all Confucian scholars could hope. Ideologically, enshrinement reflected Confucian consciousness regarding orthodoxy, or what Confucian scholar-officials regarded as the true meaning of the Confucian tradition. When Xiong He 熊鉌 (1253–1312) claimed that the establishment of the Confucius temple was done for the sake of the transmission of the Way (*daotong* 道統), he was specifically referring to the practice of enshrinement.[40] Enshrinement, taken as a whole, was indeed tantamount to the embodiment of the Confucian transmission of the Way in its totality.

Individually, to be canonized meant that one's contribution to the transmission of the authentic Way was universally recognized by the Confucian community (at least at a particular time). The value placed on enshrinement within the Confucian community can be illustrated particularly well by the case of Wang Yangming 王陽明 (1472–1529). A court meeting (*tingyi* 廷議) in 1584 was to decide whether the tablet of Wang Yangming should be enshrined in the Confucius temple. When the debate became heated, Tao Dalin 陶大臨 (1526–1574), a sympathizer with Wang, tried to calm down Lu Shusheng 陸樹聲 (1509–1605), a strong supporter of Wang and the minister of rites at that time. Tao remarked that in view of the fact that the court had already conferred the title of Count upon Wang Yangming, the honor of being enshrined in the Confucius temple would be without difficulties. In response, Lu replied, "The title of Count is merely an honor of one generation, but to be enshrined in the Confucius temple is an honor for ten thousand generations."[41] Everyone recognized the appropriateness of Lu's remark. It was precisely this mentality that led Confucian scholars to believe "enshrinement is the most important undertaking in the empire."[42]

Confucian enshrinement was markedly hierarchical. In principle, it consisted of two major classes. The higher status was "correlative worship" (*peixiang* 配享); the secondary was "subordinate worship" (*congsi* 從祀). Whether one enjoyed correlative worship or subordinate worship depended entirely on the official state assessment of his contribution to the master's teachings. Thus, the imperial government prescribed his ritual treatment—both positioned space and the ranks of offering—in the Confucius temple. Before the advent of Confucian enshrinement, both classes of rites had been practiced, from early antiquity to the Han period, in the worship of the gods of heaven, earth, and grains. Since Confucian enshrinement first developed during the Han, it was natural for it to be inspired or influenced by the traditional patterns of worship prevalent at that time.[43]

When Han emperor Ming visited the Confucius temple of Queli in the year 72, he set the first precedent for making offerings not only to Confucius but also to the seventy-two disciples.[44] Following the example of Emperor Ming, Emperor Zhang 東漢章帝 (r. 75–88), in 85, and Emperor An 東漢安帝 (r. 106–125), in 124, also made offerings to the seventy-two disciples.[45] These ritual performances could be regarded as the origin of "subordinate worship" in the Confucius temple. In addition, by at least the end of the Eastern Han, Yan Hui 顏回 (Yanzi), Confucius's favorite disciple, was already receiving correlative worship, and he continued to be so honored during the period between the Han and Tang.[46] Yet it was not until the enshrinement decreed by Tang emperor Xuanzong 唐玄宗 (r. 712–756), that these two rites were well integrated into systematic operation of the rites.[47]

The Song dynasty used architectural design to enhance the distinctions between these two rites. Those who received correlative worship, together with "ten philosophers" (*shizhe* 十哲), were worshipped in the main hall with Confucius, while those who received subordinate worship were allowed places only in the two galleries (*liangwu* 兩廡), east and west.[48] In the reform of the Confucius temple in 1530, the Ming emperor Shizong 明世宗 (the Jiajing 嘉靖 Emperor, r. 1521–1566) revoked all noble ranks that had been bestowed on canonized scholars since the Tang period.[49]

In addition, the subordinate worship underwent further differentiation through the introduction of two scholarly titles: Confucian worthies (*xianxian* 先賢) and Confucian scholars (*xianru* 先儒). According to this new classification, Confucian worthies were lower than those who received correlative worship but definitely higher than Confucian scholars. Qu Jiusi 瞿九思 (*juren* 1573), an expert in the study of the Confucius temple, had a metaphorical grasp of these distinctions. He likened canonized Confucians to Confucius's intellectual children. The "four distinguished disciples" (*sipei* 四配) with the honor of correlative worship were like the eldest sons (*zhangnan* 長男) of Confucius, the "ten philosophers" with the designation of Confucian worthies were like the middle sons (*zhongnan* 中男), and the Song Confucians with the designation of Confucian scholars came last as the youngest sons (*shaonan* 少男).[50]

The ritual space of the Confucius temple also deliberately expressed this hierarchy. The position of one's tablet in the temple strictly corresponded with the current assessment of one's contribution to Confucianism. The closer a man's tablet was to that of Confucius, the more important he was. As the diagram of the Confucius temple in figure 0.6 shows, the structure of the temple is heavily laden with this kind of value judgment.

One's ritual status might be moved up or down, east or west, or one might even be completely removed from the temple. The constant shifts of enshrinement could even consume the ruler's patience. The Qing emperor Qianlong 乾隆 (Gaozong 清高宗, r. 1735–1795) once became so irritated that he remarked: "Confucian enshrinement has been subject to change at will, suddenly moving up or down, suddenly moving to the east [gallery] or to the west [gallery]. How could it be set as a political system [*zhengti* 政體] for us to follow!" The emperor ascribed the frequency of changes to personal tastes and factional disputes in academic circles.[51]

His father, the Yongzheng 雍正 emperor (Shizong 清世宗, r. 1722–1735), also asked his scholar-officials to approach enshrinement with all solemnity and to exhaust all possibilities to find the proper candidates. In his view, only through such measures would a particular enshrinement be

Figure 0.6 The Confucius temple: a simplified form.
Illustration by Chin-shing Huang

recognized for ten thousand generations to come, and prevent anyone from having different opinions afterwards.[52] Unfortunately, neither Qing ruler perceived the underlying reasons for the fluctuations in enshrinement that they observed.

In the final analysis, two secular factors contributed to the fluctuations in Confucian enshrinement. The first factor was intellectual trends. Since the academic climate constantly changed, one's position in Confucian genealogy would be accordingly adjusted, and so would one's status in the Confucius temple. Indeed, every Confucian enshrinement in history was an officially approved version of the Confucian lineage, and enshrinement in history, seen as a whole, is a perfect indicator of the development of dominant schools in Confucianism.

The second factor that swayed Confucian enshrinement, less frequently but not less importantly, was political interference. Two examples might suffice to establish this point. During the Song period, the rise and fall of Wang Anshi 王安石 (1021–1086) in the Confucius temple precisely corresponded to the waxing and waning of his political influence.[53] Furthermore, the degree of enforced political consciousness regarding the distinction between Chinese and aliens can be clearly illustrated by Wu Cheng's 吳澄 (1249–1333) rise and fall during the Ming and his ultimate return to the Confucius temple during the early Qing.[54]

As the history of Confucian enshrinement shows, no Confucians—including even Confucius himself—were immune from changes in ritual designation. Ming Shizong's reform of the Confucius temple in 1530 perfectly demonstrates the fluctuations of Confucian enshrinement, as the title of King (*wang* 王) was removed from Confucius and his rank of worship was degraded. Moreover, this Ming emperor granted five scholars the honor of receiving sacrifice, deprived thirteen scholars of the honor, and degraded another seven to only the halls of local worthies (*xiangxian ci* 鄉賢祠).[55] These halls of local worthies differed from the Confucius temple in the scope of worship. While the Confucius temple enjoyed worship throughout the empire, the hall of worthies was confined to one locality alone. This difference was not insignificant in terms of the degree of importance and standing in the hierarchical system.[56]

Two additional points about Emperor Shizong's reform of the Confucius temple in 1530 need highlighting. First, based on the philosophical criterion of Cheng-Zhu's 程朱 teachings, the 1530 enshrinement reflected the triumph of the Cheng-Zhu version of "neo"-Confucian orthodoxy and the eclipse of classical learning. The history of the Confucius temple was full of such intellectual messages, both significant and complicated, which we must attempt to decode and interpret.[57] Second, within the Confucius temple the reform introduced a subsystem of enshrinement centered on the newly established Shrine of Giving Birth to the Sage (*Qisheng ci* 啟聖祠). Before the 1530 reform, some Confucians, such as Yan Hui, Zeng Sen 曾參 (Zengzi, 505–435 BCE), and Kong Ji 孔伋, received a higher rank of worship than their fathers. This practice seemingly violated the principle of filial piety, a cardinal virtue that served as the point of departure for Chinese moral conduct and laid the very foundation for Confucianism.

The tension brought about by Confucian enshrinement had become intense, especially since the Southern Song, when Zeng Sen and Kong Ji rose to correlative worship, a ritual status far higher than that accorded to their fathers. Afterwards, criticism of that decision never ceased.[58] Due to the increasing pressure, in 1438 the Ming government adopted a dualistic policy grounded in Pei Kan's 裴侃 suggestion to the court: "The Confucius temples of the world serve the purpose of transmitting the Way; therefore, ritual positions therein must be based on each person's intellectual excellence. Nevertheless, the Confucius temple of Queli exemplifies the relation between father and son; thus, relationship between the persons should be reckoned as the first priority."[59] In 1530, however, Ming Shizong decided to withdraw this exception for the Queli temple in order to achieve consistency in the cultural transformation of the masses. Thus, tensions arising from contradictions in previous Confucian enshrinements were resolved at last, and a model was set that endures to the present day.[60]

The actual procedure for enshrinement further confirms that the Confucius temple was a major convergence point of political and cultural forces in traditional Chinese society. Very often, it was the scholar-officials who took the initiative in proposing promising candidates for enshrinement. If the proposal was preliminarily accepted, the emperor then called a court meeting attended by designated officials to discuss the proposed enshrinement. Shen Li 沈鯉 (1531–1615), in the Ming dynasty, described the function of the court meeting for enshrinement as follows: "The matter of enshrinement is time consuming and often remains undecided. Regarding the court meeting, the court officials are able to express and debate fully the public opinions in the world. Only after that can consensus be reached and the right personages be selected. Its purpose is to achieve the unity of criterion."[61]

Hence, the emperor generally would approve the decision reached at the court meeting, though he could exercise veto power whenever he wished. Consider the example of Xue Xuan 薛瑄 (1389–1464). Although his enshrinement had received the support of the absolute majority of the ritual officials in 1540, Ming Shizong vetoed their decision.[62] This case unambiguously shows that final approval regarding enshrinement ultimately resided in the ruler's hands. Therefore, we should see the practice of enshrinement within the historical context of the subtle and complex interactions between scholars and rulers.

Enshrinement was closely intertwined with state education and the civil service examinations. In the early Tang, the twenty-two scholars who first received worship in the Confucius temple were those whose commentaries on the classics were used in the official educational system.[63] Similarly, in 1330, the Yuan dynasty approved five scholars to be enshrined in the Confucius temple either because their writings were adopted as official texts for civil service examinations or because their books were used in "classics mat" (*jingyan* 經筵) lectures to the emperor.[64] Enshrinement, viewed in this light, was an indispensable link between the political and cultural systems of the Chinese empire.

Conclusion

The Confucius temple was well integrated into the political-cultural system of the Chinese empire. From the Tang onward, only two kinds of worship were implemented throughout the empire: one for the gods of land and harvest, and the other for Confucius. However, the cult of Confucius enjoyed more esteemed rites than did the gods of land and harvest.[65] Together with royal clan temples (*zongmiao* 宗廟) and the worship of heaven (*jitian* 祭天), the Confucius temple stood among the most important ritual institutions for rulers.

In contrast to popular religions, the government imposed the cult of Confucius from above. The ritual establishments in Confucius temples were the locus of state ceremony and were not open to the public. In the Song dynasty, a court official proposed opening the Confucius temple within the National University to nonofficials and their ladies. Scholar-officials sternly criticized and condemned him.[66]

The Confucius temple has always been in a process of becoming. Overall, the rites of the Confucius temple grew at a fairly steady pace. The later a rite, the more magnificent it became. The history of the temple shows the transformation of a plain scholar into a patron, not only for cultural elites but also for political rulers. All Confucians drew cultural inspiration from the doctrine of Confucius, and thus the Confucius temple became the spiritual castle for Confucian symbols. For example, in the Ming and Qing periods, Confucian students throughout the Jiangnan area had a custom of wailing in the Confucius temple about their misfortunes.[67]

For rulers, the worship of Confucius was primarily intended to maintain political legitimacy. Frequently, when Ming Taizu took over a city from his enemies, he would first visit the local Confucius temples and then send scholars to pacify the people.[68] His actions at this point were certainly tied to Confucian teachings regarding legitimation for rulers. Cheng Xu 程徐 (d. 1369) grasped the point firmly when he advised Ming Taizu not to suspend the nationwide worship for Confucius. He offered this observation: "Based on the Way, Confucius educated the people. The reason for us to make sacrifice to Confucius is not for the sake of Confucius himself, but for his teaching and for the Way."[69] The Qing emperor Yongzheng gave this idea its fullest articulation. In an edict to the Ministry of Rites, he expressed this view:

> Without the instructions of Confucius, I wonder how one can tell the superior from the inferior and how the rules of conduct can be accomplished. This is why [the teachings of] Confucius have governed the world for ten thousand generations. He is the greatest man that people have ever had in history. Hence, if a ruler did not know to venerate Confucius, he could not establish himself as the exemplary one above and make corrections for states everywhere!

The emperor frankly confessed, "Among many, the rulers are most benefited by Confucian teachings."[70]

An inscription on a stone tablet dedicated to the Confucius temple during the Yuan also clearly articulated the interdependence of political and cultural authorities: "Without the support of rulers, the teachings of Confucius cannot reach far; without the help of Confucian teachings, the governance of rulers cannot achieve good results."[71] This statement concisely summarizes the whole story about the development of the Confucius temple in imperial China.

CHAPTER I

Expanding the Symbolic Meaning and Function of the Rites

The Evolution of Confucius Temples in Imperial China

The Way of Confucius is the paradigm for all things, and those who rule states certainly should venerate him.
—TEMÜR ÖLJEYTÜ KHAN (YUAN EMPEROR CHENGZONG 成宗, R. 1294–1307)[1]

The Way of Confucius is the model from antiquity to the present. We willingly pledge to imitate it and constantly cherish it in our hearts.
—QING SHENGZU 清聖祖 (KANGXI EMPEROR, R. 1661–1722)[2]

While the introduction describes the Confucius temple as an ideal type, this chapter deals with the Confucius temple as a dynamic and evolving institution, whose functional roles and symbolic meaning expanded at key moments in time. These quotations from Temür Öljeytü Khan and Qing Shengzu were deliberately chosen from the writings of imperial China's alien rulers, who were not of Han Chinese stock. Whether their motivations were genuine admiration or merely pragmatic, their comments reflected Confucianism's integral role in imperial rule. Since ancient times, rulers integrated Confucius temple rites into the imperial ritual system, and these rites thus became indispensable to the operations of imperial institutions. This essay explores how the rites of Confucius temples became incorporated into imperial rites, as well as the position the rites occupied and the role they played.

As their names imply, Confucius temples were built to venerate Confucius, the founder of Confucianism. All later Confucius temples descended from the first private temple—or ancestral hall—in Queli (later called Qufu) in Shandong province, which was originally established as a private place of ancestral worship of Confucius by his descendants. However, the Confucius temples established by succeeding generations were state temples that served distinctively public functions. It was only in this later form that Confucius temples were integrated into or linked with the imperial system of rites.

From Private Temple to State Temples

Before exploring the system of state temples that arose in imperial China, we will briefly survey the first Confucius temple's early history as a familial shrine for ancestor veneration. According to the early historical material in the *Zuozhuan* 左傳, Confucius died on the day of *Jichou* 己丑 in the fourth month of the sixteenth year of Duke Ai of Lu 魯哀公 (479 BCE); after that, the duke made sacrifices to Confucius and bestowed upon him the appellation "Nifu" 尼父. According to this history, Confucius's disciple Zigong 子貢 (520–446 BCE) criticized the duke for committing "a breach of propriety," because Confucius "was not called upon to serve [as an official] in life, yet received official sacrifices in death."[3] The *Zuozhuan* did not record any more detail about Confucius after he died. More than ten centuries after the original events, the Kong clan's descendants would assert dubiously that Duke Ai built a Confucius "temple" at the master's former home a year after the death of Confucius, but those claims are not supported by historical evidence.[4]

We should note that Confucius was probably buried by his disciples, as his son Kong Li 孔鯉 (532–483 BCE) passed away before Confucius did, and Confucius's grandson Kong Ji 孔伋 (known as Zisi 子思, 483–402 BCE) was too young to take charge of the arrangements.[5] Although Kong Jifen 孔繼汾 (1721–1786) was sixty-nine generations removed from Confucius, the view he advanced was the one that made the most sense:

> When the late sage passed away, his disciples buried him by the Si River 泗水 to the north of the city of Lu. After the burial, the descendants then made his residence a temple, and every generation venerated him. Yet the cemetery occupied an area of not more than 100 *mu* (畝), the earth piled [over the tomb] was no more than three *ban* 版 [about eight meters high], and the temple was comprised of just one hall of three spans.[6]

The point of the passage is to relate that Confucius's tomb and temple were modest, being smaller, lower, and containing fewer spans than those of feudal lords; thus, his family followed what was closer to his status as a member of the lowest rank of the nobility.

It is indeed likely that Confucius's disciples buried him; however, I would say that it is more probable that his descendants, several generations after the fact, were the ones who built the first ancestral hall dedicated to him. The historian Sima Qian 司馬遷 (c. 145–86 BCE), who lived three centuries after the time of Confucius, personally visited the city of Lu and was an eyewitness to the Confucius temple there, as well as its ritual carriages, costumes, and vessels; moreover, he recorded many stories and events occurring after Confucius's death. Sima Qian wrote:

> Confucius was buried by the Si River north of the city of Lu. . . . Because more than a hundred of the families of Confucius's disciples and other men of Lu settled near the grave, the district was named as Kong village. The custom of sacrificing at the sage's grave during festivals has persisted from generation to generation. Scholars discuss ceremony there, while village feasts and archery contests are held there. His graveyard covers over one *qing* (頃). His descendants and some of his disciples transformed the house in which he lived into a temple, and his cloths, hat, lute, carriage, and books are kept there. The place still exists in the Han dynasty, more than two hundred years later.[7]

This passage suggests that the home and tomb of Confucius were the two pilgrimage sites for Confucians at the time. However, the temple at Confucius's residence could serve as a model for other locations, while people could not reproduce the tomb of Confucius elsewhere; thus, the temple gained a far more important role in history. We should also note that Sima's term *miao* 廟, which came to mean "temple," referred at the time to a familial shrine, which later generations would call a *citang* 祠堂, or "ancestral hall"; hence, we should not confuse Sima's use of the term "temple" with later Confucius temples.

Sima made other comments on Confucius rites that are of interest: "When the first emperor of the Han passed through Lu, he offered a grand sacrifice there. Barons and ministers appointed to posts there pay homage to the shrine of Confucius before taking up their duties."[8] That Han Gaozu 漢高祖 (Liu Bang 劉邦, r. 202–195 BCE) felt compelled to make the great sacrificial offerings (*tailao* 太牢) of an ox, a sheep, and a pig to Confucius in Lu—in spite of being famous for his contempt for Confucians—was testament to the prestige Confucian learning had attained among the Han by the turn of Qin.[9]

Prior to this period, Han Fei 韓非 (c. 279–233 BCE) wrote, "The prominent [schools of] learning of this world are Confucianism and Mohism."[10] The *Lushi Chunqiu* 呂氏春秋 records, "Confucius and Mozi were dead for a long time, but their followers and disciples increased until they filled all the world. . . . The high nobility and great officials made their teachings eminent, and the children did [as their forebears], so that the teachings continued without interruption."[11] The prominence of Confucians explained why, when Qin emperor Shihuang 秦始皇 (r. 221–210 BCE) ordered the execution of Confucians by burying them alive, his crown prince, Fu Su 扶蘇 (242–210 BCE), pled for their lives, imploring, "The scholars all praise Confucius and take him as a model. However, in all affairs Your Majesty emphasizes the place of law and employs it as a corrective. I fear this may cause unrest in the empire."[12]

By the time Emperor Gaozu unified the Middle Kingdom, the prestige of Confucians was not a thing he wished to take lightly. Regional lords and officials obviously wanted to imitate their emperor's example, and their sacrificial offerings to Confucius then originated the localization of Confucius worship.

During the Han, the imperial court sponsored a series of changes in Confucius temple rites that ultimately resulted in the ancestral shrine's transformation into a system of official temples. First, the Han dynasty bestowed a lordly title on the legitimate firstborn son of each generation in Confucius's bloodline. Before the Qin, history did not record the identity and status of those who made sacrificial offerings to Confucius at Lu. However, Kong Teng 孔騰, the ninth-generation descendant of Confucius, became the first member of the Kong clan to be promoted to the aristocracy, when Emperor Gaozu made a pilgrimage to Lu and ennobled him as a hereditary lord in 195 BCE. The Kong clan was then granted a fief under Emperor Yuan 漢元帝 (r. 49–33 BCE) and peasant vassals under the reign of Emperor Ping 漢平帝 (r. 1 BCE–6 CE) of the Han dynasty. Each patriarch of the main Kong house was an aristocratic lord, to whom the Han government entrusted the duty of making sacrificial offerings to Confucius.[13]

The reason Han emperors worshipped Confucius was twofold. In addition to the prominence of Confucian learning during the Warring States

Period (475–221 BCE), Confucian scholars during the Han promoted Confucius by transforming him into the prophetic figure and guardian deity of the dynasty. The famous scholar Dong Zhongshu 董仲舒 (179–104 BCE) of the Western Han championed "giving exclusive honors to Confucianism and abolishing the Hundred Schools [of Thought]." He further called Confucius "the king without titles," who had "lordly virtues, but not lordly positions."[14] No honors of this sort had previously been given to Confucius. Dong proclaimed:

> Confucius journeyed westward and saw a *qilin* [Chinese "unicorn"], the omen of receiving heaven's mandate. He then wrote the *Spring and Autumn Annals* to clarify right from wrong and to explicate the meaning of political reform. [Confucius believed] the world should be united under the Son of Heaven. In his concern for the world, Confucius dedicated himself to eliminating all that ails the world. He studied what was known about early antiquity from the time of the Three Sovereigns through the Five Emperors in order to determine the Dao for a hundred later rulers.[15]

The Dao for a hundred kings clearly was not projected as a Way instituted for any particular imperial house or dynasty. Thus, Dong echoed Sima Qian's idea in "The Grand Historian's Autobiographical Afterword" 太史公自序, where he proclaimed that Confucius "authored the Six Classics to lay down good rules for all generations to come."[16] Nevertheless, with the development of the unorthodox explications of the apocryphal texts and tradition, the Confucian universalist discourse, recast in the particularistic mold of localism, transformed Confucius into the Han Empire's mythical lawgiver.[17] For example, although Wang Chong 王充 (c. 27–97) of Eastern Han agreed with Dong's interpretation of the *Spring and Autumn Annals*, Wang asserted that Confucius wrote the *Annals* specifically for the Han dynasty.[18]

Stele inscriptions from Confucius temples dated to the late Eastern Han evinced this development. The oldest inscription of this type to survive, titled *Kongmiao zhi shoumiao baidan Kong He bei* 孔廟置守廟百石孔龢碑, was found on a stele erected in the year 153, during Emperor Huan's 東漢桓帝 reign (146–167). It declared, "Confucius is the great sage, who, in imitation of heaven and earth set the pattern or rules for the Han reign." A slightly later inscription, titled *Luxiang Han Chi zao Kongmiao liqi bei* 魯相

韓勑造孔廟禮器碑, found on a stele dated to 156, during the reign of same emperor, stated, "Confucius is the sage close to our era, and paved the Way for our Han reign. Everyone from the emperor down to students admire and follow him as a model."[19]

If it was believed that Confucius, who was born centuries before the Han, had prophesied the Han dynasty's coming into being and was acting as its lawgiver, he must have been thought of as divine. On the stele's sides and back, lists of donors registered the names of people from Shandong, Henan, and Zhejiang who had contributed to furnishing ritual vessels for the Confucius temple in Queli.[20] The breadth of the geographic distribution of these donors attests to the enthusiasm that officials and literati from diverse areas had for their religious donations to Confucius, and the fervency of their veneration of him. Another inscription, titled *Luxiang Shi Chen ci Kongmiao zouming* 魯相史晨祠孔廟奏銘, found on a stele dated to 169, during Emperor Ling's 東漢靈帝 reign (167–189), largely repeated the themes of earlier inscriptions; however, two inscriptions on this stele also marked something new in the conduct of temple rites.[21]

Before highlighting these changes in the rituals performed at the Confucius temple in Queli, we need to step back several years to note how the rites at regional places, even at the original Confucius temple in Queli, differed from the rites to Confucius at the capital. Before this time, the rite of Biyong 辟雍, which the National University in the capital conducted, did not offer sacrifices to the late sage master 先聖師 (Confucius). Furthermore, the descendants of Confucius administered the sacrifices at the Confucius temple in Queli; they traveled to the site for this purpose and returned home when the ritual was completed.

Viceroy Yi Ying 乙瑛 of Lu took an earlier step, recorded in the inscription *Kongmiao zhi shoumiao baidan Kong He bei*, when he appointed an official to serve as the temple's custodian, with a stipend of one hundred bushels of grain.[22] Yi Ying's comment aligns with the historical conditions at the time. It was true that in the year 59, Emperor Ming 東漢明帝 (r. 57–75) of the Eastern Han had ordered ritual sacrifices to sagely teachers Confucius and the Duke of Zhou. However, those rites, performed by local academies at the prefectural 郡, county 縣, and borough 道 levels with sacrifices of dog meat, marked them as less prestigious than the rites of Biyong.[23]

Although Confucius's descendants were designated as feudal lords in the decades that followed, their presence was limited to visiting the temple to conduct the rites at appointed times, after which they returned home. At the same time, at the capital's Biyong National University, Confucius annually received the large-animal sacrifice of an ox, a sheep, and a pig; moreover, it was mandated that the official in charge be an elderly official who bore a noble rank. Intended to show due respect to the sagely teacher and to the importance of culture, this mandate of noble rank was an important upgrade to the status of sacrificial rites to Confucius. However, those in charge of Confucius's temple at his former residence did not conduct rites according to any regular liturgical calendar.

Therefore, Shi Chen 史晨, an official in Lu, took another step in changing the rites in Queli when he memorialized that the state pay for the ritual expenses and that the rank of the sacrificial offerings to Confucius should be equal to that of the gods of earth and grain. Shi Chen also proposed to set the dates for offering sacrifices to Confucius on a regular basis, every spring and autumn. Furthermore, he recommended giving the leftover meat to the clan elders and officials involved in performing the rites.[24] The mention of the rites for the gods of earth and grain served as a point of reference for elevating the rites of Confucius veneration to a higher status. Furthermore, the fact that Shi Chen was uneasy about the uneven solemnity between the rites of Confucius veneration at Biyong and those at Confucius's residence in Queli suggests that the imperial court also had a political stake in the orderly conduct of those rites in Queli.

Another change in ritual performance was recorded in the inscription on the back side of the stele with the *Luxiang Shi Chen ci Kongmiao zouming* inscription. This second inscription is titled *Shi Chen xiang Kongmiao houbei* 史晨饗孔廟後碑. Both inscriptions date to the year 169, during the reign of Emperor Ling.[25] In addition to preserving for posterity the details of the rites of the spring sacrifice 春饗禮, this second inscription also conveys a sense of the pomp and ceremony expected during Shi Chen's time in Qufu.

According to this second inscription, Shi Chen assumed his post in Lu on the eleventh of the fourth month, during the first year of Jianning (168), and his first order of business was to report his appointment to Confucius. Since the day coincided with the spring sacrifice, he ordered the performance of the National University's rite of Biyong; thus, he brought the capital's ritual performance to the original Confucius shrine in Queli. The daylong event, featuring rites and appropriate music, was attended by no fewer than 907 individuals, including local officials of all ranks and the official school's students and teachers. In addition, a temple custodian of one hundred–bushel rank named Kong Zan 孔讚 was present at the rites, thus documenting the implementation of the paid position that Yi Ying had instituted more than a dozen years earlier, in the year 153.[26]

The Institution of the Rite of Libations

The late Eastern Han did not establish the rites for venerating Confucius as a regular state ritual. For example, it was mandated by the *Book of Rites* (*Liji* 禮記) that the rite of libations (*Shidian* 釋奠)—the ceremonial offering of libations to late sages and teachers—was a proper ritual to celebrate the founding of a place of learning.[27] Yet historical records suggest this was not a common practice at the time of the late Eastern Han: "Though the Han founded state academies, the performance of the rite accompanying it was unheard of."[28]

The three-tier hierarchy of state rites was ancient and probably dated to the time before the Qin dynasty, although its division into great rites, intermediate rites, and minor rites occurred much later.[29] Originally, the *Rites of Zhou* (*Zhouli* 周禮) stated, "Great sacrifices make use of jade, silks, and large animals. Intermediate sacrifices make use of animals and coins. Minor sacrifices make use of animals." The Eastern Han classicist Zheng Zhong 鄭眾 (d. 83) provided this annotation, "Great sacrifices are for heaven and earth. The intermediate sacrifices are for the sun, the moon, and the stars. The minor sacrifices are for the gods ranked inferior to fortune." A century later, Zheng Xuan 鄭玄 (127–200), a master classicist of late Eastern Han, augmented the scope and explained, "Additionally, great sacrifices are for the imperial ancestral shrine; intermediate sacrifices include the gods of earth and soil, the Five Divine Offices, and the Five Mountains. Minor sacrifices are also for Si Zhong 司中 [a star in the constellation of Wenchang 文昌], winds, rains, mountains, rivers, and myriad things."[30] There is no reason to doubt that Zheng Zhong and Zheng Xuan's descriptions derived from the conduct of state rites during the Han. Therefore, the fact that Confucius was not mentioned anywhere in their list of the figures venerated by state rites suggests that Confucius worship had yet to be incorporated in the regular ritual system of the state.[31]

However, history does offer incidents that suggest how Confucius temple rites were gradually incorporated into the imperial system of rites. For example, when Emperor Guangwu 東漢光武帝 (r. 25–57) of the Eastern

Han made a pilgrimage to Lu, he ordered his grand minister of works (*Dasikong* 大司空) to perform rites to Confucius.³² More importantly, his two immediate successors oversaw rites of veneration at the Confucius temple at Queli. Guangwu's successor, Emperor Ming, also made a pilgrimage to the Confucius temple at the historic residence in Queli. He offered sacrifices to Confucius and his seventy-two disciples, while the crown prince and the princes were told to lecture on the classics for the emperor's edification.³³ Later, in the year 85, Emperor Ming's son, Emperor Zhang 東漢章帝 (r. 75–88), also came to Queli while performing a personal inspection of his realm. During his stay, this emperor offered the large-animal sacrifice to Confucius and his seventy-two disciples, with the Music of the Six Eras accompanying the sacrifices. In addition to those solemn rites, the emperor feted the men of the Kong clan and ordered scholars to teach the *Analects*.³⁴ Through the gradual process of initiation, emperors started to regularly order the teaching of the classics and to offer sacrifices to Confucius.

By the Wei and Jin dynasties, emperors were having lectures on the classics and the presentation of libations in the convenience of their own courts. The *Chronicle of the Three Kingdoms* (*Sanguo zhi* 三國志) states:

> In the second month, spring of 241, the [Wei dynasty] emperor [Cao Fang 曹芳, Prince Ai of Qi 齊哀王] began to grasp the meaning of the *Analects* [through formal studies], and ordered the minister of ceremonies (*Taichang* 太常) to make offerings of the large-animal sacrifice at the National University, with Yan Yuan 顏淵 being an auxiliary recipient [to Confucius]. . . . In the fifth month of 244, the emperor completed [listening to] the lectures on the *Book of Documents*, and ordered the minister of ceremonies to make offerings of large-beast sacrifice at the National University, with Yan Yuan being the auxiliary. In the twelfth month of the winter of 246, the emperor finished [listening to] the lectures on the *Book of Rites*, and ordered the minister of ceremonies to make offerings of large-animal sacrifice at the National University, with Yan Yuan being the auxiliary recipient.³⁵

The *Official History of the Jin* (*Jinshu* 晉書), which was compiled during the Tang, recounted the rites described in the *Chronicle of the Three Kingdoms* but merged the rites of Biyong and the ceremonial libations into the same rite. Furthermore, the *Official History of the Jin* contains numerous references to the routine performance of the libation rites at the successful conclusion of lectures on the classics for the emperor, and thus shows the linking of the rites with the completion of the lectures.[36] Furthermore, it is important to note that those rites were conducted at the Biyong—the National University of the capital—not at the ancestral hall dedicated to Confucius in faraway Queli.

I will explore in depth three developments in the rites of Confucius worship that took place during this period: the integration of Confucius temples and government academies, the "seeking out of the sage's descendants," and the proliferation of Confucius temples outside of Queli.

First, Confucius temples early on obtained an educational function. In 221, the newly crowned Wei emperor Wen 魏文帝 (r. 220–226) "sought out" Confucius's descendants and found the twenty-first-generation descendant Kong Xian 孔羨. The emperor made Kong Xian a court adviser and the Marquis of Zongsheng 宗聖侯. In addition, the emperor ordered Lu Prefecture to repair the old Confucius temple, to appoint a custodian with a stipend of one hundred bushels of grain, and to build apartments for scholars beside the temple. This was the embryonic form of the temple schools of later times.[37]

In 550, Emperor Wenxuan 北齊文宣帝 (r. 550–559) of the Northern Qi decreed the establishment of Confucius-Yanzi shrines 孔顏廟 in all prefectural academies.[38] Later, in the year 630, Emperor Taizong 唐太宗 (r. 626–649) of the Tang dynasty commanded all prefectural and county academies to establish on-site Confucius temples.[39] Those decrees resulted in the proliferation of temple schools, from the original in Queli to the entire imperium. From this point onward, Confucius temples and imperial academies became inseparable subcomponents of a single entity, regardless of geographic location.

The development in the rites of Confucius veneration also proceeded apace. During the regency of Wang Mang 王莽 (r. 9–23), coruler with the Han emperor Ping, the court conferred the hereditary title of Marquis of Baocheng 褒成侯 upon Confucius and upon his bloodline's firstborn, who were charged with overseeing the veneration of Confucius. The court soon conferred upon Confucius the additional honor of Duke Baocheng Xuanni 褒成宣尼公. These decrees set the precedent for later dynasties to honor Confucius with rites and titles.[40] The Kong clan temporarily lost its fiefdom with Wang Mang's downfall and death, but Emperor Guangwu of the Han restored the fiefdom in the year 37, along with the title Marquis of Baocheng. The Kong clan managed to pass down the fiefdom through its lineage, which remained unbroken until the fall of the Han dynasty, when historical records on them vanished.[41]

Yet, generations after the Liu family's Han dynasty met its fate, the Kong clan miraculously resurrected, and it would go on to rise repeatedly from the ashes of fallen dynasties. Like Emperor Wen of the Wei, who unified the Three Kingdoms after decades of strife, many rulers found it convenient to have a hand on Confucius's descendants in order to put the seal of legitimacy on their rites venerating Confucius. Rulers accomplished this through the ritual "seeking out" of the sage's descendants. Since the original Confucius temple was a familial shrine, it was a natural requirement that a descendant of Confucius officiate the sacrifices.

This limitation of blood, deeply impressed upon the tradition of Confucius worship, remained an enduring feature of Confucius temples well after the original ancestral hall had metamorphosed into a system of state temples. Both the Confucius temple in Queli and the Confucius temple at the imperial capital continued to demand the personal attention of Confucius's descendants for ritual purposes. The continuation of the Kong bloodline—captured in the expression "One lineage through ten thousand generations"—was a matter of the highest importance to the imperial state.[42]

Along with sacking of the Chinese capital of Luoyang in the year 311, the Central Asian chieftain Shi Le 石勒 (274–333) defeated the Han Chinese (Western) Jin dynasty and conquered vast areas of North China. These areas included Queli, and his tribesmen sacked and destroyed the Confucius temple there.[43] After regaining considerable stability in South China, Eastern Jin emperor Xiaowu 東晉孝武帝 (r. 372–396), in the year 386, conferred upon Kong Jing 孔靖 (347–422) the title of the Marquis of Feng Shengting 奉聖亭侯, with the duty of officiating Confucius worship.[44] In addition, at his capital in South China, this emperor built the Xuanni temple 宣尼廟 dedicated to Confucius veneration.[45]

Thereafter, the Northern and Southern dynasties began to build rival Confucius temples in their respective capitals.[46] Emperor Wu 南齊武帝 (r. 482–493) of the Southern Qi built a temple school at his capital, Jiankang (modern Nanjing), in 489. Likely in response to this rival's construction, Emperor Xiaowen 北魏孝文帝 (r. 471–499) of the Northern Wei also built a Confucius temple, at his capital of Pingcheng 平城 (modern Datong), during the same year. This architectural maneuvering unintentionally resulted in severing the veneration of Confucius from Queli and in facilitating the proliferation of Confucius temples.

Nevertheless, the precise ritual protocol for venerating Confucius had not yet become firmly settled. Trying to determine this very issue, Emperor Xiaowu of the Eastern Jin convened a debate among the era's most renowned scholars of ritual propriety. On one hand, Lu Na 陸納 (d. 395) and Che Yin 車胤 (c. 333–401) declared that Xuanni temple rites should be conducted according to the dignity befitting a count (*tinghou* 亭侯). On the other, Fan Ning 范寧 (339–401) believed it appropriate to extend to Confucius the same rites used for venerating the Duke of Zhou 周公 (c. 1100–1032 BCE), and Fan Xuan 范宣 argued that Confucius, as master teacher, should not be treated as a subject but rather deserved the ritual honors due to an emperor. The diversity of opinions at this time seems to demonstrate that the protocol for worshipping Confucius was underdeveloped and still a work in progress.[47]

Emperor Wu of the Southern Qi dynasty revisited this debate in 485 after he decreed the founding of an academy, and he again encountered the problem of not having a well-defined rite for the occasion. Thus, the emperor ordered a review of the Jin dynasty's conduct of rites to honor Late Sage and Ancient Master Confucius. Minister Wang Jian 王儉 (452–489) reported:

> Che and Lu [in their discussion on the rites] erred on giving [honor] too lightly; the two Fan erred on giving too lavishly. . . . Since the middle years of our dynasty, the ritual offering of fruits and vegetables [to Confucius] was discarded, and only the [more solemn] ritual offerings of meat were performed. As for ritual vessels, there are no written regulations available. I propose that the rites be done in a way lighter than the rites of "seven temples" [i.e., the highest-grade rite for an emperor's ancestral worship], but weightier than the rites of the five temples [the inferior grade of rites for feudal lords].[48]

After serious deliberation, the imperial court, in the same year, decreed to do as Wang Jian had proposed, taking another step in the long experimental process toward solidifying a ritual code for venerating Confucius.

However, the Tang was the dynasty that settled the scale and dimensions of rites at Confucius temples. During the early stage, the rites for venerating Confucius had to contend for ascendancy with the rites for venerating the Duke of Zhou. Afterwards, rites for Confucius had to contend with the newly emerging worship of the Duke of Tai 太公 (Jiang Shang 姜尚, eleventh century BCE), also called Jiang Ziya 姜子牙, a key leader in the Zhou dynasty's overthrow of the Shang. (The Tang dynastic founders regarded the Duke of Tai's grandson, Shuyu 唐叔虞, of the early Zhou state of Tang, to be their patron deity, and they paid homage to his spirit at the famous Jinsi 晉祠, near Taiyuan, on their way to overthrow the Sui dynasty and seize the Chinese throne.)

As was noted earlier, the *Book of Rites* stated, "When a place of learning is founded, the presentation of libations must be performed to honor the late sage and the late master teacher." Zheng Xuan, the Eastern Han classicist and authority on ritual propriety, identified in this passage not one but two recipients of the libations: the "late sage," referring to the Duke of Zhou, and the "late master teacher," referring to Confucius.[49] This reading triggered a controversy that would echo down the ages. During the Tang, Confucius and the Duke of Zhou alternated as the main recipient of the libations, a reflection of the fact that the controversy was playing out within the empire's ritual system.

Tang emperor Gaozu 唐高祖 (r. 618–626) decreed, in 619, that the National University should establish separate temples for the Duke of Zhou and Confucius, and both temples regularly conducted rites at seasonally appointed times.[50] The decree stated that the reason for offering ritual sacrifices to the Duke of Zhou was his contributions to the founding of the Zhou dynasty, as both a regime and a cultured way of governing. As the founding dynast, Emperor Gaozu may have honored the Duke of Zhou to emphasize his own glorious achievement in founding an empire, but his use of the term "two sages" suggests that the Duke of Zhou and Confucius were coequal in ritual status.[51]

In 624, Gaozu inspected the National University and personally attended to the presenting of the libations. In this iteration, he named the Duke of Zhou the late sage, while Confucius received offerings as a correlate. Furthermore, on that occasion, there reportedly was mingling with renowned Daoists and shaman priests, who disputed at length with Confucian erudites.[52] Therefore, we can surmise that Confucianism had not assumed a dominant position as an official ideology at the Tang imperial court, so that Confucius was relegated to a lesser status in state rites.

Emperor Taizong 唐太宗 (r. 626–649) reversed his father's policy and terminated the veneration of the Duke of Zhou in 628, while elevating Confucius as the ritual's main devotional figure and Yan Hui as a correlate recipient in the sacrifices.[53] Taizong issued this decree to accord with the advice of Vice Counselor Fang Xuanling 房玄齡 (579–648) and the erudite Zhu Zishe 朱子奢 (d. 641), who counseled:

> During his reign, Emperor Gaozu ordered the performance of the rites of libation at the National University, with the Duke of Zhou named the late sage and with Confucius as auxiliary. However, Your Majesty's subjects believe that the Duke of Zhou and Confucius should both be recognized as sages, because it is to Confucius that the libations are offered in schools. Therefore, the Jin, the Song, the Liang, the Chen, and the Sui all followed the established precedent of calling Confucius the late sage, Yan Hui the late teacher. This was always the way it has been throughout these dynasties and accords with the ancients.[54]

The principal points of their argument were as follows. First, the libations were presented in academies, which were Confucius's domain. Second, prior to the late years of the Sui dynasty, the state regarded Confucius as the late sage and Yan Hui as the late teacher. In terms of historical accuracy, Fang's and Zhu's arguments are sound. Although the imperial court sometimes referred to the Duke of Zhou as the high sage (*shangsheng* 上聖) or the supreme sage (*zhisheng* 至聖), he had received those appellations for political purposes.[55] For this reason, Confucius had been the main devotional figure to receive the libations since the Wei and Jin dynasties. Convinced by the argument, Tang Taizong decreed the change in the rites. In 630, Taizong further decreed the founding of Confucius temples in state academies at the prefectural and county levels of administration.[56] This decree was the most significant deployment of state power in the promotion of Confucianism up to that time.

Yet, the situation took another turn in the Yonghui 永徽 reign period (650–655), when Tang emperor Gaozong 唐高宗 (r. 649–683) again elevated the Duke of Zhou as the late sage and relegated Confucius as the late teacher.[57] It is important to note that in Confucius temple rites, both the primary and auxiliary figures of devotion were worshipped at the main temple hall, but correlates were relegated to the shrines on the flanks. Since the Han and Wei dynasties, the late sage—variously the Duke of Zhou or Confucius—occupied the main hall, while the late teacher occupied a shrine in a side room. Clearly, the late sage received far more respect and honor than the late teacher, and Gaozong's promulgation meant a snub to Confucius.

Many classical scholars of later generations blamed the influence of Liu Xin 劉歆 (50 BCE–23 CE) for Gaozong's change of ritual policy. For instance, Liao Ping 廖平 (1852–1932), a New Text scholar during the Qing dynasty, wrote:

> Old Text scholars used the Duke of Zhou to compete with Confucius by saying that the classics originated from the Duke of Zhou. Because succeeding generations listened to this theory, they made sacrificial offerings to the Duke of Zhou and Confucius together at schools, with one being the late sage and the other the late teacher. This is an error.[58]

As Pi Xirui 皮錫瑞 (1850–1908) pointed out, the ritual practice advocated by the Old Text scholars contradicted what the stele inscriptions made during the Han had depicted.[59]

In 657, a coterie of officials, led by Grand Commandant (*Taiwai* 太尉) Zhangsun Wuji 長孫無忌 (594–659), Minister of Rites (*Libu Shangshu* 禮部尚書) Xu Jingzong 許敬宗 (592–672), and other high-ranking officials, requested that Emperor Gaozong return to the ritual institutions of Taizong's reign.[60] Thus, these senior officials asked the emperor to rescind his own decision of a few years earlier about ritual practice regarding the Duke of Zhou and Confucius. These officials pointed out:

> When King Cheng 周成王 [c. 1042–1021 BCE] of the Zhou dynasty was a child, the Duke of Zhou acted with supreme power and created rites and music, with contributions equaling those of kings. Therefore, [Xia king] Yu 禹, [Shang king] Tang 湯, [Zhou kings] Wen 文, Wu 武, Cheng, and the Duke of Zhou were called the Six Rulers.[61]

By grouping the Duke of Zhou with other extraordinary secular rulers in antiquity, Zhangsun willed into existence the distinction between the tradition of legitimate governance and the tradition of the Way. Their advocacy for removing the Duke of Zhou from the temple of culture (*wen miao* 文廟) was part of an effort to delineate the symbolic purpose and roles of the cultural temple system.

The temple of culture provided crucial evidence for the argument set forth to Emperor Gaozong: even though the Duke of Zhou and Confucius were simultaneously worshipped as "sage teacher" beginning in Han Emperor Ming's reign, the Duke of Zhou had disappeared from the rites of temples of culture ever since the Three Kingdoms.[62] The imperial court deemed Zhangsun's argument convincing and once again regarded Confucius as the late sage. Separated from the temple of culture, the veneration of the Duke of Zhou became a part of the cult for deceased imperial rulers, as an auxiliary to King Wu of the Zhou dynasty.[63] A sharp line was drawn between the tradition of legitimate governance and the tradition of the Way, and it became courtly consensus to assign the worship of the Duke of Zhou to the tradition of governance. Thereafter, Confucius was the dominant figure of the temple of culture, and his position in state rituals was never challenged again.

With regard to the rites of libation, imperial courts from the Wei and Jin through the Northern and Southern dynasties were committed to the ritual policy for presenting libations, but their implementation was sporadic. In the Northern Qi, "When schools commence, students must offer libations to the late sage and late teacher; this rite is performed in the second month of every spring and autumn season." The Northern Qi's prefectural government academies established temples dedicated to venerating Confucius and Yan Hui. The Sui dynasty inherited those policies, but added the stipulation that regular offerings would be performed every season.[64]

In addition, the reasons for presenting the libations had increased in number; the Northern Qi made prayers in response to natural disasters and plagues at nine different classes of temples, including the temples to Confucius and Yan Hui.[65] However, succeeding dynasties rarely practiced this particular innovation, probably due to the creation of specialized rituals for addressing such natural disasters. In short, Confucius veneration did not become one of the regular "three sacrifices" (*Sansi* 三祀) of state during the Sui, but managed to do so in the Tang.[66]

According to the *Six Canons of Tang* (*Tang liudian* 唐六典), a law book compiled by the state during Emperor Xuanzong's 唐玄宗 reign (712–756), there were four categories of state rituals: ritual offerings to the sky gods, to earth gods, to the spirits of men, and to the late sage and late teacher.[67] The presentation of libations, which falls into the last category, was further divided into different rites, including offerings to Confucius and to Duke Tai of Qi. These were classified as intermediate rites by the *Six Canons of Tang* as well as by the *Rites in the Kaiyuan Era of the Great Tang* (*DaTang Kaiyuan li* 大唐開元禮). In contrast, the presentation of libations by prefectural or county governments was considered a minor rite, which was significantly less prestigious than the presentations of libations of the intermediate class, despite being similar rituals.[68]

No records of ritual offerings to Duke Tai of Qi exist prior to the founding of a temple in Panxi 磻溪 during the Tang Taizong's Zhenguan 貞觀 Era (627–649).[69] In 731, Emperor Xuanzong decreed the construction of temples to Duke Tai of Qi and to Confucius in both imperial capitals and in every prefecture, with Marquis Zhang Liang 張良 (250–186 BCE) receiving offerings as an auxiliary.[70] After this, Duke Tai of Qi was authorized to receive the rite of libations. Initially, Duke Tai of Qi was set up as a martial patron deity and temples dedicated to his veneration were fashioned after the culture temples of Confucius. For example, Confucius received the title King of Exalted Culture (Wenxuanwang 文宣王) in the year 739. Not long thereafter, in 760, Emperor Suzong 唐肅宗 (r. 756–762) conferred on Duke Tai of Qi the title King of Military Accomplishment (Wuchengwang 武成王), with ritual honors equal to those of the King of Exalted Culture.[71] In imitation of the Confucius temple, it had Zhang Liang as a devotional auxiliary and ten correlates of "philosopher" rank, all great captains of the past. For a time, the cultural and martial temple rites thus developed in lockstep.

With the rise of literati culture and the imperial examinations in the Sui and early Tang, Confucius began to eclipse Duke Tai.[72] The long-term decline of martial temples could not be halted, despite periodic attempts of revitalization, made especially during wartime. As early as Tang emperor Suzong's reign, it was evident that Confucius temples were superior in status. When Emperor Suzong suspended the observance of minor and intermediate state rituals during a drought, he made an exception for the rituals at Confucius temples, but not for Duke of Tai temples.[73]

Confucius temple rites also were more widely practiced. As Han Yu 韓愈 (768–824) said, "In all under heaven, none but Confucius and the gods of earth and grain (*sheji* 社稷) receive sacrifices [from all men of rank] from the Son of Heaven to the heads of local governments."[74] By comparison, Duke of Tai temple rites were not observed universally within the empire. The highest-ranking head of its ceremonies was a high-ranking general, whereas the Son of Heaven might personally administer the veneration of Confucius. In 788, the attendant to the Ministry of Military Affairs, Li Shu 李紓, submitted a memorial to Tang emperor Dezong 唐德宗 (r. 779–805) that implored the imperial court to curb the excessive honors given to Duke Tai temples, also known as the temples to the King of Military Accomplishment. Li wrote:

> Exalted culture has been passed down, and a hundred generations revere the master [Confucius]. Without his teachings, the five constant virtues [humaneness, rightness, propriety, wisdom, and faithfulness] and the three bonds [ruler–minister, father–son, and husband–wife] would not to be clear; if not for his regulations, countries and families could not be established. This is why Mencius said that since the birth of people, there has been no one like this one [Confucius]. Therefore, the regulations of the uncrowned king were rectified; the title of "first sage" (*xiansheng* 先聖) was added; for music, court instruments were used; for the sacrifice, the protector-in-chief was sent. The master is revered, and the Dao is worshipped; all is refined and proper. Duke of Tai wrote only "Six Stratagems," and his achievements were evident for only one generation. How can his virtues deserve such ceremony?[75]

Most court officials supported Li's memorial, and their most radical members argued that the Duke of Tai should lose the honors for military accomplishments and title of king. As this was during a time of war, the emperor followed Li's suggestion, but not the more extreme voices at court.[76]

Nevertheless, Li Shu's proposal foreshadowed the fate of the Duke of Tai temples. In 1387, the Ming emperor Taizu 明太祖 (Zhu Yuanzhang 朱元璋, r. 1368–1398) abolished sacrificial offerings at the King of Military Accomplishment temples, on the grounds that it was improper to fashion a vassal after kings.[77] Thereafter, Confucius was the only figure to whom the presentation of libations was performed.

Imperial Rulers and the Confucius Temples' Rituals

During the Tang, the basic form of the ceremonial offerings to Confucius solidified, with a nearly complete system of correlate and auxiliary worship and a well-established status as an intermediate rite of state. Moreover, rites for Confucius earned favor from the ruling class of the imperial elite and became one of the empire's universal institutions. Well integrated into the imperial ritual system, the veneration of Confucius functioned seamlessly and assumed ever-increasing importance within it. The Southern Song briefly elevated Confucius worship to the status of a great rite of state, in 1140, but returned to an intermediate rite in 1195.[78] The Western Xia granted Confucius the title Emperor of Exalted Culture (Wenxuandi 文宣帝) in 1146.[79] The propinquity of these two promulgations suggests that the Western Xia sought to compete with its contemporary rival in giving honorary titles to Confucius.

Confucian officials had earlier made the case for styling Confucius as an emperor. In 1074, an educational official, Chang Zhi 常秩 (1019–1077), recommended to the Northern Song emperor Shenzong 宋神宗 (r. 1067–1085) that this elevation of Confucius's status be made, but the emperor rejected the proposal after the officials in charge of rites advised against it.[80] Not long thereafter, in 1104, Emperor Huizong 宋徽宗 (r. 1100–1125) changed the name of the National University's King of Exalted Culture temple to the Temple Hall of Great Completion (Dacheng dian 大成殿). He further decreed that Confucius's ritual headgear was to have twelve beaded strings, which was the highest and most honored style, according to the imperial dress code. Huizong's promulgations initiated the tradition of showing respect to Confucius by designating imperial headgear and robes for him in rituals.[81]

For the most part, the rituals of Confucius worship increased in number and solemnity from the Song to the Yuan, even though intermittent warfare would cause the disruption of liturgical continuity and even the sacking of several temples. Non–Han conquest dynasties from Inner Asia fully participated in this process. For instance, Emperor Shizong 金世宗 (r. 1161–1189) of the Jurchen Jin dynasty decreed, in 1174, that Confucius's icon was to have headgear with twelve beaded strings and robes with a dozen folds.[82] Upon his ascension to the throne, in 1307, Emperor Wuzong 元武宗 (r. 1307–1311) of the Yuan dynasty granted another appellation to

Confucius by modifying his title from the King of Supreme Sageliness and Exalted Culture (Zhisheng Wenxuanwang 至聖文宣王) to the King of Great Completion, Supreme Sageliness, and Exalted Culture (Dacheng Zhisheng Wenxuanwang 大成至聖文宣王).

The ravages of war certainly were an impediment to the expansion of Confucius temple rites, because many temples were fated to endure sacking during periods of strife. For instance, the temple school system that had existed since the Tang dynasty sustained heavy wartime damage, especially in the loss of official academies, during the Five Dynasties and Ten Kingdoms. However, temples as a rule were the site of presenting libations and thus usually managed to escape destruction. As Ouyang Xiu 歐陽修 (1007–1072) wrote:

> During the Sui and the Tang, every prefecture and county established schools with students and educational officers. The rite of libations became law. Although the prefectural and county schools were in ruins, the legal code still mandated the rite of libations, and officials did not abolish it. Since there were no schools left to host the rites, [Confucius] temples were used to host them.[83]

Wang Anshi 王安石 (1021–1086), in "Fanchangxian xueji" 繁昌縣學記, observed, "In ancient times, sacrifices were offered to the late teacher and late sage at the schools and not in temples; however, the custom of recent generations is to offer sacrifices to Confucius in temples and not in schools."[84] Wang's "antiquity" referred to the period from the Han through the Northern and Southern dynasties. His "recent generations" pointed to the war-torn period from the Five Dynasties into the early Song. The ravages of those wars forced the Song to abolish many official academies and to use them as Confucius temples.[85] Ma Duanlin 馬端臨 (1254–1323) recorded, "Since the Tang, every prefecture and county had built schools, and each school had a temple of the late sage. . . . However, after times of decline and chaos, the schools in remote and crude countries frequently became dilapidated ruins and education all but forgotten, and only the temple of culture remained standing."[86] For these reasons, the Northern Song imperial court promulgated, in 1044, "the establishment of academies in prefectures and counties," which was comparable to the Tang's edict of 630 "establishing temples at the official academies in prefectures and counties."

As we have noted, Confucius temple rituals continued to develop even during periods of alien rule. Ironically, it was the Han Chinese Great Ming dynasty that dealt the first serious setbacks to the ritual system of the Confucius temples. This assault was mounted by Ming emperor Taizu and was continued by the Jiajing 嘉靖 Emperor Shizong 明世宗 (r. 1521–1566).

During the first year of his reign, Emperor Taizu followed the time-honored precedent of dynastic founders by ordering the large-animal sacrifice to Confucius. The emperor dispatched emissaries to Qufu to officiate the sacrifices and wrote a speech to mark the occasion:

> The Dao of Confucius is as vast and enduring as heaven and earth. Therefore, in the later generations, all who rule the world must pay him utmost respect and attend to sacrifices to him. We now are the ruler of the world, and it is our wish to foster the transformation of culture and to implement the Dao of the late sage.[87]

With those words, Emperor Taizu demonstrated his awareness that founders of dynasties would be wise to make ritual offerings to Confucius, because of the indispensable symbolic value in demonstrating the continuity of legitimate rule. Indeed, when Emperor Taizu first set foot in Jianghui Prefecture, his first official act was visiting the local Confucius temple there.[88]

However, Ming Taizu had had prior dealings with the Kong family in Queli during his struggle to secure the throne, and he felt they had insulted him.[89] In 1369, Emperor Taizu suddenly announced that, except for the temple in Queli, Confucius temples would no longer observe the rites of spring and autumn.[90] The timing of the edict is intriguing, because Emperor Taizu had summoned many Confucians earlier that year to discuss ritual policy and other things connected to organizing his regime.[91] Also in the same year, Emperor Taizu mandated offerings for city gods throughout the empire, a move that made his discontinuation of regular spring and autumn offerings to Confucius even more provocative. Emperor Taizu explained his policy:

> Since the Han, the spirit [Confucius] was universally worshipped in the land within the seas. We govern the people in place of preceding kings. When reading books, we chanced upon his sacred instructions [in *Analects* 2:24]: "For a man to sacrifice to a spirit which does not

belong to him is flattery. To see what is right and not to do it is lack of courage." If the wise sage did not utter this statement himself, no one would have thought of it. Therefore, we dare not order the universal offering of sacrifices, because of fear that such wastage of food would weary and belabor the spirit's sagely virtue.[92]

In intentionally breaking with centuries of tradition, Emperor Taizu was expressing and consolidating an autocratic and absolutist form of imperial authority.

In 1372, while reading *Mencius* 4b:31, Taizu came upon the passage "If the ruler views his ministers as dirt and grass, then his ministers will view him as a bandit and villain." As Taizu felt Mencius's sentiments were inappropriate reading material for his subjects, he banned Mencius from receiving sacrifice as Confucius's correlate in temples. Court officials were sternly warned that any remonstration against the imperial command would be viewed as a gross violation of Taizu's imperial majesty, a crime punishable by death. However, Qian Tang 錢唐 (1314–1394) objected anyway, remarking, "If I die for Mencius's sake, I will die with great honor." According to the official dynastic history, "The emperor appreciated his sincerity and did not punish him." In truth, making a martyr out of Qian might have precipitated a clash between political authority and cultural faith that even an autocrat like Taizu could ill afford. A year later, Taizu relented and ordered the resumption of sacrifices to Mencius as a Confucius temple correlate.[93]

It would take longer for Taizu to reinstate the empire-wide ritual offerings to Confucius, which he finally did with an edict in 1382: "Confucius made manifest the Dao of kings and emperors in order to instruct succeeding generations that sovereigns should be sovereigns, subjects be subjects, fathers be fathers, and sons be sons. He rectified the moral bonds and ordered social norms, an accomplishment comparable to the providence of heaven and earth."[94] In the same edict, Taizu cited the example of Guo Wei 郭威 (904–954), the Taizu emperor of the later Zhou dynasty: "Confucius is the teacher of a hundred generations of kings and emperors, so how dare we not venerate him?"[95] This ruler's reminder clearly articulated the political logic for rulers to be involved with the rites of Confucius worship.

Zhu Yuanzhang's descendant, the Ming emperor Shizong, took revenge in 1530 against the scholar-officials for defying his authority during the

Great Rites Controversy, which he considered a personal affront. Emperor Shizong mounted an onslaught on Confucian rites and iconography by introducing changes in four areas of ritual policy:

1. removal of all references to Confucius as "king" in posthumous titles;
2. substitution of wooden spirit tablets for Confucius sculptures, court robes, and headgear, and the reduction in the number of ritual vessels;
3. revision of sacrificial regulations to remove aristocratic titles of correlates and to change the Confucian scholars who were enshrined; and
4. renaming Dacheng halls as Confucius temples and adding the Shrine of Giving Birth to the Sage (*Qisheng ci* 啟聖祠).[96]

Altogether, those reforms inflicted a serious blow to Confucius temple rites that had blossomed since the Tang and the Song. For example, as an expression of worshipful reverence, the Tang conferred the title King of Wenxuan 文宣王 on Confucius in 739. Enshrined sages were then ennobled as lords—becoming, for example, Duke (*gong* 公) Yan Hui, Marquis (*hou* 侯) Bu Zixia 卜子夏, Earl or Count (*bo* 伯) Zengzi 曾參, and so on.[97] This institution passed from the Tang to succeeding dynasties. The Northern Song once even tried to ennoble Confucius posthumously as an emperor, an idea briefly implemented for about a half century by the alien non–Han Chinese rulers of Western Xia.

Although the Tang organized state rites into the categories of great, intermediate, and minor rites, its use of ritual vessels was not regulated in an orderly or rationalized way. For example, both the Xian Nong 先農 (ancestral god of agriculture) and the Xian Can 先蠶 (goddess of silkworm sericulture) enjoyed intermediate rites; however, they used baskets (*bian* 籩) and bowls (*dou* 豆) in different combinations of four and six, and there were no explanations for this irregularity. Later, the Tang tried to bring uniformity to the ritual code by specifying twelve vessels as proper for great rites, ten vessels for intermediate rites, and eight vessels for minor rites. According to the system, the presentation of libations was an intermediate rite with ten ritual vessels being appropriate.[98] In practice, the actual number utilized frequently exceeded the allotted number.[99] During the libation rites in 739, the Confucius sculpture was seated facing south, dressed in a king's robes and received offerings in accompaniment with music proper for an emperor. During the military campaigns of 766, a prime minister, three officials from the Department of War, and the generals of the six armies gathered at the National University to listen to lectures. At the time, the rank of the music played was higher than that which was appropriate for making sacrifices to heaven.[100]

Nevertheless, the ritual status of Confucius veneration was on the ascent overall. In 1476, the Ming emperor Xianzong 明憲宗 (r. 1464–1487) upgraded the musical accompaniment for the libations to eight rows of dancers and increased the ritual vessels to a dozen each of *bian* and *dou*, but he did not bestow the title of emperor on Confucius. In 1496, Ming Xiaozong 明孝宗 (r. 1487–1505) increased the dancers to a troupe of seventy-two, which equaled the honors given to the Son of Heaven. By 1529, during the early years of Emperor Shizong's reign, the Ming state was using the Rites of Heaven Veneration and the Rites for the Son of Heaven for offering sacrifices to Confucius. As an emperor who valorized royal absolutism, Shizong found this situation intolerable.[101]

Emperor Shizong was directing his imperial wrath against aspects of the Confucian temple that had escaped the wrath of his ancestor of the Ming dynasty. In 1370, soon after Emperor Taizu founded the Ming, he stripped the state-conferred divine titles from deified rivers, mountains, and many other entities and spared only the enshrined sages of Confucius temples.[102] Compared to his imperial predecessors in dynasties since the Han, Ming Taizu accorded less honor in the presentation of libations by reducing the musical accompaniment to only six rows of dancers and the ritual vessels to only ten. Yet Emperor Shizong went further, proclaiming, "It should be said the veneration of Confucius has reached its pinnacle, and there is nothing left that one could augment.... My own ancestor, the august Emperor Taizu, followed the Way of Confucius; nevertheless, his sagacity, humaneness, divine intelligence, martial prowess, and achievements of culture equaled Yao and Shun, and was far superior to Confucius."[103] Emperor Shizong proceeded to strip kingly titles from Confucius and aristocratic titles from the correlates, arguing that it breached ritual proprieties to portray Confucius, a mere court councilor, as a king.

Generations later, China's alien Manchu ruler, the Yongzheng 雍正 emperor of the Qing dynasty, also known by temple name Shizong 清世宗 (r. 1722–1735), would lambast his Ming counterpart of the same temple name. Yongzheng remarked, "In the ancient Three Dynasties [Xia, Shang, and Zhou], 'king' was a title that corresponds to the 'emperor' of later times, so it did not refer to the king as a prince among other feudal lords."[104] This was a jab at Ming Shizong's level of learning. Yongzheng was heir to the temple rites policy of his father, the Kangxi emperor, who once boasted that the splendor of his temple rites far surpassed the level the Han and Tang had achieved.[105]

The Yongzheng emperor proved himself a great sponsor and promoter of Confucius veneration. In 1723, he posthumously promoted five generations of Confucius's ancestors to the status of king, thus bringing Ming Shizong's 1529 demotion of Confucius into sharp relief. It is interesting to note that Yongzheng's argument was an inversion of the one set forth by Ming Shizong; as a result, although Yongzheng refrained from conferring the title of king upon Confucius, the Yongzheng emperor bestowed that royal title to Confucius's ancestors instead, a symbolically significant move.

Yongzheng's own successor, the Qianlong 乾隆 Emperor, also known by his temple name Gaozong 清高宗 (r. 1735–1795), made more pilgrimages to Queli than any other emperor of China. In 1906, near the end of the Qing dynasty, the Guangxu 光緒 Emperor (Dezong 德宗, r. 1875–1908) upgraded the rites of Confucius temples to a great rite of state, coequal to the offering of sacrifices to heaven and to the imperial ancestors; no further increase in status was possible.[106] Indeed, China's alien rulers often took extraordinary measures to glorify Confucianism because they were more keenly aware than other dynasties that "the governance of kings and emperors cannot improve the world without Confucius's teachings." An adage also said, "When governance does not improve the world, the state is imperiled." Those aphorisms, from Cao Yuanyong 曹元用 (1268–1330) of the Mongol Yuan dynasty, attests to the motivations of the rulers of China in their glorification of Confucius temples.[107]

When Inner Asian tribal peoples conquered the Middle Kingdom, they often failed at first to grasp the value of Confucius temples. For example, Jurchen raiders sacked and burned the temple in Queli during their invasion of North China and thus reduced the oldest and most venerable Confucius temple to ashes in the 1120s.[108] However, after founding the Jin dynasty, the same Jurchen leaders quickly realized that the temples were indispensable to their legitimacy. Therefore, Emperor Xizong 金熙宗 (r. 1135–1149) of the Jin dynasty built a new Confucius temple at the upper capital of Shangjing, in 1137, and attended to the offerings in person. He also paid respects to Confucius while facing north, a gesture that showed particularly high honor.[109]

Out of respect for the Confucius temple, Jin emperor Zhangzong 金章宗 (r. 1189–1208) erected a "dismount from your horse" stele (Xiama bei 下馬碑)

at the gate of the temple in 1191.[110] Emperor Wu of the Yuan decreed, in 1307, that Confucius was to receive the title King of Great Completion, Supreme Sagacity, and Exalted Culture (Dacheng Zhisheng Wenxuanwang 大成至聖文宣王).[111] After making a pilgrimage to the Confucius temple in Queli, Zhang Dai 張岱 (1597–1684) noted that the Yuan, of all the dynasties, erected the largest stone stele for Confucius. He further observed, "In the temple, none of the titles conferred by the Ming were actually used; this was a measure of the greatness of [the honors granted by the Yuan]."[112]

Another example would be Emperor Taizu 遼太祖 (r. 907–927) of the Liao dynasty. In declaring the founding of his dynasty, he was obliged by tradition to offer sacrifices to his tribal gods. Because the Khitan people were Buddhists, Emperor Taizu's ministers all anticipated that he would to make offerings to the Buddha. However, Taizu told them, "Buddhism is not a Chinese religion." Taizu then announced that he was going to follow the crown prince's counsel: "Confucius is a great sage who set the example for ten thousand succeeding generations; it is appropriate that he takes precedence." Afterwards, Emperor Taizu issued orders to build a Confucius temple and put the crown prince in charge of overseeing the temple's rites of spring and autumn. Taizu later built two more temples, one Buddhist and the other Daoist. Pointedly, when their construction was finished, the emperor visited only the Confucius temple, whereas he sent the queen to visit the Buddhist temple and the crown prince to the Daoist temple.[113]

The Expansion of Confucius Temple Rites' Symbolic Meaning

Local Administrators and Confucius Temple Rites

In 647, Xu Jingzong and other officials submitted a series of memorials that was to have an immense impact on the rites of Confucius veneration. Most importantly, Xu and his followers developed a system for designating the ritual's official in charge at various levels of imperial administration.[114] Thereafter, the state academy's educational official offered sacrifices at the capital on the emperor's behalf, while prefectural governors and county magistrates officiated the rites at local temples. This settled the pattern of appointments for the temple's ritual sacrifices.

The important place that Confucius temple rites occupied within the imperial ritual system also allowed local Confucius temples to claim ritual precedence over other rites conducted at comparable administrative levels. As we have seen, it was the custom of Han officials to make a pilgrimage to Queli if they were appointed to an administrative post overseeing that locality. As Confucius temples proliferated in other places in the empire, so too spread the custom of having administrators designated to pay visit to local temples. This was certainly the case during the Tang.[115] By the Song, a new administrator was expected to mark his arrival to take up office by first ceremoniously visiting the local Confucius temple, and only afterwards by visiting myriad other gods at their temples. Wen Yanbo 文彥博 (1006–1097) of the Northern Song wrote:

> In [1027], I obtained the *jinshi* degree and the assignment to take charge of this county. On the twenty-ninth day of the eighth month during the autumn, I assumed my duties. Following precedent, a region head must visit all officially recognized local temples to pay respect to the gods and to discipline the people, which are the foundation of political order. Therefore, I asked the local clerk to look in the county's illustrated gazetteers, which recorded the sacrificial code, to confirm that the only figure authorized to enjoy offerings was Confucius at his temple. The next day, I visited the Confucius temple.[116]

The implication of "looking in the county's illustrated gazetteers" is that the official visit to the Confucius temple was a mandatory rite in the county's records of the local government.[117] Moreover, the fact that the anecdote was an "old story" showed that the rite was old and practiced by this time. This point in the ritual code must have been inscribed in the legal terms and established for the whole empire no later than 1144, for Emperor Gaozong 宋高宗 (r. 1127–1162) of the Southern Song that year promulgated it under the advisement of Left Gentleman-Consultant Luo Changyuan 羅長源. Luo argued, "All scholar-officials must administer by studying and following the Dao of Confucius, but too many have forgotten this. I hope that a decree ordering them to pay visits to the temple school prior [to taking up office] would rectify their moral and cultural foundation." In response, Emperor Gaozong ordered, "When county- and prefectural-level civil officials first assume office, they must go to the local temple schools before they are allowed to begin performing their duties."[118]

Several texts corroborate this ritual policy. Zhang Xiaoxiang 張孝祥 (1132–1169) of the Southern Song wrote, upon assuming office, "Before beginning to perform my duties, I must pay homage at the temple and pray to the sage teacher for assistance."[119] This custom is confirmed by Zhu Xi's 朱熹 (1130–1200) narrative about the actions of a friend, Xiong Keliang 熊可量 (*jinshi* 1169), who had recently been put in charge as a local official.[120] Zhu Xi also wrote many other texts in which he discussed the tradition through his personal experience as a local official.[121]

These ritual policies passed without change to the Song's dynastic successors, the Jin and the Yuan: "When assuming office, officials must first visit the Confucius temple, and only then they are permitted to visit the temples of other gods."[122] These others were local Confucius temples whose status as a political symbol evidently had far surpassed that of other temples. In addition, peers harshly criticized officials who neglected their ceremonial duties. For instance, scholar-official Zhou Shuangxi 周雙溪 (dates unknown) angrily denounced a fellow official in a report to his superior: "Offering sacrifices to the late teacher is a great rite of the state. If an official can be remiss in even this duty, how can he be fit to govern the people?"[123]

The indignation in Zhou's report suggests that a deep sense of respect for Confucius temples had become deeply entrenched in the political culture of the literati class. However, the rule mandating that newly appointed officials visit the local Confucius temple vanished from the Ming dynasty's codes. It is my personal speculation that the omission reflected Ming Taizu's command, in 1369, to discontinue the universal observance of Confucius temple rites. His edict appeared to have ended local officials' practice of visiting Confucius temples upon assuming their office, which had prevailed during prior dynasties, even though the Ming emperor reversed his original decision in 1382.

Confucians and the System of Correlate Enshrinement in Confucius Temples

In 647, the Tang not only codified the official status for the person in charge of various temple rites but also codified the system of correlate enshrinement. Briefly, correlate veneration began in the year 72, when Emperor Ming of the Eastern Han dynasty offered sacrifices to Confucius and his

Figure 1.1 Stone rubbing of Confucius and his descendants.
Kenbunsha, Kyoto, 1989

seventy-two disciples.¹²⁴ After Emperor Ming, there were gradual developments in correlate veneration. Although the seventy-two disciples and Yan Hui received sacrifices intermittently, their status as correlates for auxiliary sacrifices was not stabilized; yet the system was becoming more sophisticated overall. In 647, Tang Taizong conferred the title Ancient Teacher upon twenty-two figures, including Zuo Qiuming 左丘明 (c. 556–452 BCE) and Yan Hui. The group of twenty-two were enshrined with the father of Confucius at the National University.

Later dynasties would base their regulations for correlate enshrinement on Tang Taizong's model.¹²⁵ Thereafter, enshrined sages would serve as virtuous exemplars for Confucians to follow both in their ethical conduct and in their responses to imperial examination essay questions. Posthumous enshrinement as a correlate was the highest honor possible for members of the literati class. However, the process of correlate enshrinement was not always seamless, because imperial rulers and the scholar-officials often contested the power to control the institution.¹²⁶

In addition, the Confucius temple served as the location where a Confucian took on new identities. Since the Sui and Tang began imperial civil service examinations, successful test takers were required to visit the Confucius temple and ceremonially pay their respect after they had obtained their certificate for civil service. In 717, the Tang dynasty decreed that the National University's Confucius temple should host the investiture ceremony for test-takers who obtained the degree of *jinshi* 進士, which was customarily the culmination of the examinations, and the successful candidates were presented to the emperor.¹²⁷ For example, the official history of the Ming dynasty stated, "In [1371], the court ordered the *jinshi* degree holders to undergo the rite of investiture at the National University, where the offerings of vegetables and libations were made."¹²⁸

In the Ming, after test takers passed the final court examination, they received ceremonial garments appropriate to their rank, which they would wear in the rite of investiture held at the National University. During the Ming and the Qing dynasties, even holders of the "recommended men" (*juren* 舉人) degree (the level below the *jinshi* degree) were qualified to serve in government posts, and thus their investitures were also held at local Confucius temples.

Imperial China's investiture ceremony, or *shihe* 釋褐, was held at Confucius temples, during which degree holders shed (*shi* 釋) their commoner's black (*he* 褐) clothes.¹²⁹ During the Ming and Qing periods, ritual weeping at the temples—the literati's symbolic act of protest against the insolence of office—further attested to the fact that the temples were the spiritual fortress of the Confucian stratum.[130]

Confucius Temples and the Rite of Reporting to Confucius

Confucius temples were among the locations for performing the rite of report (*jigao* 祭告), in which rulers reported things of ritual significance to the gods. The *Tongdian* composed in the Tang dynasty by Du You 杜佑 (735–812) stated, "In antiquity, before the Son of Heaven carried out an inspection of the realm, he would command historians to report it to the official temples, the gods of soil and grain and the famous mountains and great rivers in the region around the capital."[131] Thus, in ancient times, rulers made ceremonial reports to heaven, earth, the imperial family's ancestral shrine, and the gods of soil and grain. Because Confucius temple rites became a centrally important component of imperial state rituals in later times, Confucius joined those sacred entities designated to receive ceremonial reports. For example, in 992, Emperor Taizu of the Northern Song dynasty included the temples of exalted culture and military accomplishment in the "official temples" that received his ceremonial report about an upcoming state ritual.[132] Clearly, the rite of report underwent change and expansion throughout the ages.[133]

In its "Treatise on the Rites," the *Official History of the Ming Dynasty* declared that the emperor should mark his ascension to the throne by making a ritual report to the Confucius temple in Queli and to the mausoleums of emperors from the past.[134] Emperor Taizu's edict of 1369 established this rule: "Whenever a new emperor is enthroned, he should dispatch envoys to offer sacrifices in Queli on his behalf. This should be a perpetual rule."[135] In this, Ming Taizu followed the precedent of the alien dynasty that he had overthrown. Specifically, when Emperor Renzong 元仁宗 (r. 1311–1320) of the Mongol Yuan dynasty ascended to the throne in 1311, he dispatched officials to offer sacrifices at the Confucius temple in Queli. Thereafter, the Mongolian emperors of China would regularly order the libation rites when they first ascended the throne.[136] After that, the custom passed down from the Yuan to the Ming via Ming Taizu, and later from the Ming to the Qing dynasty. By the Qing, the ceremonies of the imperial succession, military triumph, investiture, and report to Confucius had all become essential and regular rites of state.[137]

As recorded in "Royal Regulations" in the *Book of Rites*, "[The Son of Heaven] shall lead military expeditions to punish the guilty. Upon returning, he shall offer libations at the academy to declare his victory to the first sage and first teacher."[138] Since Ming Taizu abolished the martial temples early in the Ming, subsequent emperors had found no place to commemorate their military triumphs, except at the Confucius temple. The Qing dynasty alone left at the Confucius temple a prodigious number of inscribed steles about the success of their military campaigns. The Kangxi emperor Shengzu erected such steles,[139] as did the Yongzheng emperor Shizong,[140] and the Qianlong Emperor Gaozong erected multiple steles.[141] For the Qianlong Emperor, "marking martial success at the temple of culture" became a routine matter.[142]

Thus, the symbolic meaning of the Confucius temple had expanded. In earlier times, the Confucius temple signified the imperial dedication to the source of moral transformation, to inform people about appropriate aspirations. In later times, it also stood for other ideas, including militarily punishing guilty rebels and dedicating the accomplishment at the National University.[143] As Wei Yuan 魏源 (1794–1857) wrote in *Records of His Majesty's Military Accomplishment* (*Sheng wu ji* 聖武記):

> When emperors of old embarked on a military campaign—whether led by an appointment general or the emperor himself—it was reported to the imperial shrine and the gods of soil and grain, but not the ancient teacher. The reinstatement of the ancient custom of offering the left ears taken from the enemy is the doing of our Kangxi emperor.[144]

One of my purposes is to use Anthony Giddens's (b. 1938) perspective of structuration theory to explicate the integration of Confucius temples into the system of imperial state rites.[145] Although temple rites could deviate greatly from state regulations during periods of social or political disorder, such temporary exceptions do not fall under my purview here. However, I should acknowledge such abnormal rites as, for example, the ones mentioned by Emperor Xiaowen of Northern Wei's edict in 471. Emperor Xiaowen commented, "Until very recently, the Huaixu 淮徐 region was not pacified and the temple was not in our control, which disrupted the proper conduct of temple rites and observance for ritual regulations." Xiaowen further noted that sacrilegious acts had occurred in the absence of imperial authority. For instance, male and female witches had defiled the temple by slaughtering live animals as sacrifice and by performing obscene songs and dances. In addition, actors and dancers had committed immoral acts inside the temple. For future reference, Xiaowen ordered that only libations and prepared foods are acceptable ceremonial offerings. Furthermore, the temple was to exclude women, lest they mingle with men or ask Confucius for inappropriate blessings. As the language of the edict suggests, the blasphemous actions it decried were contrary to the ritual regulations, and "violators should be dealt with for offenses against the code."[146]

The *Records of the Great Jin* contain similar examples or issues.[147] However, those extraordinary situations were aberrations to the imperial court and were invariably rectified. Therefore, we should consider these as exceptions that proved the norm. Another official dynastic history explicitly declared, "The state's work ensured that the rituals were performed with constancy."[148]

The Religiosity of Confucius Temple Rites

Confucius temples were for venerating Confucianism's revered figures. The temples comprised the sanctuaries of the imperial state cult, providing rulers and scholar-officials an exclusive place of reverence that outsiders were forbidden to enter. The uniqueness of this arrangement was not lost on Emperor Taizu of the Ming:

> Those who rule the state cannot be without assistance from Confucians, for Confucianism is the only one of the Three Religions that the state depends on. Confucius was born during the Zhou dynasty and established up its ethics, regulations, rituals, and music. Because of Confucius's great contributions to the state, the government established temples of culture for making ritual offerings to him. At the proper times for the offerings, Confucian officials would kneel and touch their heads on the ground to venerate him, but foolish commoners know nothing of this and do not partake the rituals. This is the strangest thing about Confucius.[149]

Taizu's puzzlement arose from the exclusiveness of Confucius temples, a tradition with a very long history. In the Song, a literatus once recommended opening the newly built National University and its Confucius temple to the public, including both male and female residents of the capital, so they could celebrate the achievement.[150] This unfortunate fellow became the object of universal derision by scholar-officials, which showed that the Confucius temples' exclusion of outsiders was heavily entrenched by this time.

Later, the Yuan issued a decree to refurbish the Confucius temple in Queli and gave the official in charge these instructions: "Be sure to make the temple awesome and bright, forbid people from wandering about, and make it strict and clean in order to glorify the beauty of its creation and thus respect its divine Way."[151] After visiting a Confucius temple, late Ming literati Zhu Guozhen 朱國禎 (1558–1632) reported, "Entering a [Confucian] temple is a grave and solemn matter, far different from Buddhist temples."[152] Zhu's observations pointed to the significant difference between Confucius temples and those of other Chinese religions.

In another anecdote, when the late Ming essayist Zhang Dai made his pilgrimage to the Confucius temple, he gained entry to the temple by bribing its custodians.[153] Even local Confucius temples were well guarded against trespassing, except on liturgical days, during which invited visitors were anticipated. The proscription against commoners continued well into the late Qing period; as one Confucius temple stipulated: "Not comparable to common shrine space; only designated persons may enter and tour."[154]

Small wonder, then, that during the late Qing Kang Youwei 康有為 (1858–1927) acknowledged, "For our Confucianism, only the officials involved burn incense to Confucius on the first and the fifteenth days of a month. On the other hand, students and commoners pay tribute to all gods, except Confucius."[155] Clearly, as sanctuaries, Confucius temples displayed exclusive and monopolistic characteristics to a remarkably strong degree.

A conversation at the Jurchen Jin court was also reflective of Confucianism's secular characteristics.[156] In 1194, Emperor Zhangzong of the Jin dynasty expressed perplexity that Buddhists and Taoists were doing a better job than Confucians of maintaining their temples, "whose Confucius temples were the most likely to become ruins." Why was this so? he wondered. Court advisor and Jurchen noble Wanyen Shouzhen 完顏守貞 (d. 1200) replied, "Confucians could not live in academies for protracted periods of time, unlike monks and priests, who reside in their temples."[157]

Buddhist monks and Taoist priests were dedicated clergymen at the temples where they resided, whereas Confucians were laypeople with secular duties elsewhere. According to C. K. Yang, this characteristic trait marks Confucianism as a "diffused religion," in contrast to an "institutional religion."[158]

Overall, the political character of Confucius temples increased incessantly from the time it obtained official status during the Han, a fact clearly demonstrated by analyzing the temple rites' participants. By the Tang and the Song, participation in Confucius temple rituals was the exclusive privilege of men with official status, whether they were the Son of Heaven, Confucius's sacred descendants, appointed officials, or local administrators. Ordinary subjects, forbidden to participate in the rites, naturally became alienated from Confucius temples.

Confucius worship was a ritual that fell under the exclusive control of the imperial state. Ming Taizu decreed the implementation of ritual offerings throughout the realm, but to be performed in Confucius temples alone, not in Buddhist or Taoist temples.[159] Subsequent imperial courts of the Ming and Qing dynasties repeated the proscription against inappropriate worship of Confucius in Taoist and Buddhist temples.[160] Interestingly, even in today's Taiwan, the republic forbids folk religious temples that worship Confucius to identify themselves as Confucian temples or Confucius temples.[161] At least in this sense, Confucius temples' status as an official monopolistic establishment of the state has survived into the modern era.

The official ban against associating Confucius with Gautama Buddha or Laozi in the same temple is symptomatic of the tension between the Confucian state rituals and the "unity of the three religions," which continues to be popular among the masses. First, because Confucius was the teacher of kings and emperors, only the ruling class had the right to give him offerings. Second, other temples often relegated Confucius to the inferior status of auxiliary, which was an irritation to rulers. Monk Zhipan 志磐 (fl. c. 1258–1269) of the Song said, "It has always been the case that images of the Three Religions' founders are frequently found in the cloister of monks, and the halls were named after them. Gautama Buddha is in the middle, Lord Lao is on the left, and the Sage Confucius is on the right."[162]

During the reign of Song Emperor Lizong 宋理宗 (1224–1264), Imperial Art Academy painter Ma Yuan 馬遠 (1160–1225) created a scene of the Three Religions (Sangjiao tu 三教圖, or *Portrait of the Cult of the Three*

Figure 1.2 Ming painter Ting Yun-peng's Confucius, Laozi, and Buddhist arhat. This painting illustrates the syncretism of Confucianism, Buddhism, and Daoism, with their representative figures discussing matters under a tree.
Beijing Palace Museum

Unified), a painting that is now lost. From Zhou Mi's record in *Qidong yeyui*, we learn that the painting depicts Confucius performing obeisance to the "Yellow-Faced Laozi" (Gautama Buddha), who is sitting cross-legged, and the "Dragon-like Elder" (Daoism's Laozi), who is standing upright. This was a denigrating gesture directed toward Confucianism.[163] In fact, the imperial proclamations against religious syncretism appeared rather ineffective, and the religious syncretism of the Three Religions steadily gained ground after the Song Temples that jointly display the icons of Gautama Buddha, Laozi, and Confucius sprang up all over China. By the time of the Qianlong Emperor in the eighteenth century, there were more than 590 so-called Three Religions halls in Henan province alone.[164]

In 1906, the Qing elevated the status of Confucius temples rites to that of great rites, which became its last hurrah, since imperial China fell a scant five years later.[165] To some of its contemporaries, the republic's founding was "the greatest catastrophe in all of history; the temple rites will be abolished, the ritual vessels abandoned, and the liturgical music silenced forever."[166] As the ancients say, "When the hide ceases to exist, from whence does the fur derive sustenance?" It was as though Confucius temple rites were adrift in tumultuous seas and cut loose from the government of the republic. Although Kang Youwei and his supporters attempted to write Confucius veneration into the constitution of the republic, his efforts ultimately failed (as we will see in chapter 6). Since the early twentieth century, Confucianism has existed as a disembodied and ghostly cultural presence, lingering within Chinese-speaking civilization yet awaiting a redefinition of its role.

In summary, Confucius temple rites existed under the theocratic framework of the Chinese imperial state as an organic and symbiotic component of its state ritual system. This symbiosis led to both its development as a cultural phenomenon of great significance and its downfall when the empire ceased to be. A Chinese adage aptly describes the history of the temple rites: "The waters can lift a boat or overturn it." Divesting Confucianism from politics is surely a necessary condition for its resuscitation in modern society.

CHAPTER II

Confucianism as a Religion

A Comparative Study of Traditional Chinese Religions

To treat the Confucius temple as Confucian holy ground, it must be established that Confucianism is a religion. This chapter will demonstrate that the people of traditional China unequivocally deemed Confucianism a religion in their society and felt that its temples were sacred places of worship. From a descriptive and historical approach, those facts indicate that scholars should understand the Confucius temple and the nexus of practices it represented as a religious phenomenon. To set the stage and provide context, we will first explore twentieth-century efforts to reinvent Confucianism as a Chinese response to the intrusion of Christianity into China. That endeavor reformulated Confucianism into a religion with parallels to Christianity and provoked leading Chinese intellectuals to deny the religious character of Confucianism.

Confucianism in Crisis

The controversy over whether Confucianism is a religion is a scholarly debate unique to the modern and contemporary eras; in traditional China, there was no doubt about whether Confucianism was a religion. For example, in his correspondence, even Matteo Ricci (1552–1610) stated straightforwardly that Confucianism, Buddhism, and Daoism were the "three religions or teachings" (*sanjiao* 三教) of the time, and Ricci asserted that Catholic Christianity bore a special theological compatibility with Confucianism.[1]

Although the Qing emperor Yongzheng's 清雍正帝 (Shizong, r. 1722–1735) imperial edict proscribed Christianity,[2] its efficacy in halting Christian evangelism's penetration into China was only temporary. By the late nineteenth century, Christianity had again invaded the Middle Kingdom, under the auspices and patronage of the Western powers. Chinese moralists and traditionalists, motivated by a desire to resist Christianity and the Western powers it embodied, sought to initiate China's spiritual renewal by reinventing the Confucius religion (*Kongjiao* 孔教). (Although scholars usually translate *ruxue* 儒學, *rujiao* 儒教, and *Kongjiao* 孔教 all as "Confucianism" and occasionally as "cult of Confucius," I will use "cult of Confucius" or "Confucius cult" to distinguish the explicit effort since the early twentieth century to promote a civil religion centered on the veneration of Confucius.)

The most famous among the activists were Kang Youwei 康有為 (1858–1927), the founder of the movement Protect the Cult (*Bao Jiao* 保教) during the late Qing dynasty, and Chen Huanzhang 陳煥章 (1880–1933), the founder of the Cult of Confucius Association (*Kongjiao Hui* 孔教會), also called the Confucian Association, in the early republic. The exile of Kang Youwei had the ironic result of facilitating the spread of his Protect the Cult group by bringing the movement into contact with numerous Chinese diaspora communities in Southeast Asia,[3] in addition to its already significant following in mainland China.[4] Meanwhile, Chen Huanzhang's Cult of Confucius Association established more than 130 branches in the early Republic of China—an impressive number that attested the organization's cultural influence.[5]

Naturally, movements of religious reform of this kind tend to be profoundly political. For instance, Kang Youwei declared, "To accord with its history and the nature of its people, China ought to be ruled according to the cult of Confucius."[6] Kang reiterated this point in another text: "To save China, the hearts of the people must be redeemed, morals and customs improved, evil deeds and wanton words resisted. Nothing other than cult of Confucius is capable of preserving moral principles and standards."[7] Chen Huanzhang made a similar pronouncement: "When the cult of Confucius survives, the nation survives; when the cult of Confucius prospers, the nation also prospers."⁸ These quotations clearly illustrate that concerns about the political crises of the time profoundly informed the reinvention of the cult of Confucius.

Kang Youwei firmly believed that Christianity was the spiritual pillar of the Western powers. He argued, "In all under heaven, no nation can exist without a religion."⁹ The aim of Kang and his supporters was to reinvent the cult of Confucius by endowing it with the characteristics of a "religious community" that could strengthen the nation's moral fiber. Liang Qichao 梁啟超 (1873–1929), an early supporter of Kang's project, admitted, "What is the origin of the movement to protect the cult? We feared the Christian invasion, and conceived of the movement as an instrument of resistance."¹⁰

Paradoxically, while Kang Youwei saw Christianity as antagonistic to the Chinese nation, his hostility to the Western faith in no way hindered his imitation of Christianity as the basic model for his proposed Confucian reforms. This irony is perhaps resolved in part by the fact that Kang was a dutiful follower of the (almost hackneyed) adage of Qing statecraft: "Learn from the superior techniques of the barbarians to control the barbarians."

Kang and his supporters understood that fundamental differences existed between Christianity and Confucianism. For example, they felt that Christianity put its emphasis on "the Dao (道 Way) of heaven," while Confucianism's focus is on "the Dao of mankind." Nevertheless, they did not perceive those differences as problematic to their advocacy of Confucianism as a state cult.¹¹ Their writings clearly reveal that the Confucius cult they proposed was a carbon copy of organized Christianity, and their intent to replicate the structures and institutions of organized Christianity.¹² For example, Kang gave Confucius the honorific appellation "master of the religion," and Chen discussed the functional similarity of Confucius temples and Christian churches.¹³ In the end, however, Kang's design failed to convince even his favorite disciple, Liang Qichao, let alone win over his political and intellectual opponents.

As the republic dawned, Kang continued to harp on establishing the veneration of both Confucius and heaven as the state cult.¹⁴ Unfortunately for Kang, his personal involvement in General Zhang Xun's 張勳 (1854–1923) failed monarchist coup of 1917 ruined his reputation. The movement to revive the cult of Confucius became even more highly politicized and made Kang into a magnet for the wrath of pro-republic intellectuals. In contrast, Liang Qichao championed the cause of the republic's constitution, instead of the Confucius cult; therefore, Liang became the cult's foremost critic, for which his contemporaries lionized him and made him among the most revered public figures during the early republic.[15]

It is not my intention to contrast the fates of the master and his erstwhile disciple; rather, the purpose here is to highlight the fact that the present-day controversy over whether Confucianism is a religion did not arise out of innocent scholarly curiosity. Quite the contrary, the modern debate over religiosity in Confucianism, or the absence thereof, is, and has always been, irrevocably enmeshed in the politically contingent present.

Initially, Liang was an enthusiastic advocate of Kang Youwei's Protect the Cult movement and penned many essays supporting his teacher's case. At one point, he even hailed Kang as "the Martin Luther of the Confucius cult."[16] By the time Liang Qichao was in his thirties (1902), however, his thinking on the matter had evolved considerably. Liang came to fear that an ascendant cult of Confucius would stifle free thought and, as a result, he initiated rhetorical attacks against the Confucius cult with such statements as "All religions are but zealous belief in superstition" and "Protect the Cult has nothing to do with honoring Confucius."[17] Liang also defined Confucius as "a philosopher, theoretician of statecraft, and an educator, not a religious figure." He cited many sayings from the *Analects* to support his argument, including "If you are not able to serve men, how can you serve their spirits?" and "If you do not know life, how can you understand death?" He also stated, "The master never discussed extraordinary things, feats of strength, disorder, and spiritual beings."[18] Liang Qichao's writings and citations would become a staple of the literature that argues against Confucianism's religiosity.

Zhang Taiyan 章太炎 (1869–1936), a prominent scholar during the late Qing and early republic, was irreconcilably opposed to Kang Youwei's politics and scholarship. In his critique of Chen Huanzhang's founding of the Cult of Confucius Association, Zhang Taiyan wrote, "Confucius's contribution to China was in being the first man to protect its people and enlighten its culture, not in founding any religion. . . . Confucius spurned following any religion."[19] To Zhang Taiyan, effort to promote the Confucius cult "amounts to desecrating the Queli County Shrine [in modern Qufu] and polluting the Mount Tai temple!"[20] Zhang's arguments were not particularly original, however, and were derivative of Liang Qichao's critique.

Two early republic intellectuals, Chen Duxiu 陳獨秀 (1879–1942) and Wu Yu 吳虞 (1872–1949), lauded by Hu Shih 胡適 (1891–1962) as "the two great champions who in recent years made the most effective attacks on the cult of Confucius," were representative of anti-Confucian thinkers of that period.[21] Chen Duxiu and Wu Yu inherited Liang Qichao's hostility to Confucianism but were even more radically opposed to it. Chen argued that the cult of Confucius was an aspect of autocracy and therefore "utterly incompatible with modern civilization and society."[22] Wu considered Confucian rites (*li* 禮) to be the physical embodiment of Confucianism, and coined the slogan "The cult of ritual propriety (*lijiao* 禮教) eats people."[23] As to the question of whether Confucianism is a religious cult, Chen answered with a categorical negative, whereas Wu answered in the affirmative but gave it a negative evaluation. Cai Yuanpei (Tsai Yuan-pei) 蔡元培 (1867–1940), a leading scholar of the time, also made this summary judgment: "Religion is religion, Confucius is Confucius, the nation is the nation; each has its proper bonds and cannot be conflated with one another."[24] It should not be surprising that Tsai also argued that Kang's advocacy for establishing the cult of Confucius as China's official religion was utter nonsense.[25]

In broad strokes, anti-Confucianism in the early republic was the result of a confluence of two movements: the rise of scientism in Chinese thought, and the course of political and historically contingent events. Chen's writings contain examples of scientism, such as "The path for the future of humanity's authentic apprehension and comprehension must be grounded firmly on the tracts of science, and all religions are to be discarded."[26] Cai Yuanpei similarly asserted, "In the nations of Western Europe, religion as a subject is a topic for the past, due to the fact that the substantive preoccupations of religion have already been resolved by the efforts of scholars using scientific research."[27]

At the same time there can be no doubt that from the perspective of external analysis, the political chaos of the early republic played a crucial role in enhancing the anti-Confucian ideology in such thinkers as Chen Duxiu. Lamentable incidents, such as President Yuan Shikai's 袁世凱 (1859–1916) enthronement of himself as emperor and promulgation of heaven worship as the Yuan regime's state religion, as well as Zhang Xun's military coup, all demonstrated the flagrant exploitation and abuse of Confucian cultural symbols. Those events, and many others, led to Chinese intellectuals' disillusionment with Confucianism. Excavating the past historical reality of Confucianism as a religion, therefore, requires us to extract ourselves from the political controversies of the early republic and to "bracket" the ideology of scientism. Hence, historical narrative is the most apt methodological choice for our task.

All participants in the debate over the cult of Confucius during the late Qing and early republic shared some common aspects, which continue to color scholarly discourse about the religious qualities of Confucianism. I will now identify those biased ideological presuppositions and explain why historical narrative is my choice of methodology.

All of these thinkers during the late Qing and early republic shared a predilection for philological and textual exegesis. In one debate, for example, Chen Huanzhang argued that since the word *jiao* (教) means "religion," the statement in the *Doctrine of the Mean* (*Zhongyong* 中庸) that "cultivating the Way is called *jiao*" proves that the Confucius religion is a religion. Chen Duxiu retorted that the correct meaning of *jiao* is not "religion" but "teachings" and "education," while Cai Yuanpei went so far as to argue that *Kongjiao* is not a noun.[28] These scholars were literally warring over semantics, and the debate yielded just one insight: philological explication cannot reconcile a priori assumptions that are deeply at odds.

Ultimately, this battle of semantics was merely superficial and obscured the subtext that Chinese intellectuals on both side of the debate were more alike than different. Both proponents and opponents of Confucianism used an essentialized Christianity as a comparative model in their evaluations of Confucianism. Furthermore, all participants in the debate were deeply influenced by the "apply and use" (*zhiyong* 致用) tradition of Chinese statecraft and viewed religion through the lens of social and political utility. In other words, Chinese thinkers internalized the appraisals of Christianity in Western historiography and thus overdetermined Chinese reflections on Confucianism. For example, Kang Youwei believed that the preponderance of Euro-American hegemony was not reducible to explanations of superior political institutions or material culture; rather, Christianity's ability to discipline its peoples provided the grounds for Western power. In contrast, Liang Qichao and Chen Duxiu believed that Christianity was a remnant of the ancient regime and an obstacle to the progress of modern civilization, and so modernity would abolish it.[29]

Despite disagreements among Chinese intellectuals during the late Qing and early republic regarding Confucianism, their understanding of religion did not escape the straitjacket of a definitional approach, deploying

Christianity as a universally valid archetype for all religions. Even today, scholarly discourse on Confucianism fails to overcome the definitional bias.[30] For instance, C. K. Yang's highly regarded book *Religion in Chinese Society* unfortunately failed to avoid this trap.[31] Therefore, we often encounter this bizarre claim: Confucianism is not a religion, but at the same time possesses distinctly religious characteristics.[32]

Using Western definitions of religion as the instrument to analyze non-Western religions is clearly an erroneous approach. As the father of modern sociology, Émile Durkheim (1858–1917), discovered during his research on the "primitive" religions of Australian aborigines, the traditional methodology that deploys Christianity as the definitional archetype for religion is invalid; hence, he had to critically reexamine and modify it at the very onset of his research.[33] More recently, another scholar made the sardonic comment that Hinduism is not a religion—if scholars take the Western definition of religion for granted.[34] The inflexibility of the definitional approach makes it an unproductive research methodology and makes scholars blind to a vast range of meaningful religious phenomena and experiences.

Therefore, my study brackets or suspends the definition of religion and deploys historical narrative to reconstruct the cultural meaning of Confucianism in traditional Chinese society. A careful analysis of the historical veneration of Confucius would trace the source of so much controversy among scholars during the early republic back to the cultural image of Confucius and Confucian practices during the Han Empire. Proponents of the Confucius cult, such as Kang Youwei, depended on the "holy Confucius" constructed by the esoteric, apocryphal prophecy texts (*chenwei* 讖緯) of the Han dynasty's state Confucianism as the foundation of their renewed Confucius cult.[35] The opponents of the cult of Confucius, such as Zhang Taiyan, criticized these prophecy texts as irrational and sought to delegitimize the mythical Confucius projected in Han apocryphal texts and prophecies.[36] Ultimately, Zhang's argument had even less historical consciousness than Kang's. Historians ought to acknowledge the Confucius of the Han dynasty as a Confucius in history, and it was wrong for Zhang Taiyan and similar scholars to be dismissive of historical experiences that are at odds with modern sensibilities.[37]

Having considered these factors, I will shift my focus away from the Han dynasty and onto later Chinese dynasties. In addition to avoiding the futile political struggles that have long passed as scholarship, my strategy centers on concurrent comparisons of the "three religions"—Confucianism, Buddhism, and Daoism—that are temporally appropriate and that should lead to a better historical understanding of Confucianism as a religion.

Comparative Religions in Traditional Society

By the Eastern Han, Confucianism, Buddhism, and Daoism had completely emerged onto the historical stage as full-fledged religions. Emperor Huan 東漢桓帝 (r. 146–167) of the Eastern Han, a ruler who possessed an "affinity for godly affairs," lived and ruled at this critical juncture in religious history.[38] Therefore, our inquiry into Confucianism as a religion in traditional Chinese society will begin with this emperor's religious practices and policies.

In the "Annals of Emperor Huan" in the official history *Book of the Later Han* (*Hou Hanshu* 後漢書), we find two relevant entries on the rites and sacrifices performed by the imperial court. First, Emperor Huan dispatched officials to Ku County 苦縣 to oversee the sacrifices to Laozi 老子 in the spring of 166, and again in the eleventh month of the same year. Second, in the following year, Emperor Huan performed sacrificial rites to Huang-Lao—the mythical Yellow Emperor (Huangdi 黃帝) and Laozi—in the Zhuo Long Palace 濯龍宮.[39] The most detailed historical account is probably this passage in *History of the Later Han Dynasty* (*Dongguan Han ji* 東觀漢記):

> During the seventh month [in 167], sacrifices were offered to Huang-Lao in the Northern Zhuo Long Palace. A luxuriously embroidered tapestry was laid to serve as the altar, which was adorned by vessels with lips of gold and silver, shining with light that dazzled the eye. The court provisioner prepared exquisite dishes from sacrificial meats, and music was performed. This was done so that the blessings of prosperity and harmony would be bestowed.[40]

The "Records of Rituals and Worship" 祭祀志 in *Book of the Later Han* has another account of this sacrifice: "Emperor Huan personally attended to the worship of Laozi . . . and *Music for the Imperial Sacrifice to Heaven* 郊天樂 was played."[41] That Emperor Huan would order the playing of this music in the veneration of Laozi demonstrates the extraordinary place Laozi had in the emperor's devotion. These elaborate sacrifices also show that by the time of Emperor Huan's reign, Huang-Lao, which originally referred to a school of statecraft in the early Han Empire, had been transformed into a religious cult centered on the worship of these two deified figures.[42]

In addition, it is necessary to point out that Emperor Huan also venerated the Buddha as a component of his devotion to Huang-Lao worship. The "Annals of Emperor Huan" record that he "planted fragrant forests to adorn the Zhuo Long Palace, and arranged beautifully decorated carriages to offer sacrifices to the Buddha and Huang-Lao."[43]

Buddhist missionaries introduced Buddhism to China sometime during the transition from the Western and Eastern Han, and they devised a strategy to attach Buddhism to Daoism in order to establish a bridgehead in China. In the process, they intentionally obfuscated the fact that Buddhism and Daoism were different religions; therefore, contemporaries frequently spoke of Huang-Lao and the Buddha as holy figures of the same religion.[44] For instance, according to the *Book of the Later Han*, Prince Ying of Chu 楚王英 (d. 71 CE), who lived during the reign of Emperor Ming 東漢明帝 (r. 57–75), became "in his old age increasingly fond of Huang-Lao and studied the Buddha's teachings; he abstained from meat and wine and partook of ritual baths and sacrifices."[45]

This confusing state of affairs apparently lasted for more than a century, well into the reign of Emperor Huan, without any significant change. For example, when court official Xiang Kai 襄楷 (d. c. 188) wrote a memorial to the emperor mentioning Huang-Lao and the Buddha, he still treated them as figures from the same religion: "I have heard that a Shrine of Huang-Lao and the Buddha was built in the palace. . . . Your Majesty every day refuses to abstain from the indulgence of desires and persists in ordering executions and punishments that exceeds good reason. Your Majesty disobeys their Dao [teachings]; why then expect them to confer any blessings?" The memorial suggests that Emperor Huan's new ancestral hall simultaneously venerated Huang-Lao and the Buddha. Moreover, the language of the memorial makes it clear that the court official thought the teachings of Huang-Lao and the Buddha were identical. The memorial states, "This Dao is that of serenity, abstemiousness and nonaction; it values life and despises killing; and it encourages reduction of desires and luxuries."[46]

Xiang Kai did not discuss the teachings in any more detail in the rest of his memorial, but he did try to explain why the Yellow Emperor, Laozi, and the Buddha would give the same teachings to their followers by citing a popular hypothesis: Laozi entered [the lands of] the *Yidi* (夷狄) barbarians [and] became the Buddha. Originally, this account was likely to have been made to expedite Buddhism's conversion of Chinese believers; however, the unintended consequence of this fabrication was to create a potential bone of contention between Buddhism and Daoism that would be triggered later and cause centuries of religious strife.

Since Laozi was the primary divine figure in Emperor Huan's sacrificial rites and the Buddha was a supplementary deity, Buddhism remained the junior partner in its alliance with Daoism during the reign of Emperor Huan.[47] Temple iconography provides an example. After dreaming of Laozi, Emperor Huan built a Temple to Laozi to honor the holy man in his birthplace. Upon the completion of the temple's halls, the emperor commissioned an image of Confucius, painted on a wall, to allude to Confucius's journey to seek Laozi's instruction about the rites. This temple's image of Confucius served to bestow greater glory to Laozi, the focus of the worship there.

Other examples of such iconographical practices abound. For instance, the shrine in the Zhuo Long Palace, mentioned previously, was clearly dedicated to Huang-Lao, but Emperor Huan also worshipped the Buddha there. At the temple to Laozi in Ku, which bore the image of Confucius on its walls, the chancellor of the Chen State (陳國), Kong Chou 孔疇 (c. late Eastern Han), later erected a stele (or obelisk) honoring Confucius and placed it in front of the image.[48]

Ultimately, Huang-Lao, the Buddha, and Confucius all were objects of Emperor Huan's worship because he wanted their blessings for longevity, prosperity, and political stability for himself and the Han Empire. From the auxiliary function of the Buddha and Confucius in ritual services and iconography, it is evident that Laozi occupied the most exalted place in Emperor Huan's religious devotion.

Interestingly, Emperor Wen 魏文帝 (r. 220–226) of Wei was in total disagreement with Emperor Huan's religious policy of giving greater honor to Laozi than to Confucius. When Emperor Wen heard that it was Huan who had ordered the construction of the Laozi temple, he ridiculed his Han dynasty predecessor with a scathing commentary: "How laughable indeed is Emperor Huan of Han, who, instead of learning from the sage's precepts (*sheng fa* 聖法), sought counsel from evil advisors and served Laozi and desired to gain his blessings!"[49] Emperor Wen referred, of course, to the "precepts" of the sage Confucius, and the emperor also gave solemn instructions to the governor of Yu Prefecture 豫州 in charge of Confucius's home in Lu County: "Laozi was a mere sage and it is inappropriate to honor him more than Confucius. Has the temple of Confucius in Lu County already been (re)constructed?"[50] By this time, warfare had long since destroyed the original temple of Confucius in war-ravaged Lu; however, the symbolic religious significance of Confucian temples compelled the emperor to make urgent calls for their reconstruction.

It was crucial for the development of Confucianism that during the Western Han dynasty, Emperor Wu 漢武帝 (141–87 BCE) decreed, in 136 BCE, "the abolition of the Hundred Schools of Thought and the supremacy of Confucianism alone," which elevated Confucianism from merely being one school of thought to the dignity of being the state ideology of the Han Empire. In addition, Confucius's cultural image had also undergone radical change during the Western and Eastern Han. Through the production of such prophecies as "The uncrowned king shall reign over the world, and his coming was foretold in innumerable prophecies," the historical Confucius was deified and transformed from a mortal scholar into the prophet and lawgiver of the Han imperial order. The late Eastern Han stele inscriptions in the temple of Confucius in Queli County fully reflected this process.

Of these inscriptions, the oldest extant inscription in a Confucian temple, *Kongmiao zhi shoumiao baidan Kong He bei* 孔廟置守廟百石孔龢碑, is on a stele erected in the year 153, during the reign of Emperor Huan. The panegyric proclaimed, "Confucius is the great sage, who, in imitation of heaven and earth, set the pattern or rules for the Han reign." A similar stele inscription *Luxiang Han Chi zao Kongmiao liqi bei* 魯相韓勑造孔廟禮器碑, composed slightly later, in the year 156, also during the reign of Emperor Huan, reads: "Confucius is the sage close to our era, and paved the Way for our Han reign. Everyone from the emperor down to students admire and follow him as their model." The last portion of this text also drew heavily from the esoteric sayings of the Han apocryphal texts, which even depicted Confucius as a giant figure with nine heads.[51]

The inscription *Luxiang Shi Chen ci Kongmiao zouming* 魯相史晨祠孔廟奏銘, found on a stele erected in the year 169, during the reign of Emperor Ling 東漢靈帝 (r. 167–189), not only repeats esoteric formulae similar to the quoted ones but also uses them in its summary of Confucius's life and work. This inscription completely transfigured Confucius into an omniscient prophet, preparing, centuries in advance, for the cultural needs of the future Han dynasty.[52]

As stele inscriptions indicate, by the Eastern Han dynasty, the esoteric apocryphal tradition was a decisive influence in how the Han people imagined the Confucius whom they worshipped in their temples. Another concurrent development was that Confucius temples changed from being the private shrines of the Kong clan into temples of the state cult, administered by officials from the capital. Confucian temple rites were performed not only in the capital's Royal Academy (*Biyong* 辟雍) on their appointed dates but also in the original Confucius temple in Queli, attended by local officials, members of the Kong clan, and the local elite. The Han dynasty firmly established Confucianism as the official state religion, anchored in the worship of Confucius.[53]

Veneration of Confucius and Confucian rites were crucially important to regime legitimation not only during the Han dynasty but also for successor dynasties. For instance, Emperor Wen's rebuilding of the temple of Confucius symbolically affirmed the political legitimacy of the Wei dynasty and its continuity with past traditions. In fact, the Wei dynasty had depended on Confucianism ever since its founding; to prepare for his usurpation of the Han dynasty, Emperor Wen's father, Cao Cao 曹操 (155–220), launched a shrewd propaganda campaign that exploited the popular superstitious belief in esoteric prophecies.[54]

Though Confucianism established itself as the state cult during the Western and Eastern Han dynasties, the decline and fall of the Eastern Han caused social and economic dislocation on a catastrophic scale. As a result, popular faith in Confucianism diminished to the point that Confucianism's religious supremacy, which had taken centuries to establish, was forever broken. People of all classes began to look elsewhere for their spiritual needs. Cao Cao was a very prominent example of those who took pride in challenging the conventions of Confucian statecraft.[55] In an uncanny parallel to the political–military standoff during the period of the Three Kingdoms (220–265), Confucianism's religious supremacy gave way to trilateral religious competition and the stage was set for the protracted debates and controversies among the Three Religions that characterized the next major period in China's religious history.

When Buddhism first spread to China, its missionaries relied heavily on a strategy of deliberate syncretism with Daoism to survive, as I have mentioned. However, by the third century, Buddhism had come into its own and started asserting its independence by aggressively confronting Daoism. The Buddhist–Daoist breach manifested itself in Mouzi's 牟子 Buddhist theological treatise, *Corrections to Common Errors* (*Mouzi lihuo lun* 理惑論), composed sometime between the late Eastern Han and the early Jin to Song periods.[56]

Mouzi boasted that he had mastered the Confucian Five Classics at a young age and had defeated every Daoist priest he had ever debated. In his middle years, Mouzi became "devoted to Buddhism and studied the five thousand words of the Laozi," but most people viewed his new spiritual pursuits as heresy. According to Mouzi, he wrote *Corrections to Common Errors* as a defense of his faith in response to his detractors.[57]

Readers should recall that Mouzi's professed veneration of the Buddha and Laozi echoed the religious practices of early Chinese Buddhists. People of the time often practiced Buddhism and Daoism together. Mouzi divided religions into two categories: "improving the mundane world," which Confucians exemplified; and "teaching nonaction," which the Buddha and Laozi exemplified. According to Mouzi, although these religions had different uses, they were definitely not of equal value, a point he illustrated by a gastronomical analogy: the Confucian Five Classics were the "five seasonings," but the teachings of the Buddha and Laozi were the "five staples." The indispensability of the latter two proved their superiority.[58]

Mouzi did not believe that Buddhism and Daoism had equal worth, either. He clearly asserts, "The Buddha is the originator of morals and virtue, and the progenitor of all the gods." Mouzi also manifested his opinion of Confucian religious figures when he claimed, "While Yin Shou 尹壽, Wu Cheng 務成, Lu Wang 呂望, and Kong Qiu 孔丘 were all teachers of sovereigns and emperors, Confucius was said to have sought Laozi's instruction in rites and rituals, which makes Laozi his superior."[59] Since Mouzi had already established that the Buddha was vastly superior to Laozi and the rest of the four teachers, Confucius naturally was utterly insignificant and could not begin to be compared to the Buddha.

Daoists, too, tried to denigrate rival religions as inferior by writing comparisons of religions similar to Mouzi's, which are found in many canonical Daoist texts during this period. The *Taiping jing* 太平經, for instance, categorizes into six ranks the holy men who attained mystical power, in a descending order of potency: demigods (*shenren* 神人), perfected men (*zenren* 真人), immortals (*xianren* 仙人), men of Dao (*daoren* 道人), sages (*shengren*

聖人), and worthies (*xianren* 賢人). Each rank had power over a specific domain:

> Demigods have dominion over heaven, perfected men have dominion over the earth, immortals have dominion over the winds and the rains, and men of Dao have dominion over divination and the power to change fates and fortunes. Sages have dominion over the hundred names [the common people], and worthies assist sages in their ministry of the masses and make provisions for the vicissitudes of the universe.[60]

The ulterior motive of the author of *Taiping jing* is obvious. By asserting that the highest and noblest of Confucians—sages and worthies—were the lowest and least impressive in Daoist achievements, he insinuated that Confucianism was inferior to Daoism.[61]

Daoist self-promotion like the *Taiping jing* became commonplace in popular Daoist narratives published later. For instance, in the *Baopuzi* 抱朴子, Ge Hong 葛洪 (283–363) compared the founders of Daoism and Confucianism: "Zhongni [Confucius] was a sage among Confucians, but Laozi was a sage among those who attained the Dao. Confucianism is shallow and approachable, which is why it has more followers; however, Daoism is profound and difficult and therefore only very few are capable of understanding it." Ge Hong's comparison was a mere sleight of hand designed to protect the main thrust of his argument that "Daoism is the essence of Confucianism, and Confucianism is the mere surface of Daoism." Thus, Ge Hong proclaimed the superiority of the Yellow Emperor and Laozi over Confucius and Mozi 墨子 (c. 480–389 BCE).[62]

Daoist and Buddhist challenges to Confucian orthodoxy became acute during the fall of the Han dynasty and the brief Wei dynasty, because severe social dislocation and suffering during this period discredited official Confucian ideology and created the space for Daoist and Buddhist expansion. Nevertheless, the growth of the two nascent religions also intensified mutual competition and a corresponding deterioration of their relationship. The fiction that the Buddha was an incarnation of Laozi and that Buddhism was the barbarian offshoot of Daoism, which previously served to cement the Buddhist–Daoist alliance during Eastern Han, became the point of contention between their faithful followers thereafter.

The Daoist priest Wang Fu 王浮 (290–307) triggered the conflict between Daoism and Buddhism when he demeaned the Buddha in his *Laozi huahu jing* 老子化胡經 (*Classic of Laozi's Transformation of Barbarians*), in which Wang stated that after Laozi became a Buddha in India, he invented Buddhism and taught Gautama Buddha. Wang's insult was too much for the Buddhists, who struck back by writing similar attacks on Daoism and thereby inaugurated millennia of mutual animosity between the two religions. *Laozi huahu jing* became a highly controversial text in Chinese religious discourse, and the waxing and waning of its literary reputation became a clear gauge of which of the two religions was winning the fight for religious influence and the favor of the imperial court.[63] Religious syncretism with Daoism, originally an expedient strategy for Chinese Buddhists, devolved into a thousand-year nightmare from which Chinese Buddhism could not escape.

Quite frequently, the running melee between Buddhism and Daoism caught Confucianism in the cross fire. For example, the Buddhist polemicist monk Dao'an 道安 (fl. 570s), from the Northern Zhou dynasty, asserted Buddhism's supremacy over all other religions in his *Qingjingfa xingjing* 清淨法行經, a conjured-up classic: "Buddha sent three disciples to transform China. The young Confucian bodhisattva 儒童菩薩 they renamed Kong Qiu 孔丘 [Confucius]; the bodhisattva of light 光淨菩薩 they renamed [Confucius's disciple] Yan Yuan 顏淵 [c. 521–481 BCE]; and Maha Kaya 摩訶迦葉 they renamed Laozi." Beyond Dao'an's audacity in appropriating the founding masters of Confucianism and Daoism into Buddhism, he portrayed the Buddha as projecting himself as "the chief . . . eldest . . . and foremost in the world."[64]

Taken into the proper historical context, however, Dao'an's seemingly hubristic claim belies Buddhism's modest circumstances during his day, when Buddhism was merely one of the three major Chinese religions and was not anywhere close to achieving ideological dominance over its rivals. Nevertheless, the mythical narrative found in Dao'an's book was quite popular in Buddhist texts of that era. For instance, Liang emperor Wu 梁武帝 (r. 502–549), a devout Buddhist whose reign was contemporaneous with Dao'an's lifetime, wrote: "Although Laozi, the Duke of Zhou, and Confucius were apostles of the Buddha, they were not doing right, and their achievements were no greater than doing worldly good. Therefore, they could not transcend the mundane and achieve sagehood."[65] Indeed, this narrative formed the foundation of later Buddhist discussions of Daoism and Confucianism.⁶⁶

Politically, Confucianism benefited greatly from its close association with the secular power of the empire, an advantage its competitors knew well. The Daoist Ge Hong poignantly observed, "During the time of the Three Sovereigns, Daoism was supreme; in the time of kings and emperors, Confucianism was ascendant."⁶⁷ Ge Hong's first observation was just a contrivance that allowed him to use the obscurity of antiquity to justify any statement he wished to make about the venerable antiquity of Daoism. Nevertheless, his second observation—that Confucianism enjoyed a near monopoly of political influence during most of China's imperial history—was a very keen one. Han emperors exalted Confucius over all other religions, and they revered the sage Confucius as the spiritual teacher of their line. As a result, other religions were eager to emulate the Confucian political model of endearing themselves to secular power.

During the reign of Han Emperor Huan, the Daoist Bian Shao 邊韶 (c. 147) dedicated an inscription to the temple of Laozi: "[Laozi] achieved enlightenment and transcendence, and as the cicada that metamorphosed and rose from its chrysalis. Since the times of [Fu] Xi and [Shen] Nong, [blanks in the original text] [he had returned] as the teacher to sagely rulers."⁶⁸ Laozi's cicada-like metamorphosis bears an interesting resemblance to the Buddha's cycles of reincarnation in Buddhism, which Bian Shao surely understood. For example, in Zhiqian's 支謙 (c. 200–241) translation of the *Fo shuo taizi ruiying benqi jing* 佛說太子瑞應本起經, Zhi claimed:

[The Buddha] is the lord of the heavens above and sage kings below, each happening thirty-six times, and when it ends the cycle begins anew. The form the Buddha takes depends on the needs of the times. He can be a sagely emperor, a leading master of Confucian scholars, an imperial advisor, or a Daoist priest—any form that he must, and in too many times and ways to be enumerated.⁶⁹

Daoists borrowed the idea of reincarnation or successive rebirths. Ge Hong's *Traditions of Divine Transcendents* (*Shenxian zhuan* 神仙傳) claimed that Laozi reincarnated twelve times. These reincarnations as the imperial counselor to the immortal rulers of China's mythical age spanned from the epochs of the earlier and later Three Sovereigns all the way to the reigns of Fu Xi and Shen Nong.[70] "Xiao dao lun" 笑道論 also corroborates this fact; it describes how *Wen shi zhuan* 文始傳 also presents the story that Laozi, in his many incarnations, served as the imperial counselor of emperors and kings of barbarian realms.[71]

These texts show that Daoists and Buddhists understood the Confucian advantage of being imperial councilors and desired to emulate the Confucian model of being the religious auxiliary to state power. Well did an earlier monk of the Jin period, with the Buddhist name Shi Dao'an 釋道安 (312–385), observe, "The endeavors of our faith cannot succeed without the support of the sovereign."[72]

The later Dao'an of the Northern Zhou wrote *On the Two Religions* (*Er jiao lun* 二教論) during a time when the imperial court's attitude toward the Three Religions was in a state of treacherous flux. The title of the book is misleading and belies Dao'an's concern with evaluating comprehensively all three of the major religions in China at the time. One of the crucial issues Dao'an discussed is the necessary unity between state and religion. Dao'an asserted, "Only sovereigns can be religion's founder masters (*jiaozhu* 教主)"; therefore, although Confucius and Laozi were virtuous sages, their lack of secular power meant they could not be the "founders" of their religion.[73]

Modesty did forbid the Buddhist Dao'an from stating explicitly that since the Gautama Buddha was the heir apparent of Suddhodana and the only man among the three to be both virtuous and vested with worldly authority, the Buddha alone was worthy of the title of "founding master" of a religion. Dao'an's definition for founding master is clearly prejudicial, and it is not surprising that proponents of other religions refused to engage him in a dialogue on his biased terms. However, based on his observations of the history of Buddhism in China, Dao'an insisted on combining virtue with secular power. In order to prosper in China, it was necessary for a religion to embed itself within the structures of imperial power and the ruling class, in order to shield itself from the anger of emperors, who were wont to feel threatened by religious power.

The waves of anti-Buddhist violence, known as the "disasters from the three Wu," during the Southern and Northern Dynasties, clearly illustrated this fact. The three emperors with the title Wu referred to those of the Northern Wei, the Northern Zhou, and the Tang dynasties. While longstanding religious animosity no doubt contributed to the outbreak of religious violence, it was the intentions of these three emperors—after whom the persecutions were eponymously named in Chinese historiography—that proved most crucial in initiating and conditioning these state-directed persecutions.

The imperial government's interest in regulating religions was motivated by raîson d'état, and the practitioners of the Three Religions were frequently summoned to the emperor's presence to debate the usefulness of their religion to the state. Those court debates were deadly serious affairs with grave implications for the fate of the Three Religions and their practitioners; thus, they were vastly different from the idle philosophical speculation into which they later devolved. One consequence of the debates was how much honor imperial etiquette granted each of the Three Religions; as official histories attest, an emperor frequently changed the priority order for receiving Confucian scholars, Buddhist monks, and Daoist priests to accord with the results of the most recent debate.[74]

The debates and religious policies during the reign of Northern Zhou emperor Wu 北周武帝 (r. 560–578) offer a vivid example of how capricious and devastating imperial power could be to religions. In 569, Emperor Wu summoned more than two thousand civil servants and military officers to participate in the court debate; moreover, he ordered the most prominent monks, scholars, and priests of the age to attend. All debate participants were required to advocate rigorously for the merits of the religion they favored. At the end of the deliberations, an official verdict proclaimed, "Confucianism is superior, Buddhism inferior, and Daoism superlative."[75] However, in 573, the judgment went another way: "Confucianism is superior, Daoism inferior, and Buddhism the least worthy." The following year, Emperor Wu issued an imperial decree in which he ordered "the extinction of Buddhism and Daoism, the total destruction of their icons and scriptures, the complete divestiture of shamans and priests, and their mandatory return to the lives of ordinary subjects."[76]

The period of the Northern and Southern dynasties produced other, equally frightening imperial decrees, including "Edict to Smash Icons, Burn Scriptures, and Bury Monks Alive" 擊像焚經坑僧詔, promulgated by Emperor Taiwu of Northern Wei 北魏太武帝; "Edict of Prohibition against the Proselytizing of Li Lao's Rituals" 廢李老道法詔, by Emperor Wenxuan of Qi 齊文宣帝; and "Edict of Prohibition against the Worship of Li Lao and his Rituals" 捨事李老道法詔, by Emperor Wu of Liang 梁武帝). Reading these edits readily conveys a gruesome picture of persecution and martyrdom.[77]

Although the official debates among the Three Religions during the Northern and Southern dynasties were solemn deliberations with serious implications, emperors in later dynasties transformed the debates into fashionable entertainment scheduled for the emperor's birthday. On the happy occasion of Tang emperor Dezong's 唐德宗 (r. 779–805) birthday, for example, he summoned representatives of the three major religions to the Inner Palace to debate one another and to give lectures to the emperor. In his summary of the event, the Buddhist monk Jianxu 鑒虛 wrote that all officials present agreed on this report: "The emperor of Xuanyuan [Laozi] is the sage of the whole world; king of Wenxuan [Confucius] is the sage from antiquity to the present; Buddha is the sage from the west; and Your Majesty is the sage of Jambudvīpa 南贍部洲 [China's 'continent']."[78] To understand how servile this conclusion was, the reader should recall that Emperor Xuanyuan and King Wenxuan were, respectively, honorifics bestowed on Laozi and Confucius by the Tang dynasty.[79] Thus, Jianxu hailed Emperor Dezong as a sage and an equal to Laozi, Confucius, and the Buddha—certainly an obsequious exaggeration.

More importantly, by the reign of Dezong, the religious debate held at least once in every emperor's reign (a custom the Tang emperors inherited from their Wei and Jin predecessors) had become a staged, role-playing entertainment—a diversion akin to the storytelling popular during those times. The religion-as-entertainment trend manifested itself in popular culture, too. For instance, numerous stage plays focused on the Three Religions were written and performed during the Song and Jurchen Jin dynasties.[80]

While emperors found amusement in contemplating the merits of the Three Religions, the candidates of imperial examinations did not. For them the debate remained serious business because the relative merits of the Three Religions became a topic frequently revisited in the imperial examinations and might decide their future in the civil service. Indeed, an essay topic frequently recycled in the examination was "Which of the sages of the Three Religions is the greatest?" Thus, this ghost haunted uncountable test takers preparing for the exams. Giving the essay grader what he wanted was a fine art that required both an up-to-date knowledge of current intellectual trends and a good instinct for anticipating the inclinations of the overseer of the examination that year.[81] For example, "An Overview of the Three Religions" (*Sanjiao lunheng* 三教論衡) by the literatus

Bai Juyi 白居易 (772–846) enjoyed lasting renown because test takers considered it to be among the best essay templates.[82]

Also relevant to our discussion of Dao'an's *On the Two Religions* are his two categories of "interior" and "exterior" religions. Dao'an characterized Confucianism as "a pedagogy for the salvation of exterior forms," which made it an exterior religion, while Buddhism was "the principles for the redemption of the spirit," making it an interior religion. Dao'an also consigned Daoism to the category of exterior religions, along with Confucianism.[83] This taxonomy of the interior versus the exterior became paradigmatic in Chinese religious discourse and a standard trope deployed in major religious texts. For example, Zhao Pu 趙普 (922–992) commented on Song emperor Taizong 宋太宗 (r. 976–997): "He ruled according to the Dao of Yao and Shun, [but] cultivated his mind with the Dao of the Buddha."[84] The famous court official Yelü Chucai 耶律楚材 (1190–1244), an advisor to the Mongols, commented, "For metaphysical reasoning and disciplining emotions, Buddhism is supreme; with regard to good governance and securing the peoples' livelihoods, Confucianism is peerless."[85]

Since the interactions of the Three Religions were so frequent, Daoism was eventually brought into the classificatory schema as well. Song Emperor Xiaozong 宋孝宗 (r. 1162–1189) amended the dualistic classification by arguing that "Buddhism cultivates the mind, Daoism perfects human lives, and Confucianism governs the nation."[86] The primary function of the schema was that it demarcated differences by asserting the unique utility of each of the Three Religions. This theory enjoyed exceptional popularity and lasting power in Chinese religious discourse and survived into the late Qing dynasty. For example, the provincial scholar Tang Zhen 唐甄 (1630–1704) remarked, "Laozi teaches us how to improve our lives, the Buddha enlightens us in the truths about death, and Confucius instructs us in governance."[87] The statement "the Buddha enlightens us in the truths about death" is merely a reiteration of "Buddhism cultivates the mind."

While Emperor Xiaozong emphasized the reconcilability of the Three Religions through sagacious agency,[88] Tang Zhen insisted that "the Three [Religions] are distinct and essentially incompatible."[89] Even though Emperor Xiaozong and Tang Zhen disagreed about the ultimate reconcilability of the Three Religions, it is evident that commonly accepted characterizations for Confucianism, Buddhism, and Daoism had become well established in Chinese religious discourse.

In addition to definitional essays, analogies for the three major religions were also a common literary genre that served as an arena of contesting religions. Li Shiqian 李士謙 (523–588), a renowned literatus from the early Sui dynasty and a devout Buddhist, tried to answer the question "Which of the Three Religions is the most superior?" He compared Buddhism to the sun, Daoism to the moon, and Confucianism to the five stars.[90] Just as the brilliance of the sun is unsurpassed, Li Shiqian implied that Buddhism was by far the most superior. Beizhu Luchong 孛朮魯翀 (1279–1338), a master Confucian of the Yuan dynasty, disagreed: "Buddhism is like gold, Daoism like white jade, but Confucianism is like the five grains."[91] Gold and jade are precious minerals, but the five grains were the essential staples that sustained the life of the people. By this logic, Beizhu Luchong's analogy suggests that Confucianism is the superior religion because of its indispensability, whereas Buddhism and Daoism are not as necessary, despite their usefulness.

To Mongol emperors of the Yuan dynasty—alien conquerors whose inheritance was won by force of arms and who therefore could observe Chinese religions as outsiders—Confucianism was indisputably a religion, albeit one that they found to be of little use. Emperor Xianzong 元憲宗 (Möngke Khan, r. 1251–1259) made a remark about Confucianism in his conversation with a Daoist priest:

> Now you, Master (*xiansheng* 先生), insist that Daoism is the highest, but the scholars [*xiucai* 秀才] all say the Confucianism is foremost; the Diexie 迭屑 people worship Mishihe 彌失訶 and say they will go to heaven; the Dashimans 達失蠻 worship and give thanks to heaven for its blessings. After giving this careful thought, we found none worthy to be compared with the Buddha.

Xianzong then held up his hand and used a fable to underline his point: "As five fingers extend from the palm, so the Buddhist religion is the palm and the rest are the fingers, which see not their origin, boasting and bragging, like the proverbial blind men feeling an elephant."[92]

Emperor Xianzong's terminology requires clarification: *xiansheng* was an honorific customarily used for Daoist priests, while *xiucai* was a low rank of scholar-official, but also used to refer to Confucians in general. *Diexie* and *Mishihe* are, respectively, phonetic transliterations of Jesus and Messiah, and *Dashiman* was the word Yuan dynasty Mongols used for Islamic mullahs.⁹³ This anecdote clearly shows that Emperor Xianzong was a devout Buddhist, but it also illustrates that the Mongols at the time saw Confucianism as a religion that was fully comparable to other known religions.

During the reign of the Mongols, Buddhist lamas served as the teachers of emperors and counselors of state, which gave them enormous prestige and political influence. Confucians were deprived of imperial patronage and often were condemned. Therefore, the Confucian court official Zhang Dehui 張德輝 (1195–1275) concocted the title Grand Master of the Confucian Religion (*Rujiao da zongshi* 儒教大宗師), which he gave to Emperor Shizu 元世祖 (Kublai Khan, r. 1260–1294), an honor the emperor "accepted with great pleasure."⁹⁴

Even more interesting was the case of the Uighur Confucian Lian Xixian 廉希憲 (1231–1280), who turned down Emperor Shizu's demand to convert from Confucianism to the religion of the master lama. Stubbornly refusing, Lian tersely replied, "Your humble servant has already pledged to the Confucian religion."⁹⁵ In the end, Kublai tolerated Lian's intransigence with great forbearance and did not punish him. Lian Xixian's refusal to convert points to the religious exclusivity Confucianism could and did display under the right circumstances.

Lian's was not an isolated case motivated by sanctimony or a desire for theatrics. Beizhu Luchong, who served in the post of director of the Imperial College, also contested the dominance of Buddhist lamas in the court by giving himself the honorific title Disciple of Confucius and Teacher of All Confucians under Heaven, which was an ironic appropriation of the imperial teacher's honorific, Disciple of the Buddha and Teacher of All Monks under Heaven.⁹⁶ It was also fashionable for writers of popular literature to pen anti-Daoist or anti-Buddhist propaganda. *Humble Words of a Rustic Elder* (*Yesou puyan* 野叟曝言), a popular late Qing novella belonging to the genre of Buddhist and Daoist parody, tells the story of a titleless and postless Confucian scholar who dedicated his life to battling the heresies of Buddhism and Daoism. The denouement rewards the hero with the supreme Confucian honor—to be summoned by Confucius to his divine court (that is, to be enshrined as a worthy in Confucius temples)—but only in a dream.⁹⁷

The existence of texts like *Humble Words of a Rustic Elder* suggests that the controversies over the Three Religions were not confined to the reified circles of the ruling class; instead, their influence reached the common masses and popular culture. For instance, the Ming dynasty literatus Feng Menglong 馮夢龍 (1574–1646) included a vivid account of the history of the Three Religions in his *Tales Old and New* (*Gujin xiaoshuo* 古今小說):

> Since the ending of the primordial chaos there were the Three Religions: Taishang Laojun 太上老君 founded Daoism, the Buddha founded Buddhism, and Confucius founded Confucianism. Confucianism yields sages, Buddhism yields bodhisattvas, and Daoism yields immortals. Among the three, Confucianism is the most commonplace and Buddhism is the most austere; however, Daoist teachings promise immortality and infinite transformative powers, which make it the most liberating.[98]

The author's transparent Daoist bias belied the unwitting admission that Confucian sages were fully comparable to bodhisattvas and immortals as religious exemplars.

If any doubt remains as to the religiosity of Confucianism, I submit that, in addition to religious exemplars, Confucianism also had its holy ground—Confucius temples—that were fully comparable to the temples of other religions. *Record of the Rebuilding of Qingzhen Temples*, written in 1489, clearly conveys awareness of the religious role of Confucian temples during the Ming:

> In my humble opinion, each of the Three Religions glorifies its founding master by establishing halls and shrines. Confucians have Dacheng halls 大成殿 to glorify Master Confucius; Buddhists have Shengrong halls 聖容殿 to glorify Sakyamuni Buddha; and Daoists have Yuhuang halls 玉皇殿 to glorify their Three Pure Ones 三清. In Qingzhen 清真 temples, Yisileye halls 一賜樂業殿 are erected to honor God.[99]

We should note that the "Qingzhen temples" and "Yisileye halls" in the text refer not to Islam and mosques, as is the case in modern Chinese usage, but rather to Judaism and synagogues.[100] The observations made in these passages implicitly acknowledged that, historically, Confucianism possessed all the characteristic traits of a religion, and that contemporaries considered it as such.

Confucianism had incentives to emphasize its unique religious characteristics in order to differentiate itself from its competitors during the Wei and Jin dynastic periods. At the same time, there also was a countervailing movement of religious syncretism, during the same period, which aimed to unite the three major religions; therefore, each religion was compelled to assimilate many practices and characteristics of its rivals.

The first signs of the syncretic movement, sometimes referred to by contemporaries as the movement for "unification of the Three Religions" or "the Cult of Three Unified (san jiao heyi 三教合一)," could be discerned as early as the Eastern Jin dynasty (317–420). In the writings of Sun Chuo 孫綽 (320–377), for example, we find this passage arguing for the reconciliation of Confucianism and Buddhism: "The Duke of Zhou, Confucius, and the Buddha were one and the same."[101] Another factor that facilitated syncretism of the Three Religions was the favorable political conditions encountered during the Tang dynasty, which allowed syncretism to become a powerful movement with a broad popular base.

Those favorable political conditions had much to do with the religious policies of the Tang dynasty's imperial family, the House of Li, which had long asserted that it descended from Laozi.[102] Although the Tang emperors were preferential to Daoism, they had no wish to allow religious controversy to destabilize their regime, and they took great pains to avoid alienating Confucians and Buddhists. Tang emperor Gaozu 唐高祖 (r. 618–626), in the earliest years of the dynasty, proclaimed, "Even though the Three Religions have their differences, it is nevertheless most beneficent to combine them into one."[103] Thereafter, Gaozu steadfastly refrained from taking repressive measures against Confucianism or Buddhism, and his toleration became the default religious policy for much of the Tang dynasty.[104] Emperor Xuanzong 唐玄宗 (r. 712–756), for instance, was celebrated by his contemporaries for his learned and voluminous commentaries on the *Classic of Filial Piety* 孝經 (*Xiaojing*), the *Daodejing* 道德經, and the *Diamond Sutra* 金剛經, in which he argued for their reconcilability into one religion.[105]

Religious toleration practiced by the Tang emperors proved politically astute, so emperors of succeeding dynasties imitated this Tang policy. For example, Ming Taizu 明太祖 (r. 1368–1398) made significant contributions to the movement toward religious unity by authoring a highly influential text, *On the Three Religions* (*Sanjiao lun* 三教論), in which he wrote:

I have heard that "Under heaven there cannot be two true Dao, and a sage does not have two true hearts." Yet, although the Three Religions disagreed on such matters as the desirability of luxuries and honors, the principle of aiding the needy is the same. Ours is an age benighted by foolish men, and the Three Religions are all necessary.[106]

The Qing emperor Yongzheng also promoted the Cult of the Three Unified (*Sanyi jiao* 三一教). Yongzheng's statement in 1733 was an elaboration of Ming Taizu's, which, despite its greater sophistication, remained identical in substance. Yongzheng proclaimed, "While the Three Religions differed from each other in their Dao for perfecting the mind and body, and also governing the state, it is obvious that each Way has its own advantages and disadvantages; therefore, not one of them can be discarded."[107]

Intellectually, the rise of Wang Yangming's philosophy during Ming dynasty significantly aided the spread of religious syncretism. Ji Yun 紀昀 (1724–1805) attested to this fact in his *Annotated Catalog of the Complete Imperial Library* (*Sikuquanshu zongmu tiyao* 四庫全書總目提要): "When the Learning of Mind (*xinxue* 心學) was in vogue, there was no one who did not discuss the unity of the Three Religions."[108] Yangmingism's affinity for religious syncretism can be seen in a panegyric written by He Xinyin 何心隱 (1517–1579), a left-wing follower of Wang Yangming. The subject of his praise was Lin Zhao'en 林兆恩 (1517–1598), the master of the Cult of the Three Unified: "The founding of the Three Religions of Confucianism, Daoism, and Buddhism by Confucius, Laozi, and the Buddha were great feats done in the past. Today, the only great enterprise left to be accomplished, and the only great religion yet to be founded, is to bring unification to the Three Religions."[109]

Both the learned elite and the literate public supported religious syncretism. For example, *Sanjiao kaimi guizheng yanyi* 三教開迷歸正演義, a weighty novel based on the life and work of Master Lin Zhao'en, was widely read by the literati (*shi* 士) class. Popular literature such as *Sanjiao kaimi* must have been instrumental in the transmission of Lin's ideas about unifying the Three Religions.[110] The Cult of the Three Unified appears to have enjoyed great popularity; for instance, records of Henan province from the early Qianlong era in the mid-eighteenth century counted more than 590 temples of the cult in that province alone. Such temples were distinguished by the fact that their main halls displayed the icons of the Buddha, Laozi, and Confucius side by side for veneration.[111]

Beginning in the Song and Yuan dynasties, the holy founders of the Cult of the Three Unified became a popular iconographic genre in art, and their representations in statues, portraits, and carvings were prevalent in private houses as well as in religious temples and monasteries. Zhipan 志磐 (fl. c. 1258–1269), a Buddhist monk from the Song dynasty, recounted in the *Fozu tongji* 佛祖統紀 a matter from the year 1106: "The abodes of monks in the past were frequently decorated by icons [of founders of the] Cult of the Three Unified, and the halls of the temple were named after them as well. The Buddha was central in the hall, Laozi on the left, Master Kong on the right."[112]

The Song dynasty iconographic painting *Portrait of the Cult of the Three Unified* 三教圖 by Ma Yuan 馬遠 (1160–1225), an official at the Imperial Art Academy under Emperor Lizong 宋理宗 (r. 1224–1264), offended Confucians by showing Confucius bowing to the Buddha (the Yellow-Faced Laozi) and Laozi (the Dragon-like Elder), the former meditating with crossed legs and the latter solemnly attending to the Buddha.[113] The identity of the holy man depicted in the center of iconographic paintings—the place of honor in painting as well as in seating arrangements—depended on the iconographer's religious affiliation; therefore, it is not surprising that such paintings often were the cause of religious controversies among the literati.[114] For example, the devoted Confucian Sun Fu 孫復 (992–1057) expressed the opinion that the "stalemate" among Confucianism, Buddhism, and Daoism was "humiliating to Confucians."[115]

Booksellers even retroactively amended Gan Bao's 干寶 (d. 336) *In Search of the Supernatural* (*Soushenji* 搜神記). They added text and illustrations that allowed the divine genealogy of the original to accommodate all three pantheons of the major religions, as well as adding content for new chapters, with new titles, such as "The Origin of Confucianism," "The Origin of Buddhism," and "The Origin of Daoism." The most popular of these works included illustrated books, such as the Yuan dynasty *Xinbian Liangxiang soushen guangji* 新編連相搜神廣記 and the Ming dynasty *Huitu Sanjiao yuanliu soushen daquan* 繪圖三教源流搜神大全.[116] With graphics accompanying the text, these mass-produced woodblock prints served general readers in their everyday lives; thus, these works were the ideal medium through which to propagate the idea of Confucianism as one of the three component religions of the Cult of the Three Unified.

During the epoch of mutual rivalry and competition, Confucianism had already formed its identity as a distinct religion, while its essential character was that of a state cult. During the period of the union of the Three Religions, Confucianism combined with Buddhism and Daoism and so became a virtual symbiotic organism with them and took on characteristics of a folk religion.[117] By the nineteenth century, Confucianism was widely recognized as a religion in both of its aspects, as state cult and as folk religion.[118] For example, according to the Japanese colonial government's Investigative Committee on Old Taiwanese Customs (1910), "Confucianism as formulated by Confucius and Mencius is the ancient doctrine of sage kings whose scope included the religious, the ethical, and the political, seamlessly unifying them into a systematic whole."[119] A very pithy and incisive evaluation of Confucianism, the Investigative Committee's report also expressed the universal consensus of the time.

The Collapse of Confucianism

Professor Wilfred Cantwell Smith (1916–2000) of Harvard School of Divinity argued that, as a general concept, reified religion is an invention of the West in the modern period. Despite that clear insight, there are problematic theoretical issues in Smith's work, as well as errors of historical facts in his discussion on Confucianism and Daoism.[120] My own study indicates that Confucianism, Buddhism, and Daoism had an exceptionally long history of interactions in Chinese society. The shocks and adaptations precipitated by Buddhism's extension into China during the Eastern Han were crucial to the development of systemic difference between the Three Religions, through which they asserted their unique identities.

Though he expressed himself in traditional language, Lin Zhao'en has provided an account that remains sound: "There was only one religion during the epoch of Tang [Yao], Yu [Shun], and the Three Dynasties. After the Qin and Han dynasties, the Three Religions became known, and the arts of the Dao (*daoshu* 道術) were fragmented."[121] Competition among Confucianism, Buddhism, and Daoism was among full-fledged and heterogeneous religious systems, rather than being intrafaith controversies; hence, differences among the Three Religions became sharp and systematized. Again, Lin Zhao'en provides the most useful testimony:

The religion of Confucius never did declare itself Confucianism, but the later students of Confucius named it "Confucianism." The religion of the Yellow Emperor and Laozi never did declare itself Daoism, but later students of the Yellow Emperor and Laozi declared it "Daoism." The religion of the Buddha never called itself Buddhism, but later students of the Buddha named it "Buddhism."[122]

Ming Taizu raised doubts about ancient people identifying Laozi with the Buddha and with the quest for immortality; therefore, the emperor questioned whether Laozi should be called the founding master of Daoism. Nevertheless, the founding emperor of the Ming dynasty was absolutely convinced that Confucius was the founding master of Confucianism. He wrote, "If, on the other hand, we must use the terminology of the Three Religions, then Confucianism should be named after Zhongni [Confucius], Buddhism after the Buddha, and [the quest for] immortals after Chisongzi 赤松子 and those like him. This way of naming the religions would be the most precise."[123]

Emperor Taizu's statement attests to the reality that the perception of Confucianism as a religion was deeply ingrained in Chinese minds and was accepted as fact. Even though *zongjiao* 宗教, the Chinese compound word for "religion," is a modern term (coined by the Japanese) to express a Western concept, it is by no means an exaggeration to argue that this concept refers to a phenomenon that has existed since antiquity in China. This perspective suggests that Chinese history is an invaluable treasure house of primary sources for the comparative history of religions.

Max Weber (1864–1920) poignantly wrote that when he initiated his research in the sociology of religions, he found it impossible to give a functional definition to the term "religion," and that he realized this task would only be appropriate after he had completed his work.[124] My research strategy follows Weber's wise advice on this point.

In their attempt to adapt to occidental cultural hegemony, non-Western thinkers have often examined their own religions through the optic of Christianity. Deploying Christianity as a paradigmatic model ultimately resembles fitting a square peg into a round hole. This flaw is particularly evident in the debate over the religious nature of Confucianism during the late Qing dynasty and the early republic. It should not be surprising that attempts to derive a general definition of religion from one particular faith would go awry. Protestant theologian Paul Tillich's (1886–1965) proposal to use "ultimate concern," instead of "universal religions," as a formal definition for religion was inspired by his awareness of the problems inherent in earlier expositions.[125]

Alternatively, if we translate "ultimate concern" into Confucian language as *anshen liming* 安身立命 (literally, "settling down to the state where one belongs and thus establishing one's destiny"), this term would seem to be an ideal choice, because it overcomes the formal definition's over-abstraction by placing emphasis on individual choice. In the modern context, Confucianism's spiritual strength—its ability to so effectively offer a sense of belonging in the lives of ordinary people in traditional society—has almost been extinguished by the relentless, erosive forces of history.

I would identify two principal causes for the waning of Confucianism. First, Kang Youwei's Confucian reformation—using Christianity as its model—failed because it was abandoned by Chinese intellectuals and lacked successors of an intellectual caliber to take up the banner. Second, the abuses to which politicians subjected Confucian culture during the early republic resulted in mass disillusionment and long-lasting resentment against Confucianism. "Down with the Kong family shop!" became the cause célèbre of the times. As Chen Duxiu announced on New Year's Day 1917: "Forthwith, every Confucius temple in the nation must be destroyed and all of his veneration must end!"[126]

Chen's vehemence would not have been out of place in the ranks of the Red Guards during Mao's Cultural Revolution. That the temples of Confucius—the holy of holies of Confucian holy ground—would be held in such contempt by intellectuals must have been unthinkable to Confucians of past generations. Indeed, was Chen Duxiu's assault on Confucianism anything but the herald of the violence of the Great Proletarian Cultural Revolution in the then-unseen future?[127]

From the analytical perspective of a scholar, *Ren* 仁 (humaneness) and *Li* 禮 (ritual propriety) were indisputably the twin pillars of Confucianism; but in the twentieth century, intellectuals intent on reviving Confucianism almost universally emphasized "humaneness" at the expense of "ritual propriety," because they regarded the venerable Confucian rites as only anachronistic feudal remnants without a shred of modernity to redeem them. These intellectuals were blind to the fact that the soul of Confucianism as a religion resided in the performance of its rites and rituals—the veneration of Confucius, heaven, and ancestors. Confucius himself declared that "humaneness" requires "restraining the self," on one hand, and "observance of ritual propriety," on the other; therefore, humaneness will prevail in all under heaven only when the twin ideals are actualized.[128]

The study of humaneness that ignores the need to transform Confucian rites of ritual propriety to adapt to the times would only serve to cripple Confucianism. "New Confucians," such as Feng Youlan 馮友蘭 (1895–1990) and Mou Zongsan 牟宗三 (1909–1995) and their followers, have a predilection for reconstructing Confucianism with Western philosophy that unwittingly reduces the traditional Confucius religion to mere metaphysics and dissolves its religious meaning. In the disenchanted world of late modernity, this seems tantamount to conceding that the faint hope for Confucianism rests on the ancient adage "The human mind is prone to error; the mind of Dao is only a subtle spark."

CHAPTER III

Sages and Saints

*A Comparative Study of Canonization in
Confucianism and Christianity*

Sages are those who attain the pinnacle of the Way. Therefore, learn how to be a sage, not how to be a man lacking in principles.
—XUNZI 荀子, "ON RITUALS" (LI LUN 禮論)

Be ye followers of me, even as I also am of Christ.
—I CORINTHIANS 11:1

Approached from an institutional perspective, this chapter employs the practice of enshrinement at the Confucius temple and of canonization in Catholic Christianity as the focal point of comparison, an optic that brings the unique characteristics of those religions into sharper relief. Both Confucian sages and Christian saints were exemplars of religious practice and transmitters of ethical teachings. This essay compares Confucian rites of enshrinement to the canonization of saints in Catholicism in order to call attention to Confucianism's unique religious characteristics. I will examine sagehood and sainthood from four perspectives, looking at the rites for recommending suitable candidates, outlining the standards and qualifications for sagehood and sainthood, analyzing social strata, and examining the content of religious beliefs.

In the early twentieth century, German sociologist Max Weber (1864–1920) researched the correlation between Confucianism and membership in certain social classes; however, there still is a need for deeper exploration of Confucianism's characteristics as a state cult and a public religion. I will employ a cross-cultural comparison of Confucian and Christian rites to reveal those characteristics. In general, significant differences exist between Confucianism and Christianity, because while Confucianism is a state cult and civic religion, Christianity is today primarily a private religion that responds to the individual concerns of its believers. Such differences may account for the inability of modern Chinese intellectuals, immersed in a world of private religions, to grasp Confucianism's religious nature.

Introduction

After I completed my research on Confucius temples and the history of Confucius temple rites,[1] I became increasingly interested in exploring what the Confucian system of rites might tell us about Chinese culture and society. After some deliberation, I decided that a cross-cultural approach is the most appropriate methodology for excavating the unique characteristics of Confucius temple rites and for comparing Confucian sages (*shengxian* 聖賢) and Christian saints (*shengtu* 聖徒). However, before proceeding with this comparison, I urge readers to consider the foundation laid in chapter 2, where I note that at least since the Han dynasty, the Chinese have considered the state cult venerating Confucius to be a religion. Confucianism's religious characteristics are evident in comparison with Daoism and Buddhism. Moreover, as one of the Three Religions in the syncretic movement of the Cult of the Three Unified, Confucianism even absorbed some influence from folk religion among the masses. It is necessary to understand the religious characteristics of Confucianism to ensure the appropriateness and relevance to the comparison between Confucian sages and Christian saints.

Regardless of differences in Confucian and Christian beliefs and practices, there still are grounds for comparing sages and saints functioning as religious exemplars.[2] This fact was not lost on some scholars, and Rodney Taylor even explored this comparative topic, albeit in a preliminary and theoretical way.[3] My study aims to analyze sages and saints as ritual institutions and to address specifically the social and historical conditions in which they existed.

To avoid losing our analytical focus, I will strive to bracket subjective value judgments, and I will approach the two religions' holy men from a strictly institutional perspective. To provide readers with context for the origins of those institutions, I will relate short histories of Catholic canonization and Confucian "enshrinement as correlates" (*congsi* 從祀) to Confucius (551–479 BCE). With its hierarchy for worship uniformly observed throughout China, Confucianism's rules for temple enshrinement exceeded those of Daoism and Buddhism in elaboration and sophistication.

The institutional heart of Confucian enshrinement were the Confucius temples built primarily for worshipping Confucius and secondarily for worshipping other worthy Confucian exemplars who were recognized as sages by successive dynastic governments. The practice of venerating enshrined correlates at Confucius temples dates back to at least the year 72, when Eastern Han emperor Ming 東漢明帝 (r. 57–75) paused during his travels to offer sacrifices to Confucius and his seventy-two disciples at Confucius's ancestral home in Lu 魯 County. Later, Emperor Zhang 東漢章帝 (r. 75–88), in the year 85, and Emperor An 東漢安帝 (r. 106–125), in 124, offered additional sacrifices when they too traveled to this temple at Queli 闕里 (better known as Qufu 曲阜 in the late imperial and modern periods).[4]

By the time of the Wei and Jin dynasties, the spirits of Yanzi 顏子 and the seventy-two disciples were permitted to "accompany the enjoyment [of the sacrifices]" (*peixiang* 配享), and the rites for enshrining correlates began to become systematized. The Tang dynasty, in 647, approved twenty-two Confucians who lived after the death of Confucius to "accompany the enjoyment of sacrifices," thereby setting the precedent for enshrining correlated Confucians who were not Confucius's contemporaries.[5] Even so, it was not until the reign of Tang emperor Xuanzong 唐玄宗 (r. 712–756) that the rites of enshrinement as correlate developed into a fully functioning ritual institution. Although the individuals selected as correlates changed periodically, the ritual veneration of correlates became a constant feature after Xuanzong's reign.[6]

In Christianity, canonization evolved into an official recognition of saints through rites and established rules. The word "saint" originated from the Latin *sanctus*, which means "sacred" and carries the connotation of a holy man. (It is similar to *qâdosh* in Hebrew and *hagios* in Greek.) In the Old Testament, the word referenced the "chosen people" of God. In the New Testament, usage broadened to refer to all members of the Christian church; for instance, Paul the Apostle (c. 5–c. 67) and his correspondents from churches all over the Roman Empire addressed one another as "saint."[7]

In the early history of evangelism, the persecution of Christians was frequent, and "saint" became an honorific for Christian martyrs who died for their faith in Jesus Christ. Indeed, "martyr" originally meant "witness"—a particularly faithful witness. The earliest reliable record of the public veneration of a saint described an annual Christian festival that commemorated Polycarp's (69–155) martyrdom in 155.[8]

In fourth-century Syria, "saints" referred to religious ascetics, a usage that later propagated throughout Christendom. In the sixth century, Pope Gregory the Great (r. 590–604) issued a decree forbidding the veneration of living persons as saints.[9] Thereafter, the word acquired the familiar meaning of a person who has displayed remarkable faith in life. The veneration of saints initially derived spontaneously from local folk religious practices, and the institutionalization of canonization did not take place until the Middle Ages, a process that will be examined in greater depth later. For now, I will compare the enshrinement of sages and the canonization of saints in spatial terms.

Centers and Peripheries: A Comparative Spatial Survey

The most apparent difference between the enshrinement of sages and the canonization of saints is that from the very beginning, the ruling class of China—a group that included the emperor and members of the bureaucratic apparatus—controlled the process for selecting the candidates for enshrinement. By comparison, the canonization of saints in Catholic Christianity had its beginnings in a bottom-up social phenomena derived from local expressions of folk religion.

Imperial China's temple building demonstrated this difference. Except for the original Confucius temple in Queli—the Kong clan's ancestral hall—all Confucius temples were built to serve the religious agenda of the imperial government that ordered its construction. For example, in the wake of the dynasty's evacuation of North China to its new capital in the South, the Eastern Jin emperor Xiaowu 東晉孝武帝 (r. 372–396) ordered, in 386, the construction of a second Confucius temple in order to reaffirm the cultural continuity of his regime. The construction of this temple marked the beginning of constructing Confucius temples outside of the area of the Kong clan's residence.[10] With the precedent established, the rival dynasties of the North and the South—whether ruled by native Han Chinese or by alien "barbarian" invaders—competed to build Confucius temples in their capital cities in order to assert the legitimacy of their regimes.[11]

In roughly the same era, Confucius temples began to put down local roots by merging with official academies. First, the Wei emperor Wen 魏文帝 (r. 220–226) built numerous dormitories near the Confucius temple in

Queli, thereby providing an example for temples and academies to establish mutually beneficial relations.[12] In 550, Northern Qi emperor Wenxuan 北齊文宣帝 (r. 550–559) decreed, "The imperial academies in all prefectures (*zhun* 郡) must build a Confucius-Yanzi temple."[13] Tang emperor Taizong 唐太宗 (r. 626–649), in 630, ordered all prefecture (*zhou* 州) and county (*xian* 縣) academies to build a temple of Confucius, and thus spread the temples to every administrative division of the empire.[14] By the middle of the Tang, an estimated seven hundred to one thousand Confucius temples existed in imperial China, not including those in "loose-rein" prefectures (*jimi zhou* 羈縻州) in remote frontier areas.[15] In the Ming dynasty, the number of Confucius temples increased to more than 1,560.[16]

As the Confucius temple in Queli and the Confucius temple in the capital continued to require descendants from the sacred bloodline of Confucius to be the masters of ceremonies or the deputy master of ceremonies, these two temples retained a measure of the private character of an ancestral hall. However, local administrators governed the Confucius temples in other localities of the empire, so such temples consequently became highly political entities that were quite unlike the ancestral halls from which they originated.

Power from the political center in the capital still controlled the performance of rites in all Confucius temples. As the Ming scholar Wang Shizhen 王世貞 (1526–1590) succinctly stated, the purpose of rites was to "assist its teacher [Confucius] and continue the tradition of the Way in the world."[17] Yet the interpretation of the tradition of the Way differed among scholars of different generations, and even scholars of the same generation sometimes could not agree. As a result, the emperor's court often altered the standards for recognizing sages in the enshrinement as correlates to Confucius during the sacrificial temple rites.

However, the ultimate decision about enshrinement resided in the authority on the imperial throne, which held the matter of correlates as a solemn rite of the state—not something to be decided by scholar-officials. It was the imperial state's prerogative to add or to remove a correlate from Confucius temples throughout the empire—although in accordance with precedent, central court conferences (*tingyi* 廷議) drew up lists of recommendations. The Ming literatus Chen Li 沈鯉 (1531–1615) wrote:

> The work of [approving candidates for] enshrinement takes much time to decide. The court requires this burden because court

officials can represent the public opinion of all under heaven while debating the issue, which otherwise would become fragmented into a multitude of voices and marred by arbitrary judgments. It is necessary for the court to unify them all into one discourse.[18]

The court conference provided civil officials with a forum for reaching a consensus to ensure that people throughout the empire would house and worship the same correlates, without any discrepancies.

Despite the precedent of tradition, court conferences were ultimately a formality, and the emperor was entitled to quash its recommendations. In 1540, an overwhelming number of scholar-officials wanted to enshrine Xue Xuan 薛瑄 (1389–1464); however, after letting the debate continue long enough to satisfy appearances, the Ming emperor Shizong 明世宗 (r. 1521–1566) overruled them.[19] The Ming finally enshrined Xue Xuan in 1571, when Emperor Muzong 明穆宗 (r. 1567–1572) decided to go along with the court conference's nomination.[20] The case of Xue Xuan showed that the emperors firmly controlled the authority to enshrine, or as Wang Shizhen praisingly wrote, "The rulers implemented the enshrinement with generosity and practiced it with fairness."[21] The system of correlate enshrinement was profoundly political. Only an individual selected by the imperial government could be venerated in Confucius temples, and the identities of those who received sacrifices as correlates were kept consistent in every temple of the empire.

The Christian institution for canonizing saints was a different story. In late antiquity, the occidental world experienced a sudden proliferation of localized saint cults, and their activities played a crucial role in transmitting Christianity throughout the classical world. Although most early church fathers had reservations about the cult of saints, they could not deny its obvious mass appeal, so they bowed to the inevitable and allowed believers to embrace the veneration of saints.[22] The religious practice of private individuals and private households gave rise to the adoration of saints from its incipiency; thus, church authorities merely played the role of administering the norms for veneration. The social and grassroots character of worshipping saints left an indelible mark on the cult of saints.[23]

The streamlining of the canonization processes later imposed by the church did not stamp out the regional differences that characterized the early cults of saints. Instead, after the Great Schism divided the church into the Byzantine church and the Western church, the medieval saint cults remained at least as localized as their late antiquity predecessors.[24] Emphatically, "localization" refers to a concept that goes beyond the spatial; it conveys differences of identity, such as religious confessions, monastic orders, and ethnicities, that are bound to a place. For example, the cult of Saint Patrick (c. 390–c. 461) was inseparable from Ireland.

As Pierre Delooz observed, the canonization of saints has a dialectic function. On the one hand, the canonization of a saint is a meaningful event for the wider Christian community; on the other hand, the functions that any saint could perform are essentially limited to the local.[25] In other words, the canonization of a saint was the means through which the truth of the universal church could be symbolically affirmed in a particular church. This dynamic was evident in the first millennium of the canonization system; every saint that came into being during this period began as some locally revered figure who was later made a saint by local church leaders or grassroots followers. Although Saint Augustine (Augustine of Hippo, 354–430) argued that canonization should be a prerogative of the pope, the canonization of saints continued haphazardly until late-tenth-century reforms.

The Holy See performed the first-ever rite of canonization in 993, and Rome thereby signaled its intent to actively regulate the recognition of saints, a process hitherto controlled by local authorities. However, local bishops must have continued to canonize figures that were beloved by common believers well into the thirteenth century. Finally, in a degree codified as canon law in 1234, Pope Innocent III (r. 1198–1216) abrogated the right of bishops and archbishops to canonize saints. Yet Innocent III's law conceded that many of the saints who were canonized in prior centuries without the consent of Rome were fully ingrained in the customs of the people, and so their status was to remain unaffected by the new rule.[26]

Regardless of canon law, the canonization of saints continued to be driven by the will of local believers, who pressured the religious elites in Rome until they gave official recognition of sainthood to adored figures. Candidates who were recommended to Rome for sainthood tended be persons with large followings of enthusiastic supporters. In most cases, the followers of a prospective saint were likely to be a socially varied group, and it was common to find nobles, merchants, and farmers clamoring for Rome to recognize the sainthood of the same individual. When a critical mass of support for a candidate—which frequently resembled a social movement—became impossible for the church to ignore, Rome responded by canonizing the candidate. In the late Middle Ages, local pressures to canonize saints only increased, and the best the church could do was to weed out the least desirable options; in the process of canonization, Rome only selected, but did not control.[27]

Inevitably, as the late medieval church imposed stringent standards on canonization, Rome eliminated many candidates whom local believers favored. At the same time, the hitherto interchangeable appellations of *sancti* and *beati* became differentiated, apparently a gesture to placate the disappointed supporters of local prospective saints. The term *sancti* came to denote exclusively individuals who were "sanctified" by the church, while *beati* acquired the meaning of those who were not canonized but who were no less revered by their followers than were official saints.[28]

The creation of what was effectively a subcategory of sainthood showed that the church's centralizing efforts had failed to undermine grassroots support as the decisive factor in canonization. By contrast, China's rulers tightly controlled the Confucian institution of correlate enshrinement. If the Catholic system of canonization suggests a certain deference to society by political authorities, Confucian enshrinement evokes the polar opposite—a political regime that dominated society.

Criteria and Standards for Recognizing Exemplars

The worship of sages in Confucianism and the veneration of saints in Catholic Christianity are ancient institutions with thousands of years of history. Naturally, the standards used for selecting those religious paragons shifted and changed. Such changes through historical time reveal meaningful traits of both religions.

In the following comparison, I exclude two cases as departing too far from the general rules of recognizing a paragon to be useful for my purposes. Both the Catholic church and the Confucius cult worshipped the birth parents of their divine messianic figure—the Blessed Virgin Mary and Father Kong. Despite obvious religious differences, Father Kong and the Virgin Mary both occupy a special and important place of respect within their native belief systems. Kong, also known as Shuliang He 叔梁紇 (c. 622–549 BCE), was revered by early Confucians as the father of Confucius.[29] Mary, also called the mother of God, is considered the most powerful of Christian saints and probably remains the most venerated Catholic saint in the world today.[30]

After noting those exceptions, we still find that for both religions, the first cohort of formally recognized virtuous exemplars were the disciples and students of the messiah figure. As already recounted, Eastern Han emperors Ming and Zhang, in the first century, offered sacrifices to Confucius and his seventy-two disciples. In the occident, by the third century, the apostles of Christ—especially Saint Peter (d. c. 64) and Saint Paul—were venerated in both public rituals and private prayers.[31] At the time, the identities provided by literature on the individuals who made up Confucius's seventy-two disciples were prone to change, and a similar problem exists with the identity of some of Jesus's twelve apostles.[32] However, there was little doubt that those groups were venerated as paragons of virtue next to the messianic figure they followed in life, and they were referred to by collective appellations, such as the "four distinguished disciples" (*sipei* 四配), the "ten philosophers" (*shizhe* 十哲), late worthies (*xianxian* 先賢), and late scholars (*xianru* 先儒), in the rites and rituals specific to their religion.

Beyond this superficial similarity, the disciples of Confucius and the apostles of Jesus had little in common. Historian Sima Qian 司馬遷 (c. 145–86 BCE) wrote, "Confucius, a commoner, founded a heritage that lasted more than ten generations and is honored by scholars. From the Son of Heaven to the princes and the lords, all who learn of the six arts in China owe their learning to Master Confucius; therefore, he is named the supreme sage!" Sima further commented on the enshrinement of disciples as correlates to Confucius: "Confucius taught the classics of *Odes*, *Documents*, *Rites*, and *Music*. His disciples were more than three thousand, and [among them] seventy-two mastered all six arts."[33] The criterion "mastering the six arts" elevated the seventy-two disciples over Confucius's other students of the time, eventually leading to their enshrinement as correlated sages.

The enshrinement of the seventy-two disciples for academic excellence in the six arts created the precedent that justified the correlate enshrinement of later Confucian literati. From the official perspective, all men who "assisted the teacher [Confucius] in continuing the tradition of the Way" are qualified for consideration for nomination to become correlates. This emphasis on intellectual and academic achievement was a fixed point of reference in the history of the Confucian enshrinement of sages.

Tang Taizong ordered the Confucius temple in 647 to perform the first large-scale rites to enshrined correlates, including the elevation of twenty-two scholars whose books were adopted and taught in imperial academies; the number of enshrinements carried out at this single occasion was unprecedented.[34] The emperor justified their enshrinement by saying, "Our teachings are based upon the annotations on the classics, which these scholars had made and passed down to the ages; therefore, they deserve veneration in the company of Confucius in the temple."[35]

The enshrinement ceremony that year included two major innovations. First, the ceremony set a precedent for the enshrinement as correlates of literati who lived during a period later than Confucius's own time, whereas earlier emperors only considered Confucius's contemporaries as correlates. Second, enshrining the scholars for "passing down" learning had the effect of forging a stronger bond between Confucius temples and imperial education. In addition, by the early Tang dynasty, taking the imperial examinations had become an essential step on the path to obtaining an office.[36] As such, scholar-officials were acutely aware that the correlates' scholarly texts might well have a bearing on their own political self-interest.

In later generations, the relationship between texts authored by the enshrined worthies and the prevailing doctrinal orthodoxy became even more explicit, and the rise and fall of the correlates in temples were a virtual mirror of the ideological battles waged at court. In fact, changes in the ranks of temple correlates in the Confucius temples closely mirrored the struggles between the New School (*xinxue* 新學) and the School of the Way (*daoxue* 道學) during the Song and the Yuan, as well as those within Ming Confucianism.[37]

Of course, Confucianism was not unique in emphasizing learning and scholarship. Many saints were remarkable thinkers and academics, and those who received the appellation Doctor of the Church resembled sages. For example, Saint Augustine and Saint Thomas Aquinas (c. 1225–1275) were renowned for being prolific authors.[38] Nevertheless, although the Catholic church considered Augustine's and Aquinas's works to be orthodox, it did not use them as standard textbooks on a scale comparable to the way sages' books had been employed in China since the Sui and Tang dynasties. By the thirteenth century, the Catholic church did turn its attention to scholarship and learning and canonized several great academicians, including Aquinas, who were more renowned as intellectuals than as moral paragons. Nevertheless, scholars were a decided minority among canonized saints.[39]

In contrast, China enshrined most correlates for passing down the tradition of the Way, though Confucians during the Ming did begin calling for greater attention to a candidate's moral conduct. Ju Jiusi 瞿九思 (*juren* 1573) wrote, "All Confucians learn; but the way to become sages is what is learned. Therefore, they must learn from orthodox knowledge and receive the tradition of the Dao; only then can they be included in Confucius temples as disciples of the sage."[40] Before a man could to be considered a candidate for correlate enshrinement, Ju Jiusi argued, "His conduct must be discussed before his books are discussed." Ju Jiusi wrote that prospective sages should be judged first by "moral conduct," second by "knowledge of the classics," and third by their role in their times."[41] Even prior to Ju Jiusi's proposal, the court had approved the inclusion of Lu Jiuyuan 陸九淵 (1139–1193), in 1530, and Xue Xuan, in 1571, as correlates in Confucius temples on the grounds of their adherence to Confucius's moral teachings. The renewed focus on moral conduct, which Ju Jiusi and other scholars advocated, apparently made a lasting impression on Confucian thought. For example, in an ultimately doomed effort to bolster morale in the nineteenth century, the Qing dynasty responded to extreme calamities by enshrining five Confucian martyrs as correlates in the Confucian temple.[42]

However, the share of martyrs among Confucian sages was insignificant compared to the proportion of martyrs among Catholic saints. All venerated saints of the early Christian church were martyrs. Since the deeds of those true believers who died for their faith were well known to their fellow believers, there was little need for a church authority to verify their canonization.[43] After the legalization of Christianity due to Constantine's (r. 306–337) conversion and the establishment of Christianity as the state religion of the Roman Empire, the number of martyrs to die of persecution declined.[44]

Following those favorable developments for Christianity, a new class of saints, known as "confessors," began to take the place of the martyrs. Most confessors were ascetics who confessed their own sins and renounced them by doing penance. However, the confessors also performed faith-affirming acts that glorified the Christian God. For example, confessors demonstrated faith by seeking out physical and spiritual trials in imitation of Christ.[45] Altogether, the confessor saints contributed as much as the martyr saints before them to securing Christianity's place in world history. Notably, confessors were also important leaders of the local community, a role that Roman rural elites had abandoned following the societal collapse in the wake of the fall of the Roman Empire. Acting in the capacity of evangelists and intermediary agents between the village community and the outside world, confessors began a social movement that spread from North Africa to every corner of the former empire.[46]

By the Middle Ages, the church was an increasingly bureaucratic organization, a development that enhanced the influence of popes and bishops. Consequently, grateful popes often canonized bishops who had distinguished themselves as effectual administrators, as a posthumous reward for dutiful service.[47] Popes also rewarded successful monastic orders by canonizing their founders, who were spiritual leaders or theologians, including Saint Benedict of Nursia (c. 480–c. 547), Saint Dominic of Caleruega (c. 1170–1221), and Saint Francis of Assisi (c. 1181–1226).[48]

During the medieval period, church organization was crucial to maintaining ecclesiastical authority, and leadership was as important as erudition and refinement in such church leaders as popes, bishops, and the heads of religious orders. Leaders from all these categories figured well in the ranks of canonized saints. However great their contribution to the church, such administrators, educators, and scholars by no means represented the sum of saintly values. A large portion of saints were men and women who had had personal religious experiences, such as visions and revelations. Additionally, they became renowned for doing good works as prophets, exorcists, healers, and caregivers. They had charisma and commanded popular support, which led to their canonization by the church.[49] These various kinds of saints sometimes overlapped, and their prevalence varied from time to time and from place to place.

While the standards for canonizing Christian saints were not constant in different regions and periods, one of its most venerable requirements had no counterpart in Confucianism: the necessity for a saint to perform miracles, either in life or in death.[50] Doing miracles had its origins in the collective cultural memory of Christianity. In the Old Testament, God granted Moses miraculous powers that enabled him to lead the chosen people out of Egypt. In the New Testament, Jesus performed numerous miracles, which were an important asset in evangelism, and his apostles performed miracles in his name.[51] As a result, the ability to do miracles was almost certainly the oldest criteria established for canonized saints.[52]

The importance of miracles to ordinary believers is verifiable statistically. In England between 1066 and 1300, there were more than three thousand written references to miraculous relics, in addition to undocumented rumors of miracles.[53] Since medieval theology did not rule out the possibility that Satan might bestow supernatural powers on someone, the church had to confirm the virtuous life of miracle workers before their canonization. At the same time, miracles provided evidence of virtue. Thus, the church excluded from consideration as saints apparently virtuous people who had not performed miracles, because of the lack of evidence that their virtuous conduct was holy. Virtue and miracles were two mutually dependent and equally indispensable requirements for canonization, and this has not changed, even in the modern age of reason and science.[54] In the case of Mother Teresa (1910–1997), for instance, the headline in the *China Times* read "To Canonize a Saint, Vatican Waits for Miracles."

According to the *Analects*, "The subjects on which the master did not talk were extraordinary things, feats of strength, disorder, and spiritual beings." Confucius also said, "To live in obscurity and yet practice wonders in order to be mentioned with honor in the future ages is something I do not do."[55] Because Confucians generally read these statements as excluding the supernatural, performing miracles never became a criterion for the correlate enshrinement of sages. There are stories of Confucian saints performing miracles,[56] but that is a different matter from criteria for enshrinement.

The Social Composition of Virtuous Exemplars and Religious Belief

From the perspective of quantitative and qualitative social analysis, the large disparity between the number of Confucian sages and of Christian saints must be posited as a meaningful phenomenon. The Confucian institution of correlate enshrinement reached its numerical height in 1919, when the Beiyang government enshrined the Qing dynasty scholars Yan Yuan 顏元 (1635–1704) and Li Gong 李塨 (1659–1733) as correlates, to bring the total to 182 sages. In contrast, the Catholic church, between the seventh and sixteenth centuries, canonized an estimated 4,500 saints, according to the book *Roman Martyrology*. After blatant fabrications had been excluded, the number of saints was reduced to 1,500 by the eighteenth century; however, the official number rose to 2,500 in the twentieth century.

Two factors contributed to the quantitative disparity. First, the number of sages was necessarily limited by the Confucius cult's total exclusion of women, who were forbidden to offer or to receive sacrifices in its rites. During the Northern Song, Confucian literati severely criticized a Confucian court official for suggesting that the capital's temple school (*xuedian* 學殿, a sacrificial hall used to worship Confucius and sages) be open to the public, including gentlemen and ladies of the capital city.[57] The literati and civil officials were imperial China's ruling elites. Clearly, enshrining female sages would have been unthinkable to men who could not even countenance women visiting the temple. The literati class's aversion to women surpassed that aversion in Catholicism; although women were underrepresented among saints, the church did not dogmatically oppose recognizing women exemplars of the faith.

Second, the Confucius cult's requirement for all Confucius temples to include the same correlates was an effective check on the number of sages. In 630, the Tang government ordered all academies managed by prefecture and county authorities to build a Confucius temple, and thus turned the veneration of Confucius into a universal ritual in imperial China. Han Yu 韓愈 (768–824) wrote, in *Memorial Text for the Stele at the Confucius Temple in Chu Prefecture* (*Chuzhou Kongzimiao bei* 處州孔子廟碑), "In all under heaven, none but Confucius and the gods of earth and grain (*sheji* 社稷) receive sacrifices [from all men who ranked] from the Son of Heaven to heads of local governments." According to Han Yu, the sacrifice to the gods of earth and grain did not compare to the sacrifice to Confucius in solemnity or grandeur.[58]

Every dynasty in Chinese history had carefully observed the universality of the sacrifice to Confucius. Ming emperor Xiaozong 明孝宗 (r. 1487–1505) wrote, in the *Imperial Memorial Text for the Rebuilding of the Stele of Confucius*:

> Only the deeds and virtues of the ancient sages and worthies reached all others, and successive generations have established numerous temples to venerate them, so that centrally in the capital and peripherally in prefectures and cities and even in townships, there are none without a temple. However, it is only for Confucius that everyone—from the Son of Heaven down to the major officials in prefectures and cities—understands the importance of making sacrificial offerings with their utmost seriousness and reverence.[59]

The need for uniformity imposed a demanding selection process on enshrinement. For example, the Ming dynasty official Cheng Minzheng 程敏政 (1445–1499) repeatedly urged the imperial government to be parsimonious in enshrining sages. He petitioned the throne, "Those who had virtue and achievements that contributed to one generation were venerated by one generation, not in other generations; those who had virtue and achievements that contributed to one place were venerated in that place, not in other places."[60] The local worship mentioned here referred to the "shrines of local area sages."[61]

Enshrinement in state-run Confucius temples implied holding a correlate up as virtuous paragons for all eternity; thus, the state did not take the decision lightly. Cheng Minzheng asserted, "Our late teacher Confucius had virtue and achievements that contributed to all under heaven and to ten thousand generations; therefore, all under heaven and ten thousand generations offered sacrifices to him. Those who are to serve him in his halls and temples when he receives offerings cannot be mediocre." Cheng's reference to those who were to serve Confucius "in his halls and temples" referred to the sages receiving sacrifices as correlates. As Cheng also affirmed, these correlates in the Confucius temple must be people "beyond comparison with those who are of one place and one generation."[62]

Whereas Confucius temple rites included all enshrined sages in all temples, the Catholic church has handled such things differently. As the Catholic church venerated thousands of saints, no cathedral is large enough to accommodate all their images. Moreover, the cult of saints has always been marked by the constraints of its attachment to saints of a particular time and place. Few saints were as widely and universally revered as the Virgin Mary, Saint Peter, or Saint Paul; a majority were venerated only at a limited number of locations and for some a limited length of time. In Paris, Notre-Dame and the Basilica of Saint-Denis do not have the same titular saints or the same "correlated" saints, despite being in the same city.[63] In New York City, Saint Patrick's Cathedral and Saint Thomas Church—both on Fifth Avenue and separated by few minutes' walk—house and venerate almost totally different saints.

The vast quantitative difference between sages and saints is unlikely to be random or unmotivated. I will attempt to explore this difference from the perspective of social composition.

Out of the 182 sages in the Confucius temple, a majority of ninety-six sages (52.7%) were enshrined prior to the Qin dynasty (221–206 BCE).[64]

Within this cohort of ninety-six sages, Confucius's own disciples accounted for an overwhelming majority of eighty-two sages (87.5%), but they shared the appellation "seventy-two disciples."[65] Confucius prided himself on teaching all comers, without making any distinctions based on social background. He also asserted, "I have never refused instruction to anyone, even someone offering me a bundle of dried meat."[66] According to the etiquette of the time, a bundle of dried meat was the most meager of formal gifts and designated the bearer as a man of little means.

In the biographical information about disciples in the *Records of the Grand Historian* (*Shiji*) and the *Family Sayings of Confucius* (*Kongzi jiayu* 孔子家語), there are only oblique and abbreviated accounts of the disciples' backgrounds—indirect evidence that many of them descended from nonelite families. Confucius inspired his disciples to dedicate their lives to learning about the Way and the six arts; in that, they were quite different from later literati (*shi* 士), the elite scholar-official class of late imperial society.[67]

Although there is inadequate evidence to prove the status of other sages in the Confucius clan temple, there are sufficient extant documents from the period because the Han dynasty established the Confucius cult as the state religion in 136 BCE. From the Han to the Qing dynasty, the state enshrined eighty-six sages, seventy-five of whom had served as civil officials. From the Tang to the Qing dynasty, seventy-one sages were enshrined, sixty-two of whom were government officials; moreover, forty of these had passed the civil service examinations (see table 3.1).

During the Han period, with its division of society into a four-tiered social system, only one enshrined sage—Prince Liu De of Hejian 河間王 劉德 (d. 129 BCE)—descended from a class other than the *shi*, and he belonged to the emperor's family. Civil officials accounted for 87.2% of enshrined sages since the Han and an almost identical 87.3% since the Tang.[68] The social homogeneity of the correlates showed that enshrined sages belonged to the scholar-official class. The sages were simultaneously the figureheads of the official state cult, of academia, and of the ruling class; their high level of social homogeneity reflected the integration of the Confucius cult and the imperial state.

By comparison, Christianity had an ambiguous relationship with secular power, maintaining close ties with the state without the state absorbing the church, even though the degree of the church's autonomy waxed and waned. In the late fourth century, Christianity became the official religion

TABLE 3.1
Canonization in the Confucius Temple

Candidate status	Pre-Qin	Han	Three Kingdoms, Wei, and Jin	Sui	Tang	Song	Yuan	Ming	Qing	Total
Enshrined sages	96	12	2	1	2	39	7	12	11	182
Civil official	Unknown	10 (2 unknown)	2	1	2	36	5	11	8	75
Degree holder	—	—	—	—	2	21	1	10	6	40

of the Roman Empire; under imperial aegis, Christians imitated the administrative structures of the empire for their own organization, which grew into the Catholic church. But the church was not synonymous with the state. Saint Augustine, one the church's earliest and most influential theologians, argued for the separation of secular and religious authority, which was later elaborated into the "two swords doctrine" of medieval times.[69] According to the two swords doctrine, the pope wielded the "spiritual sword" and secular rulers wielded the "temporal sword," with each sword having its own purpose.

Skirmishes between religious leaders and political leaders were a constant feature of Western history, which underscores the tension that existed between their roles. An integration of the church and state on the scale of the integration in imperial China did not occur in the West; late into the early modern period, secular authorities continued to intervene in religious disputes, but without achieving a clear victory. For example, English monarchs were unable to dictate religious policy to the Anglican church, despite being its nominal head.[70]

Tang dynasty law classified Confucius temple rites as rites of the state, synchronized with the operations of the empire's political system. So, for instances, the sacrifices of spring and autumn were observed in all Confucius temples throughout the empire.[71] However, the birthdays and death dates of the correlates had no effect on the imperial liturgical calendar. In contrast, the Catholic liturgical calendar meticulously registered each saint's heavenly birthday—the date of the saint's canonization—for ritual celebration.

Canonized saints hailed from a wide range of social classes and familial conditions, and their social composition was significantly more diverse than that of enshrined sages. In antiquity, the records of saints were scattered, much like records of sages of the same period. During the eleventh century, however, the papacy claimed the power of canonization and began to collect data for its review of saint candidates. As a result, Western scholars were able to do analytical work on saints of Western Christendom by using church records, many of which I also utilized in my research. Table 3.2 reproduces, in a slightly modified form, a table by Donald Weinstein and Rudolph Bell, which reflects my analytical framework.[72]

Utilizing Weinstein and Bell's table, we observe that saints arose from a greater range of social classes than sages did (as shown in table 3.1). Admittedly, the aristocracy, nobility, and upper and middle classes together

TABLE 3.2
Social Class of Canonized Saints (1000–1800)

Social class	Eleventh century	Twelfth century	Thirteenth century	Fourteenth century	Fifteenth century	Sixteenth century	Seventeenth century	Total (n)	Total (%)
Royalty	10.2	3.9	8.8	3.7	2.4	2.6	0	42	4.9
Nobility	39.1	41.2	31.4	29	31.4	20.7	21.2	269	31.1
Upper and middle class	8.6	20.3	22	29	20.5	35.4	36.4	209	24.2
Burghers	0	0.7	3.8	0.9	2.4	4.3	5.1	21	2.4
Urban poor	3.9	1.3	1.3	2.8	4.8	4.3	3.4	25	2.9
Farmers	2.3	3.9	3.8	4.7	13.3	6.9	6.8	47	5.4
Other	32.9	25.5	27	26.1	20.4	19.8	25.4	222	25.7
Unknown	3.1	3.3	1.9	3.7	4.8	6.0	1.7	29	3.4
Total canonized saints	128	153	159	107	83	116	118	864	100

Adapted from Donald Weinstein and Rudolph Bell, *Saints & Society: The Two Worlds of Western Christendom, 1000–1700* (Chicago: University of Chicago Press, 1982), 197.
Note: Values represent the percentage of the total number of canonized saints.

composed a large and relatively stable majority of the saints (60.2%), dwarfing the numbers of urban poor (2.9%) and farmers (5.4%). The fact that canonization was an expensive and time-consuming proposition probably accounted for the underrepresentation of commoners, whose supporters lacked the wealth and resources needed to sustain a collective social effort. Ironically, it was the elites who were better able to live up to the ideals of poverty, because they had wealth and status to renounce, whereas, the lower classes, who had little or nothing to give away, had trouble demonstrating their faith.[73]

However, a significant fact not shown in the chart was that among its 864 saints, there is a certain diversity not observed in the demographics of sages. There were 151 women (17.5%). There also were 282 laypeople (32.6%) and 49 lay tertiaries (5.7%); altogether, the share of saints who were not clergymen (that is, laypeople and lay tertiaries) represented 38.3% of the total.[74] As a whole, saints were a far more diverse group than sages in terms of social class, gender, and vocation.

The social distribution of a religion's exemplars also may provide a hint about its ordinary believers' social composition. Qing emperor Kangxi 清康熙帝 (Shengzu, r. 1661–1722) once dedicated to the Confucius temple in Queli a work of his own calligraphy that read "The teaching exemplar for ten thousand generations" (*wanshi shibiao* 萬世師表).[75] It was a pithy statement on the social homogeneity of Confucians, who were entirely made up of rulers—also known as princely teachers—and the *shi* who administered the empire, with Confucius serving as their collective figurehead.

Historical records of the social composition of those who participated in Confucius temple rites support this interpretation. The twin cartels of rulers and scholar-officials monopolized the right to participate, regardless of the temple's location, from the imperial city's temples to the most provincial ones. Moreover, the rites ranged from the most solemn rites in spring and autumn (attended to by the emperor) to the minor sacrifices during the syzygy of the sun and moon. Throughout the empire, the system of Confucius temples displayed the characteristics of an exclusive social institution.[76] As the early republic critic of Confucianism, Zhang Taiyan 章太炎 (1869–1936), remarked:

> Confucius temples are attached to official academies, and their worshippers are limited to scholars and students. The officials offer sacrifices only at appointed times of the year; the rites never extend to

the lanes and alleyways or become a folk ballad or common customs. Therefore, Confucius is only revered by students in the classroom, just as carpenters worship Lu Ban 魯班, tailors worship Xuanyuan 軒轅 [the Yellow Emperor], and petty officials and clerks worship Xiao He 蕭何 [who served the founder of the Han dynasty]. Each profession pays due respect to its master and respects its heritage.[77]

Zhang Taiyan's commentary echoes an imperial decree made in the early Yuan. Promulgated in connection to the reconstruction of the Confucius temple school in Qufu, the Yuan emperor ordered the official in charge to "make the place well-lit and clean, permit no visiting or sightseeing, be strict with cleaning and sweeping, and ensure that it is beautiful. Be respectful and avoid all things blasphemous to the Way of the gods."[78] In the Yuan dynasty, the *Rites of Temple Academies* (*Miaoxue dianli* 廟學典禮) recorded the promulgation of multiple decrees forbidding the use Confucius temples for lodging officials and foreign dignitaries, for billeting troops, and for merry-making, cavorting, or any other noise-making activity.[79] When the state forbade commoners to visit Confucius temples, even during normal hours, it also guarded the privilege to participate in temple rituals.

Christian churches took a different approach to access. No Christian (regardless of wealth, occupation, sex, or age) was forbidden to enter a church. This difference was highlighted by a Jesuit missionary to China, Guilio Aleni (1582–1649), in his Chinese-language introduction to Christianity:

> Our shrines and temples are built everywhere from the capital to the countryside. . . . Therein, all is open for rites and during worship. A ceaseless train of kings, officials, and commoners, indeed all people of the nation, go to them. Every seven days, a public rite called "Mass" is held for the public. On this day, all labors cease throughout the nation and everyone goes to the temples to listen to the clergy's lectures on the classics and on morality. Women listen to those lectures in another spot, so that there is separation between men and women.[80]

In contrast, Confucian sages were the spiritual guardians of the literati class. In regions south of the Yangzi River (Jiangnan area), literati who felt unjustly deprived of their dignity by scholar-officials of superior rank would go to a local Confucius temple to "weep ritually" (*ku miao* 哭廟).[81] Since the Middle Ages, the cult of saints has been an indelible feature of the social lives of the common people, from which the cult of patron saints developed to answer the prayers of various professions, and even of those who suffered from specific illnesses and calamities.[82] In traditional China, Daoist or Buddhist deities, instead of Confucian sages, answered those religious needs.[83] The juxtaposition of the class stratification of the cult of sages and the universalism of the cult of saints could not be any clearer.

Relics, Images, and Iconoclasm

The cult of relics is the veneration, in whole or in part, of the bodily remains of a holy person and of the objects and places related to the deceased, including clothing, jewelry, tools, utensils, and sites. Catholicism and Buddhism are widely recognized as religions with major relic cults.[84] However, the disposition of Confucianism toward relics differs from that of Catholicism.

The veneration of relics has long history in Catholicism. No later than the second century, vivid accounts already spoke of many cults surrounding the relics of saints. By the fourth century, relic cults flourished beyond the eastern diocese (North Africa and Asia Minor), and the relics of martyrs became prized possessions of nobles and bishops in the northern diocese.[85] Constantinople, the imperial capital that, like its eponymous emperor, had converted to Christianity, styled itself as the New Rome (Nova Roma) and diligently collected the relics of saints from every corner of the empire to bolster its position as the center of faith, thus inadvertently causing the mass relocation and circulation of relics.[86] During this period, Constantinople amassed a staggering number of relics, but unfortunately, crusaders pillaged almost all of its collection when they sacked the city, and the purloined relics became effective instruments for evangelism in Europe.

As the French historian Achille Luchaire (1846–1908) declared, "The true religion of the Middle Ages, to be frank, was the worship of relics."[87] As agents of intercession, saints mediated the faithful's relationship with an ineffable God, and through their words and deeds, they closed the spiritual distance between the faithful and the divine. Furthermore, pilgrimages to the holy sites of a saint's relic were much more easily accomplished than an arduous pilgrimage to Jerusalem and the Holy Land.[88]

It is very important to note that the cult of relics—especially the dismembering of the deceased saint—utterly contravened Greek and Roman civilizations' taboos. According to Roman law, grave robbing and disfigurement of cadavers were serious crimes, but as the popularity of relic cults suggests, such laws restrained Christians not at all.[89] The early church often used the relics of a saint as a spiritual focus, and it habitually built churches on the graves of martyrs and placed relics under altars. Moreover, the Eucharist, symbolizing the flesh and blood of Jesus Christ, was only a substitute for relics of a more tangible kind, when they were unavailable for use.[90]

The sacking of Constantinople by crusaders precipitated a mass redistribution of relics to the West, which the Catholic church utilized to extend its tendrils into Western Europe. By the Middle Ages, the Curia aggressively collected holy relics and gifted them to the local churches in Eastern and Northern Europe in order to bolster its prestige as the central governing body of the entire Christian faith.[91] Thus, the spread of Christianity followed on the heels of the circulation of holy relics, as this circulation and trafficking gave the cult of saints a high level of mobility. The relics of canonized saints, Jesus Christ, and the Virgin Mary metamorphosed into "sacred commodities" that supported a veritable industry on which the livelihood of many an entrepreneur depended.[92] Sometimes the scramble for relics even resulted in open warfare between armed groups, the murder of dying saints, and other horrors.

Ultimately, the importance of relics to Christianity arose from their miraculous powers, which was particularly significant for sustaining the belief among lower-class Christians.[93] Since the early days of the church, Christian theologians had given much thought to the issue of the cult of bodily relics and attempted to provide it with a theological apology. Most theologians, following 1 Corinthians 6:19, argued that the body of a saint is "a temple of the Holy Spirit," which contains mythical powers or "grace" that could not be vitiated or diminished even if the body itself were cut to pieces. As Bishop Theodore of Cyrus (c. 393–466) declared, "Though the body has been divided, the grace remains undivided."[94] Furthermore, the Book of Revelation (6:9) authorized the church's imperative to preserve relics: "I saw under the altar the souls of them that were slain for the word of God, and for the testimony which they held." Such was the intellectual foundation of the veneration of bodily relics in Catholicism.

In contrast, the Confucian institution of rites did not contain any basis for the veneration of bodily relics. According to the *Analects*, a canonical text on propriety and uprightness of behavior, Zengzi's 曾子 last words were: "Uncover my feet! Uncover my hands! It is said in the *Book of Poetry* (*Shijing* 詩經) 'We should be apprehensive and cautious, as if on the brink of a deep gulf, as if I was treading on thin ice,' and so I have been. Now and hereafter, I know my escape from all injury to my person!" A similar Confucian adage, originally a commentary on this passage, says, "To preserve one's whole body until death and to die intact, by this was meant 'escape.'"[95] In the first chapter of the canonical *Classic of Filial Piety* (*Xiaojing* 孝經), Confucius taught "Our bodies—to every hair and bit of skin—are received by us from our parents, and we must not presume to injure or wound them."[96]

The indivisibility and inviolability of the body may account for why, of the two original ritual components of offering sacrifices to Confucius, the rites of the temple successfully replicated itself in every Confucius temple in China while the rites of the grave was performed only by the original clan temple in Queli.[97] The rites of the grave were restricted in a way that the rites of the temple were not: the remains of Confucius could not be in two places at once without damaging his body, and so the grave rites remained only at the place of interment. Such Confucian teachings and practices were profoundly incongruent with the values evident in the Catholic dismemberment of the remains of saints in the veneration of relics.

Christian and Chinese conceptions of the hereafter also differed. Christians believe that the deceased will face a final judgment after their resurrection (1 Corinthians 15; Revelation 20), but Confucius agnostically waved the issue away with a rhetorical question: "Not understanding life, how can you know about death?"[98] Some Confucian canonical texts were equally dismissive of any hereafter, but others were more complex. One chapter in the *Book of Rites* (*Liji* 禮記) records that when Wu Jizi 吳季子 (576–484 BCE) buried his son, he said, "That the bones and flesh should return again to the earth is what is appointed; however, the spiritual energy (*hunqi* 魂氣, often glossed as 'spirit' and even as 'soul') can go anywhere! It can go anywhere!"[99] Wu Jizi did not elaborate on where spirits go; however, another chapter in the *Rites* did recount "The spiritual energy returns to the heavens, but the body and ghost [*xingpo* 形魄] return to the earth."[100] As the chapter on rituals in the *Xunzi* 荀子 explains regarding the deceased, "Burial is reverently storing his bodily form. Ritual sacrifices reverently serve his spirit."[101] Scholars of rites attested, "The ancients did not offer sacrifices at grave sites" because they believed the spiritual energy (*hunqi* 魂氣) of the deceased is insensate.[102] The doyen of Tang dynasty classical scholarship, Kong Yingda 孔穎達 (576–648), issued the opinion "When man is born, his spirit is potent and his soul is strong; however, when he dies, his form disintegrates and his energy dissipates."[103] Thus, although there are inconsistencies in Confucian canonical texts regarding notions of the afterlife,[104] there is a shared absence of any belief in a resurrection.

While Confucianism did not practice relic veneration, it did use icons in its rites, and it experienced iconoclasm; therefore, these areas provide further grounds for comparisons with Christianity. The use of icons in Confucianism and Christianity dates back to the third century;[105] moreover, iconoclasm reached its height in the sixteenth century, when iconoclasts targeted all holy images in both religions. There are more similarities in the approach to images in Confucianism and Christianity than these coincidences. In recent decades, the power of images has become a larger academic subject for art historians,[106] but historians have always viewed the relationship between icons and faith as a significant one. The Dutch historian Johan Huizinga (1872–1945) wrote in his magnum opus, *The Autumn of the Middle Ages*:

> For the daily understanding among the mass of people, the existence of a visible image made intellectual proof of faith entirely superfluous. There was no room between what was depicted, and which one met in color and form—that is, depictions of Trinity, the flames of hell, the catalog of saints—and faith in all this. There was no room for the question, Is this true? All these representations went directly from picture to belief. They existed in the mind fully defined and grabbed in all the reality that the church could demand of faith and then some.[107]

Images have the power to convey ideas and doctrines implicitly to the believer via direct visual experience, and historians specializing in Confucius temples discovered numerous recorded instances of people experiencing epiphany after viewing the iconography of sages.[108] Since Confucianism and Christianity benefited greatly from the use of icons, it appears perplexing that people would turn on the very same images in iconoclastic movements. Therefore, I will attempt to explain the context, origins, and development of icons and iconoclasm in the two religions.

Icons can be either two-dimensional (murals) or three-dimensional (statues). We know from the extant fragments of the "Treatise on Literature" (Yiwenzhi 藝文志) in the official *Book of Han History* (*Hanshu* 漢書) that two scrolls of material existed under the heading "Icons of Confucius and the Disciples" 孔子徒人圖法, which suggests that conventions for depicting Confucius and his disciples were already established at the time.[109] There is other supporting evidence. One Western Han literati surnamed Dan purportedly made a painting of Confucius.[110] Later, the Hongdu Gate School 鴻都門學, built by Eastern Han emperor Ling 東漢靈帝 (r. 167–189) in 178, displayed the iconography of both Confucius and the seventy-two disciples.[111] It was also recorded that engravings of the icons of Confucius and the seventy-two disciples once graced the beams beneath the roof of the Temple for Rites to the Duke of Zhou 周公禮殿, built by Gao Zhen 高眹 in 194.[112]

In addition to their presence in academies and temples, paintings and engravings of Confucius and his disciples were common in ancestral halls and tombs, such as in the stone antechamber of the tomb of Lu Jun 魯峻 (c. 111–172), a deputy ambassador of the Han Empire. According to historical records, the walls of this antechamber contained "the icons of loyal court officials, dutiful sons, and virtuous women, which were recorded in history, as well as Confucius and the seventy-two disciples."[113] The text *Stele for Han Chi's Restoration of the Temple of Confucius* 韓勅修孔廟後碑, inscribed on a stele erected in 157, contains references to the renovation of the old temple building and the "painting of new holy icons" 改畫聖象.[114] As the textual evidence clearly suggests, the use of painted images of Confucius became increasingly commonplace during the Han dynasty.

Scholars do not know the origins of the statues of Confucius in Confucius temples, which played such a prominent role in Confucian rites and practices.[115] The earliest reference to the use of statues in the Confucius temple can be found in *Shuijing zhu* 水經注 by Li Daoyuan 酈道元 (c. 466–527). Li Daoyuan describes a temple that Wei Emperor Wen renovated in 221: "There are icons of Confucius accompanied by two disciples holding scrolls, expressing a respectful countenance suggestive of those seeking for instruction." Although Li did not specify whether the icons were paintings or statues, the text is suggestive of latter possibility.[116] A later temple of Confucius at the National University (*Guozijian* 國子監)

in the capital of Luoyang, built during the Northern Wei dynasty, displayed, according to one source, icons not only of Confucius but also of "Yan Yuan 顏淵 seeking instructions on humaneness and Zilu 子路 on statecraft."[117] We may therefore deduce that the icons in the Confucius temple renovated in 221 were most probably of Yan Yuan and Zilu.

During the reign of Western Jin emperor Hui 晉惠帝 (r. 290–306), in 293, the National University (*Taixue* 太學) performed a sacrificial rite to Confucius with Yanzi as an enshrined auxiliary sage. Court official Pan Ni 潘尼 (c. 250–c. 311) wrote a firsthand account as a participant. During the offering of sacrifices, "the swept floor and hung curtains were treated as the halls and walls of a temple. Confucius took his place at the western wall, and Yan served him at the northern wall."[118] The likenesses of Confucius and Yanzi to which the text refers were definitely statues. By 541, during the Eastern Wei dynasty, Li Ting 李珽, an inspector (*cishi* 刺史) of Yan Prefecture, recorded that the Confucius temple in Queli was "furnished with the icon of Confucius and in addition those of ten disciples," which suggests an increasing number of disciples represented in iconography.[119] By the early Tang dynasty, patterns of iconography of Confucius temples stabilized and would remain unchanged until the early Ming period.[120]

The rise of iconography in Confucius temples was concurrent with the spread of Chinese Buddhism. An ancient name for Buddhism in China was the "icon religion" (*Xiang jiao* 像教), due to its extensive use of iconography in evangelistic efforts. The popularity of images of the Buddha after the Han and Wei dynasties probably inspired Confucians to imitate them.[121] That Confucian iconography began during the Wei-Jin and the Six Dynasties period was therefore no coincidence. Moreover, as Qiu Jun 丘濬 (1421–1495), an ardent opponent of Confucian iconography, argued, "The use of images has no precedent in antiquity and is an innovation created when Buddhism spread to China. Sacrificial rites during the Three Dynasties [Xia, Shang, and Zhou] used the *zhu* [*muzhu* 木主, memorial tablets], and no images were used."[122] Qiu's account agrees with other evidence, which enhances its credibility.[123]

Although Qiu fiercely opposed icons in Confucian rites, his arguments were not original. Rather, they derived from Zhu Xi 朱熹 (1130–1200), the master of the Southern Song School of Principle (*lixue* 理學). Zhu Xi's famous treatise "On Genuflection" (*Gui zuo bai shuo* 跪坐拜說) mocked Su Shi 蘇軾 (1036–1101) for having once crawled and knelt before the icons in a Confucius temple, and took no position on the abolition of icons.¹²⁴ In the early Ming dynasty, Zhu's text was specifically cited by Song Lian 宋濂 (1310–1381) in his memorial recommending the abolition of icons; moreover, he convinced Emperor Taizu, who subsequently ordered its implementation in the Imperial University's own Confucius temple.¹²⁵

In Song Na's 宋訥 (1311–1390) commissioned text *Stele for the Building of the National University by the Great Ming Empire* 大明敕建太學碑, he reported, "The master and his followers have no graven images of clay, and memorial tablets are used in their sacrificial rites; thus, a barbaric custom of hundreds of years was reformed."¹²⁶ The reference to "barbaric custom" (*yi xi* 夷習) suggests that the "reform" was motivated by more than the intention to simply address a controversy over ritual and was in fact also a political gesture to signify the end of the barbarian rule of the Mongols and the rise of a restored Han Chinese empire.

Taizu's reform of the rites was abortive and, despite sporadic proposals by dissidents, was not adopted again by several generations of Ming emperors who succeeded him. The imperial court's determination to continue the old rites and institutions was demonstrated in 1481, during the reign of Emperor Xianzong 明憲宗 (r. 1464–1487). When Zhu Lang 祝瀾 (1436–?), an administrator from the National University, proposed installing memorial tablets in Confucius temples to replace iconic images, the emperor censored and exiled him posthaste for his offense.¹²⁷

However, the situation suddenly reversed when Emperor Shizong 明世宗 (r. 1521–1566) succeeded to the throne. In 1530, Shizong began reforms in the rites of Confucius temples as an excuse to reduce the prestige and influence of the scholar-official class (to be discussed in chapter 4). He ordered the discontinuation of the honorific "king" when referring to Confucius in favor of the title Late Teacher, the demotion of the rank of enshrined sages, the reduction of iconoclasm in the temples, and the elimination of several ritual robes and vessels used in the offering of sacrifices. The edict provoked "uproarious disapproval" from the scholar-official class.¹²⁸ Summoning a conclave of thirteen official historians to oppose the decree, court official Li Quan 黎貫 (1483–1542) criticized the emperor's decision as "laughable here and now and surely mocked in future histories."¹²⁹

Nevertheless, Shizong brushed aside their criticism, and his edict became established law. The imperial court ordered all Confucius temples to adopt memorial tablets, smash icons, abrogate the practice of honoring Confucius with noble ranks, and cease the display of his statues. Officials who refused to obey those orders "took to hiding the images of the sages in secret compartments between the walls."[130]

After several decades, a Confucian official, Wang Shizhen, boldly pleaded with Emperor Wanli 萬曆 (Shenzong, r. 1572–1620) to reverse the Confucius temple policies of Shizong's reign: "We who carry the table book and wear the belt of the court [that is, scholar-officials] have swallowed our distress and dared not utter what we have felt for sixty years. We only beg that now will be the time to return to what is right."[131] The memorial's palpable sense of pain articulated genuine expressions of grief felt by the literati class. Later historians did not forget to castigate the Shizong Emperor: "Changing the title of King for that of the Teacher, destroying icons and replacing them with memorial tablets—for those things, Confucians to this day nurse grievances."[132] Such condemnations were what most Confucians at the time could not say in public and did not need to articulate to one another.

In short, the iconography in Confucius temples, originally conceived as a component in ritual and worship, inadvertently became the arena for the power struggle between the throne and the scholar-official class and culminated in the iconoclasm that signified autocracy's final victory. The lone survivor, the statue of Confucius in the Confucius temple in Queli, only temporarily postponed its fate, for the iconoclasts of the Cultural Revolution (1966–1976) would finally destroy it as the last iconographic victim of arbitrary power.[133] The relationship of the iconography of Confucius temples and the power of secular rulers verified the observation by Mengzi 孟子 (c. 372–c. 289 BCE), "Those Zhao Meng exalts, Zhao Meng can also humble."[134]

The history of iconoclasm in Christianity is more complicated. Origen of Alexandria (c. 185–c. 254), an important theologian, argued, in his apologia for Christian iconoclasts, "Christians and Jews are led to avoid temples and altars and images by the command . . . 'You shall not make a carved image for yourself nor the likeness of anything in the heavens above, or on the earth below, or in the waters under the earth. You shall not bow down to them or worship them.'"[135] The code, to which Origen referred, is the Second Commandment of the Mosaic law, from Exodus 20:4.[136]

Nonetheless, the appreciation of art was not idolatry, and early Christians did not shun the use of the visual arts to tell the story of Jesus Christ for the purposes of evangelism.[137] From the very beginning, the veneration of icons was inseparable from the veneration of relics, and the rise of icons was probably a result of the popularity of the relics.[138] Particularly after the ban on Christianity was lifted in the fourth century, Christians publicly displayed the objects of art, formerly hidden in crypts or on one's person. These forms of Christian art included murals, embroidery, and sculpture; moreover, they usually depicted either biblical stories or the likeness of Jesus, the Virgin Mary, or saints.

Leaders of the church had long recognized the effectiveness of art as instruments of evangelism.[139] In the sixth century, Pope Gregory declared, "It is one thing to adore a picture, another to learn from the history [that is, the subject] of the picture what is to be adored. For what scripture shows to those who read, a picture shows to the illiterate people as they see it; because in it the ignorant see what they ought to imitate, they who do not know letters can read it."[140] In other words, objects of art had great mass appeal for illiterate believers, and the church was opposed only to the idolatry of representation, not to its legitimate uses as outlined by the pope.

Despite of the distinction between worship and veneration, there still were two waves of iconoclasm in the history of Christianity. The first, occurring in the Byzantine Empire between 711 and 843, was precipitated especially when Emperor Leo III (r. 717–741) attempted to unify secular and religious powers in his person, an effort bitterly opposed by the patriarch of the Eastern church and the pope of the Latin church. Influenced by Islam and Judaism, as well as by Christian sects in Asia Minor, Leo III, in his contempt for idolatry, ordered the destruction of images and the confiscation of ecclesiastic properties. Iconoclasm swept through Byzantine domains and horrified monks and believers. From the perspective of a consolidator of central power, the veneration of icons and the cult of saints represented hostile centrifugal forces that must be crushed, and their resistance was inevitably met with harsh persecution.[141] This roughly one-century-long iconoclastic movement lost its fervor, however, when regime change at the top put an end to its political backing.[142]

This century of iconoclasm was not merely a facade for political self-aggrandizement but also the era's most important theological controversy, whose partisans engaged each other in lively theological debates in multiple ecclesiastical councils.[143] As a result of the internecine struggle, the influence of the Greek church receded from Western Europe, while the Latin church washed its hands of the dioceses of the Byzantine Empire and thus damaged both churches' claims to universality.[144] My point here is that politics was not the only motivation for iconoclasm, and this observation is equally valid for the second wave of iconoclasm, from sixteenth-century Protestantism.

It is widely acknowledged that by the time of the Reformation in 1517, the Catholic church had lost much of its moral luster, and a once inspiring faith was by then decried as the cesspool of superstition.[145] The Curia's graft and simony, buying or selling of ecclesiastical pardons or benefices, as well as the counterfeit relics and saints prevalent in local churches, undermined the credibility of the Catholic church. One contemporary sardonically remarked that if all splinters of the true cross were gathered in one place, a team of three hundred men could not have lifted its weight.[146] A similar remark could aptly apply to the jars that contained the alleged breast milk of the Virgin Mary, which were so numerous that they were rendered commonplace. The indignation against abuses of the cult of saints and relics gave rise to a movement of religious reform, and the second wave of iconoclasm was one of its multifarious consequences.

Criticism against the Curia was not a calamity that suddenly arose against the church. Rather, the humanist Desiderius Erasmus (c. 1466–1536) was among the first internal critics who began the movement. A common saying during the Reformation was "Luther hatched the egg Erasmus laid."[147] While the aphorism contained an element of truth, Erasmus remained merely the generator of negative criticisms and did not give form to a new faith, which more accurately characterized the work of Martin Luther (1483–1456) and John Calvin (1509–1564).

The gist of Lutheran theology was its appeal to "Christian liberty," which rested on Luther's affirmation of the value of faith over works. The source of faith came from the word of God, through reading the scriptures, without the superfluous meditative authority of the church or the intercession of enshrined saints. Luther also believed that human nature contains dualistic aspects of spirit and flesh; moreover, faith exists to elevate the inner spirit in a union with the Holy Spirit.[148] He condemned the veneration of relics and images as blasphemous; however, when iconoclasm escalated into wholesale social conflict, Luther retreated from his originally uncompromising position.[149]

Calvin could accept no compromise, and he was the man who pushed Luther's doctrines to their utmost logical extreme or expression. Calvin's doctrine of predestination represented the logical conclusion to the supremacy of faith over good works,[150] and he emphasized the sublimation of the spirit to complete the exclusion of the flesh's weakness. He believed that God only allowed the performance of miracles in remote antiquity, during the age of evangelism, whereas in modern times miracles are impossible. Within this theological framework, there was no place for relics and images, with their suspicious reification and emphasis on materialism.

Calvin denounced as a fraud Pope Gregory's defense of images as "textbooks for the illiterate" and questioned the distinction between "worshipping" God (*latria*) and "serving" saints (*dulia*).[151] He ruthlessly mocked the cult of saints and relics in his *Inventory of Relics*, where he declared forthrightly, "Attributing a visible form to God is impiety. Setting up idols is a defection from the true God."[152] Calvin's ideas became the cornerstone of the new Ten Commandments of Protestantism, and the controversy over saints was among the causes of the separation of Western Christianity into the camps of Protestant and Catholic. Wherever Protestantism held sway, the religious landscape totally transformed; in Protestant churches, austerity replaced luxury and explication of the scripture replaced images. The veneration of saints and relics so prevalent in medieval society vanished and, along with it, the mediation between mankind and God that saints once performed. Confronted with an ineffable God and the insurmountable abyss of transcendence, believers could only respond with "fear and trembling" (1 Corinthians 2:3).[153]

While there were political and economic dimensions to iconoclasm in the West, the dominant factor was religion.[154] Anthropologists Victor Turner (1920–1983) and Edith Turner (1921–2016) used technical terms from Ferdinand de Saussure's (1857–1913) linguistic theory to explain the meaning of iconoclasm, arguing that the purpose of iconoclasm was to rupture the link between signified and signifier and to replace it with a new worldview (a new signification).[155] This observation is appropriate for Protestantism, since the destruction of icons also annihilated the basis of the belief in saints, which in turn allowed a rerouting of all beliefs to return to the figure of Jesus Christ.

In other words, it was Protestant Reformation's refashioning of belief that led to iconoclasm, and its influence even reached secular scholarship.[156] In contrast, iconoclasm did not lead Confucianism to undergo to any such theoretical readjustment. The iconoclasm of the sixteenth century signified the mentality of autocratic secular rulers who unilaterally dominated the institution of rites in Confucius temples, and the only meaning signified by the replacement of images with memorial tablets was the jealousy of a lord who would not "spare even ritual robes to glorify another." We could aptly sum up this predicament by quoting a rustic ancient Chinese idiom: "Without the skin, where will the hair attach?"[157]

Conclusion

Whether as exemplars of virtue or propagators of doctrine, sages and saints share family resemblances.[158] I have juxtaposed their general similarities on a macro level and their particularities on the micro level to highlight their fundamental differences and the origins of those differences.

The German sociologist Max Weber expounded the class stratification of Confucian belief,[159] but much of Confucianism's aspects as a state cult or public religion remains underexplored. I have sought to reveal those unique characteristics through a cross-cultural comparison between Confucianism and the rites of a culture from a different context.

Zhu Xi, the doyen of Southern Song Confucian scholarship, tried to explain why "all contemporary sacrifices offered to Confucius are performed solely in schools" by citing the idea of the homogeneity of *qi* (氣類).[160] By "schools," Zhu Xi really meant "temple schools," academies with built-in temples for the veneration of Confucius and the offering of sacrifices that, by the Southern Song period, were ancient and venerable institutional practices. What is important here is the fact highlighted in Zhu Xi's account: the mechanism that animated the Confucian institution of rites was the Confucius temple. In addition, the temple had a trilateral relationship with rulers, Confucians, and commoners, which is crucial for our understanding of the temple's role in Confucian rites.

Most importantly, the "sacrifice to Confucius" and the "sacrifice to heaven" were in the domain of the ruling class, and dynasties performed these rites in such extraordinary circumstances as the naming of a new reign era, the changing of dynastic colors, or the enthroning of a new emperor. In ordinary times, the sacrifices to Confucius were solemn rites of the state and were performed every spring and autumn. In other words, sacrifices to Confucius were an indispensable part of the imperial ritual calendar, and the privilege of participating in them was beyond the reach of the common people.

The mutually beneficial relationship between the ruling class and Confucianism was aptly expressed by Ming emperor Chengzu 明成祖 (r.

1402–1424). In a short prayer to Sage Confucius engraved on a stele celebrating the renovation of the temple of Confucius, the emperor requested, "Grant us a great sage from among the literati in every generation to help the Great Ming last ten thousand years."[161] The Qing emperor Yongzheng 清雍正帝 (Shizong, r. 1722–1735) more bluntly asserted, "The teachings of Confucius is of great use to princes."[162] Little wonder, then, that emperors exerted total control over the rites of Confucius temples and even over the granting of ritual enshrinement, the most highly prized honor to Confucians.[163]

Besides the declarations of emperors, there are numerous texts, such as the genres of Prayerful Reports to the Venerable Sage (*gao xiansheng wen* 告先聖文) and Records of the Temple Schools (*miao xue ji* 廟學記), in the collected writings of prominent Confucians.[164] Such documents attest that the purpose of offering sacrifices to Confucius was to promulgate Confucian teachings and to pray for divine favors for the state. Personal relationship with the divine or blessings for individual worshippers were simply irrelevant. Thus, the sacrifice to Confucius clearly displayed the public and civic qualities that characterized Confucianism as a religion.

Another significant point of divergence between Confucius temples and Christian churches was that the holy ground of the Confucius cult and the rites performed in a Confucius temple could be accessed only by officials and Confucian scholars. When a local official assumed his office, he had to perform a special rite to introduce himself and to give homage to the local temple. This practice originated in the early Han, when Emperor Gaozu 漢高祖 (r. 202–195 BCE) passed through Lu County and ordered the offering of the highest sacrifice of beef, mutton, and pork at the Confucius temple there. The emperor thus set the precedent for his underlings: "Whenever a new feudal lord or procurator was appointed to the region, he would first pay respects to Confucius in the temple prior to assuming his duties."[165]

At the time, the practice was limited to Lu County only. However, the Yuan dynasty mandated that all local administrators, "upon arrival, first pay respects and give homage at the temple of the venerable sage, and only then is permission to visit other shrines granted."[166] The temple of the venerable sage referred to the local Confucius temple, and the government's order clearly showed that as important political symbols, Confucius temples had supremacy over all other shrines and temples. Moreover, officials who failed in their duties to minister rites in local temples were subject to immediate and severe censure. For example, Ming Confucian Zhou

Shuangxi 周雙溪 posed this stinging rhetorical question in a memorial to his superior: "Offering sacrifice to the late teacher [Confucius] is the greatest rite of the state. If you are even negligent in the ministry of this [rite], how are you supposed to minister to the welfare of the people?"[167] Such brazen confidence about holding the moral high ground illustrates how deeply ingrained temple rites were in Confucian political culture.

In addition, Confucius temples also served as the place of transformation where the status of Confucian scholars changed. Following the institution of the imperial examination system by the Sui and Tang dynasties, it was customary for all those who had passed the exams and had advanced to the status of examination degree holders to participate in rites at the temple to honor Confucius.[168] Therefore, the temple of Confucius at the National University conveniently served as the place where those successful in the highest examination underwent *shihe* (釋褐), a Confucius temple rite of investiture during which the degree holder takes off (*shed* 釋) the commoner's black (褐) clothes.[169] These highest degree holders, called "presented scholars" (*jinshi* 進士), passed a palace examination overseen by the emperor, who bestowed their degrees. In the Ming and Qing, those passing the province-level exam qualified for civil service positions, so the temple in the province's administrative city became the place to conduct investiture for the holders of the *juren* degree.

Even though Confucians claimed possession of the moral truth, "used daily without being known, practiced habitually without being noticed" by the common people, commoners were, in reality, indifferent to Confucius temple rites. For instance, one famous student of the rites, Qin Huitian 秦蕙田 (1702–1764), commented, "People honor Confucius but feel no familiarity; however, remoteness does not hinder our devotion.[170]

In contrast to Catholic churches that celebrated the dates of each saint's canonization,[171] Confucius temples venerated sages on special spring and autumn dates that were universal throughout the empire and that bore no connection to the birthday of Confucius or any other sage. This difference in designating dates on respective ritual calendars reflects their distinctive orientation toward either the private or the civic.[172] It was not until 1727 that the Qing emperor Yongzheng honored the birthday of a sage, when he designated the birthday of Confucius as a fasting day to refrain from eating meat, and it was a Manchu, not a native Han Chinese, who made that declaration.[173]

Even then, members of the scholar-official class largely ignored this mandate. In the late Qing, reformer Liang Qichao lamented, "Upon entering school, a pupil immediately learns to venerate Wenchang 文昌 and Kuixing 魁星 as gods; however, regarding the most sanctified founder of our religion, the fire of his legacy has all but burned out, his sacrificial vessels almost empty, his dates of birth and death scarcely known by anyone." He observed the same situation even in temple schools: "In our Yue 粵 [Guangdong], Wenchang 文昌 and Kuixing 魁星 enjoyed the sacrificial offerings; in contrast, people rarely worship Confucius."[174]

Wenchang and Kuixing were the deities of destiny and wealth, concerns immediately relevant to the masses; to them the elevated character of Confucius appeared distant and nebulous. Although late Qing reformers tried to imitate the "open door policy" of Christian churches to encourage mass participation, the conservative Ye Dehui 葉德輝 (1864–1927) responded skeptically. He retorted, "If this policy is addressed to foolish commoners, they have no use going to the temple, since Confucius temples do not perform divinations; and womenfolk have no need to enter the temples either, since Confucius temples do not bestow the blessing of having children."[175] Ye's reasons for opposing the reforms reveal the remoteness of Confucius temples from commoners.

On this point of the chasm between the masses and Confucian temples, Lu Xun 魯迅 (1881–1936) wrote a particularly vivid critique:

> Various powerful men have powdered him [Confucius's statue] with all manner of cosmetics and raised him on pedestals of ever more terrifying heights. Yet he has fared rather poorly compared to the later-imported Buddha. Admittedly, every county has a sacred temple, also known as the temple of culture, but it always appeared desolate and abandoned, and ordinary folk avoided that place. If they go anywhere to worship, it is a Buddhist temple or a Daoist shrine. Ask the common folk who Confucius was, quite naturally they answer, "A sagely man." However, this answer merely echoes the gramophones of the powerful elite.[176]

Lu Xun's "pedestals of ever more terrifyingly heights" is a literary flourish, but one that accurately portrayed the use of Confucianism by various dynastic regimes as the foundation of their rule.

The social distance between Confucius temples and the common people is also readily observable during the period of iconoclasm. In the eighth and sixteenth centuries, ordinary believers resisted iconoclasm in the West by rioting in the streets, which resulted in large-scale social unrest.[177] In comparison, resistance to sixteenth-century Ming iconoclasm was confined to the indignation of the literati class, without much, if any, participation of the lower classes. The difference in the class composition of the believers had a clear role in shaping the disparate responses of the two religions' faithful to iconoclasm.

After Ming iconoclasm, Confucian images were replaced by memorial tablets inscribed with the names of the worthies (often in arcane scripts, as in the case of pre-Qin enshrined sages), which would have made the Confucius temples even more mysterious and inscrutable to illiterate commoners and therefore even more distant from their concerns. In short, as sacred grounds of Confucianism, Confucius temples traditionally rejected the participation of the ordinary people. One result, as we illustrated in chapter 2, was that modern Chinese intellectuals, immersed in the paradigm of the private religion, were ill equipped to grasp its religious nature.

Confucianism and Christianity once were the spiritual pillars of traditional society, and their significance was undeniable. The year 1919 saw the end of the Confucian institution of enshrined sagehood, while Catholic Christianity's canonized sainthood remains a vigorous living tradition.[178] Do the fate of these ritual traditions portend their overall destiny in the coming hundred years? Will Confucianism vanish while Christianity finds second life in the new century? The nature of Confucian and Christian rites perhaps provides hints to answers those questions.

CHAPTER IV

The Cultural Politics of Autocracy

The Confucius Temple and Ming Despotism, 1368–1530

The ritual system of the Confucius temple was the converging point of political and cultural power in imperial China. This chapter uses two incidents that occurred during the Ming dynasty as examples of the interactions between rulers and scholars, and how they sought to manipulate the operations of the ritual system of the Confucius temple, to conflicting ends.

In imperial times, the Confucius temple symbolized the tradition of, and succession to, the Way (*daotong* 道統); it also was well integrated into the imperial tradition of legitimate governance (*zhitong* 治統). Both emperors and Confucian scholars continually manipulated the ritual practices of the temple to serve their own interests. Because of this, the Confucius temple was in a perpetual process of becoming. From the Tang period, Confucius temples spread throughout China at a steady pace. Despite the growing influence of Confucius temple rites, however, the changes in ritual ordered in 1530 by the Ming emperor Shizong 明世宗 (r. 1521–1566) ran counter to the main tenets of this liturgical tradition. This chapter is devoted to showing how Shizong drew on the political resources of the ruler to weaken the morale of the scholar-officials and thereby strengthen despotism.

The Confucius Temple Reforms of 1530

When Emperor Wuzong 明武宗 (r. 1505–1521) died without leaving an heir, the Empress Dowager Cishou 慈壽 and Grand Secretary Yang Tinghe 楊廷和 (1459–1529) invited Zhu Houcong 朱厚熜 (1507–1567), the deceased emperor's cousin and the eldest son of Prince Xingxian 興獻王, to ascend the throne, in accordance with Wuzong's posthumous decree. This new emperor was Emperor Shizong, also known as the Jiajing 嘉靖 Emperor. Shortly after assuming the throne, Shizong announced his desire to worship in the imperial ancestral shrine his own natal father as a deceased sovereign, rather than having himself adopted into his cousin's line as precedent dictated. The resulting conflict with court officials became known as the Great Rites Controversy (*daliyi* 大禮議). At issue was Shizong's insistence on "continuing the imperial order" (*jitong* 繼統) without "continuing the dynastic line" (*jisi* 繼嗣) of his predecessor. Court officials argued that the late emperor's line had to be continued if the imperial order were to continue. Neither side was willing to compromise.

Then, in 1524, Shizong removed the word "natal" (*bensheng* 本生) from the title of his natural mother, Lady Zhang, the empress dowager. When court officials demurred, imperial guards beat sixteen of them to death on the spot and imprisoned another 143. The protest immediately subsided, and the controversy temporarily ceased.[1]

The Qing editors of the *Ming History* elaborated on the relationship of this controversy to the principle of "serving one's lord according to the Dao":

> Basing his argument mostly on the Puyuan 濮園 debates of Sima Guang 司馬光 [1019–1086] and Cheng Yi 程頤 [1033–1107] of the Song, Yang Tinghe promoted [Shizong's] "Great Ritual" and drew the court to speak out in one accord.... Yet, since Shizong inherited the throne by imperial decree, succeeding Wuzong, the situation was different. All the officials accepted the arguments of these wise scholars of the past as reliable. They attempted to avoid offending the world and later generations, yet did not help Shizong plan thoroughly or handle the situation with refinement. They did not help him reflect on his reasoning in order to obtain absolute appropriateness. The harder they struggled, the more they lost. What a pity![2]

The Qing scholar Mao Qiling 毛奇齡 (1623–1716) attributed the disaster of the Great Rites Controversy to shallow learning on both sides and their failure to consider ancient rituals.³ Mao's command of the sources was broad, and he was familiar with both recent and ancient developments. His views were truly unique, yet the controversy over Shizong's reforms cannot be explained as simply a matter of shallow learning. Rather, the debates were a test of autocratic authority and its legality.

For this reason, it is difficult to reach a judgment about whether Shizong's ritual changes did more harm than good. Although Shizong was not a direct natal descendant of the previous emperor, he was in complete control after succeeding to the throne and was not swayed by his court officials. This is a good example of Ming autocracy. After the ritual debates of 1524, Shizong proceeded to overhaul all rituals in order to validate his actions. For example, in 1525 he had a comprehensive account of the ritual changes, *Collected Debates on the Great Rites Controversy* (*Dali jiyi* 大禮集議), distributed throughout the empire. After completion of the *Great Statutes of Ming Ethics* (*Minglun dadian* 明倫大典), in 1528, charges were brought against the officials who had opposed him in the debates; Yang Tinghe and others were demoted to commoners.⁴

Such actions indicate that Shizong understood how to use power to accomplish his aims and how to use principle (and ritual) to defend his actions. The editors of the *Ming History* made an acute observation on Shizong's behavior: "The emperor [Shizong] personally charged the court to debate and determine the 'great rituals,' but he then used his authority to create the rites and music himself."⁵ Shizong's interest in changing the rituals was not naturally inspired but grew out of the Great Rites Controversy.

Shizong made the most numerous revisions to the rituals in 1530. He created a rite in which the empress personally tended to silkworms in the northern suburbs, changed the enshrinement positions of the gods of soils and grains at the altar, reestablished the four suburban sacrifices, and reinstituted separate sacrifices to heaven and earth.⁶ In the eleventh month, he began to revise the liturgy for the temple of culture (*wenmiao* 文廟), also called the Confucius temple. The Confucius temple reforms were an important link in this chain of ritual changes, and the implications were indeed extraordinary. If Shizong was following a whim in revising the other rituals—merely exercising authoritarian fiat—then his Confucius temple reforms were a challenge to "institutionalized" orthodoxy and an intentional act of degradation.

Scholars have claimed that the revision of the temple of culture originated with Grand Secretary Zhang Cong's 張璁 (1475–1539) proposals,[7] yet full consideration of the sources shows that this is not the case. Before the temple changes of the tenth month of 1530, Shizong instructed Zhang Cong to "order and compile all sacrificial ceremonies for clouds, rain, wind, and lightning, and those of the late sage and master," in *Established Precedents of Ritual Ceremonies* (*Siyi chengdian* 祀儀成典).[8] In a memorial to the throne, Zhang Cong reported:

> The sacrifices to clouds and lightning and the allocation of state spirit tablets have all been revised under your sagacious wisdom, but the liturgy of the late sage and master still requires revision. Shuliang He 叔梁紇 was the father of Confucius, and Yan Lu 顏路, Zeng Xi 曾皙, and Kong Li 孔鯉 were the fathers of Yan [Hui] 顏回, Zeng [Sen] 曾參, and Zisi 子思 [Kong Ji 孔伋], respectively. The three sons are enshrined in the main hall, but Shuliang He and the other fathers are all in the side cloisters. Could the original intentions of the sages have been thus? This ought to be urgently corrected. I, your subject, request that a new hall be erected behind the main hall to worship Shuliang He and that Yan Lu, Zeng Xi, and Kong Li receive secondary sacrifices.[9]

The enshrinement in the temple of culture was in accordance with established rankings. Yan Hui, Zeng Sen, and Kong Ji were enshrined in correlate positions; thus, their position greatly exceeded their fathers in the two cloisters, not to mention Confucius's status in relation to Shuliang He.[10] Therefore, Zhang Cong found fault with the existing regulations.

We can see that the reforms in the Confucius temple came from Shizong and that Zhang Cong perceptively used the model of the ritual debates about the emperor's status in relation to his natal parents—rooted in the immutable moral principle of father and son—to affirm the aims of Shizong's changes. The ultimate power was nonetheless held by Shizong himself. Clearly, the phrase "Although the son be equal to a sage, he should not take precedence over his father" was appropriated from the Great Rites Controversy.[11]

Shizong agreed. Immediately after Zhang Cong presented his memorial, Shizong announced his judgment:

> If we enshrine Confucius in the main hall and relegate his father to the side cloisters, the spirits will surely be very displeased. How could there be peace [if we did this]? If a person shows respect for his parents in this fashion, can we see how he respects heaven? Using twelve sacrificial vessels and prepared sacrificial meat closely copies the great sacrifice. This reasoning cannot be doubted; the rites must be corrected to show respect for heaven.

Shizong then ordered Zhang Cong to "further apprehend Confucius's mind and elaborate on it."[12]

We have no way of knowing whether Zhang Cong did "further apprehend Confucius's mind" before elaborating on it, but Zhang Cong's statement in his memorial in response, "I followed the emperor's will" (*Cong yuan di yi* 璁緣帝意) in revising the regulations for the temple of culture, supports the view that the emperor initiated the changes. In his memorial, Zhang Cong wrote:

> The rites to Confucius have been in chaos since the Tang and Song dynasties, and no one has been able to correct them. We should now call [Confucius] the "first sage and master" and not call him "king." In the sacrifice, it is better to refer to [the building as] "the temple" and not "the court." During the sacrifice, wooden spirit tablets should be used; the sculptures [of Confucius and the other honorees] should be destroyed. Ten sacrificial vessels [rather than twelve] should be used, and six rows of dancers [rather than eight]. Shuliang He should receive sacrifices in a separate temple, with the three [other fathers] as his correlates. The noble titles should be eliminated in favor of "worthy" and "scholar." The sacrifices to Shen Dang 申黨, Gongbo Liao 公伯寮, Qin Ran 秦冉, Yan He 顏何, Xun Kuang 荀況, Dai Sheng 戴聖, Liu Xiang 劉向, Jia Kui 賈逵, Ma Rong 馬融, He Xiu 何休, Wang Su 王肅, Du Yu 杜預, and Wu Cheng 吳澄 should cease. Lin Fang 林放, Qu Yuan 蘧瑗, Lu Zhi 盧植, Zheng Xuan 鄭玄, Fu Qian 服虔, and Fan Ning 范寧 should receive sacrifices in regional [temples]. Hou Cang 后蒼, Wang Tong 王通, Ouyang Xiu 歐陽修, Hu Yuan 胡瑗, and Cai Yuanding 蔡元定 should be added [to the temple].[13]

Zhang Cong's proposed reforms may be grouped into four main areas, related to posthumous titles, substitutions and reductions of temple elements, revised regulations, and renamings.

Posthumous Titles

Confucius was not to be referred to as "king." In this, Zhang Cong claimed to be continuing the business left unfinished by Wu Chen 吳沈 (d. 1386) of the early Ming. In "Disputing Confucius's Ennoblement as King" (*Kongzi feng wang bian* 孔子封王辯), Wu had argued that Confucius was only a minister and that conferring the title of king on one who was not born into the nobility was a transgression of ritual. According to Wu Chen, "It is permissible to say the master [Confucius] possessed the way of a king, but not to say that the master had the title of king."[14] Zhang Cong also used Qiu Jun's 丘濬 (1421–1495) argument that the imperial worship of Confucius began during the reign of Emperor Ping of the Han 漢平帝 (r. 1 BCE–6 CE), when the "traitorous follows of Wang Mang 王莽 (r. 9–23) appeared and falsely worshipped the teachings of the Confucians to elevate their own reputations."[15] Zhang Cong thus argued that later generations referred to Confucius as the " 'First Master Confucius' to show that the reason the sage was revered lay in the Dao, not in noble rank."

Substitution of Wooden Spirit Tablets for Sculptures, Elimination of Court Robes, and Reduction in the Number of Ceremonial Dancers and Vessels

Emperor Taizu 明太祖 (r. 1368–1398) ordered that wooden tablets be used at the National University in Nanjing. This precedent was invoked by Zhang Cong. In addition, Qiu Jun had argued that "China did not have the practice of installing sculptures until the arrival of Buddhism."[16] In fact, since the founding of the Ming dynasty, and even during the Song, there had been intermittent debates about removing the sculptures and installing tablets.[17] Zhang Cong proposed that this change be ordered. Once the sculptures were removed, there was no need for court robes.

There also was a reduction in the number of dancers and vessels. Initially, Ming regulations called for six rows of ceremonial dancers and ten sacrificial vessels. In 1476, at the request of Chancellor Zhou Hongmo 周洪謨 (1420–1491), the number of ceremonial dancers had been increased to eight rows and the number of sacrificial vessels to twelve, thus creating rites appropriate for the Son of Heaven.[18] Now they were reduced to the original number.

Revision of the Sacrificial Regulations by Removal of Titles of Nobility and Reordering of the Scholars

Once Confucius no longer had a title of nobility, the other enshrined did not need them either. Zhang Cong's reordering of the honorees was based on the writings of Cheng Minzheng 程敏政 (1445–1499).[19] This change originated in the shift of scholarly fashion, from an emphasis on transmitting the classics (*chuan jing zhi shi* 傳經之師) to an emphasis on transmitting the Way (*chuan Dao zhi shi* 傳道之師).[20] The enshrinement of Cai Yuanding (1135–1198) drew on the arguments of the brothers Gui Hua 桂華 and Gui E 桂萼 (d. 1531) that Ouyang Xiu 歐陽修 (1007–1072) was enshrined because of his position during the Puyuan debates of 1063.[21] Wu Cheng 吳澄 (1249–1333) was removed from the temple because he had served in the Yuan court after originally serving in the Song court. He previously had been denounced by Xie Duo 謝鐸 (1435–1510).[22]

Renaming the Hall of Great Completion (Dacheng dian 大成殿) the Confucius Temple and Adding the Shrine of Giving Birth to the Sage (Qisheng ci 啟聖祠)

Since Confucius was no longer a king, the sacrifice had to take place in a temple (*miao* 廟) and not a court (*dian* 殿). The establishment of the Shrine of Giving Birth to the Sage had been discussed for a long time. Hong Mai 洪邁 (1123–1202), during the Song dynasty, and Xiong He 熊鉌 (1253–1312), during the Yuan, had noted the moral dilemma of "revering the son and humbling the father" (*zi zun fu bei* 子尊夫卑) in the enshrinement of the sages and worthies in the Confucius temple.[23] During the Ming, Cheng Minzheng had even more emphatically attacked this contradiction.[24] Zhang Cong's advocacy of establishing the Shrine of Giving Birth to the Sage in order to emphasize the primacy of ethical relations neatly paralleled the deeper significance of the Great Rites Controversy of 1524.

Zhang Cong's proposed reforms in the Confucius temple coincided with Shizong's intentions, but generations of scholars have considered them an insult to Confucianism.[25] According to a contemporary record, "The scholars of the time, whose eyes and ears had been polluted for a long time already, argued and debated vigorously, all with differing views."[26] In other words, the scholar gentry had long been used to the old institutions and did not approve of the new institutions. The censor Li Guan 黎貫 (1483–1542) pointed out: "[If Confucius] is called 'first master' and not 'king,' . . . not only would eight rows of ceremonial dancers and twelve sacrificial vessels constitute a breach, using six rows of ceremonial dancers and ten sacrificial vessels would also be a breach. Not only should the sculptures be destroyed, but the multiple halls and double eaves as well."[27]

From the beginning, many people found fault with the Shrine of Giving Birth to the Sage, especially after the removal of Confucius's title of king. It was also considered highly unsuitable that Shuliang He retained a noble title.[28] At the conclusion of the debates, Shizong ordered the sculptures destroyed and tablets installed. Many local prefects could not bear to destroy the sculptures and hid them in walls.[29] The sculptures in Queli (Qufu) were preserved unharmed.[30]

Destruction of the sculptures went against human conscience, and the officials could not do much to enforce the regulations. At the time, Junior Compiler Xu Jie 徐階 (1503–1583) submitted a memorial opposing the elimination of the noble titles and the destruction of the sculptures and went on to strongly criticize the emperor:

> All of Your Highness's actions have been in accord with the founding emperor, Taizu. Taizu demoted the rank of many spirits, but he spared Confucius's title as king. This was because he did not think lightly of this change. Even if the great mountains and rivers are made sacred and Confucius is humanized, there will still be some debate on the significance of these changes.[31]

Shizong and Zhang Cong had based their reform of the Confucius temple on the dynastic founder's decision. Xu Jie challenged them, using their own weapon:

The tradition of sacrificing to Confucius has been handed down throughout the empire for a long time. Scholars and students of the classics have become accustomed to it, and peasants and commoners are extravagant in their worship. If it is decreed that the title of king be removed, the populace will be stupefied and become anxious and fearful, not understanding the reason behind Your Highness's action. After some speculation, they may believe Your Highness has no regard for others and lightly robs Confucius of his nobility. It is difficult to predict people's fickle suspicions.[32]

On the one hand, Xu Jie elevated Taizu, and on the other hand he provoked Shizong by pointing out that people's emotional responses must be considered. An angry Shizong had Xu Jie exiled. Although Xu Jie gained a reputation for virtue throughout the empire, he was not able to shake Shizong's determination.[33]

In response to the doubts of other officials, Zhang Cong wrote a point-by-point rebuttal entitled "Inquiries on the Sacrifices to the First Teacher Confucius" (*Xianshi Kongzi sidian huoda* 先師孔子祀典或答). Two points in this document are worthy of attention. First, at the beginning of the dynasty, Song Lian 宋濂 (1310–1381) had submitted a memorial entitled "Debate on the Confucius Temple Hall" (*Kongzi miaotang yi* 孔子廟堂議), whose main point was that "to not use the ancient rites in sacrificing to Confucius is to desecrate the sacrifice. A desecrated sacrifice is disrespectful, and if one is disrespectful, one shall have bad luck."[34] A careful reading of Song Lian's text suggests that his purpose was to persuade Taizu to respect Confucius and Confucianism. Zhang Cong, on the other hand, used it as a base for the reforms in the Confucius temple.[35]

Another question raised in Zhang's rebuttal was "If the reform of the Confucius temple sacrifice ceremony is enforced throughout the empire, what about Queli [the temple of Confucius in Qufu]?"[36] This question suggests that opponents of the reforms had retreated and were defending their second option, to shield the temple in Queli from the reforms. This sort of two-track policy had been apparent earlier in the Ming, although the situation was vastly different. In 1438, Pei Kan 裴侃 had noted the tendency toward "respecting the son over the father" in the Confucius temple rites and stated, "The temples of culture throughout the empire stress the transmission of the Way in the ordering of the tablets. The family temple in

Queli must preserve [distinctions of] father and son to promote the cardinal human relationships."[37]

The court established the Shrine of the King Who Gave Birth to the Sage (*Qisheng wang ci* 啟聖王祠), with the fathers of the four masters, Yan Hui, Zeng Sen, Kong Ji, and Mencius, as correlates.[38] This was done only in Queli. Zhang Cong evoked the words of Zisi as a basis for extending this practice throughout the empire: "Today, all vehicles of the empire use the same axle width, and everyone writes with the same characters. Action is in accordance with ethics. This is called greater unification. How can this be doubted in Queli?"[39] According to Zhang, the Queli temple could not be an exception.

As a highly ranked official, Zhang Cong represented the court in demanding a unified position on education. After his memorial was submitted, the texts of the debates at the Ministry of Rites were collected. Most of the ritual treatises issued by the court were based on Zhang Cong's views.[40] Shizong ordered that ritual practice follow these treatises, which thus became the definitive statutes for the empire.

Shizong's Confucius Temple Reforms of 1530

Just as the contention over the great rituals was at its peak, Senior Compiler Yang Shen 楊慎 (1488–1559) sighed, "This dynasty has nurtured scholars for 150 years. Now is the time to fight and die for ideals." Yang and more than two hundred other officials knelt outside a gate to the palace in the hope of persuading Shizong to rescind his order.[41] On the contrary, Shizong angrily had sixteen men beaten to death, and many more exiled. In 1525, Yu Shan 余珊 (*jinshi* 1508) submitted a statement on the event: "When officials speak of rituals today, if they disagree [with the throne] on one point, they are charged with treason. They are exiled or sentenced to death, so that the court is empty."[42]

Shizong thought himself knowledgeable about matters of ritual and considered himself a lover of antiquity. In fact, he was opinionated and often at odds with court officials. He attempted to awe his officials and establish an air of imposing authority. When Zhang Cong submitted his memorial on reforming the Confucius temple, Shizong ordered the Ministry of Rites to meet with the members of the Hanlin Academy (翰林院) to discuss it. Xu Jie objected to the reforms and was immediately demoted. Shizong personally drafted "Explanation of the Corrected Sacrifices to Confucius" (*Zheng Kongzi sidian shuo* 正孔子祀典說) and "Extensive Record of the Corrected Sacrifice to Confucius" (*Zheng Kongzi sidian shenji* 正孔子祀典申記) and ordered the Ministry of Rites to discuss these two essays.[43]

In response, Xia Yan 夏言 (1482–1548), a favored minister of Shizong, praised Shizong for "using a sage's mind to deduce the Sage's mind; the analysis is detailed and clear, and the inquiry precise and accurate." He followed this, however, by saying, "In the past few days, debates have been rampant. In all loyalty, I request that Your Highness . . . temporarily postpone your ritual of sacrifice to Confucius."[44]

Clearly, the opposition was enormous. The censor Li Guan even said that if Shizong insisted on reforming the Confucius temple, he would only "be criticized by contemporaries and laughed at by later generations."[45] Zhang Cong, however, seems to have been prepared for this response, for after he recited Shizong's essays, he said:

> The difficulties in changing customs cannot be understood by the average fools, who will defend themselves by claiming to "respect Confucius." They are directed by profit and never have been directed by righteousness. It is only the emperor who is justly righteous. Acting on authority of his own heart is what is meant by "only a sage can understand a sage."[46]

Shizong wished to confer further with other court officials, and perhaps to divine some instruction from the imperial ancestors. Because of Shizong's resolve, Zhang Cong was able to unite his supporters and attack his opponents and thus achieve Shizong's demand.[47] This imperceptibly helped advance Shizong's authoritarian power. By advising Shizong to reform the Confucius temple "on authority of his own heart," Zhang Cong was in fact handing over the "creation of rites and music" (the authority of cultural creation) to an autocratic ruler.

The two essays by Shizong are useful for understanding the emperor's reforms of the Confucius temple. In the first month of 1525, over the strong objections of many officials, Shizong stubbornly insisted on creating the Rite of the Empress Personally Tending the Silkworms. The emperor announced: "The institutions of rites and music originate from the Son of Heaven. This is purely the way of antiquity. Thus, Confucius wrote this saying in order to inform all later generations."[48] The passage from the

Analects reads, "When all under heaven is in accord with the Way, rites, music, and military action originate from the Son of Heaven."[49] Shizong's selective quotation of this passage was meant to use the name of Confucius to oppress Confucian officials. Ironically, Shizong's target was Confucius himself.

In the introduction to the "Extensive Record of the Corrected Sacrifice to Confucius," Shizong wrote, "It is our view that the Way of Confucius was the Way of a king, his virtue was the virtue of a king, his accomplishments were the same as a king's, and his work was the same as a king's. It is only that his position was never that of a king."[50] Confucius "had the virtue without the position" and hence ought not receive the rites of a king. Shizong criticized the "conferring of the title of king" on Confucius and described it as an error repeated from the time of Tang Xuanzong 唐宣宗 (r. 846–859) to that of Yuan Wuzong 元武宗 (r. 1307–1311). He pointed out that in the *Spring and Autumn Annals* 春秋 Confucius had reprimanded all those in his own day who had usurped the title of king. Some might call misunderstanding the intentions of the sage and recklessly conferring the title of king on him reverence, but in fact it "villainously inflicts extreme harm on the sage."[51]

In his "Extensive Record of the Corrected Sacrifice to Confucius," Shizong elucidated—in great detail—the meaning of the word "king" (*wang* 王). "King," as it is used as Confucius's posthumous title, is not the same as the "heavenly king" (*tianwang* 天王) of the Zhou institution, "the king who rules over all under heaven." Rather, it is the later noble title of king "as conferred on a [feudal] ruler" (*zhuhou wang* 諸侯王). Rulers throughout history have conferred the posthumous title of king on Confucius and have not elevated him to the position of emperor, "not wishing him to be of equal status [with themselves]." The title of king thus confers on Confucius the position of subject. How can this be considered a sign of reverence?[52]

Shizong used this argument not only to refute Xu Jie's argument but also to rebut the arguments of earlier scholars, such as Zhou Hongmo, who wished to elevate Confucius to the status of the Zhou dynasty's heavenly king.[53] If Confucius retained the title of king yet received the rites due an emperor, he could not escape allegations of transgression and usurpation. Scholars such as Zhu Yizun 朱彝尊 (1629–1709) would later disagree with Shizong's opinion. As Zhu delicately explained, "The emperor rules over the National University. The rites of the emperor are administered in accordance with the learning of the emperor, performing the music of the emperor, sacrificing with twelve vessels, and dancing in eight rows."[54]

Shizong put unprecedented stress on the rank of sacrifice in the ritual hierarchy. When he objected, in 1530, to placement of his royal ancestors Taizu 太祖 and Taizong 太宗 as subordinate to the sacrifice to the altar of the gods of soils and grains, he stated very clearly, "Every time we sacrificed to the gods of soils and grains and presented offerings to Taizu and Taizong as correlates, we had doubts. Heaven and earth are the most highly respected, followed by the imperial ancestral temple, and only then the altar of soils and grains. This is the underlying principle of the order of ritual sacrifices." Thus Shizong permitted only the principle of "respecting the ancestor who attended to heaven," and not "offering to the ancestor who attended to earth."[55] In Shizong's view, there was no comparison between the importance of country and that of the ancestral temple. The ritual of the Confucius temple can thus be imagined.

Shen Defu's 沈德符 (1578–1642) subtle analysis of Shizong's reform of the Confucius temple is quite astute: "Replacing the statues with tablets and the title of 'king' with that of 'master' can be justified. As for replacing eight rows of dancers with six and reducing the sacrificial vessels, this was because the emperor [Shizong] did not want master to be on the same level as the ruler."[56] Shen Defu's conclusions are supported by the events of the time. As the court was debating the Confucius temple reforms, Li Guan led a group of thirteen censors in jointly submitting a strong objection. This memorandum said that Shizong's rituals honoring heaven and imperial ancestors had been grand indeed. Why then did he call into question only Confucius's title of king? This criticism struck a nerve, and Shizong had Li Guan and the others arrested, saying, "Rectifying the sacrificial ceremony arises from my respect for the master and the Way. Li Guan has absurdly brought up ancestral worship ceremonies, with the intent of slandering the Great Ritual. He collaborated with others and insolently harassed the court with petitions. Let him be stripped of his office and title." At Censor-in-Chief Wang Hong's 汪鋐 (*jinshi* 1496) request, Shizong disciplined only Li Guan.[57]

Shizong's continuing anger over the Great Rites Controversy unmistakably revealed itself in the reformed rituals of the Confucius temple. In speaking of the issue of "respecting the son and humbling the father" in the Northern Song rites for the Confucius temple, Shizong could not help placing blame on the Confucian officials involved in the Puyuan debates.[58] He said:

> How can the son sit in the main hall while the father eats below? This is called unrectified names. Once the standards were muddled, all details were destroyed as well. By the time of the Song, Cheng Yi claimed to have received the tradition of the Way and advised Song Yingzong 宋英宗 [r. 1063–1067] against recognizing King Pu 濮王 as his father. If this can be endured, what cannot be endured![59]

The extent of Shizong's anger is apparent.

Shizong claimed, time and again, that he had no intention of using his position to oppress the former master. He also said that if the Confucius temple rituals were not reformed,

> sons would not treat fathers as fathers, subjects would not treat rulers as rulers, families would break down and rebels would revolt, and much more.... We cannot but defend ourselves and our official [Zhang] Cong. What he is doing is for the sake of obligation (*mingfen* 名分) and principle, not to flatter us, not to demote the master. This is the way we, too, would correct matters.[60]

What is surprising is that Shizong boldly criticized Xianzong 明憲宗 (r. 1464–1487) for accepting the arguments of the Ministry of Rites that to "increase the dancers to eight rows, use twelve sacrificial vessels, use prepared meat, and follow the rituals of serving heaven" was "without problem."[61] Throughout history, it has been truly rare for a ruler to criticize a dynastic predecessor.

Shizong often made himself responsible for continuing in the footsteps of Taizu, and the Confucius temple reforms were no exception. When Taizu first took control of the empire, he ordered that the sacrifices to Confucius in Nanjing use tablets rather than statues, six rows of dancers, and ten sacrificial vessels. Shizong felt that this was utmost respect, and so he did not add to it. As to why Taizu still retained Confucius's title of nobility, Shizong explained, "How could he not have expected this of a later generation?"[62] The implication is that Shizong himself is the "later generation" that would remove the noble title.

Strictly speaking, Shizong did not blindly accept all rituals set by Taizu. In fact, in his later years, he made many amendments to the rituals established by Taizu. Shizong was very conscious of this, and in the third month of 1530, he expressed his position very clearly:

> The world created by Taizu was vast and open; the number of exemplary virtues that could be retained and emulated were many. But as for rites and music, there could not but be some matters to be left to later generations. As for upholding and expanding these, despite the sagacious mind of our ancestor [Taizu], how could there not have been matters left to sagely sons and spirited descendants? These are the matters now at hand. How can we sink into the view that our founding ancestor is indubitably correct, daring not to change a thing?[63]

In 1533, a student from Puzhou 蒲州 named Qin Tang 秦鏜 (1463–1541) submitted a petition saying that the separate suburban rites and the revision of the Confucius temple "were not consonant with the intentions of the sagely founder. Please return them to their original states."[64] Qin Tang may have understood how to use ancestral precedent to limit the whims of Shizong, but he ignored Shizong's self-image. In addition to being condemned to death for his improper petition, Qin was unable to change what had already been done. As it turned out, from Shizong's point of view, the "Son of Heaven" mentioned in the passage from the *Doctrine of the Mean* that reads "None but the Son of Heaven determines rites, sets measures, and defines the forms of written characters" meant not only the dynastic founder Taizu but also successive rulers. This is why, in the "Extensive Record of the Corrected Sacrifice to Confucius," Shizong said the ritual of the Confucius temple "must be appropriate to the times. When it comes to maintaining social order, [errors] must be speedily corrected."[65]

The State Teachings of Ming Taizu

Upon close examination, it is evident that although Shizong did not leave the rituals as set by Taizu untouched, he retained their general spirit. It is not difficult to recognize a similarity in the attitudes of Taizu and Shizong toward the Confucius temple and other sacrificial rites. In the second month of 1368, Taizu followed precedence in establishing a new dynasty and offered a great sacrifice to Confucius at the National University (*Guoxue* 國學); he also sent a representative to Confucius's home in Qufu to hold a sacrifice. On this occasion, he said:

> Zhongni's 仲尼 Way is as broad and ancient as heaven and earth. Therefore, no one who has since taken possession of the empire has not shown reverence and exhausted the rites by maintaining the sacrifices to him. Now that we rule the empire, [our] hopes lie in the brilliant transformation of the realm through the propagation of the master's Dao.[66]

This passage clearly expresses Taizu's understanding that the sacrifice to Confucius was an indispensable symbol of the dynastic founder's resolve to continue the imperial order. The following year, however, his attitude changed precipitously. He suddenly announced that the spring and autumn sacrifices at the Confucius temple would be held in Qufu only, and no longer throughout the empire.[67]

> Since the time of the Han dynasty, [Confucius's] spirit has been sacrificed to throughout the land. We have unified the people in the name of the earlier kings. While going through Confucius's writings, we saw such teachings as "To sacrifice to spirits not of one's own ancestor in flattery" [*Analects* 2.24]; "Respect spirits but keep them at a distance" [6.22]; "Sacrifice according to the rites" [2.5]. If the sages and worthies had not clearly stated this, how could he say it? Therefore, we dare not sacrifice [to Confucius] throughout the land and exhaust resources to burden the sagely virtue of [Confucius's] spirit.[68]

The founding of the Ming dynasty was a time of reconstruction. Taizu often ordered officials to reform rites.[69] In the same year, he ordered that the city god, *Chenghuang* 城隍, should receive sacrifices throughout the land. It was thus inconceivable that Confucius would not receive sacrifice in official temples throughout the empire. Both Minister Qian Tang 錢唐 (1314–1394) and Vice Minister Cheng Xu 程徐 (d. 1369) submitted petitions strongly protesting this decree. Cheng wrote:

Of all the sacrifices of ancient and present times, only those to the soils and grains, the Three August Ones, and Confucius are held throughout the land. If the people throughout the realm do not sacrifice to soils and grains, then the Three August Ones would have no means to thrive; if they do not follow Confucius's Way, then they would have no means on which to establish themselves... Confucius established his teachings based on the Way, and so all under heaven sacrifice to him. They do not sacrifice to the man but to his teachings and to his Way. To have all people read his books, follow his teachings, practice his Way, and yet not be allowed to sacrifice to him is not the way to secure the hearts of the people and uphold the teachings of the world.[70]

Taizu would not listen. In 1371, Song Lian submitted "On the Confucius Temple," in which he spoke of the advantages of sacrificing to Confucius throughout the temple. And not surprisingly, he was banished and exiled.[71]

It is evident that, on the one hand, Taizu understood the importance of the sacrifices to Confucius in the founding of a dynasty, but on the other hand, he discontinued the sacrifices in state temples throughout the empire for the sake of minor sacrificial quibbles. There must have been a deeper reason for this. Indeed, when Taizu's general Xu Da 徐達 (1332–1385) advanced into Jining 濟寧 in the third month of 1368, the Yansheng Duke 衍聖公, Kong Kejian 孔克堅 (1316–1370), who had been ennobled in 1335 by the Mongols, pleaded illness and sent his son (Xu) Xixue (徐)希學 (1336–1381) to the capital to have an audience with Taizu. Taizu was upset about this and personally wrote to Duke Kong Kejian:

> I am told that you have been sick for a long time, but I wonder if this is true. Your Kong family is a distinguished house known for your ancestor's teachings, which generation after generation of rulers have followed. Your family has served different dynasties over time and should surely make no exception to this rule when it comes to my regime. I have received the mandate of heaven to lead the Chinese people and drive away the barbarians in order to bring peace to China. This despite the fact that I came from among the common people, but so did the Han dynasty founder, Gaozong [sic, Gaozu] in antiquity. Hence, it is not permissible for you to neglect my state on the pretext of illness![72]

Taizu obviously was well aware of the importance of Confucius's ancestral line to the legitimation of his political power. Kong Kejian's hesitation to respond to Taizu's summons may have been a sign that the combat in North China was not yet over and the victor not yet clear. Later, when Kong Kejian did come to court, Taizu broke precedent and did not confer an office on him. Taizu held an audience with him in court but said, "Although your age is not advanced, illness plagues you. Thus, I will not trouble you with an office." Taizu explained to his officials, "The reason I did not confer an office on Kong Kejian was because he is the descendant of the late sage. To be especially polite to him, I am giving him a salary, but not burdening him with work."[73] The same month, Taizu nonetheless conferred the title of Yansheng Duke on Kong Kejian's son, Xixue. Taizu's displeasure could not be veiled.

When reading *Mencius* in 1372, Taizu came upon the passage "If the ruler views his ministers as dirt and grass, then his ministers will view him as a bandit and villain" (*Mencius* 4b:31). Taizu felt this was inappropriate reading matter for his subjects, and he banned Mencius from receiving sacrifice as a correlate in the Confucius temple. He also announced that any remonstration would be regarded as treason. Nonetheless, Qian Tang objected, saying, "If I die for Mencius's sake, I will die with great honor." The official histories comment, "The emperor appreciated his sincerity and did not punish him."[74]

Qian Tang's willingness to sacrifice his life for his ideals exemplifies the conflict between political authority and cultural belief; the price of this conflict was too high for an autocratic ruler to sustain. In 1373, Taizu reinstated Mencius in the sacrifices.[75] Not until 1382 did he restore the sacrifice to Confucius in state temples throughout the empire. The edict said, "Confucius understood the Dao of the sovereign and taught it to the world by allowing rulers to be rulers, subjects to be subjects, fathers to be fathers, and sons to be sons, setting standards and ordering ethics. His accomplishments are equal to heaven and earth."[76]

Allowing rulers to be rulers, subjects to be subjects, fathers to fathers, and sons to be sons is truly a Confucius teaching, but in this context, Taizu's emphasis is worth consideration. In 1380, Taizu had executed his prime minister, Hu Weiyong 胡惟庸, on suspicion of treason, and the repercussions were extensive and long lasting.[77] Taizu may have wished to make use of Confucius's teachings to dissolve the political strife then rampant at court. Later, during the Wanli era (1573–1619), while explaining that sacrificing to Confucius throughout the empire was not blasphemous, Qu Jiusi 瞿九思 (*juren* 1573) said something interesting about Taizu:

> Looking over the lands of the empire, our emperor on high feared there were those who were not loyal and so intended to use the spirit of the great sage to pacify them. He thus had no choice but to make use of Confucius's importance. . . . Once this had been completed, Confucius received sacrifices throughout the empire. It is precisely because he relied upon the sage that he cannot be criticized.[78]

Qu Jiusi was renowned as a pure Confucian, and his defense of Confucianism was not unusual. This passage, however, has other implications about which the histories say nothing. What these implications may be, we may never know.

In 1370, Taizu revoked the titles of nobility of all spirits except Confucius. Since the Tang dynasty, the spirits of mountains and rivers had been honored with such titles as "emperor" and "king." Taizu explained his action by saying that "for the relations between spirits and humans to be appropriate, titles must be correct and appropriate to the rites."[79]

In 1371, Taizu proclaimed that the Three August Ones 三皇 could not receive sacrifices in the provinces and counties. In 1295, the Yuan emperor Chengzong 元成宗 (r. 1294–1307) ordered the establishment of temples to the Three August Ones in the provinces. Sacrifices were to be held in the spring and autumn, to be led by a pharmaceutical master.[80] Taizu felt this was an improper rite and forbade the provinces from conducting such sacrifices.[81] The unintentional result of this was that there were no sacrifices to the Three August Ones.

In 1373, a temple of kings and emperors (*Lidai diwang miao* 歷代帝王廟) was built in the capital for the sacrifices to the Three August Ones, the Five Emperors, and the founding emperors of the Han, Tang, Song, and Yuan dynasties.[82] In 1388, thirty-seven eminent officials throughout history were included as correlates in the temple of kings and emperors.[83] The temple's form and regulations imitated those of the Confucius temple, but the offerings and ceremonies exceeded those of the Confucius temple. Every spring and autumn, the emperor conducted the ceremonies in person, to emphasize the glory of imperial legitimacy. There was a strong suggestion of competition with the Confucius temple.[84]

In 1387, Taizu eliminated the temple of the King of Military Accomplishment (Wuchengwang *miao* 武成王廟). This temple, originally called the *Taigong* 太公 temple, had been established in 731, during the Tang dynasty, for sacrifices to Taigong Wang 太公望. In 760, Taigong Wang was given the title of King Wucheng, with a liturgy comparable to that of Confucius, King of Exalted Culture. In imitation of the Confucius temple, there were ten correlates, all great military generals of old.[85] Later generations also added seventy-two worthies as correlates.

The original intention was to build two peaks of exalted culture and military accomplishment, with equal status. Because of the civil service examination system, Confucianism had subsequently become the basis of official learning. As the literati gained confidence, there was a tendency to value the literary over the martial. In 788, the attendant to the Ministry of Military Affairs, Li Shu 李紓 (d. 834), suggested that the sacrificial ceremonies of the Confucius temple and the Wucheng temple ought not be equal:

> Exalted culture has been passed down, and a hundred generations revere the master [Confucius]. Without his teachings, the five constant virtues [humaneness, righteousness, propriety, wisdom, and faithfulness] and the three bonds [ruler–minister, father–son, husband–wife] would not to be clear; if not for his regulations, countries and families could not be established. This is why Mencius said that since the birth of people, there has been no one like this one [Confucius]. Therefore, the regulations of the uncrowned king were rectified; the title of "first sage" (*xiansheng* 先聖) was added; for music, court instruments were used; for the sacrifice, the protector-in-chief was sent. The master is revered, and the Dao is worshipped; all is refined and proper. Taigong wrote only "Six Stratagems," and his achievements were evident for only one generation. How can his virtues deserve such ceremony?[86]

Li Shu's petition is representative of the attitude of civil officials. For this reason, although the sacrificial ceremonies of the Wucheng temple were grand, they could not compare with those of the temple of culture.[87]

In any case, Taizu did not eliminate the sacrifice at the temple of King Wucheng solely because he emphasized the temple of culture. He had other intentions. The Qing scholar Qin Huitian 秦蕙田 (1702–1764) misunderstood

Taizu's reason for elimination of the martial temple and wrote, "How can Taigong's accomplishments be compared with those of Confucius?" He even praised Taizu's actions for "breaking from a millennium of blasphemous sacrificial rites."[88] Taizu's reasons were clear: "Taigong was ennobled as a lord of Zhou. If he receives the sacrifices of a king, he would be equal to the Zhou Son of Heaven. If he is given a false title, he shall surely not receive the sacrifice."[89] For this reason, Taizu eliminated Taigong's title of king, closed his temple, and ordered that he receive sacrifices as a correlate in the temple of kings and emperors.

Shizong eliminated Confucius's title of king for the same reason. Shizong's intention was clear: a subject must not receive an emperor's rites. To do so infringes on the emperor's privileges. In the policy question for the palace examinations in 1388, Taizu expressed his opinion concerning ritual: "The way of serving spirits is no different from that of leading the people. All sacrifices, from the beginning of time to the present, have been instituted for a reason, but the ritual regulations of the sages and worthies have distinctions. From the Son of Heaven to the common people, the sacrificial titles and the distinctions have deep roots."[90]

Taizu's revoking of the feudal titles of the spirits reflects his attitude. Nevertheless, despite Taizu's strict adherence to the order of the sacrifices, when Wu Chen argued that Confucius should not be called king, Taizu still refused to deny Confucius his royal title.[91] Perhaps he remembered the enormous protest that had arisen when he ended the empire-wide sacrifices to Confucius in 1369 and wanted to avoid aggravating the scholar-officials too much.

The Cultural Legitimation of Autocracy

Shizong's reign began more than a century after the founding of the dynasty. Autocratic government was already accepted, the ruler's power consolidated. Shizong shared none of Taizu's concerns. Indeed, he had higher praise for Taizu than he did for Confucius:

> Of the rulers of later generations who have been in the position of king, although many have been similar to Confucius, there has been none whose virtue could equal that of Confucius. As for my lofty ancestor [Taizu], although he followed Confucius's Dao, his sagely

benevolence, martial prowess, and literary virtues were equal to those of Yao and Shun. I fear Confucius could not compare.

Thus, Shizong believed that "the title of a king ought not to be falsely used, and the virtue of a king ought not to be falsely imitated."[92]

In the early years of the Hongwu era, Wu Chen said, "The two emperors and three kings [of archaic times] fulfilled their roles as rulers and teachers. Since Confucius was not able to be ruler, he was a teacher."[93] Once put in Shizong's hands, this attitude became even more amplified. In rebutting Li Guan, Shizong said, "The ruler concurrently holds the role of teacher, but a teacher must never feign the title of ruler. Confucius was originally a subject of the Zhou dynasty, no different from Taigong Wang. The teachings he transmitted were originally the teachings of [Fu]xi and [Shen]nong [who were both rulers]. He only expounded them."[94]

In the second month of 1520, Shizong decided to establish the sacrifice to the Sagely Matters. The nine sage rulers—Fuxi 伏羲; Shennong 神農; the Yellow Emperor Xuanyuan 黃帝軒轅; Yao 堯; Shun 舜; the founder of the Xia dynasty, Yu 禹; the founder of the Shang dynasty, Tang 湯; and the founders of the Zhou dynasty, kings Wen 文王 and Wu 武王—were placed in the ruling position facing south. The sage Duke of Zhou was placed in the left correlate position and Master Confucius on the right.[95]

In 1371, Song Lian suggested following the argument of Xiong He of the early Yuan dynasty and considering Fuxi as the founding ancestor of the tradition of the Way, followed by Shennong, the Yellow Emperor, Yao, Shun, Yu, Tang, Wen, and Wu, with Gao Tao 皋陶, Yi Yin 伊尹, Taigong Wang, the Duke of Zhou, Ji 稷, Xie 契, Yi 益, Fu Yue 傅說, and Jizi 箕子 as correlates. The emperor and court officials, Song Lian said, should take these people as models. If sacrifice to these people were ordered, the tradition of the Way would be even more respected.[96]

Taizu did not follow this advice. Since Xiong He and Song Lian were in favor of increased respect for Confucius, it is significant that they advocated having everyone from the emperor to the common people sacrifice to Confucius separately rather than as a correlate of the sage rulers throughout history.[97] Shizong implemented this model, but he replaced Gao Tao and the others with the Duke of Zhou as the "sage" (*xiansheng* 先聖) and Confucius as "master" (*xianshi* 先師). This was in accordance with Shizong's statement that the teachings transmitted by Confucius were based on those of [Fu]Xi and [Shen]nong and that Confucius had only "expounded them," providing illumination.

In Shizong's sacrifice to the sagely master, Confucius was returned to his early Tang status as correlate of the Duke of Zhou. Although he was not the correlate of the Duke of Zhou as sage, the implication is the same. Fei Mi 費密 (1599–1671) argued that the demotion of Confucius from sage to master was very unjust:

> The titles "sage" and "master" are different. In the *Rites of Zhou* 周禮, there are many kinds of masters. Later generations called anyone who taught disciples a master but did not dare call him a sage. Thus, "sage" is respectful and "master" is subordinate. Now, a sage has been demoted to a master for no reason. . . . I do not know on which canonical source this is based.[98]

Such was Fei Mi's displeasure with Confucius's designation as master, let alone Confucius's demotion to the position of correlate. For Confucians, Shizong's action amounted to a nightmare. No wonder that even Zhang Cong, who so strongly supported the Confucius temple reforms, tried to prevent Shizong from going through with his plan of the sacrifice to sagely masters by saying, "The world of the Three August Ones was chaotic, and many matters remain mysterious."[99] But Shizong was obstinate, and this sacrifice was implemented. Confucius, revered in the "tradition of the Way," became subservient to "political legitimacy" in the imperial register of sacrifices.

In the context of Chinese political history, the combination of the tradition of the Way (*daotong*) and tradition of legitimate governance was the last step in the growth of autocracy. Full autocracy implies a ruler with absolute and unrestrained political power. In history, the tradition of the Way symbolized the cultural power of Confucianism and was political in that it was used as the criterion for judging the legitimacy and the competence of a government. The independence of the Way from the political establishment served as a check on political power and so was an obstacle to autocracy. No one understood this better than Lü Kun 呂坤 (1536–1618), in his reflections on the relation between power and truth:

> Although ministers dispute one another at court, after the issuance of an edict from the emperor, no one dares to defy it and speak out

against it. Although scholars argue with one another in school, when someone invoked the words of Confucius, everyone agrees and keeps silent. Therefore, in the world, only principle (*li* 理) and political power (*shi* 勢) are the most respected, but principle is supreme. The emperor cannot suppress principle with his power at court. Even if he did so, principle nevertheless would exist in the world forever. In fact, political power lies within the realm of emperors, whereas principle lies within the realm of the sages. If the reign of an emperor is not legitimated by the principle of the sages, it will decline. Thus, political power needs principle for the justification of its existence.[100]

To be sure, just because a political ruler claims absolute power does not necessarily mean that he has identified with the tradition of the Way, nor does it necessarily mean that political and cultural authority are united in the ruler. The ruler might attempt to challenge or even destroy the tradition of the Way and the power of the Confucian authorities as a means of expanding his power over that tradition. Such were the measures adopted by the founder of the Ming dynasty, Taizu, and followed by Shizong.

Undermining an independent tradition of the Way was a perfectly logical step in the process of strengthening autocracy. However, the methods used to do this were varied—as is clear from the differences between the tactics of Ming Taizu and Ming Shizong, on the one hand, and those of the Qing emperor Kangxi 清康熙帝 (r. 1661–1722), on the other. In retrospect, the Qing emperor, although an alien ruler, was much more successful. Unlike the Ming founder, the Kangxi Emperor did not directly confront the tradition of the Way as the symbol of cultural authority. The Kangxi Emperor was more sensitive to, and more conscious of, the subtle influence of Confucian symbols on Chinese politics and society.[101] His promotion of Confucius temple rituals was only one of many demonstrations of this sensitivity. The Qing emperor used the Confucian cultural heritage as a means of reinforcing his political legitimacy. Through his restructuring of the relationship between the tradition of the Way and the tradition of imperial governance, the Kangxi Emperor assumed the leadership of both, an ideal that had never been actualized by the Ming rulers.

CHAPTER V

Xunzi

The Confucius Temple's Absentee

Remembering his childhood, Nobel laureate Lee Yuan-Tseh 李遠哲 said he used to frequent the Confucius temple with his friends and, using the spirit tablets as the net and the altar as the table, they played table tennis. Fortunately, the great pre-Qin philosopher Xunzi 荀子 (c. 310–238 BCE) escaped this blasphemy by the virtue of his centuries-long absence from the temples.

In 1084, Xunzi was enshrined as a sage of the Confucius temple, then deprived of that privilege in 1530. The rise and fall of Xunzi's fortunes demonstrates that the roster of canonized Confucian sages at the temple was not fixed and has in fact been subject to frequent changes.

As the name implies, Confucius temples are places of worship dedicated to the veneration of Confucius and of the sages enshrined by the imperial state to receive posthumous offerings as Confucius's correlates. In imperial China, Confucius temples were the sacred grounds of Confucianism, and the ceremony of offering libations to Confucius was among the most solemn and grand rites of the state.

In the modern age, however, Confucius temples have been reduced to pale ghosts of their former selves, not living, breathing institutional bodies. Confucius temples and the rites are rarely on the mind of the people. The historical processes of modernity reduced Confucius temples' cultural prominence and led to the loss of religious belief in Confucius and the displacement of Confucianism as the dominant social and political ideology.

It is fair to say that restoring the institution of correlates is as important to the revitalization of the culture of Confucius temples as finding meaning for the temples' rites. However, as I have stated elsewhere, "The restoration of the institution of enshrinement is a huge question, with implications for the cultural and spiritual well-being of the modern Chinese-speaking peoples. We are in need of a genuine movement for the 'creative transformation' of Confucian culture."[1]

To enshrine or not to enshrine? That is the question.

In traditional China, Confucius temples were the nexus of political power and cultural authority. The temples were the site of power struggles between imperial rulers and the Confucian scholar-officials to control enshrinement; nevertheless, the Chinese seriously sponsored state enshrinement. The enshrinement of correlates was a visible sign of a dynasty's continuity with the tradition of the Way, and the tally of sages a dynasty enshrined at Confucius temples was a measure of its glory.[2] Therefore, promoting Confucian culture and learning was a matter of prestige for the imperial court, because its enshrinement of sages from the past would increase its own glory in the eyes of future generations.

Today, the position of Confucianism in the cultural mainstream is insecure, and most people regard those individuals who are striving to restore its traditional position as more idealistic than practical. Even the less ambitious goal of forging a consensus among self-identifying Confucians could prove a daunting project. In imperial China, ideological conformity and intellectual orthodoxy was of paramount importance, but those proclivities run counter to modern societies' preference to encourage diversity and individuality.

For example, enshrining a sage in imperial China required the nomination of the candidate by court officials, as well as the emperor's agreement that the enshrinement of the sage should take place. As the empire's supreme political authority, the emperor was free to accept or reject the recommendation of his officials. It was commonplace for a nomination to languish through many decades and the reigns of multiple emperors before the candidate was finally enshrined as a correlate.

Today, the authority to enshrine would also carry with it the responsibility to define the tradition of the Way for the contemporary world and to adapt Confucian thought to the spirit of the age. Finding an authoritative decision-making body that could be trusted with responsibility is a daunting prospect. Yet when Confucians in the past tried to rise to the challenges of changing times, they turned to enshrinement. In fact, the most recent changes to temple enshrinement took place in 1919, when Yan Yuan 顏元 (1635–1704) and Li Gong 李塨 (1659–1733) were enshrined as correlates to Confucius. Their enshrinement was almost certainly a response to the pragmatic and empirical intellectual spirit of early twentieth century.

Here is a dilemma. One the one hand, leaving the correlates as they were in the past is not an option, because inaction is tantamount to allowing the last enshrinement of 1919 to become the final historical judgment on Confucianism. Such a refusal to address new enshrinements might possibly preserve Confucianism for all eternity, but only as an ossified artifact without relevance to modern life. On the other hand, introducing changes willy-nilly is as problematic as the alternative. Confucius temples were a transnational or universalistic system, and the same correlates are still enshrined in temples throughout East Asia. Changing correlates in any single temple would lead to repercussions in the entire region. Although it is a necessary condition for the restoration of Confucianism to the East Asian mainstream, a misstep in restoring the process of correlate enshrinement would only accelerate the collapse of the Confucius temple culture. Yuan Shikai 袁世凱 (1859–1916) may have realized this fact only after his cynical exploitation of Confucianism backfired and sparked the collapse of his attempt to establish himself as emperor.

In the modern age, the valorization of cultural diversity and pluralism makes enshrining great Confucian thinkers of the recent past impractical, no matter how revered they might be. As continuing debates about the merits of recent Confucian thinkers have shown, the time to pass judgment on them is yet to come. From this perspective, it is worth considering the compromise of selecting a figure of indubitable stature from antiquity, Xunzi. Anyone who has visited a Confucius temple and paid attention to the correlated sages could attest to Xunzi's curious absence from the temples. In light of the crucial role Xunzi played in the development of Confucian learning, his absence is all the more extraordinary.

Actually, Xunzi was not always absent from Confucius temples, because the Northern Song had enshrined him as a correlate in 1084. However, after Emperor Shizong 明世宗 (r. 1521–1566) of the Ming dynasty eliminated him from the ranks of the correlates, in 1530, he was never again enshrined. Yet, as this example shows, the proposal to enshrine Xunzi is not an innovation, since Confucius temples included Xunzi veneration for almost five centuries.

Xunzi's Rise and Fall as a Correlate in the Confucius Temple

Xunzi, or Xun Kuang 荀況, also known by his courtesy name Xun Qing 荀卿, was born in the state of Zhao during the late Warring States period. More than a millennium later, Emperor Shenzong 宋神宗 (r. 1067–1085) of the Northern Song enshrined Xunzi in 1084, along with Yang Xiong 揚雄 (53 BCE–18 CE) and Han Yu 韓愈 (768–824). However, Mencius 孟子 (c. 372–289 BCE) was the true star of Shenzong's enshrinement ritual that year, to whom this trio collectively played second fiddle. The court declared Mencius to be an "auxiliary," just like Confucius's favorite disciple Yanzi, while Xun, Yang, and Han became "correlates," inferior in status to auxiliaries. The distinction was marked in a number of ways. For example, auxiliaries were venerated in the central temple structure while correlates were relegated to the side halls. In addition, Shenzong conferred on Mencius the title of duke, whereas the emperor ennobled Xunzi only as a count.[3]

Xunzi and Mencius, in fact, shared a relationship that was at once complementary and antagonistic, in terms of personality and intellectual positions. Shenzong's decision to enshrine Yang Xiong and Han Yu as correlates was based on their connection to Mencius's thought. Although Mencius toured the states of the Middle Kingdom to promote Confucius's ideas, he could not find employment as a court adviser, so he became known for his philosophical positions and his arguments against the adherents of Yang Zhu 楊朱 (c. 395–335 BCE) and Mozi 墨子 (c. 480–389 BCE). As Mencius claimed, "I, too, wish to follow in the footsteps of the three sages [Yu the Great, the Duke of Zhou, and Confucius] in rectifying the hearts of men, laying heresies to rest, opposing extreme actions, and banishing excessive views. I am not fond of disputation. I have no alternative."[4] Mencius argued that the Way of Confucius would flourish only if the teachings of the Yangists and Mohists were extinguished; therefore, only those able to refute Yang and Mo deserved consideration as true disciples of the sage.[5]

Both Yang Xiong, in the Western Han, and Han Yu, in the Middle Tang, invoked that aspect of Mencius's spirit in their struggle against heresies. Yang had explicitly modeled himself after Mencius: "In ancient times, Yangzi's and Mozi's philosophies obstructed the path. Mencius dismissed and refuted them, extending to those like them. Later, heresies again obstructed the path. I want to be like Mencius."⁶ By the Middle Tang, Confucianism had experienced several centuries of declining influence because of competition from the "heresies" of Buddhism and Daoism. In response to these two heresies, Han Yu promoted Mencius as equal in merit to the legendary Yu the Great 大禹; moreover, Han Yu mounted attacks on Gautama Buddha and Laozi:

> The calamity from Gautama Buddha and Laozi is greater than from Yangzi and Mozi, and my virtue does not reach that of Mencius. Mencius could not rescue us from the unanticipated catastrophe that would come, while I must try to preserve what was already destroyed. Alas! The task greatly exceeds my powers. Yet, when we see another in mortal danger, we do what we can, even though we may perish in the attempt. If I somehow manage to revive the Way and pass it on, I will never have any regrets even if I perish.⁷

Han Yu's temple enshrinement as a critic of the Buddha and Laozi sought to parallel Mencius's criticism of Yang Zhu and Mozi. The trio of Mencius, Yang Xiong, and Han Yu thus symbolized the collective embodiment of courageous defenses against heresy through different eras.

However, such symbolic logic did not extend to Xunzi, for although Xunzi was a relentless critic of non-Confucian thought, he also was a rigorous critic of fellow Confucians. In particular, he lambasted Zisi 子思—Confucius's grandson, Kong Ji 孔伋 (c. 483–402 BCE)—and Mencius for their interpretations, saying, "Peculiar and unreasonable in the extreme, they lack proper logical categories. Mysterious and enigmatic, they lack a satisfactory theoretical basis. Esoteric and laconic, they lack adequate explanations."⁸ Therefore, we must look elsewhere to explain Xunzi's enshrinement.

In the Northern Song, attention began to be given to the human mind as an object of inquiry, and Confucian scholars engaged in heated debates over the inherent quality of human nature. In fact, the enshrinement of 1084 was an attempt to represent all four major Confucian philosophical interpretations of human nature. Mencius represents the position that human nature is originally good, Xunzi represents the position that human nature is inherently dysfunctional or prone to bad behavior, Yang Xiong represents the position that human nature is both good and bad, and Han Yu represents the position that human nature has a tripartite differentiation.[9] Conferring sagehood on all four Confucians was a declaration of the imperial court's broad-mindedness, which was possible because the enshrinement occurred before the emergence of an inflexible Confucian orthodoxy centered on Zhu Xi 朱熹 (1130–1200). Yet the imperial court's decision to enshrine Mencius as an auxiliary and Xunzi as a correlate clearly showed that the Northern Song court regarded Mencius as superior to Xunzi.

Nonetheless, Xunzi was renowned for erudition and learning. As Yang Jing 楊倞 of the Tang dynastic era proclaimed, Xunzi "gave wings to the Six Classics and glory to Confucius."[10] After the ravaging fires of Qin, Xunzi's learning played an important role in the renaissance of culture during the Han. Wang Zhong 汪中 (1745–1794) said of Xunzi, "Between the passing away of the seventy disciples [of Confucius] and the rise of the Han scholars, he preserved the Six Classics through the calamity of the Warring States and the tyranny of the Qin."[11] Indeed, Xunzi's importance to the continuity of Confucian learning was great. In the *Records of the Grand Historian*, Sima Qian 司馬遷 (c. 145–86 BCE) not only took note of the fact that men like Xun Kuang wrote books that spread through the world[12] but also combined the lives of Xunzi and Mencius into a single shared biography.[13] Clearly, Sima Qian considered Xunzi and Mencius to be comparable in stature and importance. Decades after Sima, Liu Xiang 劉向 (77 BCE–CE 6) would acknowledge that Xunzi's theory of mankind's dysfunctional nature was diametrically opposed to that of Mencius, but he still considered both scholars worthy of a place of honor accompanying Confucius.[14]

However, Mencius's prestige seems to have overshadowed Xunzi even during the Han dynasty. For instance, Emperor Wen 漢文帝 (r. 180–157 BCE) of the Western Han briefly established a doctorate for the study of Mencius, which Western Han emperor Wu 漢武帝 (r. 141–87 BCE) soon abolished.[15] Yet the study of Xunzi had never become an official category of scholarship during the Han.

Another metric for judging the popularity of Xunzi and Mencius is to compare the quantity of textual commentary that accrued around their texts. By the Eastern Han, it was intellectually fashionable to write commentaries on the *Mencius*, with Zhao Qi 趙岐 (108–201) certainly the most famous commentator of the period.[16] One could not claim that commentaries on the *Xunzi* became fashionable until the Tang, when Yang Jing wrote his commentaries on the text. It is evident that the Mencius school was gradually gaining the upper hand over the Xunzi school of thought.

Yet Xunzi and Mencius remained comparable figures all the way from the Han to the middle period of the Tang dynasty. For example, Xu Gan 徐幹 (170–217) of the Wei dynasty wrote in his *Zhonglun* 中論, "Xunzi and Mencius had talents second only to Confucius, and developed their own teachings to continue Confucius's mission."[17] Playing a key role in this development was Han Yu, known to history because "his writings countered the decline of the previous eight dynasties, and his Way saved those in distress in the empire."[18]

In Han Yu's day, Mencius, Xunzi, and Yang Xiong were all under consideration for enshrinement, and their chances appeared to be about equal. For instance, the then newly built Confucius temple in Chu Prefecture (in modern Zhejiang) prominently displayed the trio. Moreover, later in the Northern Song dynasty, the trio also figured in the Shrine of the Five Worthies (Wuxiantang 五賢堂), which suggests their continuing important status in the eyes of Confucians.[19]

In this context, Han Yu's contribution to Mencius's ascendancy was to create a genealogy for those in the tradition of the Way that elevated Mencius and at the same time entirely excluded Xunzi and Yang Xiong from the lineage of orthodox thinkers. In the famous essay "Seeking the Origin of the Way" (*Yuan Dao* 原道), Han Yu proclaimed the transmission of the Way through the sage kings of early antiquity to Confucius and culminating with Mencius:

> What I call the Way is not the so-called Way of Laozi and the Gautama Buddha. Yao passed the Way to Shun, Shun passed it to Yu, Yu passed it to Tang, Tang passed it to Wen, Wu, and the Duke of Zhou; thereafter, the three passed it to Confucius, and Confucius passed it to Mencius. When Mencius died, no one received his transmission of the Way.

Han Yu further argued that Mencius was a superior thinker to Xunzi and Yang Xiong, both of whom "lacked discrimination in their choices and precision in their speech."[20]

As Han Yu had only written "Seeking the Origin of the Way" to stake out his position, a closer reading of his other texts is required before reconstructing his larger meaning. In "Reading Xunzi" (*Du Xun* 讀荀), Han

Yu said reading Mencius convinced him that the Way of Confucius was awesome and thus confirmed Mencius's contribution in transmitting the Way. Later, reading Yang Xiong strengthened his confidence in Mencius. Thereafter, he obtained and read the *Xunzi*. Han Yu reflected, "Studying his words, [I find that] sometimes there are things that appear impure; but overall, there is little that disagrees with Confucius." Han Yu concluded, "Mencius was the purest of the pure, whereas Xun and Yang were mostly pure, but marred by small blemishes."[21] Furthermore, Han Yu rated Xunzi's greatness as somewhere between that of Mencius and Yang Xiong and thus rated Xunzi among the most worthy disciples of the Sage Confucius. For instance, he said of Mencius and Xunzi, "Their spoken words were classics, penetrating into the realm of the sacred."[22]

To a large degree, it was due to Han Yu's praise of both Mencius and Xunzi as "the propagators of the Way" that the imperial court included Xunxi in the enshrinement of 1084.[23] In many ways, the ritual libation to Confucius held that year was emblematic of Northern Song Confucian scholars' evaluation of their forebears as a whole. In other words, the high honors that the Song court paid to Han Yu encouraged the court to follow his view in elevating both Mencius and Xunzi. Han Yu's writings thus played a role in shaping the Song court's selection of Confucian sages for enshrinement in 1084 and its organization of the ceremonial honors each sage received.[24]

In fact, before and during the Tang dynasty, Yan Hui occupied an important place in Confucius temple rites, second only to Confucius. Late in the Tang, Han Yu championed Mencius over Yan Hui. Afterwards, in the Northern Song, Wang Anshi 王安石 (1021–1086) employed the *Mencius* as a key text to justify his own major reforms of Song government; moreover, Wang and his followers threw their support behind Han Yu's scholarship, precipitating Mencius's eclipse of Yan Hui. After this period, "Confucius–Mencius" gradually overshadowed "Confucius–Yan Hui" in both texts and temple offerings. In the Yuan, Emperor Mingzong 元明宗 (r. February 27–August 30, 1329), also known as the Khutughtu Khan Kuśala (1300–1329), finalized Mencius's rise to prominence by conferring the title "second sage" (*yasheng* 亞聖) on Mencius and "third sage" (*fusheng* 復聖) upon Yan Hui.[25] This change of titles established the ritual framework that put Mencius in the place of honor next to Confucius while relegating Xunzi to a minor status.

After that, Xunzi's status steadily declined. To a large extent, Xunzi's fall from grace was due to the increasing rigidity of Confucian orthodoxy after the Yuan. The ascendant Zhu Xi version of Confucian thought elevated Mencius as the progenitor of its school and his theory of humanity's inherent goodness became entrenched. As a result, Zhu Xi's followers judged other Confucian thinkers according to their adherence to, or deviations from, Zhu Xi's interpretation of Mencius's ideas.

Cheng Yi 程頤 (1033–1107) of the Northern Song best encapsulated the dismissive attitude toward Xunzi, "Xun and Yang [Xiong] did not even know [human] nature. How can they speak of the Way?"[26] This ossification in the Cheng-Zhu version of Confucianism affected even Han Yu's reputation, because he had argued that mankind has a tripartite human nature. For example, Song men employing this narrow view of Confucianism condemned Han Yu, saying, "He was more than adequate as a literary man, but his knowledge of the Way was deficient."[27] Naturally, Xunzi and Yang Xiong fared even worse than Han Yu did in estimation of such Cheng–Zhu Confucians.

Cheng Yi was the key figure in the rise of the Cheng–Zhu variety of Confucianism. While he had a mixed evaluation of Han Yu, Cheng Yi was unsparingly critical of Xunzi and Yang Xiong. Particularly galling to Cheng Yi was the fact that Yang Xiong had served under Wang Mang 王莽 (r. 9–23) the usurper of the Han dynasty's throne. Cheng Yi also objected to Han Yu's opinion that Yang Xiong was only "marred by small blemishes."[28] A man whose integrity was as compromised as Yang Xiong's, Cheng Yi argued, could in no way be honored or revered as a sage.[29] In 1396, Cheng Yi's strenuous objections to Yang Xiong's character influenced Emperor Taizu 明太祖 (r. 1368–1398) of the Ming dynasty to issue an order forbidding Yang Xiong from receiving offerings at Confucius temples.[30] Although Xunzi's personal morals were beyond reproach, Cheng Yi did not moderate his criticism of Xunzi's scholarship. He sneered, "Xun Qing had great talent but little learning. By arguing that rituals were a pretense and human nature is bad, he became blind to the worthies and the sages."[31] Cheng Yi concluded that Xunzi marked the point in time when people lost the Way of the sages.

Zhu Xi brought Cheng Yi's version of Confucianism to such completion that the Song government enshrined them in the Confucius temple in 1241 as the recognized state and educational orthodoxy, and thus expelled

Wang Anshi and repudiated his learning. Zhu complained, "Xun had nothing more than [the ideas of the Legalists] Shen [Buhai] 申不害 (c. 385–337 BCE) and Han [Fei] 韓非 (c. 279–233 BCE)"; moreover, Zhu scoffed that Xunzi was outclassed even by the likes of Wang Tung 王通 (584–617) and Han Yu.[32]

Some of his contemporaries shared Zhu Xi's views on orthodox purity. In 1170, Li Wengang 李文綱 included Mencius in "A Genealogical Diagram of the Sage's School" (*Shengmen shiye tu* 聖門事業圖). Li proclaimed Mencius to be "one of the sages of past generations," because Mencius had "transmitted the utmost upright and central Way, which has been put into practice for over ten thousand generations without any flaws." At the same time, Li listed Xunzi and Yang Xiong, alongside such heretics as the Gautama Buddha, Laozi, Yang Zhu, and Mozi, as "solitary sages or men of virtue," or those "whose Way could help temporarily but could not be transmitted down through the ages."[33] By the accepted standards of imperial temple rites, "Those whose virtue and merit benefit for a time period should be venerated for that time; when the times change, their veneration should cease."[34] The implication was that Han Yu could keep his place in the Confucius temples of later generations but Xunzi's and Yang Xiong's days were numbered. Disagreement in scholarship was one thing, but enshrinement was the supreme honor for Confucians and "a matter of eternal significance."[35] Attacking Xunzi and Yang Xiong in order to expel them from temple rites became a popular activity among Song Confucians.

Xiong He 熊鉌 (1253–1312) lambasted Yang Xiong for the moral defect of serving the usurper Wang Mang; furthermore, he also castigated Xunzi: "In treating human nature as bad and ritual proprieties as an affectation, he had lost sight of the foundations. Why then would we have any need of his learning?"[36] Xiong He displayed his interest in changing the system of enshrinement, hitherto based on Han Yu's ideas of "finding a balance of virtue and scholarship." Xiong He also put forward the idea that the Shrine of Five Worthies should also change the sages venerated therein so that they were coordinated with Confucius temples. Thus, the most orthodox line of Song Confucians—Zhou Dunyi 周敦頤 (1017–1073), the two Cheng brothers, Zhang Zai 張載 (1020–1077), and Zhu Xi—should replace the then current Xunzi, Han Yu, and others. This proposal reflected the pronounced shift in the dominant orthodoxy within Confucian learning.[37] Xiong He's bombastic attack on Xunzi and Yang Xiong caught the attention of other Cheng–Zhu school Confucians, who joined the long-term campaign to expel Xunzi and Yang Xiong from Confucius temples.

During the early Ming, Song Lian 宋濂 (1310–1381) set forth his "Opinions on the Confucius Temple Halls" ("Kongzi miaotang yi" 孔子廟堂議) to discuss establishing the correlates that would set the liturgical tone for the Ming dynasty. Song Lian designated Xunzi and Yang Xiong for expulsion from the temple because "Xun Kuang said human nature is bad, and Yang Xiong served Wang Mang."[38] Another scholar, Wang Yi 王禕 (1321–1372), repeated this statement verbatim.[39] Although Yang Xiong was soon excluded from receiving offerings, Confucians were not satisfied with this partial success. In fact, in 1499 Cheng Minzheng 程敏政 (1445–1499) argued that Xunzi's and Yang Xiong's defects were comparable in severity and thus should be dealt with accordingly. Cheng advised the emperor:

> [Xun] Kuang viewed human nature as bad and ritual proprieties as artificial. In his view, Zisi 子思 and Mencius had disordered the world, while [Confucius's major disciples] Zizhang 子張, Zixia 子夏, and Ziyou 子游 were debased scholars. Therefore, Cheng Yi said that Xun Qing's faults were numerous and Yang Xiong's were few. People today quite appropriately think that [Xun] Kuang should also be excluded from receiving ceremonial offerings.[40]

In the following year, Zhang Jiugong 張九功 (1528–1565) further lobbied against Xunzi and increased the severity of the charges against him:

> As for the Xun Kuang, Count of Lanling 蘭陵, his words are close to those of [Yellow Emperor] Huangdi and Laozi, but his methods were mixed with those of [legalists] Shen [Buhai] and Han [Fei]. He sought patronage from Huang Xie 黃歇 and shamelessly associated with this notorious rebel. His learning was transmitted to Li Si and caused the disaster of scholars buried alive and books burned. He [Xun] viewed human nature as bad and ritual proprieties as artifice, Yao and Shun as dissembling, Zisi and Mencius as causing disorder in the world. Therefore, Master Cheng [Yi] ridiculed him as extremely biased, while Master Zhu [Xi] deliberately called him the magistrate of Lanling to associate him with the state of Chu and thus to profoundly demean him.[41]

Such arguments had the objective of getting Xunzi barred from receiving sacrifices at Confucius temples.

Notably, Zhang Jiugong had found that Xunzi was a teacher of the infamous Li Si 李斯 (c. 284–208 BCE), the legalist chancellor of the state of Qin; therefore, Zhang added the relationship as a new charge in his case against Xunzi. There was some historical basis for this accusation. As Sima Qian recorded, "Li had learned statecraft from Xun Kuang," even though Sima did not hold Xunzi guilty by association for Li's evil actions.[42] Although the imperial court's eventual expulsion of Xunzi from the Confucius temple cited his links to Li Si's burning of books and burying scholars alive, the purported causation was nevertheless extremely tenuous.

Actually, Zhang Jiugong's attack on Xunzi was not the first time the sage suffered guilt by association. In the late Tang dynasty, Lu Guimeng 陸龜蒙 (d. 881) wrote that he rejected the commonly attributed status of "great Confucian" to Mencius, but especially to Xunzi. Regarding Xunzi, Lu proclaimed: "Li Si learned the Way of Confucius through Xunzi and rose to the position of chancellor. As he put his Way into practice and fulfilled his ambitions, he destroyed the classic *Book of Odes* and *Book of Documents* by burning them, and he massacred scholars by burying them in pits—deeds that are malevolent to the extreme."[43] Therefore, according to Lu Guimeng, Xunzi did not deserve the status of a great Confucian; moreover, he ranked Xunzi as inferior to Mencius.

The Song dynasty's renowned literati scholar Su Shi 蘇軾 (1036–1101) added fuel to the flames of blaming Xunzi, further excoriating him:

> People in the past were surprised that Xun Qing mentored Li Si, who consigned books to the fire and greatly adulterated the laws of the ancient sage kings. Li seemingly treated the Way of his mentor like a hated enemy. However, reading Xun Qing's book now, I can understand that Li's service to Qin originated from Xun Qing, which should not be the least bit surprising.[44]

Later, Zhang Jiugong incorporated into his own bombastic attacks on Xunzi Su Shi's opinion that Xunzi should be blamed for his erstwhile disciple Li Si's burning of books and burying scholars alive. When Zhang Cong 張璁 (1475–1539) restructured Confucius temple rites in 1530 to curry favor with the Ming emperor Shizong, he excluded Xunzi from the temple's list and set a precedent for the remainder of the Ming as well as for the Qing dynasty.⁴⁵

Although Ming Shizong's ritual reforms of 1530 were informed by political self-interest, the induction and removal of correlate sages that he instituted was also made in a way that was responsive to the shifts in Confucian thought taking place at the time. Therefore, even though Confucians disliked the reduction of ritual honors enjoyed by Confucius temples that Shizong also decreed, they responded positively to the emperor's changes in the enshrined correlate sages. Indeed, later scholars would conclude, "Although [Shizong's] intentions were selfish, his arguments themselves are fair." Prior to it, for instance, Hu Juren 胡居仁 (1434–1484) had already echoed the view handed down from the Song by saying, "Making the statement that human nature is bad, [Xunzi] ruined everything. If the fountainhead is corrupted, the flow [of the school of thought] will not have one good end." Similarly, Luo Qinshun 羅欽順 (1465–1547) felt that Han Yu was "too lenient" in only criticizing Xunzi for "lacking discrimination in his choices and precision in his language."⁴⁶

As these scholarly attacks on Xunzi clearly show, anti-Xunzi discourse had radicalized during the Ming dynasty; moreover, such radical views reflected changes in contemporary standards of enshrinement, from "transmitting the classics" to "transmitting the Way." The Way of the Ming Confucians referred to the Cheng-Zhu orthodox version of "neo-Confucianism" and its interpretation of Confucius–Mencius orthodoxy, which differed from the Way of Xunzi.⁴⁷

Almost five centuries had passed since the Ming emperor expelled Xunzi from Confucian temples during the reformation of rituals in 1530, yet there have been sporadic cries for the reinstallation of Xunzi to his rightful place as a revered sage. These outcries became particularly loud during the middle period of the Qing dynasty. In part, appreciation of Xunzi was a result of the growing academic interest in the study of pre-Qin philosophers during the late Ming and into the Qing era. Naturally, Xunzi was a figure of great importance to such scholars, because of his stature among pre-Qin thinkers.

Originally, Han Yu claimed, in "Reading *Xunzi*," that he "wanted to cut out the unfitting words in the *Xunzi*, and in so doing, reincorporate the *Xunzi* among the books of the sages." In short, it turned out that when the importance of textual study received more and more attention, several scholars during the Song engaged in the reevaluation of the *Xunzi* project, a trend that flourished in the Ming and continued into the early Qing.[48] During the Ming, Gui Youguang 歸有光 (1507–1571), in his emended edition of *Xunzi*, said:

> During the Warring States Period, scholars wrote many books that threw the world into confusion. Only Xunzi brought light to the Way of Confucius, and in that regard, he was a match for Mencius. . . . In terms of subtlety, Mencius could not surpass him. Yang Xiong and Han Yu both promoted him as a complement to Mencius. However, Song scholars later deprecated him to the point that he became unknown to the world today.[49]

Li Zhi 李贄 (1527–1602), another man whom orthodox Confucians spurned as a heretic, also emphasized the learning of the Hundred Schools of the Warring States Period. In particular, he designated Xunzi as the first of the "virtuous scholar-officials," while he relegated Mencius to second level. Li Zhi came to the defense of Xunzi: "[Xunzi] and [Mencius] were almost contemporaneous, and while their literary talents were equal in beauty, Xunzi's literary style was superior in magnificence; moreover, in his implementation, he was more thorough and forthright. I do not understand why some chose to promote Mencius and suppress Xunzi."[50] By the Qing, revising the verdict on Xunzi had become a fashionable intellectual pursuit,[51] which marked a sharp contrast with the rampant critique of Xunzi during the previous dynasty.[52]

Additionally, during the Qianlong (1736–1795) and Jiaqing (1796–1820) reigns, scholarly preoccupation with philology resulted in a greater awareness of Xunzi's role in preserving and transmitting the classics. For example, Wang Zhong attributed the preservation of the classics almost entirely to Xunzi. Wang Zhong wrote in the first section of his "Xun Qing tonglun" 荀卿子通論, "[Xunzi's] learning descended from Confucius and especially contributed to the classics." Regarding the transmission of the classics, he further remarked, "The Duke of Zhou's contribution was that of creation and Confucius's was interpretation, while Xunzi's was transmission, so their standard was the same."[53] Wang Zhong's text was highly influential, and his reappraisal of Xunzi would play a major role in Xunzi's rehabilitation among Qing literati.

Finally, the revival of the learning of ritual proprieties also led to greater appreciation of Xunzi, justifiably renowned for his solemn attitude toward, and deep learning of, ritual proprieties and ritual regulations.[54] Scholar of ritual proprieties Lin Tingkan 凌廷堪 (1755–1809) observed, "When Xun spoke of humaneness (ren 仁), he traced it to back to its source in ritual proprieties." He pointed to Xunzi's superior understanding of rituals: "[Mencius] only grasped the main points and beginnings of ritual proprieties. As for [Xunzi], his writings discussed all the outstanding texts on rituals, and what he promoted was the essential ideas about rituals." Lin further charged, "When later generations honor [Mencius] at the expense of [Xunzi], they put themselves beyond the pale of the ritual proprieties and ritual regulations."[55] The late Qing expert on Xunzi, Wang Xianqian 王先謙 (1842–1917), said, "Xunzi's discourses on scholarship and statecraft took ritual proprieties as their principal aim."[56] Even the great advocate for Mencius's learning, Kang Youwei 康有為 (1858–1927), conceded, "Mencius's learning about ritual proprieties was shallow."[57]

Such ideological and scholarly shifts were reflected in the arguments and memorials presented to the Qing imperial court in favor of restoring Xunzi to his former place in Confucius temples. This is confirmed in Yan Kejun's 嚴可均 (1762–1843) "Xunzi dang congsi yi" 荀子當從祀議 and in Yao Chen's 姚諶 (1835–1864) "Ni shang Xun Qingzi congsi yi" 擬上荀卿子從祀議. Both Yan Kejun and Yao Chen repudiated Su Shi's attribution of guilt to Xunzi for Li Si's tyrannical deeds, and they charged Su with being absurd and biased. Even the early Qing scholar Yan Ruoqu 閻若璩 (1636–1704), who advocated the exclusion of Wang Yangming 王陽明 (1472–1529) and Lu Xiangshan 陸象山 (1139–1193) from veneration in Confucius temples, admitted that Xunzi had no notable moral flaws and that his exclusion from Confucius temples was solely due to his theory of human nature.[58]

Yao Chen and Yan Kejun were well aware that Xunzi's theory of human nature was the fundamental reason for his exclusion from Confucius temples. As Yao Chen said:

> The school of Mencius was what Song Confucians themselves came out with, while Han Confucians singularly passed down the school of Xunzi. Teachings derived from the works of Song Confucians have enjoyed currency for centuries, which was inadequately favorable for Xun Qing's views. The world's opinion of Xun Qing is limited to the one statement that human nature is bad and that he differed from Mencius.[59]

Therefore, Yao Chen argued, Confucians should base their understanding of human nature on the view of Confucius, from whom both Mencius and Xunzi deviated. Furthermore, in spite of the Song Confucian attacks on Xunzi, Yan Kejun pointed out that, in fact, their prevailing ideas of moral principles (*yili* 義理) and physical constitution (*qizhi* 氣質) arose, respectively, from the teachings of Mencius and Xunzi. When they spoke of the disciplined cultivation of *qizhi*, they implicitly acknowledged the validity of Xunzi's argument that the application of will or discipline can transform and improve human nature.[60] Yan Kejun's commentary on Song scholarship deserves its own book, but it is sufficient here to say that he accepted Qian Daxin's 錢大昕 (1728–1804) and other scholars' efforts to reconcile the schools of Xunzi and Cheng-Zhu Confucianism.[61]

On the scholastic front, Yao Chen and Qian Daxin tried their hand at affirming Xunzi's contributions to the Six Classics. Qian Daxin observed, "Confucius's Way exists in the Six Classics, and with the exception of the *Book of Documents*, Xun Qing passed down all of them."[62] Yao Chen insisted, "After Confucius, the passing down of the Six Classics' texts depended on Xun Qing." While commending Xunzi for his "particularly profound knowledge of ritual proprieties," Yao Chen also asserted, "Mencius's learning for inquiring and writing seems not to be as meticulous as Xun Qing's." In proposing that offerings to Xunzi be restored in Confucius temples, Yao insisted that Xunzi's "tablet be placed just below Confucius's seventy disciples, and his book be issue throughout the empire and made an official text for education, along with the *Mencius*."[63]

In terms of official learning, when Ji Yun 紀昀 (1724–1805) edited the *Annotated Catalog of the Complete Imperial Library*, he chose to put the controversy over Mencius and Xunzi under the heading "Zhu Lu yitong" 朱陸異同 (Similarities and Differences between Chu and Lu), symbolically subsuming the controversy under the rubric of Confucian internal disputes,[64] instead of "Miscellaneous Schools" (*Zaxue* 雜學) or "Heterodoxies" (*Yiduan* 異端).[65]

At this point, a rehabilitation of Xunzi's reputation was well under way. For instance, the Qing literatus Wang Zhong changed his son's name from Wang Xisun 汪喜孫 to Xixun 喜荀 (1786–1848),[66] while another Qing literatus, Li Ciming 李慈銘 (1829–1894), named his study the Hall of Xun Learning 荀學齋 and titled his journals *Hall of Xun Learning Diaries*.[67] Evidence from these and other examples suggests a revival in the literati's acceptance of Xunzi as a great Confucian. Court historian Pang Zhonglu

龐鍾璐 (1822–1876) even included Xunzi in the *Biographies of Correlated Sages*, seemingly in preparation for official restoration of Xunzi's status in the Confucius temple.⁶⁸

However, the impact of Western thought and the renewed controversy between Old Text and New Text schools were to put an abrupt end to the progress made toward reinstating Xunzi as a sage. In the words of Chinese of that era, China's encounter with Western imperialism during the late Qing constituted "a revolution unprecedented in two thousand years of history." In any event, Xunzi, whose reputation was just beginning to recover, suffered fresh blows. Anti-absolutist reformers such as Liang Qichao 梁啟超 (1873–1929) renewed the assault on Xunzi and charged him with monarchism, narrow-mindedness toward heterodox thought, rigid adherence to ritual proprieties and social norms, and a pedantic preoccupation with philological exercises.⁶⁹

We could roughly divide these objections into those arising from disagreements with either Xunzi's sociopolitical views or his scholarship. Charges of monarchism and stiff adherence to ritual proprieties and social norms fall into the class of sociopolitical views, while accusations of narrow-mindedness and pedantry relate to scholarship. In the eyes of New Text scholars, Xunzi's school was the embodiment of the philology of "Han learning" or the school of "evidential research" of the Qianlong and Jiaqing reign periods of the eighteenth and early nineteenth centuries. Having turned against the philologist school that he followed in his youth, Liang Qichao expressed his hostility vividly: "The Qing scholars of evidential research called their learning 'the school of Xun.' Since we wanted to crush evidential research's monopoly on learning, we used the stratagem of 'capturing bandits by first capturing their ringleader,' so we mounted our attack by aiming at their spiritual ancestor, Xunzi."⁷⁰ Once again, intellectual trends turned against Xunzi.

Critics in this period also revived the unfair criticism that Xunzi was a supporter of autocratic rule. For instance, Liang Qichao argued, "It is fair to say that Xunzi led to the disaster of Li Si's burying scholars alive."⁷¹ He further charged, "Xunzi had given rise to a polity [of imperial authoritarianism] that prevailed for two thousand years."⁷² Liang's schoolmate, Tan Sitong 譚嗣同 (1865–1898), even proclaimed, "For two thousand years, the government has been the Qin's government of vicious bandits. For two thousand years, learning has been Xunzi's study for servility."⁷³ Liang's and Tang's attitude toward Xunzi was informed by their mentoring under Kang

Youwei, who led his students in the so-called Movement to Exclude Xunzi. In addition to promoting the orthodoxy of Mencius, this movement combated the philosophies of its named enemies—Xunzi and Shen Buhai.[74]

The opposition in the late Qing and early republic affected Xunzi's intellectual standing for the worse. The spiritual mentor of the May Fourth Movement, Hu Shih 胡適 (1891–1962), lambasted Xunzi's philosophy with such choice epithets as "an extremely shortsighted form of utilitarianism" and "an ideology that exclusively normalizes autocracy."[75] Wu Yu 吳虞 (1872–1949), who styled himself as the "the lone pugilist fighting against the Kong family shop," said Xunzi's philosophical reverence for monarchical rule and hierarchy made his thought susceptible to political exploitation by tyrannical autocrats.[76]

By the late Qing, therefore, whereas Mencius's stock went up with his reinvention as a champion of the rights of the people, Xunzi's went down for his purported function as autocracy's megaphone.[77] Those charges against Xunzi were the result of Chinese history's sudden change of course, and their unfairness did not prevent the further savaging of Xunzi's reputation that resulted. Although Zhang Taiyan 章太炎 (1869–1936) trumpeted Xunzi's learning as "more profound than that of Mencius," he could not halt Xunzi's deterioration throughout this period.[78] Although in its last decades of existence the Qing issued more edicts conferring sagehood than in any comparable period of history, Xunzi still was not elevated to that status. He was even absent from the Beiyang (Northern) government's only performance of Confucius temple rites, in 1919.[79] Xunzi's fall from grace was definitive.

In fact, the edifice of Confucian tradition as a whole had crumbled under pressure, as wave after wave of reformers adopted the anti-Confucianism battle cry "Destroy the Kong family shop." For instance, Wu Yu paid a backhanded compliment to Xunzi: "The Confucius cult's survival into later generations was in large part due to Xun Qing's efforts." Any doubt as to what he meant was clarified by the following sentence: "The blame for the Confucius cult's calamitous legacy for posterity, as well, in large part fall upon Xun Qing's head."[80]

In the republic, movements of Confucian revival rallied around Confucius and Mencius but increasingly pushed Xunzi into the margins. For example, Qian Mu 錢穆 (1895–1990) acknowledged the rough parity of intellectual stature of Xunzi and Mencius; however, Professor Qian added, "Ultimately, it is an indisputable fact that the philosophy of humanity's inherent goodness is Confucian orthodoxy."[81] Modern New Confucianism's master, Mou Zongsan 牟宗三 (1909–1995), also asserted that Xunzi "was not a part of Confucianism's orthodox tradition."[82] However, the remarks of the Chinese Communist Party's cofounder, Chen Duxiu 陳獨秀 (1879–1942), was probably more damaging: "We should destroy all the Confucius temples in this nation and abolish all their rituals."[83] Chen Duxiu's zeal would not have been out of place at the anti-Confucian iconoclastic rallies of the Cultural Revolution.[84] Thus, external and internal factors have intertwined to continue depriving Xunzi of both his former title of sagehood and his former place in Confucius's sanctuary.

Conclusion

This chapter has outlined with broad strokes the rise and fall of Xunzi's posthumous reputation in Chinese history. Certainly, Xunzi—both the man and the book he left behind—have become another historical text, and readers can ascribe various meanings, both to him and to his text, that are at odds with one another. While the historical existence of Xunzi's learning is undeniable, it is equally undeniable that the significance and value of Xunzi's learning are open to interpretation. Indeed, this pre-Qin scholar has been an endless source of controversy for more than two thousand years.

Xiong He wrote, during the Yuan era, "We revere the Way with shrines to continue the tradition of the Way."[85] The "shrines" referred to in his statement were Confucius temples. As Xiong's writings implied, the history of the temples' correlated sages would also be the history of the shifting Confucian tradition of the Way, a living tradition that tried to present itself as continuity with the past even while adapting its ideology to the present. The effort necessarily required imperial regimes to update the enshrined sages by removing old ones and installing new ones who better represented the spirit of the age and better fit with the needs of the present.

Outwardly, Confucius temples asserted that enshrined sages were exemplars in perpetuity and for all times, but the institution in practice was flexible and adaptable. Correlate enshrinement had three main engines of change: shifts in the understanding of what constituted the tradition of the Way, generational differences in the literati's evaluation of past Confucian scholars, and state intervention for political considerations. All three factors left indelible marks on the historical controversies over Xunzi's sagehood that accompanied his enshrinement in, and then expulsion from, Confucian temples.

After the late Qing, the Chinese-speaking world experienced an intellectual revolution that led to Western thought overtaking traditional Chinese thought and thereby further complicated efforts to interpret Xunzi. Viewing Xunzi through an occidental philosophical lens produced images that contained the reflections of—or rather, distortions of—Western sociology,[86] logic,[87] psychology,[88] and philosophical materialism.[89] Thus, Xunzi became a palimpsest for interpreting readers' preconceptions, and much of the tradition of the Way dissolved into abstract insubstantiality. Returning Xunzi to a Confucian context is the only way to discuss enshrining Xunzi in a way that avoids the pitfalls of anachronism or obsolete antiquarianism.

Resuming sage worship as a viable and relevant practice at Confucius temples requires the development of proper historical understanding. Huo Tao 霍韜 (1487–1540) made an incisive remark when he submitted a memorandum requesting the Ming dynastic court to enshrine Xue Xuan 薛瑄 (1389–1464): "The Confucians venerated as correlates in the past dynasties were Confucius's seventy-two sagely disciples who in person received the sage's teachings, the Han Confucians who compiled and edited the sage's classics, the Tang Confucians who annotated the sage's classics, and the Song Confucians who clarified the sage's classics."[90]

While Xue Xuan's own learning was not as profound as that of former sages, Huo proposed that Xue should be enshrined because he was active during a period of brilliant scholarship, learned from and modeled himself after Confucius, and lived a morally exemplary life.[91] Huo's arguments showed that although standards for enshrinement varied from dynasty to dynasty, the essential conditions were the candidate's importance to the development of Confucian learning and his current relevance. From this perspective, Xunzi is well qualified to be a correlated sage for our own era.

First, Xunzi was highly important in Confucianism's development during antiquity. Modern New Confucians' emphasis on metaphysical and transcendent benevolence comes at the expense of ritual proprieties. They have forgotten that Confucius said, "Benevolence is constituted by subduing the self and returning to ritual proprieties."[92] Mencius represented benevolence or humaneness and Xunzi represented ritual proprieties, the twin pillars of Confucianism. In Confucius's teachings, benevolence is the accomplishment of perfect virtue, which was given shape and reality through fulfilling righteous duty and following ritual proprieties. Mencius said, "Benevolence is a man's heart. Righteousness is a man's road."[93] He also said, "To dwell in benevolence and to follow righteousness constitutes the sum total of a great person."[94] In comparison, Xunzi's school of "rituals and law" emphasized the study of the classics and knowledge of the ritual regulations.[95] The two traditions are complementary paths to virtue. In addition, Confucius said, "Learning without thought is labor lost; thought without learning is perilous."[96] Giving equal importance to learning and reflection is a defining trait of Confucian learning; Xunzi and Mencius each claimed part of that heritage.

Second, from the perspective of current relevance, Xunzi's emphasis on learning is especially important now. Xunzi said that human nature is inherently bad, but he also posited that learning could ameliorate and transform human nature. Zhang Xuecheng 章學誠 (1738–1801) made the incisive observation that, in fact, Xunzi's theory of bad human nature could be explained by his realization that "innate, nature-gifted qualities are not to be relied upon. Rather, human artifice or effort is required to weld learning."[97] Zhang Xuecheng's statement suggests that he grasped the centrality of learning in Xunzi's thought. In fact, the very first chapter of the *Xunzi* is focused on learning. Even though Kang Youwei was an advocate for Mencius, Kang also conceded, "Mencius's main teaching is to extend the human inner goodness without needing to learn. Xunzi's main teaching is that since their innate nature is bad, humans must change their constitution by exerting the will to knowledge."[98] Encountering Western learning, Yu Yue 俞樾 (1821–1906) proposed that Xunzi serve as a bridge to accessing occidental knowledge:

> Mencius held that we should follow the model of ancient rulers, but Xunzi held that we should follow the model of later rulers. Without Xunzi, we would be unable to open the path to development after the Three Dynasties [China's mythical golden age]. . . . Now I want to be Xunzi's follower. Western knowledge is here, and I want to engage and learn it."[99]

Although modern New Confucian master Mou Zongsan had, as we noted, decried Xunzi as lying outside of Confucian orthodox thought, even he acknowledged that Xunzi could be "the lifeline that connects the civilizations of China and the West."[100]

The modern age needs Xunzi's thought to play a balancing role in Confucianism, from the perspective of seeking a more complete understanding of Confucianism and openness to Western civilization. The Jin-era classical scholar Zhao Bingwen 趙秉文 (1159–1232) anticipated this need when he wrote, "Mencius followed the ancient rulers, Xunzi followed the later rulers. Put Mencius and Xunzi together and we have Confucius."[101] Or, as Kang Youwei put it, "As Mencius's fortunes rose for two thousand years, so Xunzi's fortunes fell for two thousand years."[102] By embracing Xunzi, we may transcend the cycle of dispute between the camps of Mencius and Xunzi that has plagued Confucianism for centuries.

CHAPTER VI

The Disenchantment with Confucianism in Modern China

Confucius, who founded Confucianism, is the great founder of religion on this earth.
—KANG YOUWEI (1897)

Today, the Chinese people are almost unanimous in their belief that Confucianism is not a religion.
—WING-TSIT CHAN (1953)

Historically, the health of the Confucius temple system depended on Confucianism's status as imperial China's state cult. As China entered the twentieth century, however, Confucianism was confronted by challenges from secular forces, whose escalating attacks ultimately caused a general disenchantment with Confucianism. In turn, Confucianism's loss of official status and religious fervor resulted in the decline of the Confucius temple, which can still be observed in the modern age. Our contemporary tendency to attribute to Confucianism the qualities of a secular philosophy is a psychocultural artifact produced by modern Chinese. Here, I attempt to tell the story of the process through which Confucianism was first dismantled as China's state religion and then reimagined as a secular philosophy.

The teacher Kang Youwei 康有為 (1858–1927) and his former student Liang Qichao 梁啟超 (1873–1929) were the two figures who best embody the opposing Confucian paradigms in the late Qing and early republic. Kang wanted to reform Confucianism by using organized Christianity as its model. Liang embarked on a very different project of deconstructing Confucius as the founder of a religion and reimagining him as a secular scholar. As history would show, Liang emerged as the victor in that ideological contest.

Although Confucians in recent decades have launched a program to salvage the remaining religious components of Confucianism, with the aid of what we may politely refer to as "creative" exegesis of classical texts, the ancient adage applies: "When the hide ceases to exist, from whence does the fur derive sustenance?" The chasm between Confucianism and modern society will not be overcome without the social and institutional practice of ritual propriety (*li* 禮) to sustain humaneness (*ren* 仁).

Preface

For more than a century, academics have argued over the question of whether Confucianism is a religion; yet no definitive conclusion has emerged from that debate. Both chapter 2 of this book and another of my published essays have sought to excavate Confucianism's religious characteristics in imperial China and to explore their specific forms.[1] Even when we set aside the syncretic movement to unify Confucianism with Daoism and Buddhism as the "Three Religions," Confucian practices in Confucius temples were the principal areas for performing rituals of the state cult. Moreover, the religious characteristics displayed therein were those of public religions and state cults.

In short, using private religions as a model for understanding all religions is a Western paradigm that deeply influenced modern Chinese intellectuals, leading to their inability to discern the role of Confucius temples in representing the scholar-official elite's collective agenda within the regime of a state religion. Blinkered to the uniquely public orientation of Confucianism, they came to the erroneous conclusion that Confucianism is not a religion. Thus, a historical analysis of the attempted reforms of Confucius temple rites is a necessary corrective to this scholarly blind spot, and offers perhaps the best hope of finding an answer to the century-old question.

Confucianism's appeal lay in its promises of collective blessings for "a prosperous state and a restful people" and a "flourishing future for the culture," which are distinct from a private religion's appeal to personal happiness and fulfillment. Moreover, the privilege of partaking in Confucius temple rites—which can be seen as approximating recognition as a member of the Confucius cult or of Confucianism—was monopolized by the rulers and the elite scholar-official class.

With that in mind, the alienation from Confucianism that commoners reportedly felt should not surprise us. For example, Qin Huitian 秦蕙田

(1702–1764) of the early Qing wrote that the common people's feeling for Confucius was "respect, not affection."[2] Yan Fu 嚴復 (1854–1921), an eyewitness of the late Qing, wrote that members of the common classes "never prayed to Confucius." He added, "The women and children of China today know all about heaven, Naraka [hell], bodhisattvas, and Yama [the god of death]. But if you ask them who [Confucius's most famous disciples] Yan Hui 顏回, Zilu 子路, Ziyu 子游, or Zizhang 子張 were, they would say that they do not know." Yan Fu further observed that every Chinese village, no matter how small or provincial, would have a Buddhist monastery or convent; processions of crawling pilgrims were always abundant on holy days. However, he could not find any incidence of a villager praying to Confucius.[3] Kang Youwei, one of the most influential champions of the movement to preserve the Confucius cult (*Kongjiao* 孔教), admitted, "For our Confucius cult, only the officials involved burn incense to Confucius on the first and the fifteenth days of a month. On the other hand, students and commoners pay tribute to all gods except Confucius."[4] Those accounts are almost certainly based on direct observation of the religious behavior of the Chinese people.

The apathy of commoners toward Confucius is the product of Confucianism's long historical evolution. Ever since Confucius temples obtained official status during the Han, the temples' political character continually strengthened, as the social composition of temple rites participants would readily demonstrate. By the Tang and Song dynasties, all participants in temple rites were men bearing official titles and offices—whether they were the Son of Heaven, the revered descendants of the Kong clan, high officials, or local administrators. While the literati of the temple schools did attend the sacrificial rites, their role was as a passive audience. The strict barring of commoners from the temples led to their attitude of "respect, not affection" for Confucius and his temples.

In the Song, the literati elite severely censored a scholar-official for suggesting that the recently renovated Confucius temple in the capital open its doors to visits by nonofficials and their ladies.[5] The Mongol Yuan emperor Shizu 元世祖 (Kublai Khan, r. 1260–1294) decreed, in 1261, not only that the renovated Confucius temple in Qufu must be clean and beautiful but also that touring and sightseeing would be specifically forbidden.[6] Zhu Guozhen 朱國禎 (1558–1632) of the late Ming wrote of his pilgrimage to a Confucius temple, "Entering the temple, [I sensed] its solemnity and gravitas, so far removed from the likes of Buddhist temples."[7]

Zhu's comment underscored the difference in the bearing of Confucius temples in contrast to other religious temples.

Another late Ming essayist, Zhang Dai 張岱 (1597–1684), managed to visit the Confucius temple in Qufu only after "paying a bribe to the gate-keeper, who guided [him] therein."[8] An account from the late Qing described Confucius temples similarly: "They are unlike the ordinary shrines and temples that freely allow touring and visiting by all and sundry."[9] Confucius temples were exclusive spaces, as demonstrated by the thoroughness with which they shut out all but those of high station in society. The official state was firmly in control of the rites that took place within the confines of Confucius temples, the holy grounds of the Confucian religion.

By the last decades of the Qing, some Confucians began to connect the exclusiveness of Confucian temples with the lack of popular support for Confucianism. Tan Sitong 譚嗣同 (1865–1898) observed, "Although the prefecture and county governments built Confucius temples, only men of the court and the academy venerate him there. Meanwhile, farmers and village elders milled about around the gates and walls to peer inside, too far to hear or see the rites or music, let alone to whom or for what the sacrifices are all about."[10] In a late Qing lecture on reform, Liang Qichao complained, "Upon entering school, a pupil immediately learns to venerate Wenchang 文昌 and Kuixing 魁星 as gods; however, regarding the most sanctified founder of our religion, the fire of his legacy has all but burned out, his sacrificial vessels almost empty, his dates of birth and death scarcely known by anyone."[11] As the gods of fortune, Wenchang and Kuixing were relevant to the lives of commoners. By comparison, Confucius's awesome character was vague and distant. In short, the evidence does not support the stereotype captured by the saying, "Even a child of three *chi* 尺 [Chinese feet] in height may venerate and honor Confucius."[12] Kang Youwei's Confucian reformation arose from this obvious sociopolitical chasm.

A Stillborn Reformation: Kang Youwei's Cult of Confucius

Although people commonly call Kang Youwei the "founder" of the Confucius religion or state cult, this attribution is inaccurate. Before they parted ways, Kang's greatest disciple, Liang Qichao, once praised him as

"Confucius religion's Martin Luther,"[13] a tacit acknowledgement that Kang's project was that of reformation, not creation.

From the very beginning, Kang Youwei argued that the Confucius cult (孔教) is fully a religion, in the same way that Buddhism, Christianity, and Islam are religions.[14] In "On the Learning of Nature" 性學篇, which Kang authored in 1877, before he was twenty years of age, he proclaimed:

> Under heaven, there now are many religions. In China, there is the Confucius cult, the religion passed down from [early antiquity by] the two emperors (*di* 帝) and Three Sovereigns (*huang* 皇). In India, there is Buddhism, which it created. In Europe, there is Jesus, and in the Muslim (Hui 回) lands there is Islam. From these descended many other religions, uncountable in their numbers.[15]

In Kang's eyes, the Confucius cult was not created ex nihilo; instead, it has always been a Chinese religion, since the mythical times of early antiquity, when it was "passed down from the two emperors and Three Sovereigns," which Kang presented as irrefutable historical fact. Although Kang did not belabor himself with enumerating the characteristics of the Confucius cult, he was clearly convinced that it had always been a religion.

As a thinker, Kang was reacting to the shocking impact of Christian missionary activities and the eruption of religious violence in China. Kang's movement to "save the cult" (保教) was a means to an end, an instrument for "saving the nation" (保國) and "saving the race" (保種). In fact, "preservation" entailed modifying Confucianism into a religious ideology capable of mobilizing the Chinese people, competing with Christianity, and confronting the challenges of the new century.

After the First Sino-Japanese War, Kang submitted the "Second Memorandum for the Emperor of the Qing," which included many recommendations in response to China's precarious situation. Kang noted, "[Christian] churches dot the provinces under direct imperial rule like chess pieces on a board" and far outnumbered the single Confucius temple established for each county. He advised the court to "renovate all of the dilapidated shrines of the countryside as Confucius temples, and order all charity houses and compatriot halls to only venerate Confucius." Additionally, he wrote that the empire should imitate Christians in sending Confucius missionaries overseas, especially into the South China Sea area, where many Chinese immigrants lived; each island in that sea should have a Confucius temple staffed by an "educational official," that is, a religious officer. In this recommendation, Kang showed that he was cognizant of how "religious missions could be used as a justification for traveling, collecting information about barbarians, and propagating a national reputation."[16]

Later, Kang tried to end officialdom's monopoly of Confucianism by establishing private charity houses under the name "sacred learning society" 聖學會, supplementing the relatively small number of existing Confucius temples. Although charity houses were numerous in China, he claimed that most of them were established for the benefit of urban laborers and merchants. At the same time, isolated dwellers of the nation's remote regions were acquainted with such Daoist gods as Wenchang and Guangong but ignorant about Confucius, a situation about which the literati did nothing. Kang lamented, "The foreigners preached their own religion and spread them over the earth, which had lately penetrated even into the Middle Kingdom. In Wuzhou 梧州 [Guangxi], where aliens trade, there are a great number of preachers who exclusively venerate Jesus. But we do not even know how to venerate Confucius exclusively and propagate his sacred teaching."[17] Kang recommended that China establish Confucius-venerating charity halls and schools throughout the nation as Confucius missions, which were to provide the common masses with a wide variety of charitable benefits, including free medicine, clothes, and coffins.

Kang's program for a Confucius cult reformation did not occur in a vacuum. During the same era, Song Shu 宋恕 (1862–1910), who styled himself "China's Martin Luther," advocated a broadly similar program. Song justified his innovations by invoking the venerable authority of Confucius; moreover, the appellation he gave himself showed a shrewd appreciation for his place in the history of the Confucius cult.[18] Song observed that in sharp contrast to Confucianism's high national status, many of its temples had fallen into disrepair, while the educational officials in charge of temple schools occupied their time with teaching the art of passing imperial civil service examinations, instead of being of use in rectifying the people's morals. He wrote:

> Now is the time to give weight to the office of educational officials. County native residents should be employed for this office on the recommendation of an assembly of local gentry. Adopting the system of a seven-day week [culminating in a worship day] in Western countries, students should assemble to worship Confucius with hymns and

lectures. Except for those who are traveling outside the county, students who dwell in the town must not be absent from weekly worship, and those who dwell in the countryside must take turns in attending. Farmers, artisans, merchants, and people of all other statuses, etc., should follow the students in weekly worship and listening to the hymns and lectures.[19]

Song's proposal to ask "farmers, artisans, merchants, and people of all other statuses" to attend weekly worship and listen to the hymns and preaching at the temple is a striking break with tradition. Moreover, he proposed that China should imitate the West by "convincing private imperial subjects to establish churches that venerate Confucius, using a cycle of seven days to arrange worship, hymns, and lecturing, and having the same regulations in state temples."[20]

By "state temples," Song was referring to Confucius temples established by the imperial government for purposes of state cult rites. The Tang dynasty, in the year 630, had first instituted by imperial decree, "All prefectural and county schools must establish a Confucius temple."[21] Thus did the Chinese empire create the precedent for all subsequent dynasties to make the temple schools an integral component in the operations of the imperial ritual system. However, that decree was silent with regard to establishing Confucius temples at administrative divisions beneath the county.

The motivation behind proposals by such leaders as Song and Kang to establish private charity houses and schools arose from the perceived need to compensate for the low number and density of Confucius temples. Zhou Huanshu 周煥樞 (1856–1899), a close friend of Song Shu, even proposed to create an organization—modeled after the Jesuit order—called the Church for Assisting the Sage 翼聖教會. Zhou also advocated for colloquial Chinese translations of the *Analects* and the *Classic of Filial Piety*—inspired by the vernacular translations of the New Testament by Protestants—in order to encourage ordinary people to read the Confucian scriptures.[22]

In imitating Christianity, reformers hoped to overcome Confucianism's exclusivity as the religion of elite literati by broadening its appeal to all social classes. Nevertheless, as conservative Ye Dehui 葉德輝 (1864–1927) remarked, "Confucianism is the anchor of mankind's heart, and scholar-officialdom is the anchor of Confucianism."[23] In the modern language of the class-conscious philosopher Feng Youlan 馮友蘭 (1895–1990), "Confucius was the progenitor of the literati class, or at least he gave voice to its highest expression. As China's dynastic regimes throughout history were in the hands of the literati class, Confucius was honored as the teacher and the sage, just as carpenters worshipped Lu Ban 魯班 and winemakers worshipped Ge the Immortal 葛仙."[24] Indeed, despite the best effort by reformers to "adopt the rites and customs of Christian churches for use at Confucius temples," Ye Dehui retorted, "If implemented for the sake of village yokels, since the Confucian temple does not allow *beijiao* 杯筊 for divination, the village yokels would have no reason to come. If implemented for womenfolk, since Confucius temples do not give blessings for fertility, womenfolk would have no reason to come."[25] Ye's stated reasons for his opposition to the reformation of the Confucius cult is a concise description of the masses' alienation from Confucius temples.

Kang's ideas for Confucian reforms could be traced to his earliest works, such as *A Study of the "New Text" Forgeries* 新學偽經考 (1891) and *A Study of Confucius as a Reformer* 孔子改制考 (1892–1898). In *Confucius as a Reformer*, Kang wrote, "Confucius was the founder of the religion, the holy and divine king. He is the auxiliary of heaven and earth, the cultivator of all beings. No man, no thing, no doctrine lies outside the boundaries of Confucius's great Dao. He is the greatest of sages since humanity came into being."[26] Portraying Confucius as a reformer of institutions and the author of the Six Classics allowed Kang to remake Confucius as a founder figure for the Confucius cult and thereby lend legitimacy to the movement.

Kang's most elaborate and sophisticated case for Confucius temple reforms may be found in two separate texts. The first text is a memorandum he submitted to the imperial court in 1898 under the title "Memorandum for Instituting the Veneration of Holy Confucius as the State Religion, Promulgating a Calendar Based on the Confucius Era, and the Abolition of Unworthy Shrines."[27] The second text, which he submitted to the Beiyang government in second year of the republic (1913), had the title "An Advisory for Making the Confucius Cult, in Conjunction with Veneration of Heaven, the State Religion."[28] The first memorandum was written during the Hundred Days Reforms of the late Qing, and the second was penned during the regime of Yuan Shikai 袁世凱 (1859–1916). Though submitted fifteen years apart and to two different regimes, they were very much an inalienable part of the contemporary political fray. Ultimately, the twin events of the defeat of the Hundred Days Reforms and Yuan's abdication would seal the fate of Kang's abortive reform agenda for the Confucius cult.

A historical puzzle remains: If sacrifices to Confucius were still a de jure state ritual—which it surely was—why did Kang Youwei find it necessary to petition the ruler to declare the Confucius cult to be the "state religion" at this particular historical moment? Liang Qichao's remark provides a short answer: "We were afraid of Christianity's invasion and thought it [the Confucius cult] up to combat it [Christianity]."[29] However, Liang omitted another part of the answer: whereas state rites are a matter involving only a few of the officialdom's elites, a state religion would involve the Chinese public and the common masses.

Though Kang long championed making Confucius worship China's state religion, he submitted the memorandum on May 1, 1898, only after hearing news in Beijing that German troops had recently desecrated the temple of culture in Jimo, Shandong. Following this incident, Kang's student Liang Qichao initiated a movement among the literati to sign a petition to the Censorate (*Yushitai* 御史台), urging diplomatic action.[30] The public petition proclaimed, "In the temple of culture in Jimo, Shandong, the German [army] destroyed the statue of Confucius and gouged out the eyes of the statue of Zilu 子路. . . . The fortune of our religion and the survival of our nation hinge upon this act."[31] Kang's writing of the May 1 memorandum was the direct result of these events.

Concisely, Kang's "Memorandum for Instituting the Veneration of Holy Confucius as the State Religion" urged the government to "allow Confucius worship in the people's shrines and temples" because the survival of Confucianism and China had to take precedence over petty niceties and scruples. Kang lamented that the proliferation of "unworthy shrines"—a reference to the shrines to folk deities—had led to the mockery of China by Europeans and Americans as a nation without religion. In contrast, "The peoples of Europe and America devote their worship only to their heavenly god, perform temple sacrifices only to the founder of their religion, fast and cleanse themselves every seven days, recite their scriptures and perform rites to glorify the name of their god. . . . Through this, they have realized the meaning of having a true and godly religion." In China, Kang wrote, "only little children who went to school would read the classics and worship the sage [Confucius]; however, from the moment they were mature enough to leave school to their death in old age, not one day would be spent in the veneration of [our] religion's founder."[32]

Kang proposed thoroughgoing reforms on a broad spectrum. On the one hand, he proposed that private imperial subjects should be encouraged to build Confucius-worshipping charity houses and schools. On the other hand, he urged the imperial court to order "the abolition of all unauthorized or illicit shrines and rebuilding them as Confucius temples." He further suggested that the court promote "the exclusive building of Confucius temples, from the capital city to the wildest provinces and counties, with both Confucius veneration and heaven worship, and with all people—men and women—allowed to participate in the rites." Temples should saturate the country at a rate of "at least one temple to each borough with a thousand or hundreds of people." Kang also suggested, "Each borough or town should have a society of the Confucius cult." Clearly, Kang's proposals were informed by his earlier observation: "Their [Christians'] churches spread throughout the land, where lords and vassals, men and women all worshipped together," but in China "temples of culture are found only in cities and not villages, and where there is one temple, a second temple is never to be found."[33] In other words, Kang was setting up his reforms in direct competition to the spread of Christian churches on the local level.[34]

How had "unauthorized shrines" proliferated throughout China? Kang explained:

> Now, the temple schools venerate Confucius, but when the educational official performs rites on holy days, men of other statuses and also women are forbidden to partake in the rites. Where one place rejects the hearts of the people, another will necessarily take the adoration and donations they offer. Just as each place must have a temple, each temple must honor a deity. Although this should be an issue of great import, the imperial decrees are not setting and rectifying which deities may receive sacrifices; the imperial court lets people build shrines freely and without any prohibitions, and allows the people to do things there in complete liberty. Nonetheless, among the vulgar masses, the wise are few and the foolish are many. Witches and shamans lord over them, illicit shrines are built with wanton abandon, and weird deities are worshipped. All this is the natural result of affairs that have gather momentum for a long time. Illicit shrines [are so busy that they] barely have time to receive worshippers, so who dares to contend with them?[35]

Kang rightly understood that polytheism was China's long-standing tradition: "Zhang the Immortal 張仙 is for those who pray for children, the

God of wealth for those who pray for riches, the laborers and artisans venerate Lu Ban."[36] Although Kang's comments were a vivid and accurate description of the situation, he did not mention the crucial fact that the sacrifice to Confucius was a state rite, hitherto jealously guarded from commoners.

An account by one of Kang's contemporaries provides supporting evidence as well:

> [Foreigners] have a contempt for us as a land without any religion. In fact, this state of affairs is caused by excessive strictness of our nation's governance. Though it venerates Confucius, this is true only of the temples of culture built by the provincial, prefectural, and county governments under direct imperial control, while the common people exclusively venerate Siddhartha Gautama and Laozi, Lord of the Way. Buddhist temples and Daoist shrines are as stars in the sky or chess pieces on a board. Even those that study the classics—who recite Confucius's and Mencius's books by day and bear the weight of the Way upon their shoulders—venerate the deities, like Wenchang and Kuixing, but neglect Confucius in their devotions.[37]

Kang Youwei blamed Wu Pei 吳培, an official of the Censorate during Emperor Kangxi's reign, for commoners' alienation from Confucius temples. Fearing that women might be an affront at Confucius temples, Wu brought forward the proscription against incense burning by women in the temples, which led to an eventual ban against all Confucius veneration by commoners. According to Kang, Wu's actions cut off commoners from the reach of religion and thus constituted an offense that "ought to have been punished by death."[38] However, as we have already seen, Confucius temples historically excluded even women of high social status at least as early as the Song dynasty.

Another notable turn of phrase by Kang was his complaint that "unauthorized temples have spread throughout the land," voiced in the same breath as his assertion that China was "a nation without religion." Why did Kang not sense the contradiction in those statements? The explanation resides in the "ideal type" Kang used to designate "religion," which he had derived from occidental monotheism. The logic of this "ideal type" makes it clear why Kang felt compelled to present Confucius as the founder of his religion. Kang's Confucius cult was a conscious program to restructure Confucianism to parallel Christianity, with a one-to-one correspondence between the components. Jesus Christ became Confucius the Founder; the Roman Curia becomes the Ministry of Religion; local churches became Confucius churches; and the Christian Era became the Confucius Era.

My interpretation helps us to make sense of Kang's other strange proposition, that is, that Confucius veneration be conjoined to heaven worship, a rite that, by tradition, was reserved only for the emperor himself and was forbidden to imperial subjects great or small.[39] However, because worship of heaven was such a commonplace practice among ordinary people, imperial officials found it difficult to enforce this proscription.[40] Combining heaven with Confucius was an expedient move to satisfy the religious yearnings of commoners, and thus sought to universalize Confucius worship. Nevertheless, underlying this project was an archetype of an essentialized Christianity, with heaven standing in for God and Confucius as a kind of substitute Jesus.

Additionally, in the May 1, 1898, memorandum, Kang suggested the development of Confucius cult associations on Chinese soil, by placing the Duke of Sacred Continuance—the patriarch of the Kong clan—at the head of the associations. The overall structure of Kang's Confucius cult association mirrored the papacy in many ways, such as in allowing all people to join the ranks of its faithful. He proposed that the association ask Protestants and the Jesuit order to each send a representative to negotiate binding rules for religious organizations in China. He wanted religious organizations to handle outbreaks of religious violence and take those thorny issues out of the imperial government's jurisdiction. For instance, in accordance with the agreed-upon rules, the Duke of Sacred Continuance's authorized agents would deal with Confucius cult members who might get involved in antimissionary violence. This was obviously a mechanism designed to avoid embroiling Chinese and foreign governments in open conflict over cases of religious violence between missionaries and Chinese subjects.[41]

The intentions behind Kang's program was not mysterious to many of his contemporaries. For example, reformist Chen Baozhen 陳寶箴 (1831–1900) wrote:

> When the ban on overseas travel was completely lifted, Kang Youwei saw how European nations honored the pope, who held sway

over the political governance of nations, and he believed it was the cause of foreign nations' strength.... Confucius's religion had become disorganized and ineffectual. In sharp contrast, the European pope has great power, and wherever his disciples go, they exert great influence over the policy of the state. Thus, [Confucius's disciples] became indignant. They used Confucius's title of the uncrowned king and the doctrine of heaven to make Confucius the founder of the religion, in order to compete with the Christian God and Jesus. The purpose was to enlighten the people and to implement their theocratic program.[42]

Chen's comments are an insightful exposition of Kang's aims in restructuring the Confucius cult. However, we should note that post-Enlightenment Christianity, with which Kang was familiar, is only one of the many forms, with only some of the many different characteristics, that the religion had displayed in the past.[43]

Though Kang's Confucius cult movement was ultimately fruitless, it did have a large following for a time.[44] In the early republic, Confucius cult associations spread to hundreds of counties, and Kang's speeches sometimes attracted tens of thousands, including the society's upper crust, merchants, and intellectuals.[45] Kang's movement even achieved an international reach to members of the Chinese diaspora.[46] After the republican revolution in 1911, Kang journeyed all over China to muster support for Confucius cult associations, because he feared the overthrow of the empire would lead to a debacle for Confucianism and its rites. "We are at the cusp of a crisis that is unprecedented any time in ancient history. The sacrifices will be abolished, and the chanting and the ritual music will be silenced forever," he wrote in despondent reflection.[47]

Kang's fears were well founded. A wave of anti-Confucian iconoclasm soon swept across the early republic and wreaked havoc that was unprecedented in history—though it would not be the last time.[48] Furthermore, one of the first official acts by Minister of Education Cai Yuanpei 蔡元培 (1867–1940) was the abolishment of the recitation of Confucian classics at the nation's schools.[49] Such body blows against the Confucius cult made Kang even more anxious to find a place for Confucius within the ascendant political edifice of the republic.[50]

Kang was fully aware that Confucius veneration was an inseparable part of the imperial regime, the demise of which threatened to cut

Confucian rites loose from their institutional moorings. In this context, Kang's haste in trying to make his budding Cult of Confucius Association the basis of China's official religion was understandable. However, by initiating a crisis of constitutional proportions, Kang garnered support only from reactionaries and warlords.[51] The defeat of Kang's proposal to amend the secular constitution not only dashed his reputation but also marked the utter failure of the project to transform the Confucian tradition into a new state religion.

As Lu Xun 鲁迅 (1881–1936) put it:

> Various powerful men have powdered him [Confucius's statue] with all manner of cosmetics and raised him on pedestals of ever more terrifying heights. Yet he has fared rather poorly compared to the later-imported Buddha. Admittedly, every county has a sacred temple, also known as the temple of culture, but it always appeared desolate and abandoned, and ordinary folk avoided that place. If they go anywhere to worship, it is a Buddhist temple or a Daoist shrine. Ask the common folk who Confucius was, quite naturally they answer, "A sagely man." However, this answer merely echoes the gramophones of the powerful elite.[52]

By raising Confucius to ever more terrifying heights, Lu referred to the historical fact that China's dynastic regimes had frequently relied on Confucius for legitimation of their rule.

In fact, Kang Youwei and Chen Huanzhang's 陳煥章 (1880–1933) reform movement was a response to Confucianism's lack of mass appeal to the common people, which they tried to address by adopting the model of Western churches. This entailed a break from the Confucian tradition, a difference in attitude that Chen Huanzhang illustrated by comparing the old adage "Those who hear of the Way come to learn; going away to teach them is unheard of" with his own motto, "To proselytize with vigor."[53]

To sum up, the two failures of Kang Youwei's Confucius cult reformation movement were rooted in the epochal shifts of history that took place in the late Qing and the early republic. The first failure, occurring in the late Qing Empire, stemmed from Confucianism's frustrated transition from a state religion for collective purposes to a personal and private religion. However, the failure of Kang's attempt to rekindle Confucian reforms in the early republic was more foundational; by misreading the trends of history, Kang actually accelerated the collapse of Confucianism as a state religion. After this point, the Confucian religion lost all traction in the political system of the republic and quickly became a ghost of a past culture. It is in this light that we should interpret Gu Jiegang's 顧頡剛 (1893–1980) comment that "the Confucius cult is a religion that was incompletely engineered."[54] As the insistent exclusion of Confucianism from the family of religions by Chinese-speaking intellectuals from China and Taiwan shows, the aftereffects of the events discussed above are still felt today.[55]

The Countermovement Against the Confucius Cult

The initial opponents of the Confucius cult movement were antireformists, a broad camp that included a heterogeneous set of political alignments. At one end of the spectrum was Ye Dehui, who believed that "Confucius cult is the most righteous principle under the natural order and accords with human hearts." But he also wrote, "There is no need for melancholy about [the fate of] Confucius and no need to save the religion." In addition, Ye was vehemently opposed to treating Confucius as the founding figure of a religion.[56]

At the other end of the political spectrum were the Old Text Confucian scholars, including Zhang Taiyan 章太炎 (1869–1936) and Liu Shipei 劉師培 (1884–1919), who opposed Kang's school of New Text Confucianism. Zhang contemptuously dismissed Kang's Confucius cult movement,[57] while Liu Shipei opposed the New Text interpretation that Confucius was a reforming lawgiver who crafted the classics by using antiquities as a source of legitimation. Instead, based on Liu's assumption that Confucius's Six Classics were written in Zhou-era characters and circulated during the Zhou, he argued, "The man known as Confucius was [just] a Chinese scholar; the view that he was a Chinese religionist is in error."[58] Liu's remarks directly responded to Kang's program to reimagine Confucius as the founder of Confucianism and "a great founder of religion on earth."

Ironically, the most influential opponent to Kang's project was his formerly most loyal and zealous disciple, Liang Qichao, who defected from Kang's camp after falling under the influence of Yan Fu and Huang Zunxian 黃遵憲 (1848–1905). Liang's attacks accusing the movement to preserve the Confucius cult of not having been motivated by a desire to honor Confucius would prove telling.

When Liang was still an early follower of Kang's movement, in 1896, Yan Fu wrote him a missive in which he stated, "The religion cannot be preserved, nor should it." Yan added the logical conclusion, "If the religion is changed for the purpose of its salvation, then it ceases to be the religion which was meant to be saved."[59] Yan's arguments shook Liang's faith, but for a time he still tried to press on, spending much energy organizing the Union to Save the Religion.[60] Liang persisted because he viewed saving Confucianism and saving China as an indivisible project; the abandonment of the one necessarily endangering the other. As Liang cautioned, "Those today who do not take the preservation of the state and the religion as their task must have failed to fully grasp the causes of our moral crisis."[61] The charter of the Association to Save the Nation, whose founding figures included Kang, reiterated Liang's rallying call. This association's principal causes were "saving the nation, saving the race, and saving the religion," and Liang was a major contributor to its advocacy work, forums, and publications.[62]

However, in 1902, the third year of his exile to Japan, Liang began to oppose attempts at instituting the Confucius cult as China's state religion and made a public break from his established position. The reversal arose from Liang's changing calculus regarding what was beneficial to China's national interest. Religion as such held little interest for Liang, to whom the significance of a religion was solely in its usefulness to China's national cause. In his later years, for instance, Liang became an advocate for Buddhism, after he came to regard it as the apt vehicle for nurturing a unified Chinese identity and spirit of self-sacrifice.[63] In fact, Liang remained disinterested in religions in their pristine forms. Nonetheless, like Yan Fu, he saw the role religious faith could play as an agent of ideological mobilization in modern nation-states, because religion could serve as a catalyst for sparking and unleashing latent political energies. From the beginning to the end, the object of Liang's ultimate concern was always the state.[64]

In 1898, a consensus had existed between Liang and Kang that Christianity was the driving force behind the rise of the Western world. Liang had given his unreserved support to Kang's campaign to make the Confucius cult China's state religion, because Liang believed China's national salvation required it. Liang's "Letter in Response to My Friend on the Preservation of the Religion" 復友人論保教書 (1897) and "On China's Religious Reformation" 論支那宗教改革 (1899), which he penned during his exile to Japan, were written during his period of promoting the pro-Confucius cult.[65]

Nonetheless, Liang's attachment to the Confucius cult movement was short-lived. Beseeched by Yan Fu and Huang Zunxian, Liang changed his opinion and concluded, "'Religionists' is a term that specifically refers to those with superstitious beliefs about religious faith." Additionally, they convinced him that instituting the Confucius cult as China's state religion would stifle freedom of thought and thus hinder national progress and reforms. Christianity's decline in the West was also a factor in his opinion that the project to save Confucianism was doomed to fail.[66]

Huang Zunxian reflected on his criticism of Kang, which influenced Liang's thinking:

> [Kang] perceived the blossoming of Catholicism since two hundred years ago and mistakenly believed that the wealth and power of the West was due to its religion, so he attempted to honor our Confucius as its rival. Unknown to him, [the West] has long cast aside the propagation of religion, like pomace dregs. In modern Europe, such nations as Germany, Italy, and France mightily suppressed all religionists who tried to usurp political power. Those trying to aggrandize religion are aping the waste products of others and are in grave error![67]

In a similar vein, Liang later wrote: "Intoxicated by Western customs, some men thought the religion of Europeans and Americans is the reason for their power, so they wanted to abandon our customs to adopt those [of the West]. Such thought arose from an erroneous understanding of the most essential facts."[68] Liang's remark was a thinly veiled criticism of Kang.

Huang told Liang that the separation of church and state is the appropriate strategy in the context of the contemporary world:

> In Western countries, the separation of politics and religion is practiced. Their good governance is due to the flourishing of learning. Our country practices the unity of church and state. When kept separate, the church may compensate for the shortfalls of the state. When kept in unity, there is no religion beyond politics and learning. Today, we should adopt Western politics and Western learning to repair the defects of our politics and learning. We do not need to promote our religion in competition with others or dispute with them.[69]

Huang's claim that Western governance arose from "the flourishing of learning" was a deliberate attack aimed at severing the causal relationship that Kang posited between occidental religion and Western power. Huang's highly influential call for the separation of church and state would later form China's mainstream political thought.

Bracketing Liang's historical impact for the moment, it should be noted that, for Liang, the salvation of the nation had always taken precedence over its racial or religious preservation.[70] Liang drew his battle lines in the following passage: "Henceforth, we must direct our efforts to saving the nation alone. Race and religion have no claims to our urgency whatsoever."[71] Taking another shot at his erstwhile mentor, Liang reiterated, in "A Discourse on the New Citizen," "As I dare not blame the Confucius cult, I have no recourse but to detest and revile those who use the Confucius cult as a disguise, by exploiting and deceitfully distorting it, to be thieves of themselves and of the nation's people."[72]

Liang defined Confucius as a "scholar of philosophy, statecraft, and pedagogy," but not a religionist, by highlighting selected passages in the *Analects*. The most notable passages were "If you are not able to serve men, how can you serve their spirits?" and "If you do not know life, how can you understand death?" He also noted, "The master never discussed extraordinary things, feats of strength, disorder, and spiritual beings."[73] Generations later, modern scholars, seeking to refute the idea that Confucianism is a religion, have cited Liang's arguments almost verbatim. Liang also pointed out, "Westerners often compare Confucius to Socrates, but rarely do they compare him to the Buddha, Jesus, or Muhammad; they are quite right."[74]

Such remarks on the part of Liang and others marked the metamorphosis of Confucius's historical image during this period. However, Kang decried their absurdity. "Many contemporaries make the absurd claim that Confucius was a thinker of philosophy, statecraft, and education."[75] Nevertheless, Liang's faction was to win the cultural battle and establish his claim: "The *jiao* 教, to which the Confucius cult refers, actually connotes the same meaning as *jiao* in education (*jiaoyu* 教育), and not the *jiao* in religion (*zongjiao* 宗教)."[76]

Liang's characterization echoed among scholars. For instance, in the early republic, Feng Youlan proclaimed, "Confucius much resembled Socrates" in being "a sage," and "by virtue of being the Chinese Socrates alone, Confucius's greatness is assured." Feng also said that Confucius "was truly a [great] teacher."[77] The historian of classical textual scholarship, Zhou Yutong 周予同 (1898–1981), observed that Confucius "was not a religionist" but "a man of ancient China whose character was developed fully and perfectly into that of a sagely man,... a pragmatic educator,... a political thinker whose career was unsuccessful,... [and] an ethicist who was especially interested in the research of moral issues."[78] Although such portrayals of Confucius were not necessarily faithful ones, they effectively drowned out Kang's opposing understanding of Confucius as a religious founder.

Another major factor in Kang's loss was his activity in the early republic, when he again promoted the dual veneration of Confucius and heaven[79] and the institution of the Confucius cult as the state religion, and supported Zhang Xun's 張勳 (1854–1923) 1917 military coup to restore the dynasty. Those miscalculations backfired, ruining Kang's credibility and politicizing Confucius veneration as a partisan issue. The reputation of Confucius temples fell to the point that, in 1919, heavily armed soldiers had to stand guard over the rites of worshipping Confucius.[80]

Those developments also pitted Kang against supporters of the Chinese republic, like Zhang Taiyan, who opposed both Kang's scholarship and his politics. "Confucius's contribution to China was being the bearer of protection and enlightenment for its people, not the founding of any religion.... Religion was what Confucius had spurned," Zhang wrote in an article criticizing the Cult of Confucius Association. He added that those who venerated Confucius as a religious figure were committing actions that "amount to no more than violating Confucius's temple in Queli and leaving filth in his house on Mount Tai!"[81] However, in form and substance, those arguments were repetitive of Liang's writings.

The ambivalent stance toward Confucianism, adopted by the early republic potentate Yuan Shikai at various times, is illustrative of this struggle. On one hand, he showed great deference to Confucius and promulgated "The Order for Revering Sage Confucius" in June 1913. On the other hand, in a letter offering his congratulations on the establishment of the Confucius society (Kongshe 孔社), he spoke out against making the Confucius cult the state religion: "Confucius was never a religionist. Superficial people do not understand this and feel compelled to venerate him formulaically. They forced Confucianism into the ranks of religions, such as Buddhism, Daoism, Islam, and Christianity. They not only lose sight of their original intention to honor Confucius but also might cause Confucianism to be constrained by laws."[82]

Claiming as he did on this occasion that "national education should teach the Way of Confucianism as the foundation to self-cultivation" was very different from the objective, which he previously outlined in a tentative proposal to the National Assembly, to "institute Confucianism as China's religion."[83] Thus, Yuan's comments on Confucius marked a retreat from his prior commitment. Yuan's policy shift reflected the fact that the course of history had turned against the Confucius cult.

Another note of ambivalence was struck by the monarchist Lao Naixuan 勞乃宣 (1844–1927) in his "Oration for the Confucius Cult Association," a speech authored for the Duke of Yansheng, which opened with the assertion that Confucius had "explicated without authoring" the classics. Lao added, "The founding of the Cult of Confucius Association is aimed toward propagating Confucius's teachings over the world; it is not a religion."[84] Those comments are certainly at odds with Kang's ideas about religion. In addition, although Zhang Dongsun 張東蓀 (1886–1973) was sympathetic to Kang's religious conception of the Confucius cult, he opposed the dual veneration of Confucius and heaven, because he viewed it as a superfluous innovation that failed to do Confucius justice.[85]

If conservatives were not on board with Kang's project, it is not surprising that radical reformers Chen Duxiu 陳獨秀 (1879–1942) and Wu Yu 吳虞 (1872–1949) would earn praise from Hu Shih 胡適 (1891–1962) as "the two champions that in recent years struck the mightiest blows against the cult of Confucius."[86] Chen and Wu not only were heirs to Liang's animosity toward the Confucius cult but also broadened their attacks to bear on all things Confucian. Chen claimed that the Confucius cult and autocracy were inseparable, and thus concluded that Confucianism was "absolutely incompatible to modern civilization and society."[87] Wu considered the institution of ritual proprieties to be Confucianism's physical embodiment, which he attacked with the famous apothegm "Ritual propriety eats people."[88] On the question of whether Confucianism is a religion, Chen answered in the negative while Wu affirmed that it was a religion but gave it a negative valuation.

Cai Yuanpei, China's foremost educator of the era, declared, "Religion is religion, Confucius is Confucius, and the nation is the nation; each has its proper bounds and should not be conflated with the others."[89] Stating that Confucius's learning was confined to the realms of "pedagogy, politics, and ethics," Cai asserted that Confucius had nothing to do with religion and even that *Kongjiao* 孔教 (the term Kang used for the Confucius cult) was never used as a noun. From this perspective, the effort to elevate the Confucius cult as China's state religion was utterly nonsensical.[90] It is notable that during the early republic, and especially in the wake of Yuan Shikai's monarchical push, Cai Yuanpei appointed himself the "deconstructor" of the Confucius cult, for earlier, during the late Qing, he had argued exactly the opposite. In his 1910 book on the history of Chinese moral philosophy, Cai had argued that Confucianism had been China's state religion since the Han instituted it, and that it broadened its mass appeal to become a popular religion during the Song dynasty. The contradiction between his earlier and later assertions is obvious.[91]

The convergence of two factors accounted for the anti–Confucius cult movement in the early republic: the rise of scientism and contingent political events. The twentieth century was not an epoch for religion, and with the advent of Western science in China, which appeared at around the same time as Christianity, the survival of all religions was threatened.[92] Chen Duxiu stated, "In the future, the orthodoxy of science is to govern all of humanity's truthful apprehension of facts, and all religions are to be abolished and cast aside."[93] Cai Yuanpei claimed, "As an object, religion is a problem relegated to the past in occidental Europe, because scholarly scientific research has resolved the concerns raised by religion."[94] Additionally, Cai's proposal to replace religious instruction with aesthetic education reflected the contemporary instinct—coinciding with the May Fourth Movement—to support science and denounce metaphysics.

It seems clear in hindsight that the political chaos during the early republic certainly hardened animosity toward the Confucius cult. Confucian cultural symbols were incessantly abused by Yuan Shikai during his enthronement and performances of heaven worship, as well as during Zhang Xun's monarchist coup. Those events—and many others like them—resulted in enhanced disillusionment among Chinese intellectuals about Confucianism. Chen Duxiu welcomed New Year's Day of 1917 by declaring, "We should not only reject the institution of the Confucius cult as the state religion in any future constitution but also destroy all Confucius temples of the nation and abolish their rites!"[95]

At the same time, it is undeniable that the word "religion" had acquired a negative connotation in the intellectual circles of the early republic. Chen Duxiu announced, "I object to the Confucius cult because it should not have been thought of as a religion. On the subject of religion, I am against its each and every iteration."[96] Hu Shih summarized a widespread view when he said, "China is a nation without religion, as the Chinese are not a superstitious people."[97] The antireligious turn of Chinese history affected even Liang Shuming 梁漱溟 (1893–1988), among the pioneers of the "new" twentieth-century Confucianism, who conceded, "The school of Confucius did not appear to be religious . . . [and] in truth, Confucius was quite opposed to religion."[98] Liang added that the Chinese people "lived lives that were nearly devoid of all religion." Reaching to Feng Youlan for support, Liang paraphrased Feng as confirming, "Confucius was not religious; although religious rites are present, the fact that he and his thought were not religious was unaltered."[99] Bertrand Russell (1872–1970), who visited China, further muddied the waters with his comments that one of China's identifying characteristics was "the substitution of the Confucian ethic for religion among the educated classes."[100] Liang Shuming reinforced the point: "Chinese replaced religion with moral philosophy."[101]

Another New Confucian trailblazer of the twentieth century, Xiong Shili 熊十力 (1885–1969) echoed, "Mister Cai [Yuanpei's] argument that Confucians were textual scholars rather than religionists was absolutely on mark. . . . Textual scholarship is the pinnacle of philosophy and more than adequate as a replacement for religion."[102] Additionally, Liang Shuming and Feng Youlan further echoed one another in saying that Confucianism's scriptures and rituals were poetic and artistic expressions instead of having a religious nature.[103]

Xie Youwei 謝幼偉 (1905–1976), a scholar with the self-described aspiration to master Chinese and occidental philosophy, noted that a large number of academics believed "religion did not exist in traditional Chinese thought at all" and that "Chinese philosophers from the very beginning were apathetic to religion."[104] Such comments showed that Chinese intellectual circles were markedly disinterested in religion during most of the twentieth century, and most thinkers seemed to believe that Confucianism could plausibly be described as almost anything but a religion.[105]

In 1922, a group of self-described progressive intellectuals banded together to form the Antireligion League, specifically in opposition to Christianity but also to the Confucius cult, because "religion is an object that impedes human progress."[106] One of its cofounders was Cai Yuanpei, the principal advocate for "replacing religion with aesthetic education."[107] He declared, "An ideology that valorizes the stale and the old binds the various religions today; they use bizarre rituals and hyperbolic propaganda to lure the ignorant into blind obedience in order to maintain the livelihood of their missionaries. This invasion of the personal spiritual world by outside forces should be considered a violation of human rights."[108] Li Dazhao 李大釗 (1889–1927), author of the Antireligious Declaration, proclaimed, "Religious legends are mythical and superstitious. Instead of believing in Confucius, the Buddha, or Jesus, we believe in truth."[109] Such attitudes toward religion were of course greatly at odds with Kang's understanding or valuations. Although Liang was not a wholehearted supporter of the league, he had condemned "those who ate the rice of the Cult of Confucius Association."[110]

An additional complication was that the institution of the Confucius cult as a state religion would interfere with religious freedom and provoke Christians, Buddhists, and Daoists.[111] Both untimely and unpopular, the movement to establish the Confucius cult as the state religion lost its momentum and faded away.

However, reinventing Confucianism was not unprecedented in Chinese history. In fact, attempts to create a religion from Confucian thought were little more than restructuring the imperial state cult into a private religion. The difference was that prior to Kang, those projects imitated Buddhism, Daoism, or folk religions, while Kang's model was Christianity from the West.[112]

From the late Qing to the early republic, the Confucius cult's opponents and proponents shared common beliefs that continue to shape contemporary understandings of Confucianism and its nature as a religion. First, both proponents and opponents shared a predilection for applying "creative" interpretations to classic Confucian texts to support their own beliefs. Moreover, in their creativity, they shared an inclination toward textual exegesis and philology. For instance, Chen Huanzhang argued that the Confucius cult was a religion because the *Doctrine of the Mean* proclaimed, "Cultivating the Way is called *jiao* 教." As we have seen, Chen Duxiu countered with an alternate "correct" reading in which *jiao* merely meant "teaching" or "education," while Cai Yuanpei even attacked the reading of *Kongjiao* as a noun.[113] Their polemical war of words solved nothing, save proving that philological explications could not resolve fundamental conflicts over values.

The dispute over the meaning of words and the interpretation of classical texts was a superficial phenomenon and obscured the way in which, at their core, both sides used Christianity as a religious archetype for judging

Confucianism. Although their views all were mediated by the "apply and use" (*zhiyong* 致用) tradition of pragmatic statecraft, their perceptions of the value and role of Christianity in the West differed greatly. Kang believed that the spiritual foundation of Christianity was as important to the West's wealth and power as its political institutions and resources, if not more so. In contrast, Liang Qichao and Chen Duxiu believed that Christianity was an anachronistic force in modern civilization and needed to end.[114]

Conclusion: Confucianism Without Form or Spirit— Intellectualized Confucianism and Its Remaining Religious Nature

In 1926, Gu Jiegang spoke at Xiamen University, saying:

> In the Spring and Autumn period, Confucius was a gentleman; in the Warring States, Confucius was a sagely man; after the Eastern Han, he was a religious founder; and today he is becoming a gentleman again. Making Confucius a gentleman is not to treat him disrespectfully. It is the truth regarding what he was, which he gladly chose for himself.[115]

Sadly, Fu Sinian (Fu Ssu-nien) 傅斯年 (1896–1950) did not grant Confucius even that much. "Confucius may not have been a pure gentleman; he was about half a gentleman and half something else." Lu Xun remarked, "The ordinary people of China, especially the so-called ignorant commoners, would call Confucius a sagely man, but they do not think he was a holy man. To him, they are diffident and respectful, but not intimate. Yet I think it is most likely that no one in the world knows Confucius better than China's ignorant commoners."[116] Such judgments by leading public intellectuals during the republic reflected their alienation from Confucius, and their project to remove religiosity from Confucianism was all but complete.

In a retrospective overview of modern Chinese religious developments, Wing-tsit Chan 陳榮捷 (1901–1994) wrote, in 1953, "Contemporary Chinese are almost unanimous in denying Confucianism is a religion."[117] But another narrative arose in the wake of Chinese disenchantment with

Confucius. As sociologist C. K. Yang 楊慶堃 (1911–1999) argued, rather than denying that Confucianism was a full-fledged religion in a theistic sense, it is better to understand Confucianism as a social and political theory with a certain religious quality.[118] Because he was a functionalist, Yang was preoccupied with Confucianism's social, political, and educational roles in traditional China. Nevertheless, he was simply providing a sociological spin to Liang Shuming's much earlier remark that Confucianism "has all the effects of religion but none of the absurdities and ridiculousness of most religions."[119] Although such views continued to strip the form and spirit from Confucianism, they largely continued the widespread judgment among May Fourth intellectuals and extended similar understandings of Confucianism in humanistic fields in the West.

In China, Liang Shuming articulated a similar interest in replacing older terminology for Confucianism. In a 1966 publication, he remarked, "'Confucius cult' (*Kongjiao* 孔教) and 'Confucian religion' (*rujiao* 儒教) are both problematic terms, so I have used 'Duke of the Zhou's teachings' to avoid confusion."[120] Due to its religious connotation, use of the term "Confucian religion" disappeared from contemporary Chinese and was replaced by the secularized term "Confucian" (*rujia* 儒家) and the intellectualized "Confucian learning" (*ruxue* 儒學).[121]

Likewise, traditional Confucianism does not meet the standard Western definition of religion, and contemporary scholars often say that Confucians and Confucianism have "religious characteristics" or "religiosity" (*zongjiaoxing* 宗教性) but that Confucianism is not a religion.[122] For instance, historian Mou Zhongjian 牟鍾鑒 claims, "We can only say 'Confucian learning' possesses religiosity, but we must not say it is a religion."[123] Meanwhile, many Western Sinologists use the term "spirituality" in reference to Confucianism's religious dimensions, to avoid using the loaded term "religion."[124] But those words do not capture the soul of Confucianism as it was practiced in history.

Mou Zongsan 牟宗三 (1909–1995), Xu Fuguan 徐復觀 (1904–1982), Tang Junyi 唐君毅 (1909–1978), and Zhang Junmai 張君勱 (1887–1969) first used the terms "religiosity" and "religiousness" when they coauthored "A Manifesto on the Reappraisal of Chinese Culture: Our Joint Understanding of the Sinological Study Relating to World Cultural Outlook."[125] All four men were second-generation New Confucians. In a speech entitled "Confucianism as a Religion," Mou would later write:

Religions have two dimensions. One is their [eternal] substance, another their [inner] logic. According to its substance, Confucianism is not a religion, as it is commonly called. It does not possess the rituals common in religions. It has transformed religious rituals into the proprieties and music, practiced in ordinary actions of daily life. But according to its logic, it possess a high religiosity and a fully developed religious spirit. Moral consciousness and moral actualization saturate its religious consciousness and spirit, because its higher focus is the realization of the Way of heaven (Tiandao 天道).[126]

The phrase "according to its substance" can be read as the characteristics of a "diffused religion" in sociology,[127] which Kang Youwei and Chen Huanzhang had called "humanistic religion."[128] The phrase "according to its logic" would refer to the "inner and transcendent" religiousness that is the pride of modern New Confucians.

Additionally, Mou Zongsan developed the idea of Confucianism being a "moralistic religion" 人道之教 and a "humane religion."[129] Building on Mou's ideas, the third-generation New Confucian Tu Weiming 杜維明 has elaborated the theory that Confucianism's religiosity springs from its "ultimate concern with personal transformation" 內在既超越, through which believers achieve transcendence and unity with the divine.[130] As historian (and my mentor) Yu Yingshi (Yü Ying-shih) 余英時 has insightfully observed, after basing itself on theories of mind and human nature, New Confucianism's Way is both hard to achieve and easily lost. It is worrisome that New Confucianism cannot provide religious experience beyond residual religiosity and intellectual discourse on the "subtle and precarious" quest for the Way.[131] Thus, New Confucians' turning of Confucianism into an intellectual and scholastic pursuit risks the elitist pitfall that disconnected traditional Confucianism from the lives of ordinary Chinese.

Modern Confucianism's preoccupation with using textual exegesis and creative interpretation of the classics to prove preconceived notions imposes further limitations on its usefulness[132] and opens it to accusations of intellectual reductionism.[133] The line between New Confucian "religiosity" and becoming an inaccessible elite culture is precariously thin.

In addition, New Confucianism has thus far failed to rise above textual exegesis and the reliance on creative interpretation to prove its preconceived ideas. The approach employed by New Confucians suggests an intellectual reductionism that confuses belief and religious experience with knowledge. Its lack of an anthropological dimension leads to an inability to account for past Confucians' subjective experiences, practices, and beliefs.

In summary, modern Chinese intellectuals continue to be troubled by the question "Why does Confucianism resemble a religion without being one?" The Qing dynasty's fall marked the Chinese empire's disintegration, which left its embedded Confucian system of rites rootless and without sustenance. Moreover, the impact of attacks from many sides soon destroyed Confucian ritual proprieties, which had supported traditional society. As Liang Shuming aptly pronounced, "Ritual propriety and music were the Confucius cult's only important activities, so with their demise, the Confucius cult passed away."[134]

Without the practice of ritual proprieties to give Confucianism its form and social function, we cannot fault New Confucians for trying to promote "the learning of the mind and human nature" to comfort the Confucian spirit through transcendent humaneness (*ren* 仁). However, Confucius taught that the perfection of humaneness that leads to the Great Unity follows from "overcoming oneself" (*keji* 克己) and "observing ritual proprieties," which are mutually interdependent.[135] The mere "religiosity" of a spirituality that is not sustained by the formal trappings and practices of religion—such as institutions and rites—cannot gain social traction in modern society; it becomes nothing but a ghost of a religion.

From the perspective of comparative religions, the Reformation in the West enabled Protestantism to shed excessive rituals and center itself on personal faith; the movement toward secularization following the Enlightenment further resulted in religion's relocation in the West from the public sphere to private belief.[136] Modern Confucians who have found themselves in a cultural world without Confucian ritual proprieties and music are somewhat comparable to the Protestants of yore. However, the question of whether the Confucian cult or Confucianism is a religion is not a philosophical question but a historical one. Confucianism generated a variety of different religious meanings in accordance with its time, place, and stage of development; moreover, such diversity was able to coexist despite the existence of tensions or contradictions. In short, the question "Is Confucianism a religion?" does not have an ahistorical answer that transcends temporal and geographic boundaries.

CHAPTER VII

The Lonely Confucius Temples Across the Taiwan Straits

The Difficult Transformation of Modern China's Traditional Culture

The eminent Sinologist Joseph R. Levenson (1920–1967) once sensationally remarked that modern Chinese intellectuals were intellectually alienated from Chinese traditional culture in spite of their affective attachment to the Chinese past. Which is to say, for Chinese intellectuals, traditional culture was like mummies in a museum—nice to look at, but not terribly useful.[1]

Naturally, such remarks are anathema to cultural conservatives. But the fate of Confucius temples and their associated ritual system presents sobering proof that, if anything, Levenson had understated his argument. Confucius temples and rites were rejected intellectually and affectively not only by the public at large but also by intellectuals. Those who neglected Confucius temple rites even included the twentieth-century New Confucians, who had limited themselves to rarefied discourse on *ren* 仁 (humaneness) but uttered not a word on *li* 禮 (ritual or propriety), despite their self-proclaimed status as defenders of Confucian culture.

Yet, according to no less of an authority than Confucius himself, in the *Analects*, the achievement of *ren* in the world requires the exercise of self-restraint and returning to submit to *li*.[2] Furthermore, ancient Confucianism was distinguished by an animating spirit of historical consciousness, a fact that its modern disciples seem to have lost sight of in their contentment with being passive historical objects. Little wonder that

[198]

Confucianism today has little purchase in the "real world," to say nothing of its traditional goal to "manage the affairs of state and aid the people" (*jingshi jimin* 經世濟民).

In fact, in traditional China—or more precisely, in imperial China—Confucius temple rites were among the most celebrated and significant of state rituals, dwarfing other state ceremonies and religious rites in terms of their historical continuity and antiquity and the span of territory in which they were practiced.

However, in Taiwan and China today, Confucian rites are treated either as antique window dressing (in Taiwan) or as a commodified brand-name product for the new market economy (in China). For example, my colleague who is a retired humanities professor at a university in southern Taiwan once said that he had never set foot in the Tainan temple of Confucius, even though he lives near the site. My colleague's indifference to the temple is not an isolated case.

In September 1992, I went on a research sabbatical to Qufu 曲阜 to see the original temple of Confucius in Shandong, China. Right before the visit, I toured the Buddhist Lingyin monastery 靈隱寺 in Hangzhou. Although my visit took place on a regular weekday, the huge throng of devotees and their passionate worship at the Buddhist monastery made a profound impression on me. However, when I visited the Confucius temple, I found that its halls were empty of visitors and tourists, and its prominently displayed donation boxes at the temple's Dacheng hall 大成殿 were a reflection of the temple's pitiless commodification. The tomb of Confucius, located in a nearby forest, was not without its share of visitors, but except for me, no one bothered to offer respect to Confucius at the tomb. As a simple gesture of respect to a figure from antiquity who was one of the most significant human beings in the course of world history, I bowed toward the tomb three times.

Nevertheless, my greatly abbreviated performance of the traditional ceremony—the kowtow of "three genuflections and nine dips of the forehead"—unfortunately made a scene and caused embarrassment to a friend who was acting as my guide.

"Why are you not happy with one bow? You really are pushing it at three," I remember him saying.

To give context to my inadvertent faux pas: I later learned the appalling fact that during the Cultural Revolution, anyone caught bowing to the tomb of Confucius was incarcerated on trumped-up charges and frequently suffered various tortures at struggle sessions.[3] Obviously, China's anti-Confucian movement in the 1960s and 1970s was thoroughly political, but it profoundly influenced people's behavior.[4] For example, the *People's Daily* editorialized, on February 2, 1974:

> The struggle against Kong [Confucius] is indeed an important element in the struggle against Lin [Lin Biao 林彪, 1907–1971], a means to upend the old roots of Lin Biao's revisionism, to more perfectly carry out the struggle against Lin. The struggle against Lin and the struggle against Kong are the most serious class struggles of the nation; a total revolution in the realm of ideology; a declaration of war against feudalism, capitalism, and revisionism; a heavy blow against imperialism, revisionism, and counterrevolution; the first priority of the all-national party, all-national army, and all-national people.[5]

Texts of this kind appear absurd to readers today, but in context of the hysteria that gripped China at the time, people probably saw it as commonplace, and even after political passions cooled, the Cultural Revolution's legacy of indifference to, and contempt for, Confucianism remains palpable in many modern Chinese minds.

From a historical perspective, the dismissive attitude toward the Confucius temple and its culture in Taiwan and China is actually an extension of the anti-Confucian movement that occurred during the era of the republic in the early twentieth century. Beginning with Hu Shih's 胡適 (1891–1962) famous one-sentence summary of Wu Yu's 吳虞 (1872–1949) scholarly contribution as having "torn down the Kong clan's corner shops,"[6] the slogan "Down with the Confucian shop" took on a life of its own as the emblem for the spirit of that era. Chen Duxiu 陳獨秀 (1979–1942), on January 1, 1917, advocated, "We should destroy all the Confucius temples in the nation and abolish all their rituals!"[7] Chen Duxiu's fury would have been right at home in the Cultural Revolution's anti-Confucian struggle sessions, and it is likely that the widespread modern indifference to Confucianism is but a distant echo of Chen's battle cry of a century ago. The fall from grace of Confucius temples and their embodied Confucian culture would have been astonishing to Confucians of earlier eras, had they been unfortunate enough to witness it.

Political Power and the Rise and Fall of Confucius Temples

Throughout the history of Confucianism, state power and its interventions determined whether Confucius temples, as well as their rites as intertwined institutions, flourished. Indeed, as the history of the May Fourth Movement, beginning in 1919 (as well as its immediate antecedent, the New Cultural Movement, 1915–1919), clearly showed, the political and the cultural were deeply intertwined. As an intellectual movement, the May Fourth Movement was a reaction to the self-proclaimed emperor of China, Yuan Shikai 袁世凱 (1859–1916), and the notorious monarchist supporters, such as Zhang Xun 張勳 (1854–1923), who had abused Confucian symbols during their brief imperial restoration.[8] Among other things, Yuan Shikai's personal character and his performance of sacrificial offerings to Confucius evoked collective disgust and disdain from Chinese intellectuals and soured them on Confucian rites; furthermore, their antipathy quickly catalyzed into a full-throttled anti-Confucian movement. The chain of events also proved the correctness of Mencius's 孟子 (c. 372–c. 289 BCE) observation, "Those Zhao Meng exalts, Zhao Meng can also humble."[9] Clearly, politics was decisive in causing the decline of Confucius temples and temple rites.

However, we must understand that the rise of Confucianism in ancient China also was a result of political factors. In imperial China, Confucius temples belonged to the system of state cults that were used for official rites by the imperial state. Emperors of the Western Han dynasty orchestrated the process when they transformed the family ancestral rites of the Kong clan's private ancestral hall into a state-managed temple of Confucius. Thus, more than two millennia ago, Han emperors set the precedent for the incessant political manipulation of Confucianism that became the historical norm.

In terms of religious rites, Confucius temples had roles for two distinct kinds of presiding celebrants. First, for more than two millennia, members of the Kong clan, the nominal descendants of Confucius, were indispensable to the veneration of Confucius at the site of their original family shrine in Queli (modern Qufu), although their appellations changed from dynasty to dynasty. Second, the master of ceremonies at a Confucius temple was always the imperial chief administrator of the province, prefecture, or county in which the temple was situated, with the only exception to this tradition being at the Confucius temple in Qufu. In addition, the imperial capital's Confucius temple always played a special role as the stage for the emperor's rites and political proclamations. Because the Confucius temple in Qufu was the original one and thus viewed as the progenitor of the temple system, it was unique in simultaneously displaying both of the temple's characteristics: that of the state temple and of the private ancestral hall. As a private ancestral hall, the Qufu Confucius temple has always required men descended from Confucius's bloodline to lead its devotions.

Even so, historical records showed that in the late Eastern Han dynasty, the Kong clan became extinct in Qufu. In order to protect the legitimacy of the rituals in the Qufu Confucius temple, imperial rulers had to make a show of searching the realm for the clan's true descendants and verifying their legitimacy in order to maintain the legal fiction that the "perpetual continuity" of the sacred descendants remained inviolate. Furthermore, before and during the Eastern Han dynasty, the veneration of Confucius was practiced only in Qufu, the sage's native birthplace.

In the wake of the nomadic invasion and conquest of North China by Central Asians, whom the Han Chinese regarded as barbarian tribal peoples, the remnant Han Chinese Jin regime fled to South China, where it erected a Confucius temple in its capital. Inadvertently, the catastrophe became a precedent and the impetus for Confucius temples to be constructed far beyond Qufu and eventually throughout the lands under Han Chinese administration. Competing Confucius temples were built during the Northern and Southern dynasties period by rival regimes.

After the unification of China by the Tang dynasty, Emperor Taizong 唐太宗 (r. 626–649) decreed in 630, that all prefectural and county imperial academies were to serve as the local centers of Confucius worship. As an expression of the top-down promotion of Confucianism by the state, Tang Taizong's decree was the most remarkable in scope, but it was far from being the last. According to one scholar, there were more than 1,560 Confucius temples within China's borders by the Ming dynasty. This figure does not include temples situated in the Chinese empire's many tributary states and allies, such as Vietnam and Korea. Evidently, it was imperial might that enabled Confucius temples to spread far and wide and to grow to a density and depth that was unrivaled by native folk religions. For example, in spite of the local popularity of Matsu temples, they never extended beyond the confines of China's southeastern coastline and outlying islands.

The ruling class took pains to promote the system of Confucius temple rites because they regarded Confucian teachings as beneficial for the stability of their regime. The Qing emperor Yongzheng 雍正 (r. 1722–1735) noted that to solidify effective rule, it paid to promote the Confucian ideal "Ritual propriety is fulfilled and thus the hierarchical order is secured." Moreover, this was the greatest service Confucianism could render to the ruling class, a fact the Yongzheng emperor plainly acknowledged, saying, "for rulers it is especially beneficial."[10]

From a realpolitik perspective, the history of Confucius temples is an integral part of the history of the symbiotic relationship between rulers and Confucian scholar-officials. The mutual dependence was succinctly described by Cao Yuanyong 曹元用 (1268–1330) during the Yuan dynasty: "The teaching of Confucius will not extend far without the [support of] rulers' governance; without the teachings of Confucius, it is impossible to perfect social customs. When Confucian teaching is not widespread, there is no loss (or harm) to the Way; governance that fails to improve social customs will certainly imperil the state."[11] Cao's assertion that "when Confucian teaching is not widespread, there is no loss (or harm) to the Way" should certainly be understood as a Confucian scholar-official's self-serving flattery or exaggeration. Nevertheless, this assertion does not detract from his crucial message: "governance that fails to improve social customs will certainly imperil the state." This speaks both to the value of Confucian teachings to governance and to their reciprocal dependence.

Beginning in the Han dynasty, when Confucius temples became state temples, their politicization increased by degrees, and the class composition of the participants in Confucius temple rites reflected this politicization. For example, from the time of the Tang and Song dynasties, the master of ceremonies at every Confucius temple was a man of official rank, whether he was the Son of Heaven himself, an officially recognized descendant of the Kong clan, or an official designated by the court or local administrators. All such men represented the official state. Although Confucian scholar-officials of the National University did appear at the rites, they were present only as "those who attended the sacrifice"; moreover, the state forbade all commoners to trespass on the temple's sacred grounds. For ordinary men and women, those practices made the Confucius temple a place of solemn but forbidding power.

Anecdotal evidence illustrating the exclusionary nature of Confucius temples could be found in the Song dynasty, when a scholar-official proposed to open the doors of the capital's National University to visiting nonofficials and their ladies. His views made him an object of ridicule in the learned opinion of his peers.[12] An imperial edict from the Yuan dynasty to a local administrator in charge of restoring the Qufu Confucius temple further reinforces our impression that Confucius temples were the proprietary reserve of the ruling class and scholar-officials. The order declared that people be forbidden from wandering around or doing anything disrespectful within the temple compound.[13] It is more than safe to assume that members of the general public, who were banned from entering temple grounds for the purposes of "visiting or touring," would have been barred from watching or participating in the official Confucian rites held in the temple.

In the late Ming dynasty, Zhu Guozhen 朱國禎 (1558–1632) wrote in a comment marking his visit to a temple of Confucius, "Entering a [Confucian] temple is grave and solemn matter, much unlike Buddhist temples."[14] Zhu's comment illustrates how Confucius temples were set apart from other religious temples. Another charming anecdote, by the late Ming dynasty essayist Zhang Dai 張岱 (1597–1684), recounted that he bribed his way past the gatekeeper and into the Qufu Confucius temple, demonstrating that entering a Confucius temple was no trivial matter for nonofficials.[15]

The Abandonment of Confucius Temples

Regarding the common masses' lack of affection for Confucius temples, Lu Xun 魯迅 (1881–1936) had this to say:

> Various powerful men have powdered him [Confucius's statue] with all manner of cosmetics and raised him on pedestals of ever more terrifying heights. Yet he has fared rather poorly compared to the later-imported Buddha. Admittedly, every county has a sacred temple, also known as the temple of culture, but it always appeared desolate and abandoned, and ordinary folk avoided that place. If they go anywhere to worship, it is a Buddhist temple or a Daoist shrine. Ask the common folk who Confucius was, quite naturally they answer, "A sagely man." However, this answer merely echoes the gramophones of the powerful elite.[16]

When Lu Xun wrote about the ruling class raising Confucius to "ever more terrifying heights," he was referring to historical dynasties that had used Confucian ideas as the foundation of their statecraft; moreover, rulers who worshipped other gods usually kept their personal religion to themselves. For example, while the Jiajing 嘉靖 Emperor (r. 1521–1566) of the Ming dynasty had an affinity for Daoism, the Yongzheng Emperor of the Qing favored Lamaism; nonetheless, both presented a Confucian public facade to the bureaucracy while continuing to confine their personal worship in their private quarters of the inner court. For such reasons, state confidence in Confucianism as the foundation for rulers to manage the state and aid the people was rarely shaken. From dynasty to dynasty, emperors promoted the image of Confucius to ever more awe-inspiring heights, carrying Confucius temple rites to ever-greater heights of ritual sophistication and prestige.

From the available evidence, it seems that Lu Xun's scornful observation that the common people avoided Confucius temples might well be true. Foundationally, Confucianism's lack of mass appeal was likely the result of the absence of the metaphysical, the anthropomorphically divine, or any otherworldly moorings in Confucian beliefs. Best characterized as a rational humanism, Confucianism could perhaps be satisfying to the collective consciousness of Confucian scholar-officials and the ruling class, but when people confronted human psychological needs, Confucianism was of no comfort or help in explaining personal and individual suffering. Consequently, as Lu Xun remarked, people were far more far likely to consult Daoist gods and the Buddha, rather than Confucius, about their personal needs. Lu Xun was writing during the era of the republic, when Confucius temples had already opened to the public, but a belated embrace of inclusion could not overcome centuries of inherited religious habits among the common people, who had some awe of the Confucius temples even as they avoided them.

In addition, while it is not surprising that other types of temples of culture (*wen* 文) outside of the Confucian system, such as the Wenchang shrines 文昌祠 and the Zitong shrines 梓潼祠, did in fact attract popular devotion, the contrasting lack of public interest in Confucian temples of culture does suggest that this matter deserves a closer look. In the late Qing dynasty, Liang Qichao 梁啟超 (1873–1929) observed, "In our Yue 粵 [Guangdong], Wenchang 文昌 and Kuixing 魁星 enjoyed the sacrificial offerings; in contrast, people rarely worship Confucius." Liang added, "Upon entering school, a pupil immediately learns to venerate Wenchang and Kuixing as gods; however, regarding the most sanctified founder of our religion, the fire of his legacy has all but burned out, his sacrificial vessels almost empty, his dates of birth and death scarcely known by anyone."[17] Wenchang and Kuixing were deities with authority over an individual's destiny and attainment of official status, so they were intimate and relevant to the concerns of the common people. In comparison, Confucius's sagely personhood projected a rather remote and inscrutable image with scant relationship to a commoner's needs and aspirations. Why did this difference arise?

Perhaps the answer rests largely in the role and function of Confucius temples as the loci of public rituals for the state cult and not a private religion. Like the rite of sacrifice to heaven (*ji tian* 祭天), the rite of the veneration of Confucius (*ji Kong* 祭孔) was the domain and privilege of rulers. In extraordinary times these rituals marked political revolution or dynastic succession, and in peacetime these rituals were perpetually reinforced as the rites of the state and held every spring and autumn. In other words, the veneration of Confucius was integral to the workings of imperial machinery—something kept away from the blasphemous touch of common hands.

However, the Qing Empire was toppled from within by the literati class of scholar-officials. Cut loose from its institutional moorings in the imperial theocratic state, the system of Confucian rites began to drift within modern Chinese society, in search of a reason for its being. Furthermore, the founding of the republic brought only new challenges and no amelioration of its dire straits. Confucius temples and their rites do linger on today, but they do so without defined status and in a marginalized social space. Except on the official Confucius Day (also known as Teacher's Day), when the public's memory is briefly and temporarily stirred by the performance of the rites at Confucius temples, the presence of Confucius temples is scarcely acknowledged by the Chinese-speaking peoples across the Taiwan Straits.

The reason for this sad state of affairs is simple: far from the political and theological center that Confucius temples hitherto occupied, the temples became marginal to contemporary Chinese life. For example, in 1992, China organized a group of academics to make a field survey of Confucius temples in Korea and to consult Korean experts of Confucian rituals. Reading reports of that mission calls to mind the lines from Wang Yangming's 王陽明 (1472–1529) satirical poem titled "Singing Four Poems on Liangzhi to Students" 詠良知四首示諸生, about "throwing away one's own adequate treasure and acting like a beggar wandering the streets alone."[18]

In addition, we should note that China's rites for the sacrifice to Confucius still, for the most part, continue the rite performed during the Manchu Qing dynasty, whereas Taiwan returned to the earlier rites of the Han Chinese Ming dynasty. One of the most obvious differences is found in the eight-row dancing (*bayiwu* 八佾舞); in China, it is performed by red-clad dancers, but in Taiwan the dancers wear yellow clothes. Moreover, in 1991, Taiwan's Taoyuan city government was reported to have "restored" a Confucius temple.

These examples are not intended to establish the superior state of Taiwan's knowledge and practice with regard to Confucius temples. In fact, the "restorers" of the Confucius temple were apparently ignorant of the basic characteristics of Confucian architecture and filled the gaps in their knowledge by using features commonly found in Buddhist monasteries and Taoist temples. To add insult to injury, the restorers even built a dome over the Pillar to the Heavens (*Tongtian Zhu* 通天柱). This space should to be open to the sky, as a symbol of the honorific couplet praising Confucius: "His virtue is comparable with heaven and earth, and his Way links together antiquity and the present" (*de mou tiandi, dao guan gujin* 德侔天地，道貫古今). As a final indignity, the restorers installed a random number of knobbed nails into the temple gates, even though specific numbers had historically vested ritual significance.

Depoliticization: A Sine Qua Non for a Viable Confucianism

One may argue that Confucianism and its institution of temple rites is dying out because its day and political function have passed. However, an alternative is to consider that Confucians need to take time to process the political symbols that Confucianism has accrued through its long history. In other words, a movement of depoliticization might be necessary for Confucian culture to jettison its political baggage. Such a program might conceivably restore vitality to Confucius temples and thereby facilitate a search for its meaningful cultural place in contemporary society.

For instance, every year in Taipei, Taiwan, a political firestorm inevitably and invariably arises when the city government is obliged to choose between the rite of imperial *bayiwu* (eight-row dancing) or the less noble *liuyiwu* 六佾舞 (six-row dancing) for the Taipei temple of Confucius, which is still under public control. In imperial China, *bayiwu* was the exclusive realm of the Queli Confucius temple and the Confucius temple in the imperial capital, while county and prefectural temples performed *liuyiwu*. Thus, if the Taipei city government announces that the temple will perform six-row dancing—which it often does, citing space concerns—that announcement carries the implication that the city of Taipei is only a seat of a local government, not the capital of a sovereign nation. Therefore, the Chinese regard a decision to have only six rows of dancers to be a servile political gesture to Beijing. The key to resolving this controversy is to avoid and to refuse to be mired again in the quagmire of ancient ritual law. Rather, the answer is to depoliticize the political significance of *bayiwu* and *liuyiwu* inherited from ancient China.

Another example would be the decision about which government office is responsible for Confucius temples according to Confucian ritual regulations. In Taiwan, there was once a lively controversy—now completely forgotten—about whether the proper governmental authority was the Presidential Office, the Ministry of the Interior, or the Ministry of Education. The protracted fight yielded no discernible results insofar as scholarship was concerned. Nevertheless, in practical terms, the controversy led all state authorities to abandon their duty to take care of the nation's Confucius temples and the Taiwanese branch of descendants of the Kong clan. In the past, dynastic governments and scholar-officials considered Confucius temple rites to be "great rites of state," which the Tang dynasty had defined as rites of the "middle rank" and the Qing dynasty elevated to rites of the "supreme rank." At one time, then, the sacred descendants of the Kong clan were the emperor's honored guests and the figurehead of civil officials. Thus, the obvious contrast between the past and the present cannot be overstated.

However, if we dismiss the institution of Confucius temple rites as moribund vestiges of feudalism, already doomed by modern progress, we would be ignoring clear evidence to the contrary in the neighboring countries of South Korea and Japan. Modern Korea and Japan have protected their Confucius temples as worthy cultural heritages. Moreover, these modern societies have preserved this component of cultural heritage without any of the embarrassment or awkwardness about Confucius temples that we find in Taiwan and China.

There is no reason to doubt that Confucian temple institutions can integrate with modernity and find new roles to perform in modern society—if Confucian rites shed anachronistic elements of imperial politics. For example, a crucial step would be for governments to allow civil society to take over the care of the temples. Regaining the approval of the general public is an initial condition for resuscitating the cultural functionality of Confucius temple rites.

Whether Confucius temple rites are to be restored or to be reformed to adapt to the new age is a question that requires serious consideration. For instance, the master of ceremonies in Confucius temple rites has always been a ranking public official. However, in the modern democratic age, would civic groups, rather than the government, be the more appropriate custodians of Confucian rituals and the better enablers of public participation? It certainly is necessary for those who desire Confucianism to become vibrant and relevant to the larger society to ponder such alternatives.

In fact, the key to Confucianism regaining its crucial traditional function—of providing "moral training for the masses, instructive models for hundreds of rulers, and ritual paths for thousands of years" (*da xun sheng min, shifan bai wang, yi gui qian zai* 大訓生民，師範百王，儀軌千載)—is surely dependent on the ability of its rites to involve the public at large. Otherwise, Confucius temples and the cultural values they represent would fade into meaningless formalities even in the societies where Confucianism managed to still exist.

An additional issue is that the institution of enshrinement (*congsi* 從祀) has become profoundly problematic in the modern social context of pluralism, in which Confucianism is not the dominant culture. In traditional China, the enshrinement of outstanding Confucians was the core of Confucian ritual institution. It had symbolically embodied the transmission and succession of the Way (*daotong* 道統) and had facilitated the recruitment of the best and brightest into the ranks of Confucian officials. Moreover, Confucianism runs against the grain of pluralistic modern societies that respect individual difference. Even if Confucianism pulls back from its absolute, universal claims and seeks only internal coherence and uniformity, its prospects for significant revival in a modern society remain unclear.[19]

In contrast to the pluralism and diversity of modern societies, the paramount concern in an imperial structure was to maintain order through the uniformity and integrity of an orthodoxy. Thus, the decision to enshrine a sage was a laborious and time-consuming process: an assembly of courtly

Confucian scholar-officials had to agree by consensus on the nomination of an individual candidate, and the emperor had to act in his capacity as the supreme political authority to approve the selection. As a result, it was quite common for the process to approve the enshrinement of a sage to span decades; moreover, the process could include the reigns of multiple emperors when an emperor deferred making a decision and passed the issue to his successor.

Can those living in a pluralistic modern society really assume that there is an authoritative voice to determine the nature of the transmission and succession of the Way, or to decide what the spirit of contemporary Confucianism is in today's world? Who could be invested with the power to nominate, approve, and change the list of Confucian sages worthy of enshrinement?

We also should be mindful that the institution of enshrinement has, in the past, been the vital mechanism that enabled Confucius temples to keep abreast of the recent advances or new directions in Confucian scholarship and philosophy. The last enshrinement of Confucian sages took place in the eighth year of the republic—that is, in 1919—when Yan Yuan 顏元 (1635–1704) and Li Gong 李塨 (1659–1733) became recognized sages. This enshrinement reflected the pragmatic and utilitarian bent that characterized the spirit of the epoch of the late nineteenth and early twentieth centuries. If we were to accept the enshrinement of Yan Yuan and Li Gong as the final judgment of Confucian history, we would essentially also be conceding that we had relegated Confucianism to an eternity that is as ossifying as it is everlasting. Confucianism would then become devoid of connection to the spirit of our own and future times, which are alive and ever changing.

Confucius advised, "Learning without thought is labor lost; thought without learning is perilous."[20] "Learning" and "thought" are the two strands of Confucianism, with Mencius and Xunzi 荀子 (c. 310–238 BCE) historically representative of the principal emphasis of each strand.

Since the Western Han dynasty, Xunzi and his school of Confucianism have been lauded for their vital role in providing continuity for the classics and for promoting the Dao; however, the ascendant Zhu Xi's 朱熹 (1130–1200) orthodox view of mind and philosophy of human nature had so eclipsed Xunzi by the mid-Ming dynasty that Xunzi was removed from his enshrined position in Confucius temples. From a modern perspective, Xunzi's disenshrinement was unfortunate, and the restoration of his veneration in Confucius temples would provide a representative or symbolic bridge to our own contemporary intellectual trends, because he was an arch representative of learning and scholarship. Thus, chapter 5 makes a case that restoring Xunzi's status in the Confucius temple might have a salutary effect on the vitality of Confucianism.

In theory, the enshrinement and the disenshrinement of notable Confucians resulted from the institutional intent to mirror the rise and fall of philosophies and approaches to learning within the Confucian intellectual mainstream. From the perspective of cultural structure, the institution of enshrinement best engendered the Confucian spirit of historical consciousness; furthermore, enshrinement played the role far beyond serving as a record of past deeds and thus kept Confucius temples from fading into history. In other words, the cessation of enshrinement as a functioning institution signaled the ritual death of Confucianism and symbolically ended Confucianism and its system of rites at Confucian temples as a living culture. As a result, Confucianism figuratively became like curated physical relics in historical museums. Metaphorically, Confucian thought became a passive object of archaeological inquiry—good for provoking philosophical musings about the past but irrelevant to modern life.

To paraphrase Shakespeare: To enshrine or not to enshrine? That is the question. The restoration of the institution of enshrinement is thus a fundamental issue, with implications for the cultural and spiritual well-being of the modern Chinese-speaking peoples. We are in need of a genuine movement for the "creative transformation" of Confucian culture.

Kong Qingrong 孔慶鎔 (1787–1841), the Duke of Yansheng 衍聖公 and the seventy-third patriarch of the Kong clan during the Qing dynasty, once wrote, "I guarded my mouth to avoid topics of the affairs of the world / With scarcely two or three persons to know my heart." It is hard to imagine that the author of such guarded, melancholy prose was the master of what was historically the first house of the empire and a man who had received almost every conceivable earthly honor in the China of the era. I do not propose reexamining the issue of Confucius temples to serve the Kong clan's interests but rather to confront the decline of traditional culture and its modern predicament.

Conclusion

Reflections on My Study of Confucianism as a Religion

> There is a story of a drunkard searching under a streetlamp for his house key, which he had dropped some distance away. Asked why he didn't look where he had dropped it, he replied, "It's lighter here!"
>
> —ABRAHAM KAPLAN, *CONDUCT OF INQUIRY*, 11

As my exploration of the Confucius temple concludes, this chapter furnishes a reflection on the approach and the conceptual presuppositions I used for undertaking this project. Gu Jiegang 顧頡剛 (1893–1980) reminisced, in the preface of his book *Debates on Ancient History* (*Gushi bian* 古史辨, 1926), "A friend visited my home once and saw on my desk books on Confucian temple rites and rituals. He said derisively, 'These are useless. They have nothing to do with human life and I cannot understand why earlier scholars prize them so.' I replied that I do not agree.¹ Although Gu did not explain the reasons for his disagreement, I would argue that he had good cause.

My own research on Confucianism took form after I encountered, by chance, the Qing dynasty text *A Study of Confucian Temple Rites and Rituals* (*Wenmiao sidian kao* 文廟祀典考),² which inspired me to deploy the concept of "Confucian holy ground" as an analytical tool to conceptualize Confucian temples. Taking a partly anthropologically informed approach, my research focused on believers' interactions with sacred space—an approach that differs from previous scholars' emphasis on religious doctrine and canonical texts. Generally, I found purely theoretical discussions tend to become ungrounded and detached from historical reality. For example, overtly religious content in the *Analects*—the Confucian canonical text—is, in the current view, quite thin when compared to the scriptures of other historical religions, such as the Bible for Christianity, the Koran for Islam, and the Vedas for Hinduism.

Unlike other major religions, which are defined by canonical texts and textually derived religious doctrines, Confucianism was unique in displaying its religious character primarily through the performance of ritual sacrifices and veneration. We will return to this point later. For the moment, it should suffice to note that in conventional scholarly discourse, there are just two major approaches to understanding religion, either by way of Émile Durkheim (1858–1917) or by way of Max Weber (1864–1920).[3] Both Durkheim and Weber were trendsetting scholars who wrote epochal texts in the field of religious studies, and meticulous and cogent methodology clearly informed their works.

Durkheim grasped the fact that from a methodological perspective, the then prevalent use of Christianity as a definitional archetype for the study of non-Western religions was a deeply flawed practice; therefore, he worked to correct this flaw in scholarly discourse. At the same time, he still insisted on clear definitional boundaries, which he not only considered foundational to religious studies but also practiced scrupulously during his study of the religion of Australian aborigines.[4] The absence of clear definitional boundaries, Durkheim warned, would inevitably lead to the failure to delineate the proper object of inquiry and thus would threaten to invalidate the analysis. William James (1842–1910), a scholar of the psychology of religion, had earlier expressed his dissatisfaction with the inflexibility of the definitional approach to religious studies when he argued, "The word 'religion' cannot stand for any single principle or essence, but is rather a collective name." However, in terms of practical research strategy, James did not essentially differ from the Durkheimian approach.[5]

In contrast, Max Weber's approach was substantively different from Durkheim's. Weber did not believe the definition of religion could be determined at the beginning of an inquiry; instead, Weber proposed that religion only becomes definable at the conclusion of one's research. Furthermore, Weber recommended that the scholars of religion should not be concerned with questions of essentialism. Instead, the important task for scholars is to shed light on, or to enhance understanding of, the conditions and effects of social behavior—a concern that obviously speaks to his interest in the meaning of religious behavior on the individual level. For Weber, the most foundational of religiously inspired behavioral patterns are those that influence action in "this world."[6]

It follows that Weber's methodology informed his approach to "definitions" as a theoretical concept. He asserted, "Methodology can only bring us reflective understanding of the means which have demonstrated their value in practice by raising them to the level of explicit consciousness; it is no more the precondition of fruitful intellectual work than the knowledge of anatomy is for 'correct' walking."[7] Although the act of giving definition to a problem is an initial step in any research method, Weber claimed that it is in solving substantial problems, not in reflecting on epistemology or methodology, that a science is established and improved. Therefore, Weber preferred the historical approach in his academic work, and his methodological strategy was characterized by improvisation and flexibility.[8] Like Weber, modern anthropologists are inclined to reject "universality" as a definitional qualification for religions, because they recognize that the conceptual elements of "universal religion," as well as the relationship thereof, are historically idiosyncratic. Indeed, the defining of "universal religion" itself is a discursive and historical construct.[9]

Durkheim's and Weber's strategies each possess its own advantages, but my own approach most closely resembles Weber's. The major conceptual inspiration of my method, however, is the later Ludwig Wittgenstein (1889–1951).[10] Wittgenstein's replacement of philosophical essentialism with "family resemblances" allows me to overcome the conceptual obstacle of the definitional approach and the futile controversies that it spawned. Moreover, this insight enabled me to direct my energies to what really was problematic: the religious characteristics of Confucianism.

Wittgenstein's concept of family resemblances is similar in spirit to Friedrich Nietzsche's (1844–1900) concept of genealogy.[11] Furthermore, Nietzsche repeatedly argued that history's convoluted passage through time and place revealed that ahistorical definitions were nonsensical; moreover, he even proclaimed, "Only that which has no history is definable."[12] In this frame of analysis, religion is itself a culturally constructed category in history. Although idealists armed with philological tricks had exhausted the potential of the word "religion" during the nineteenth century,[13] the game of definitions in China was still quite new in the early twentieth century and thus not yet spoiled.

Both the Chinese proponents and opponents of Confucianism as a religion have sidestepped the challenge of identifying Confucianism's true historical origins. Instead, both sides engaged in a mining operation in the vastness of canonical texts to furnish "proofs" they needed to bolster their own claims about history. Above all, the proponents and opponents shared a predilection for appropriating Confucian classics and imposing their subjective interpretation on the canon to prove their arguments. (A more charitable characterization would be "creative appropriation.") Players on both sides frequently resorted to philological exercises and the exegesis of texts. For example, Chen Huanzhang 陳煥章 (1880–1933) made a case for Confucianism as a religion, that is, a Confucius cult (*Kongjiao* 孔教), by quoting the phrase from the classic *Doctrine of the Mean*: "Cultivating the Way is called *jiao*" (*xiu Dao zhiwei jiao* 修道之謂教). However, Chen Duxiu 陳獨秀 (1879–1942) countered that "*jiao*" in this context refers to "education" or "teachings" rather than religion, while Cai Yuanpei 蔡元培 (1867–1940) even made the argument that *Kongjiao* was never meant to be read as a noun.[14] This controversy over the proper definition of words yields only one insight: philology and semantics cannot resolve ideological conflicts.

In fact, the argument over canon and definition was only superficial and disguised the subtext that both sides of the debate had aped the definitional approach, which naturalized Christianity as the archetype of all religions. In other words, Chinese intellectuals were measuring Confucianism against the backdrop of Christianity. The most crucial difference from how Western scholars had employed Christianity as the measure for characterizing other religions was due to Chinese intellectuals' commonly shared immersion in the "apply and use" (*zhiyong* 致用) tradition of pragmatic statecraft. Thus, these Chinese valuations of Confucianism arose from their mediated understanding of Western historiography, and Christianity was a hotly contested topic among them. Therefore, Kang Youwei 康有為 (1858–1927) believed that Euro-American hegemony over the world could be attributed not only to political and matériel superiority but also to the superior discipline that Christianity provided in society. In contrast, Liang Qichao 梁啟超 (1873–1929), Chen Duxiu, and other like-minded intellectuals believed that Christianity was reactionary and anachronistic to modern civilization and thus needed to be abolished in the name of progress.[15]

Liang Qichao used quotations from the *Analects* of Confucius to define Confucius as "a scholar of philosophy, statecraft, and pedagogy" but not "a religionist."[16] In the *Analects,* Confucius said, "If you are not able to serve men, how can you serve their spirits?" and "If you do not know life, how can you understand death?" He also noted, "The master never discussed extraordinary things, feats of strength, disorder, and spiritual beings."[17] Liang Qichao's argument became the standard text for those who would deny that Confucianism was a religion, properly defined. Liang also said, "Westerners often compare Confucius with Socrates, but rarely do they compare him to the Buddha, Jesus, or Muhammad; they are quite right."[18]

Liang Qichao and his followers' portrayal of Confucius evidenced the transformation of the cultural image of Confucius that was occurring during the early twentieth century, a phenomenon that Kang Youwei, who had been Liang Qichao's teacher, observed with disgust: "Recently, some people mistakenly claimed Confucius was a philosopher, a statesman, an educator. Because of this wrong assertion, China misses the chance to claim a religious founder."[19] Later events would establish that Liang's side, not Kang's, was the victor in this conflict over the legacy of Confucius.[20] Indeed, Liang's surely unintentional activation of the secularization of Confucianism was to reverberate down through the ages and resulted in the establishment of the dominant discourse that Confucianism is not a religion, an idea that is still widely accepted by the overwhelming majority of the global community of the Chinese-speaking people.

During the late Qing dynasty and the early republic, three major factors led to the formation of the mainstream consensus that denied the religious character of Confucianism. First, Chinese intellectuals followed the definitional approach, and deployed Christianity as an archetype that provided standards against which Confucianism was evaluated. It is necessary here to note that this evaluation is ahistorical, since Christianity has taken on many different forms throughout its history.[21] Furthermore, intellectuals during the late Qing and early republic perceived only the most recent forms of Christianity in their time, that is, merely the latest incarnations mediated through its missionaries to China. Despite the rising tide of the "social gospel" during this period, almost every confession and sect within the Christian faith dedicated itself to the salvation of the soul, which is the characteristic of a private, personal religion. Therefore, Christianity during the same period bore more than a passing resemblance to Buddhism and Daoism, which also had an emphasis on individual happiness. All of these made a sharp contrast to Confucianism, which in imperial China functioned as a public or collective state religion. This explains why Chinese intellectuals took the classification of Buddhism and Daoism as religions for granted but repeatedly debated Confucianism's definitive status as a religion.

The second factor was that Chinese intellectuals during the late Qing and early republic were trapped in controversies over philosophical and textual "doctrines" but ignored the religious function and role of Confucianism in imperial China's social and political system.[22] A prime example of this blind spot is Liang Qichao's argument against Confucianism's classification as a religion, which relied on textual exegesis of the *Analects*. In fact, the interpretation of texts and debates over quasi-doctrinal verities were predominantly indulged in by elites but were of little concern to the masses, for whom efficacy and miracles were far more important in informing their religious practice.[23]

Finally, yet importantly, the issue of normative values also colored the debate over Confucianism's religious characteristics during the late nineteenth and early twentieth centuries. Specifically, the word "religion" had taken on a distinctively negative meaning (that of superstition) to intellectuals of the age, and Confucianism's proponents often wished to distance Confucianism from the taint of religion, or to reform it by purging it of religious trappings.

Fortunately, my research on the history of Confucian temple rites has uncovered phenomena and characteristics of Confucianism that were distinctly and uniquely religious. I hope that readers will have a clearer perception of the historical truths of the Confucian religion, which the passage of time has obscured.

The most straightforward method to reveal Confucianism's religious characteristics was not to engage in further theoretical disputes but to listen to the voices of the ancient people in traditional Chinese society. For example, in his collected *Stories Old and New* (*Gujin xiaoshuo* 古今小說), Feng Menglong 馮夢龍 (1574–1646) vividly described Confucianism as one of the "Three Religions" of China, and compared them in this way:

> Since the ending of the primordial chaos, there were the Three Religions: Taishang Laojun 太上老君 founded Daoism, the Buddha founded Buddhism, and Confucius founded Confucianism. Confucianism yields sages, Buddhism yields bodhisattvas, and Daoism yields immortals. Among the three, Confucianism is the most commonplace and Buddhism is the most austere; however, Daoist teachings promise immortality and infinite powers of change, which makes it the most liberating.[24]

Even though the author was obviously partial to Daoism, it is more relevant that he designated Confucian sages (and worthies) (*shengxian* 聖賢) as religious exemplars that were fully comparable to bodhisattvas (*Fo pusa* 佛菩薩) in Buddhism and "immortals" in Daoism. All these revered figures were enshrined and venerated. However, Confucian sages and worthies were additionally distinguished by the sophisticated system through which the imperial Chinese state selected them. Furthermore, the internal hierarchy of the ranks bestowed on them were uniformly observed throughout the empire.[25]

Chen Huanzhang, an intellectual in the early republic, observed, "Every proper religion has its churches. . . . Since we use the word 'churches' to refer to Buddhist monasteries, Daoist temples, Islamic mosques, and Evangelical halls, we cannot single out the temple halls of Confucius and refuse to call them churches." He concluded, "The church of the Confucius cult is in its schools, which some call temples of culture (*wenmiao* 文廟) yet others call the sage's temples (*sheng miao* 聖廟) or palaces of learning (*xue gong* 學宮)."[26] Chen was referring to the traditional "temple schools," which were symbiotic entities that conjoined Confucius temples with the National University. These "Confucius temples" were the temples of the Confucian cult and the sacred sites of the Confucian religion.[27]

For centuries prior to Chen Huanzhang's writings, Confucian literati made similar remarks about Confucius temples. For example, *Record of the Rebuilding of a Qingzhen Temple* 重建清真寺記, written in 1489, during the Ming dynasty, clearly expressed this view:

> In my humble opinion, each of the Three Religions glorifies its founding master by establishing halls and shrines. Confucians have Dacheng halls 大成殿 to glorify Master Confucius; Buddhists have Shengrong halls 聖容殿 to glorify Sakyamuni Buddha, while Daoists have Yuhuang halls 玉皇殿 to glorify their Three Pure Ones. In Qingzhen 清真 temples, Yisileye halls 一賜樂業殿 are erected to honor God.[28]

We should note that the Qingzhen temples 清真寺 referred to in the original Chinese is not an Islamic mosque, as in modern usage, but rather refers to a Judaic synagogue.[29] From this passage, it is clear that Confucian temples—regardless of their many differences from the temples of the other religions to which they were compared—was the holy ground of its religion and were considered a functional equivalent, in that respect, to other religious temples.

In fact, many in China considered Confucianism to be a religion fully comparable even to Christianity and Islam. Möngke Khan (Yuan emperor Xianzong 元憲宗, r. 1251–1259), remarked, in a dialogue with a Daoist priest, "Now, the *xiansheng* 先生 insists that Daoism faith is the highest, but the *xiucai* 秀才 all say the Confucian faith is foremost; the Diexie 迭屑 worship Mishihe 彌失訶 and say they will go to heaven; the *Dashimans* 達失蠻 worship and give thanks to heaven for its blessings. After giving this careful thought, we found none worthy to be compared with the Buddha."[30]

To explain a few intricacies of the text, *xiansheng* (elder) was an honorific for Daoist priests; *xiucai* (scholar) was of course a reference to Confucian scholars; Diexie and Mishihe 彌失訶 were phonetic transliterations in Chinese for Christians and Jesus Christ; and *dashiman* was the Yuan dynasty term for mullahs.[31] Here, Möngke Khan declares his higher evaluation of Buddhism, but it does not distract from the parallels in the comparison of Confucianism to other religions.

This understanding of the religious character of Confucianism did not change appreciably even in the first half of the nineteenth century, when a literatus identified with the self-styled name Fu Qiu Shi 浮邱士 (also known as Tang Peng 湯鵬, 1800–1844) wrote:

> This one was the only religion in [the golden age of] the Three Dynasties [*sandai* 三代, or the early reigns of the Xia, Shang, and Zhou dynasties]. After the Zhou and Qin periods, there were three religions. However, later and down to the present, we have five religions. The "one religion" is Confucianism; the so-called Three Religions are Daoism and Buddhism in addition to Confucianism. The so-called Five Religions add Christianity and Islam, beyond the Three Religions.[32]

It is thus apparent that literati in imperial China considered Confucianism as an institution or entity to be equivalent to other established and venerable religions—a perception that remained unchanged until almost the end of the Qing dynasty.

My examination of extant sources shows that to the worshippers partaking in Confucian rites, Confucianism was indeed a religion. These sources encompassed surviving stele inscriptions, local histories, and collected private writings, including *Records of Academies and Temple Schools* (*Xue ji* 學記), *Dedication to Temple Schools* (*Miaoxue ji* 廟學記), and *Dedication to the Veneration of Confucius* (*ji Kong wen* 祭孔文), or even local bureaucrats' routine records, such as "Report to Confucius, the Sage" (*gao xiansheng wen* 告先聖文) and "Report to Confucius, the Master" (*gao xianshi wen* 告先師文). The countless number of such texts reveals Confucianism's characteristics as a public religion, more commonly called a state religion.[33] Hence, comparisons with the standards of private religions have missed the point, even though these standards are certainly far more familiar to modern men and women.

There exists representative evidence from several texts to support my assertion that Confucianism in imperial China was a state religion that expressed its religious characteristics in the ritual system for Confucius temples. As their name implies, Confucius temples were sites that housed enshrined Confucian exemplars and served as the sacred ground of the religion and the embodiment of its "transmission and succession of the Way" (*Daotung* 道統).

In 1684, the Kangxi 康熙 emperor Qing Shengzu 清聖祖 (r. 1661–1722) came to pay his respects at the Confucius temple in Qufu and dedicated a hagiographical plaque to adorn the main Dacheng hall: "The exemplar of teachers for ten thousand generations" (*wanshi shi biao* 萬世師表).[34] The subtext of these words is that it was always the rulers and the scholar-officials who worshipped at Confucius temples.

The class composition of the members of the Confucian religion was the result of its development within imperial China and its political culture. Specifically, during the Western Han dynasty, Confucius evolved from a learned man to the prophetic lawgiving figure of the Han political regime. The *Kongmiao zhi shoumiao baidan Kong He bei* 孔廟置守廟百石孔龢碑, dated to 153 and the earliest extant inscription about Confucius, bore witness to this transformation. It read, "Confucius is the great sage, who, in imitation of heaven and earth [*Qian Kun* 乾坤], set the pattern or rules for the Han reign." Soon thereafter, in 156, the *Luxiang Han Chi zao Kongmiao liqi bei* 魯相韓勑造孔廟禮器碑 stele inscription read, "Confucius is the sage close to our era and paved the Way for our Han reign." Another stele inscription, *Luxiang Shi Chen ci Kongmiao zouming* 魯相史晨祠孔廟奏銘, dated to the year 169, echoed the same proclamation.[35]

Such inscribed attributions of the Han political system to Confucius implied that he was at least a prophetic being, having effected the institutions of a Han Empire that was founded hundreds of years after he passed from this world. Following the demise of the Han Empire, successive dynasties replicated such laudatory precedents, and the veneration of Confucius became a symbol of theocratic continuity that conveyed legitimacy by heaven's mandate (*tianming* 天命) and tradition. For example, in preparation for his inauguration, Emperor Wen of Wei 魏文帝 (r. 220–226) traveled to the residence of the descendants of the Kong clan to request that they perform the ritual veneration of Confucius. Moreover, this emperor declared in an edict, "Confucius is certainly a great sage, and a model for ten thousand years to come."[36]

Employing similar rhetoric, Temür Khan, as Emperor Chengzong of Yuan 元成宗 (r. 1294–1307), also asserted that since Confucius was traditionally regarded as a paradigm for all rulers, Confucius was able to extend humaneness to the whole world.[37] That naturally gave rise to the established precedent, "Whoever rules the state should venerate and make sacrifice to him."[38] Yuan dynasty literati Cao Yuanyong's 曹元用 (1268–1330) insightful comment on the veneration of Confucius by Chinese rulers grasped this point very well: "The teaching of Confucius depends on the statecraft of the rulers to reach far; on the other hand, the statecraft of the rulers cannot improve the world without Confucius's teachings. When Confucius's teachings are not widespread, his Way is not diminished, but when statecraft fails to improve the world, the state is imperiled."[39]

Cao's assertion that "when Confucius's teachings are not widespread, his Way is not diminished" is a biased comment from a Confucian scholar, but it is more important to note that he had accurately observed the mutual dependence between Confucius veneration as an institution, on the one hand, and the power of rulers, on the other hand.

Zhu Yuanzhang 朱元璋 (Ming Taizu 明太祖, r. 1368–1398), the founding emperor of the Ming dynasty, made a similar point in conversation with descendants of Confucius. With characteristic bluntness, he roared, "Your ancestor provided the legacy of the Three Bonds and Five Relationships and passed down the good moral example of statutes for myriad generations; however, your family [now] doesn't read books and doesn't preserve the moral example of your ancestors."[40] The Yongzheng 雍正 Emperor (r. 1722–1735) of the Qing dynasty acknowledged, in an edict in 1727, "Confucius's teachings clarify human relationships, distinguish personal status, rectify the hearts of the people, make social customs proper, because they also know that when human relationships are clear, when personal status is distinguished, when people's hearts are rectified, and social customs are made proper, those who benefit the most are the rulers above."[41] Indeed, Yongzheng's statement that "those who benefit the most are the rulers above" illustrates just how crucial the veneration of Confucius was to rulers.

In fact, the Chinese ruling class had a nearly continuous tradition of making such prayers to Confucius as "Protect the state's lineage and comfort the life of the people" and "Your cultural teachings are promoted clearly, and the whole country receives blessings."[42] The Yongle 永樂 Emperor (Ming Chengzu 成祖, r. 1402–1424) wrote, in one prayer, "Grant us great worthies from the literati in every generation to help our great Ming dynasty to last ten thousand years."[43] Similarly, when Külüg Khan (Yuan emperor Wuzong 元武宗, r. 1307–1311) bestowed the posthumous honorific Dacheng Zhisheng Wenxuanwang 大成至聖文宣王 on Confucius, the Yuan emperor added the prayer "Please employ your spirit powers to bless our reign."[44] The prayers of emperors showed that Confucianism possessed the religious characters of a public, state religion, a fact that modern scholars too often ignore.

Confucianism's status as a public religion of the state meant the veneration of Confucius was not a private matter of Confucius's descendants. As Ming emperor Wuzong 明武宗 (r. 1505–1521) wrote, in his imperial missive to the Kong clan, "This is an auspicious affair of our state and not the sole honor of your clan."[45] Actually, the veneration of Confucius was a glorious event not only for the Kong clan but also for the entire class of Confucian scholar-officials. As an official appointed by the imperial court proclaimed, "Glory covers not just the sons and grandsons of the Kong surname but all men under heaven who wore Confucian robes."[46]

We should acknowledge that not all emperors honored Confucian temple rites. In fact, emperors who wanted to consolidate their rule, especially those wishing to suppress the factions of Confucian scholar-officials, frequently targeted Confucius temples and the rites for destruction. For example, Emperor Ming Taizu once promulgated the abolition of the sacrifices to Confucius throughout the empire, and the Jiajing 嘉靖 Emperor (Shizong 明世宗, r. 1521–1566) orchestrated a wave of iconoclasm and the abrogation of temple rites.

Yet those attempts ultimately failed to eliminate the Confucian class's regard for Confucius temples as the holy ground of their religion. For educated men and scholar-officials, pilgrimages to the Confucius temples, particularly the one near Qufu, was an event of extraordinary spiritual significance. Upon the completion of a pilgrimage, for instance, a scholar in the era of the Chongzhen 崇禎 emperor Ming Sizong 明思宗 (r. 1627–1644) wrote, "I am lucky enough to fulfill my lifelong wish to visit this sacred ground."[47] When the celebrated master Zhu Xi 朱熹 (1130–1200) served in a local administrator's post, he dedicated prayers to Confucius on each major event of his career there. These included "Reporting to Confucius" (*gao xiansheng wen* 告先聖文), upon assuming an office; "On Paying a Visit to Confucius" (*ye xiansheng wen* 謁先聖文), upon receiving a new appointment; and "Reporting to Confucius on the Discharge of Local Service" (*ci xiansheng wen* 辭先聖文), about his resignation, which informed both Confucius's spirit and fellow Confucian scholar-officials that he had discharged his duty.[48]

In Confucianism, the performance of the veneration of Confucius made collective appeals to "declare the civilized rule of a dynasty"[49] rather than focusing on personal welfare, a difference acknowledged by the traditional taxonomy of the Three Religions. Confucianism was meant to "govern the world," while Buddhism and Daoism were consigned to the personal goals of "cultivating the mind" and "nurturing life."[50] Corresponding to its function, Confucian temple rites were restricted to officials and Confucian scholars. Well into the late Qing dynasty, we find a contemporary making the remark that Confucian temples were "quite unlike ordinary temples and halls that permit entrance to anyone who wanted to visit and sight-see."[51]

In terms of the social composition of the Confucius religion's membership, among the traditional four-tier class system of literati scholar-officials (*shi* 士), farmers, artisans, and merchants, only those hailing from the *shi* class had the right to participate in the rites or to worship at Confucius temples, which made the religion highly exclusive and monopolistic. It is not surprising that commoners typically felt alienated from the state religion. As a middle Qing specialist on ritual propriety (*li* 禮), Qin Huitian 秦蕙田 (1702–1764), aptly described it, commoners' feelings toward Confucius were "respect without intimacy."[52]

Another scholar of the late Qing, Yan Fu 嚴復 (1854–1921), wrote that in all his years, he had "never seen one [member of the common classes] make an appeal to Confucius." Moreover, Yan Fu added, "The women and children of China today know all about heaven, Naraka [hell], bodhisattvas, and Yama [the god of death]. But if asked who [Confucius's most famous disciples] Yan Hui 顏回, Zilu 子路, Ziyu 子游 or Zizhang 子張 were, they would say that they do not know." Every Chinese village, no matter how small or remote, had a Buddhist monastery or nunnery that on holy days could summon worshippers, who came reverently crawling on all fours; yet Yan wrote that he had never seen even one villager worship Confucius.[53]

Even Kang Youwei, who made it his life's mission to protect Confucian orthodoxy, professed, "As for our Confucianism, only the officials are involved in burning incense to Confucius on the first and the fifteenth days of a month. On the other hand, students and commoners pay tribute to all gods except Confucius."[54] Without a doubt, those remarks were based on the reality of traditional Chinese religious phenomena that these writers had personally observed.

Similarly, Feng Youlan 馮友蘭 (1895–1990) wrote, in the preface to his memoir *Sansongtang zixu* 三松堂自序:

> A joke: The martial temple to Guan Yu 關羽 and the temple to the Money God 財神 burn a lot of incense, but the Confucius temple had no visitors. Confucius was unhappy. Therefore, a smart man asked Confucius, "Do you have Guan Yu's glaive [a large bladed weapon fixed upon a pole]?" Confucius answered, "No." [The man] then asked, "Do you have the Money God's money?" Confucius replied, "Not that, either." The man then said, "You have neither Guan Yu's glaive nor the Money God's money, so of course they don't care about you, and there is no reason for you to complain about it!"

Feng added a comment to the story: "Though told as a joke, this story is a reflection of social realities."[55]

A popular saying further underscored this point: "There was scant worship at the temple of Confucius, and there wasn't much that could be done about that." However, Zitong temples 梓潼廟 and Wenchang temples 文昌廟 enjoyed great popularity—even among literati and students—that far exceeded the popularity of Confucius temples. This gap in popularity, even among the literati, is startling because these folk temples were under the rubric of temples of culture (*wen*), just as Confucius temples were. As a seventeenth-century classical scholar observed, there were no literati who did not burn incense to Zitong.[56]

This phenomenal disparity in popularity among literati is even more remarkable because in imperial China the Confucian classics and other Confucian texts were the basis for the civil service examinations for obtaining official rank and positions. Yet it was to either Wenchang or Kuixing 魁星—not Confucius—that an aspiring examination candidate would most frequently pray for divine blessing during the exams. This apparently bizarre contradiction showed the vast emotional distance between mortal men and Confucius, which still exists in shrunken form in modern-day Taiwan. Every year, students about to take the state's educational tests, as well as candidates about to take the civil service examination, still pray with considerable fervor at Taipei's Wenchang temple, which routinely sells out its annual supply of seven thousand wish lamps. Scarcely any students or civil service candidates visit the holy ground of the same city's Confucius temple.

A Christian evangelist, Liang Fa 梁發 (1789–1855), confirmed these observations when he noted, on the eve of the Taiping Rebellion:

> The reason Confucian [students] erect statues of Wenchang and Kuixing as spirits and pay their respects is their desire to ask for blessings to enhance their wisdom and advance their abilities in order to pass the official examinations. However, Chinese people are mostly engaged in the study of Confucian books but still feel compelled to set up these two statues and worship them. Everyone seeks blessings for passing the provincial exams and then the palace examination, in order to win appointment as Hanlin scholars and become an official to govern the people.[57]

Liang Qichao spoke of the situation at the imperial academies in the late Qing dynasty in similar terms: "In our Yue 粵 [Guangdong province], Wenchang and Kuixing enjoyed sacrificial offerings; in contrast, people rarely worship Confucius. Continuing his lamentations, Liang Qichao noted that people even failed to remember Confucius's birthday—even though celebrations of birthdates of deities were especially marked at their temples. Liang observed, "Upon entering school, a pupil immediately learns to venerate Wenchang and Kuixing as gods; however, regarding the most sanctified founder of our religion, the fire of his legacy has all but burned out, his sacrificial vessels almost empty, his dates of birth and death scarcely known by anyone."[58]

In fact, over most of the centuries in imperial China, the vast majority of people—even officials—did not actually celebrate Confucius's birthday. His birthday became an official holy day only in 1721; moreover, it was a non-Han Chinese ruler, the Yongzheng Emperor of the Manchu Qing dynasty, who bestowed that honor on Confucius.[59] Furthermore, that Qing emperor's immediate successor, the Qianlong 乾隆 Emperor (r. 1735–1795), soon overruled this edict, declaring, "The legends about Confucius's birthday are taken from Buddhist and Daoist sources, but there is no record in the Confucian classics. Therefore, it [the birthday celebration rites] should be abolished."[60] In terms of popularity, the day of Confucius's birth did not come close to competing with those of either the Buddha or Laozi. Celebration of Confucius's birthday was not even competitive when compared to the birthday festivals for folk deities such as Goddess of Mercy Guan Yin 觀音, Lord Guan (Yu) 關帝, Lu Ban 魯班, or Luo Zu 羅祖.

Folk temples, such as Wenchang temples and Zitong temples, welcomed all worshippers, regardless of class background, putting into sharp relief the active exclusion of the masses from Confucius temples.[61] The fact that Confucianism was a state religion likely accounted for this disparity in inclusivity. The state both institutionalized and regulated the rites of the Confucian religion, whereas the worship and rites of Wenchang and Zitong naturally expressed organic folk beliefs and had characteristics of private, personal religions.

In addition, shifting attitudes in the modern age encouraged intellectuals to intentionally overlook the religious characteristics of Confucianism and its temple rites. Since the late Qing dynasty, Confucians who were interested in furthering the philosophical development of Confucianism emphasized humaneness and benevolence (*ren* 仁) at the expense of rituals and propriety (*li* 禮), and one of their motives was to protect Confucianism from increasingly common attacks on ritual decorum. This development found its most classic and emblematic expression in the work titled *Renxue* 仁學, *The Learning of* Ren (humaneness), by Tan Sitong 譚嗣同 (1865–1898).[62] As for the self-styled New Confucian movement in the period of the republic, all three generations of its adherents followed the original mold of emphasizing theoretical discussions about humaneness, and for such reasons, *Renxue* remained the theoretical centerpiece around which modern Confucian thought revolved.

After the Qing dynasty fell in the 1911 revolution, imperial China's institutions also collapsed, one by one, including the Confucian system and teachings of rituals (*lijiao*) that had always been the pillar of traditional society but that came under comprehensive and acrimonious attack by Chinese intellectuals after the revolution. Liang Shuming 梁漱溟 (1893–1988) wrote, "Ritual propriety (*li* 禮) and music (*yue* 樂) were the only important activities of Confucianism; if rituals and music die, then Confucianism ceases to be."[63]

Therefore, the modern New Confucian paradigm that emphasizes the transcendent metaphysics of humaneness (*ren*) could be seen as a compensatory mechanism that arose in reaction to the demise of ritual propriety (*li*), which had been written off as a total loss in the realm of physical reality. Yet this New Confucian preoccupation with the subtle spark of humaneness at the expense of gentleness of ritual decorum is deeply problematic. It seems New Confucians essentially forgot Confucius's teaching, which declared, "To subdue one's self and return to propriety is perfect virtue [humaneness]. If a man can for one day subdue himself and return to propriety, all under heaven will ascribe perfect virtue to him" (*Analects* 12:1).[64] Preserving the metaphysics of humaneness but abandoning the practices of ritual decorum runs the risk of reducing Confucianism to a disembodied spirit, an incorporeal wandering ghost that has no connection or relevance to the real world. From this perspective, the New Confucians' single-minded preoccupation with abstractions, such as "religious characteristics" and "spirituality," at the expense of ritual and practice—a quintessentially Western fixation[65]—raise troubling questions about the viability of their project.

Philosopher Herbert Fingarette (1921–2018), who relocated ritual to the heart of primitive Confucianism in *Confucius: The Secular as Sacred*, a book published in 1972, was among the few scholars who have gone against the grain of conventional wisdom. Fingarette argued that Chinese and Western scholars of Confucianism have allowed the influence of Western philosophical idealism to distort their reading of the *Analects* and have unduly exaggerated the role of inner subjectivity in the text. Influenced by John Langshaw Austin's (1911–1960) theory of performative utterance, Fingarette emphasized that the meaning of the term "humaneness" (*ren*) was found in active expression, and he set out to prove that humaneness and ritual comprised the two aspects of a coherent totality; when separated from ritual, humaneness would be a signifier without a referent.[66] Setting aside questions about the degree of Fingarette's theoretical correctness, we may at least safely credit him with bringing some balance to Confucian studies that have long been decidedly biased in favor of humaneness. Fingarette's work led to great debates among Western sinologists, but it was virtually unknown in East Asia.

At the same time, Fingarette had theoretical differences with New Confucians. He criticized their limiting of the scope of inquiry to canonical texts and their ignoring of the actual ritual practices of historical Confucian traditionalists. These actual ritual practices, of course, included rites of Confucius temples; moreover, these rites were important on an institutional level as well as on the level of subjective emotions felt by individual worshippers. From this perspective, exploring the ritual role of Confucius temples in Confucian religion is an urgent task. This is especially true because Confucius temples—historically at the heart of Confucian rites—have, since the early republic, suffered so much damage and defamation that their religious significance became obscure.

Overall, if there has been any special method to my research into Confucianism, it is the approach—inspired by Wittgenstein—to liberate researchers from definitional questions about religion.[67] This methodological turn falls into the category of removing conceptual obstacles—a task that is mostly destructive of existing paradigms. The more creative aspect of my work would be my treatment of the Confucius temple as sacred ground, which provides a new framework to explore the religious characteristics of Confucianism. My work not only adjusts the focus of scholarly inquiry to view spatial practices but also brackets controversies over interpretations of canonical texts. It is my profound hope that my work may serve scholars as a key that will provide enhanced access to explore unsolved mysteries about Confucianism as a religion.

Notes

Preface

1. Mircea Eliade, *The Sacred and the Profane: The Nature of Religion*, trans. Willard R. Trask (New York: Harcourt Brace Jovanovich, 1959).
2. "Zhang Daoling qi shi Zhao Sheng" 張道陵七試趙昇, in *Gujin xiaoshuo* 古今小說, ed. Feng Menglong, in *Guben xiaoshuo congkan* 古本小說叢刊 (Beijing: Zhonghua, 1990), vol. 31.1–4, *juan* 13, 1a (553).
3. Xu Ke 徐珂, "Qing Huihuijiao" 青回回教, in *Qing bai leichao* 清稗類鈔 [Qing Petty Matters Anthology] (Taipei: Commercial Press, 1966), *juan* 15, 40. *Qingzhen* here refers to Judaism, rather than to Islam (as the term does today). See Chen Yuan 陳垣, "Kaifeng yisileyejiao kao" 開封一賜樂業教考, in *Chen Yuan shixue lunzhu xuan* 陳垣史學論著選, ed. Wu Ze 吳澤 (Shanghai: Shanghai Renmin chubanshe, 1981), 77. Three Pure Ones (*san qing* 三清), or three founding masters, are Yuanshi *tianzun* 元始天尊, Lingbao *tianzun* 靈寶天尊, and Daode *tianzun* 道德天尊.
4. For example, see *On Sacred Grounds: Culture, Society, Politics, and the Formation of the Cult of Confucius*, ed. Thomas A. Wilson (Cambridge, Mass.: Harvard University Press, 2002).

Introduction

This introduction is based on talks given at Yale, Princeton, and the University of Chicago. I would like to thank all the appreciative audiences. My thanks particularly extend to professors Kang-i Sun Chang, Frederick Mote, Susan Naquin, Willard Peterson, Prasenjit Duara, Denis Twitchett, and Ying-shih Yü for their comments and encouragement. The original version was published as "The Confucius Temple as a Ritual System: Manifestations of Power, Belief, and Legitimacy in Traditional China," in *Tsing Hua Journal of Chinese Studies* 25, no. 2 (1995): 115–136.

1. Chen Duxiu 陳獨秀, *Chen Duxiu xuanji* 陳獨秀選集 (Tianjin: Tianjin Renmin chubanshe, 1990), 43–46.
2. The term "Confucius temple" is an English translation of *Kongzi miao* 孔子廟, *Kong miao* 孔廟, *Xuanni miao* 宣尼廟, and *Wen miao* 文廟. The first two terms have been used from ancient times to the present. *Xuanni miao* was most often used in the Northern and Southern dynasties between the Han and Tang eras. The term *Wen miao* began during the mid-Tang, in contrast to the newly established martial temple (*Wu miao* 武廟). See also Huang Chin-shing, *Entering the Master's Sanctuary: Power, Belief and Legitimacy in Traditional China* 優入聖域：權力、信仰與正當性 (Taipei: Asian Culture Press, 1994).
3. My description here is rather different from the conventional accounts offered by Kong Chuan 孔傳 of the Southern Song. See Kong Chuan, *Dongjia zaji* 東家雜記, in *Jingyin Wenyuange sikuquanshu* 景印文淵閣四庫全書 (Taipei: Commercial Press, 1983–1986), vol. 446, *juan* 1, 6b. For a detailed analysis, see Huang Chin-shing, "Power and Belief: The Formation of a National Cult, the Worship of the Confucius Temple in Imperial China" 權力與信仰：孔廟祭祀制度的形成, *Continent Magazine* 大陸雜誌 86, no. 5 (May 1993): 8–34. This is also collected in Huang Chin-shing, *Entering the Master's Sanctuary* (Asian Culture Press), 164–216.
4. Sima Qian 司馬遷, *Shiji* 史記 (Beijing: Zhonghua, 1982), *juan* 47, 1945. See also Wang Su 王肅, ed., *Kongzi jiayu* 孔子家語, in *Jingyin Wenyuange sikuquanshu*, vol. 695, *juan* 9, 12a.
5. Sima Qian, *Shiji*, *juan* 47, 1945.
6. Han Fei 韓非, *Han Fei Zi jishi* 韓非子集釋, ed. Chen Qiyou 陳奇猷 (Taipei: Heluo tushu chubanshe, 1974), 1080; Lü Buwei 呂不韋, *Lüshi chunqiu jiaoshi* 呂氏春秋校釋, ed. Chen Qiyou 陳奇猷, *juan* 2, 96 (Taipei: Huazheng shuju, 1985).
7. Sima Qian, *Shiji*, *juan* 6, 258.
8. Sima Qian, *Shiji*, *juan* 97, 2692.
9. Kong Chuan, *Dongjia zaji*, *juan* 1, 33b; and Ban Gu 班固, *Hanshu* 漢書 (Taipei: Dingwen shuju, 1986), *juan* 81, 3352.
10. Ban Gu, *Hanshu*, *juan* 10, 328; Kong Zang 孔臧, *Lian cong zi* 連叢子, in *Jingyin Wenyuange sikuquanshu*, vol. 695, *juan* 1, 1a–1b.
11. Ban Gu, *Hanshu*, *juan* 67, 2925. Queli has been called Qufu 曲阜 since the Ming period, so modern scholars often simplify by referring only to Qufu.
12. Ban Gu, *Hanshu*, *juan* 12, 351.

13. Ban Gu, *Hanshu*, juan 99a, 4044–4045; Kong Zang, *Lian cong zi*, juan 1, 1a–1b.
14. Hong Gua 洪适, *Lishi lixu* 隸釋・隸續 (Beijing: Zhonghua, 1985), juan 1, 15a–15b.
15. Kong Yuan-cuo 孔元措, *Kongshi zuting guangji* 孔氏祖庭廣記, in *Congshu jicheng chubian* 叢書集成初編 (Shanghai: Commercial Press, 1936), vol. 3316–3317, 8; Chen Hao 陳鎬, *Queli zhi* 闕里誌 (Jinan: Shandong Friendship, 1989), juan 1, 7b–8a; Zhang Zuoyao 張作耀, *Dazai Kongzi* 大哉孔子 (Hong Kong: Peace, 1991), 21.
16. *Kongfu dang'an xuanbian* 孔府檔案選編 (Beijing: Zhonghua, 1982), juan 1, 17.
17. Li Dongyang 李東陽, *Ming huidian* 明會典, ed. Shen Shixing 申時行 (Beijing: Zhonghua, 1989), juan 91, 520.
18. Kong Jifen 孔繼汾, *Queli wenxian kao* 闕里文獻考 (Chengdou: Sichuan daxue chubanshe, 2005), juan 9, 6b.
19. Fan Ye 范曄, *Hou Hanshu* 後漢書 (Taipei: Dingwen shuju, 1983), juan 79a, 2563; Chen Shou 陳壽, *Sanguo zhi* 三國志 (Taipei: Dingwen shuju, 1983), juan 2, 77–88.
20. Cheng Minzheng 程敏政, *Huangdun wenji shiyi* 篁墩文集拾遺, in *Jingyin Wenyuange sikuquanshu*, vol. 1253, 1a–4b.
21. Kong Jifen, *Queli wenxian kao*, juan 5, 2b–3b.
22. Fan Ye, *Hou Hanshu*, 3108. Also see Huang Chin-shing, *Entering the Master's Sanctuary*, 203–210.
23. Chen Shou, *Sanguo zhi*, juan 4, 119–121.
24. Fang Xuanling 房玄齡, *Jinshu* 晉書 (Taipei: Dingwen shuju, 1987), juan 19, 599.
25. Liu Yuxi 劉禹錫, *Liu Yuxi ji* 劉禹錫集 (Shanghai: Shanghai Renmin chubanshe, 1975), juan 20, 184.
26. Chen Shou, *Sanguo zhi*, juan 2, 77–78.
27. Fang Xuanling, *Jinshu*, juan 14, 442.
28. Shen Yue 沈約, *Songshu* 宋書 (Taipei: Dingwen shuju, 1980), juan 14, 366.
29. Xu Song 許嵩, *Jiankang shilu* 健康實錄 (Beijing: Zhonghua, 1986), juan 9, 235.
30. Xiao Zixian 蕭子顯, *Nan Qishu* 南齊書 (Taipei: Dingwen shuju, 1980), juan 9, 143–144.
31. Xiao Zixian, *Nan Qishu*, juan 3, 56; Wei Shou 魏收, *Weishu* 魏書 (Taipei: Dingwen shuju, 1980), juan 7b, 165.
32. Linghu Defen 令狐德棻, *Zhoushu* 周書 (Taipei: Dingwen shuju, 1980), juan 7, 123; Liu Xu 劉昫, *Jiu Tangshu* 舊唐書 (Taipei: Dingwen shuju, 1981), juan 1, 9; juan 3, 48.
33. Pan Xiang 潘相, ed., *Qufu xianzhi* 曲阜縣志 (1774; repr., Taipei: Taiwan Xuesheng shuju, 1968), juan 21, 11b.
34. Ouyang Xiu 歐陽修 and Song Qi 宋祁, *Xin Tangshu* 新唐書 (Taipei: Dingwen shuju, 1981), juan 15, 373.

35. Ouyang Xiu 歐陽修, "Xiangzhou Guchengxian fuzimiao ji" 襄州穀城縣夫子廟記, in *Ouyang Xiu quanji* 歐陽修全集 (Taipei: Shijie shuju, 1961), 273; Ma Duanlin 馬端臨, *Wenxian tongkao* 文獻通考 (Shanghai: Commercial Press, 1936), in Wanyou wenku shitongben 萬有文庫十通本 (Beijing: Zhonghua, 1986), *juan* 43, *kao* 考 411.
36. Lü Yuanshan 呂元善, *Shengmen zhi* 聖門志, in *Congshu jicheng chubian*, vols. 3318–3321), *juan* 1b, 18.
37. Kong Jifen, *Queli wenxian kao, juan* 33, 296.
38. Shen Shixing, ed., *Ming huidian, juan* 91, 2090; Xiao Song 蕭嵩, *DaTang Kaiyuan li* 大唐開元禮, in *Jingyin Wenyuange sikuquanshu*, vol. 646, *juan* 53, 1a–2a; *juan* 54, 1a–1b; *juan* 69, 1a–2a.
39. Wei Liaoweng 魏了翁, *Heshan wenji* 鶴山文集, in *Jingyin Wenyuange sikuquanshu*, vols. 1172–1173, *juan* 45, 6a.
40. Xiong He 熊鉌, *Xiong Wuxuan xiansheng wenji* 熊勿軒先生文集 (Shanghai: Commercial Press, 1936), *juan* 4, 48.
41. Sun Chengze 孫承澤, *Chunmingmeng yulu* 春明夢餘錄 (Hong Kong: Longmen shuju, 1965), *juan* 21, 36b; Sun Chengze, *Tianfu guangji* 天府廣記 (Beijing: Tianjing chubanshe, 1962), *juan* 9, 89.
42. Qu Jiusi 瞿九思, *Kongmiao liyue kao* 孔廟禮樂考, *juan* 5, 45b. Published in the Wanli reign of the Ming dynasty.
43. See Huang Chin-shing, *Entering the Master's Sanctuary*, 222–228.
44. Fan Ye, *Hou Hanshu, juan* 2, 118. "Seventy-two" is a symbolic figure rather than seventy-two in number. See Wen Yiduo 聞一多, *Wen Yiduo quanji* 聞一多全集 (Beijing: SDX Joint Publishing, 1982), 207–220. As for the meaning of "seventy-two disciples" in history, see Huang Chin-shing, "Knowledge and Belief: Confucian Enshrinement and the Confucian Conception of Orthodoxy" 學術與信仰：論孔廟從祀制與儒家道統意識, *New History* 新史學 5, no. 2 (June 1994): 1–82; also collected in Huang Chin-shing, *Entering the Master's Sanctuary*, 217–311.
45. Fan Ye, *Hou Hanshu, juan* 3, 150; *juan* 5, 238.
46. Mi Heng 彌衡, "Yanzi song" 顏子頌, in *Liang-Han Sanguo wenhui* 兩漢三國文彙, ed. Gao Ming 高明 (Taipei: Zhonghua congshu bianshen weiyuanhui, 1960), 2250; and Wang Pu 王溥, *Tang huiyao* 唐會要 (Kyoto: Chubun Shuppansha, 1978), *juan* 35, 635–636.
47. Between the years 720 and 739, Tang Xuanzong completely systematized Confucian enshrinement.
48. Pang Zhonglu 龐鍾璐, *Wenmiao sidian kao* 文廟祀典考 (1877; repr., Taipei: Zhongguo liyue xuehui, 1977), *juan* 3, 10a.
49. *Shizong shilu* 明世宗實錄, in *Ming shilu* 明實錄, ed. Huang Chang-chien 黃彰健 (Taipei: Institute of History and Philology, Academia Sinica, 1966), *juan* 119, 3b–4a.

50. Qu Jiusi, *Kongmiao liyue kao, juan* 1, 44a.
51. Pang Zhonglu, *Wenmiao sidian kao, juan* 1, 17a–17b.
52. Eertai 鄂爾泰, *DaQing Shizong Xianhuangdi shilu* 大清世宗憲皇帝實錄 (Taipei: Wen Hai, n.d.), *juan* 20, 19b–20a.
53. Wang Anshi was enshrined in the Confucius temple with the honor of correlative worship in 1104; moreover, in 1113 he was given the title King of Shu (Shu-wang 舒王), a title that was equal to that of Confucius in the temple. His son, Wang Pang 王雱, was also enshrined, with the honor of subordinate worship. Wang was degraded to the honor of subordinate worship in 1126 because of the threat from the north. After the fall of central China, Wang Pang was deposed from the temple, in 1177, and Wang Anshi himself was also cast out, in 1241.
54. Wu Cheng received sacrifice in the Confucius temple in 1435. Due to the increased threat of invasion from northern nomads in 1530, Wu Cheng was deposed from the temple because he had once served an alien regime—the Yuan dynasty. In 1731, Wu was rehabilitated by the Qing regime.
55. See Huang Chin-shing, "Between Orthodoxy and Legitimacy: Reflections from the Debates on Ritual Reforms of the Confucius temple in 1530" 道統與治統之間：從明嘉靖九年孔廟改制論皇權與祭祀禮儀, *Bulletin of Institute of History and Philology, Academia Sinica* 中央研究院歷史語言究所集刊 61, no. 4 (1990): 917–941; also collected in Huang Chin-shing, *Entering the Master's Sanctuary* (Asian Culture Press), 125–163; or (Zhonghua), 107–137.
56. Cheng Minzheng, *Huangdun wenji* 篁墩文集, in *Jingyin Wenyuange sikuquanshu*, vols. 1252–1253, *juan* 10, 3a.
57. For a detailed discussion of this subject, see Huang Chin-shing, "Knowledge and Belief," 217–301.
58. Criticism was voiced, for example, by Hong Mai in the Song, Xiong He in the Yuan, and Cheng Minzheng in the Ming. See Hong Mai 洪邁, *Rongzhai sibi* 容齋四筆, in *Rongzhai suibi* 容齋隨筆 (Shanghai: Shanghai guji chubanshe, 1978), *juan* 1, 615; Xiong He, *Xiong Wuxuan xiansheng wenji, juan* 4, 52; and Cheng Minzheng, *Huangdun wenji, juan* 10, 10b–12a.
59. Zhang Tingyu 張廷玉, *Mingshi* 明史 (Taipei: Dingwen shuju, 1980), *juan* 50, 1297.
60. In the Qing dynasty, "*Qisheng ci*" was renamed "*Chongsheng ci* 崇聖祠"; see Pang Zhonglu, *Wenmiao sidian kao, juan* 1, 8a.
61. Sun Chengze, *Tianfu guangji, juan* 9, 88–89.
62. *Shizong shilu, juan* 235, 2b–3a. Only after 1571, when Xue Xuan received support from the court meeting and the approval of Ming emperor Muzong 穆宗 (the Longqing 隆慶 emperor, r. 1566–1572), was he permitted to be enshrined in the Confucius temple.

63. Wang Pu, *Tang huiyao, juan* 35, 636. The twenty-first year of Zhenguan's 貞觀 reign was misprinted in this source as the thirty-first year of Zhenguan's reign.
64. Song Lian 宋濂, *Yuanshi* 元史 (Taipei: Dingwen shuju, 1980), *juan* 77, 19021–19027.
65. Han Yu 韓愈, *Han Changli wenji jiaozhu* 韓昌黎文集校注 (Taipei: Huazheng shuju, 1975), *juan* 7, 283.
66. Tuo Tuo 脫脫, *Songshi* 宋史 (Taipei: Dingwen shuju, 1978), *juan* 351, 301.
67. Chen Kuo-tung 陳國棟, "Lamenting in the Confucius Temple and Burning of the Confucian Garments: Two Social Gestures of the Licentiates in the 17th Century" 哭廟與焚儒服——明末清初生員層的社會性動作, *New History* 3, no. 1 (March 1992): 69–94.
68. Zhang Tingyu, *Mingshi, juan* 1, 6–10.
69. Zhang Tingyu, *Mingshi, juan* 139, 3982.
70. Pang Zhonglu, *Wenmiao sidian kao, juan* 1, 12b.
71. Chen Hao, *Queli zhi, juan* 18, 63b.

1. Expanding the Symbolic Meaning and Function of the Rites

The Chinese-language version of this chapter was originally published as Huang Chin-shing, "The Symbolic Expansion of the Meaning and Function of the Rites of Confucian Temples in Imperial China," *Bulletin of the Institute of History and Philology, Academia Sinica* 中央研究院歷史語言研究所集刊 86, no. 3 (September 2015): 471–511.

1. Anonymous 佚名, *Miaoxue dianli* 廟學典禮, ed. Wang Ting 王頲 (Hangzhou: Zhejiang guji chubanshe, 1986), *juan* 4, 85.
2. Qing Shengzu 清聖祖, "Yuzhi zhongxiu Queli Kongzimiao bei" 御製重修闕里孔子廟碑, in *Shitou shang de Rujia wenxian: Qufu beiwen lu* 石頭上的儒家文獻：曲阜碑文錄, ed. Luo Chenglie 駱承烈 (Jinan: Qilu shushe, 2001), 2:795. For evidence on dating this stele inscription to 1693 instead of 1683, see Ma Qi 馬齊 and Zhang Tingyu 張廷玉, eds., *DaQing Shengzu Renhuangdi (Kangxi) shilu* 大清聖祖仁 (康熙) 皇帝實錄 (Taipei: Xinwenfeng chuban gongsi, 1978), *juan* 160, 17b–19b.
3. Hong Liangji 洪亮吉, *Chunqiu Zuozhuan gu* 春秋左傳詁 (Beijing: Zhonghua, 1987), *juan* 20, 882–883.
4. Kong Chuan 孔傳, *Dongjia zaji* 東家雜記, in *Jingyin Wenyuange sikuquanshu* 景印文淵閣四庫全書 (Taipei: Commercial Press, 1983–1986), vol. 446, *juan* 1, 6b. This popular assertion deserves skeptical evaluation. Nonetheless, it was

accepted as genuine in the Southern Song by Wei Liaoweng 魏了翁 (1178–1237) and by Confucius's fiftieth-generation descendant, Kong Yuancuo 孔元措 (1182–1251), who lived under the Jurchen Jin dynasty. See Wei Liaoweng, "Luzhou zhongxiu xueji" 瀘州重修學記, in *Heshan wenji* 鶴山文集, in *Jingyin Wenyuange sikuquanshu*, vols. 1172–1173, *juan* 45, 8b; and Kong Yuancuo, *Kongshi zuting guangji* 孔氏祖庭廣記, in *Congshu jicheng chubian* 叢書集成初編 (Linlang mishi congshu 琳琅秘室叢書; repr., Shanghai: Commercial Press, 1936), vols. 3316–3317, *juan* 3, 21. For a detailed analysis, see Huang Chin-shing, "Power and Belief: The Formation of a National Cult, the Worship of the Confucius Temple in Imperial China" 權力與信仰：孔廟祭祀制度的形成, in *Entering the Master's Sanctuary: Power, Belief and Legitimacy in Traditional China* 優入聖域：權力、信仰與正當性 (Taipei: Asian Culture Press, 2003), 168–171.

5. Sima Qian 司馬遷, *Shiji* 史記 (Beijing: Zhonghua, 1982), *juan* 47, 1946; Hu Zi 胡仔, *Kongzi biannian* 孔子編年, in *Jingyin Wenyuange sikuquanshu*, vol. 446, *juan* 3, 19b. Scholars such as Yang Hsien-yi, Gladys Yang, Burton Watson, and William Nienhauser have provided useful English translations of portions of Sima Qian's *Historical Records*.

6. Kong Jifen 孔繼汾, *Queli wenxian kao* 闕里文獻考 (1762), in *Ru Cang* 儒藏, *shibu* 史部 (Chengdu: Sichuan daxue chubanshe, 2005), vol. 2, *Kong Meng shi zhi er* 孔孟史志二, *juan* 11, 1a.

7. Sima Qian, *Shiji*, *juan* 47, 1945. In this first-century BCE source, Sima used the land unit of one *qing* (頃), which Kong Jifen (*Queli wenxian kao*) estimated as one hundred *mu* (畝) in his eighteen-century Chinese units. If we take Kong Jifen's view to be correct, the land area would be roughly sixteen acres in U.S. land units.

8. Sima Qian, *Shiji*, *juan* 47, 1945–1946; *Records of the Historian*, trans. Yang Hsien-yi and Gladys Yang (Hong Kong: Commercial Press, 1974).

9. "'The governor of Pei does not care for Confucian scholars,' replied the cavalryman. 'Whenever a visitor wearing a Confucian hat comes to see him, he immediately snatches the hat from the visitor's head and pisses in it, and when he talks to other people, he always curses them up and down. He will never consent to be lectured by a Confucian scholar!'" Sima Qian, *Records of the Grand Historian*, trans. Burton Watson (New York: Columbia University Press, 1993), 220; for the Chinese text, see Sima Qian, *Shiji*, *juan* 97, 2692.

10. Han Fei 韓非, *Han Fei Zi jishi* 韓非子集釋, ed. Chen Qiyou 陳奇猷 (Taipei: Heluo tushu chubanshe, 1974), *juan* 19, 1080.

11. Lü Buwei 呂不韋, *Lüshi chunqiu jiaoshi* 呂氏春秋校釋, ed. Chen Qiyou 陳奇猷 (Taipei: Huazheng shuju, 1985), *juan* 2, 96.

12. Sima Qian, *Shiji*, *juan* 6, 258.

13. Kong Chuan, *Dongjia zaji*, *juan* 1, 33b; Kong Zhencong 孔貞叢, ed., *Queli zhi* 闕里志 (Taipei: Institute of History and Philology, Academia Sinica), *juan* 2, 19a–20a, originally published in the Wanli reign of the Ming dynasty (1573–1620), prefaced by Li Dongyang 李東陽 in 1605, and by Huang Kezuan 黃克纘 and Kong Zhencong in 1609.
14. Ban Gu 班固, *Hanshu* 漢書 (Taipei: Dingwen shuju, 1987), *juan* 56, 2508–2522.
15. Dong Zhongshu 董仲舒, "Furui dishiliu" 符瑞第十六, in *Chunqiu fanlu* 春秋繁露 (Taipei: Shijie shuju, 1975), *juan* 6, 126–127. A *qilin* is a mythical and auspicious creature, traditionally compared to the unicorn of Western mythology.
16. Sima Qian, *Shiji*, *juan* 130, 3310.
17. See Huang Chin-shing, "Power and Belief" (Asian Culture Press), 184–195.
18. Wang Chong 王充, *Lunheng jijie* 論衡集解, ed. Liu Pansui 劉盼遂 (Taipei: Shijie shuju, 1990), *juan* 12, 249.
19. Hong Gua 洪适, *Lishi lixu* 隸釋·隸續 (Hongshi huimuzhai 洪氏晦木齋; repr., Beijing: Zhonghua, 1985), *juan* 1, 15a–15b; 18a.
20. Han Chi 韓勑, "Luxiang Han Chi zao Kongmiao liqi bei" 魯相韓勑造孔廟禮器碑, in *Shitou shang de Rujia wenxian: Qufu beiwen lu*, 1:19–26.
21. Hong Gua, *Lishi lixu*, *juan* 1, "Luxiang Shi Chen ci Kongmiao zouming" 魯相史晨祠孔廟奏銘, 25b. For three slightly different titles of this stele, see Huang Chin-shing, "Symbolic Expansion," 477.
22. For the slightly different titles used to refer to this stele, see Huang Chin-shing, "Symbolic Expansion," 477. Imperial officials and the nobility received a stipend in bushels of grain, or its equivalent in value, according to their rank. An official of one hundred bushels was of a junior rank.
23. Fan Ye 范曄, *Hou Hanshu* 後漢書 (Taipei: Dingwen shuju, 1983), *juan* 14, 3108. See also Kong Jifen, *Queli wenxian kao*, *juan* 14, 484b; Du You 杜佑, *Tongdian* 通典, ed. Wang Wenjin 王文錦 (Beijing: Zhonghua, 1988), *juan* 53, 1472; Liu Xu 劉昫, *Jiu Tangshu* 舊唐書 (Taipei: Dingwen shuju, 1981), *juan* 24, 917, note "Zhenguan ershiyi nian Xu Jingzong deng shangzou" 貞觀二十一年許敬宗等上奏; and Qin Huitian 秦蕙田, *Wuli tongkao* 五禮通考 (Weijingwo 味經窩; repr., Taoyuan: Shenghuan tushu gongsi, 1994), *juan* 117, 9a.
24. Hong Gua, *Lishi lixu*, *juan* 1, "Luxiang Shi Chen ci Kongmiao zouming," 25b–26b.
25. For variations in the title, see Huang Chin-shing, "Symbolic Expansion," 477.
26. Hong Gua, *Lishi lixu*, *juan* 1, "Shi Chen xiang Kongmiao hou bei" 史晨饗孔廟後碑, 27b–28a.
27. Sun Xidan 孫希旦, *Liji jijie* 禮記集解, ed. Sheng Xiaohuan 沈嘯寰 and Wang Xingxian 王星賢 (Beijing: Zhonghua, 1989), *juan* 20, 560.

28. Fang Xuanling 房玄齡, *Jinshu* 晉書 (Taipei: Dingwen shuju, 1987), *juan* 19, 599.
29. For a declaration of the three levels of state rituals, see Xiao Song 蕭嵩, *DaTang Kaiyuan li* 大唐開元禮, in *Jingyin Wenyuange sikuquanshu*, vol. 646, *juan* 1, 1a.
30. Quoted in *Zhouli* 周禮, "Chunguan zongbo disan, Sishi" 春官宗伯第三‧肆師. See also Sun Yirang 孫詒讓, Wang Wenjin 王文錦, and Chen Yuxia 陳玉霞, eds., *Zhouli Zhengyi* 周禮正義 (Beijing: Zhonghua, 1987), *juan* 37, 1465.
31. Although there were three levels of sacrifices, it was not until the Sui dynasty that these were officially declared in the imperial ritual system. See Gao Mingshi 高明士, "Suidai de zhili zuoyue: Suidai liguo zhengce yanjiu zhier" 隋代的制禮作樂──隋代立國政策研究之二, in *Studies on the Sui and Tang Dynasties* 隋唐史論集, ed. Joseph Wong 黃約瑟 and Lau Kin-Ming 劉健明 (Centre of Asian Studies, University of Hong Kong, 1993), 19–20.
32. Fan Ye, *Hou Hanshu*, *juan* 1, 40.
33. Fan Ye, *Hou Hanshu*, *juan* 2, 118. Emperor Ming went to Queli in the third month of the year 72.
34. Fan Ye, *Hou Hanshu*, *juan* 79a, 2562.
35. Chen Shou 陳壽, *Sanguo zhi* 三國志 (Taipei: Dingwen shuju, 1983), *juan* 4, 119–121.
36. Fang Xuanling, *Jinshu*, *juan* 19, 599. For more examples, see Du You, *Tongdian*, *juan* 53, 1472–1474.
37. Chen Shou, *Sanguo zhi*, *juan* 2, 78. On historical corrections to the date and title, see Huang Chin-shing, "Symbolic Expansion."
38. Pan Xiang 潘相, ed., *Qufu xianzhi* 曲阜縣志 (1774; repr., Taipei: Taiwan Xuesheng shuju, 1968), *juan* 21, 11b.
39. Ouyang Xiu 歐陽修 and Song Qi 宋祁, *Xin Tangshu* 新唐書 (Taipei: Dingwen shuju, 1981), *juan* 15, 373.
40. Ban Gu, *Hanshu*, *juan* 12, 351.
41. Fan Ye, *Hou Hanshu*, *juan* 79a, 2563. On Guangwu's restoration of Confucius's title, see *juan* 1a, 63.
42. See Huang Chin-shing, "Power and Belief" (Asian Culture Press), 195–198.
43. Fang Xuanling, *Jinshu*, *juan* 14, 442.
44. Fang Xuanling, *Jinshu*, *juan* 9, 235.
45. Xu Song 許嵩, *Jiankang shilu* 建康實錄 (Beijing: Zhonghua, 1986), *juan* 9, 283. The *Jinshu* does not record the establishment of this Xuanni temple.
46. Xiao Zixian 蕭子顯, *Nan Qi shu* 南齊書 (Taipei: Dingwen shuju, 1980), *juan* 3, 56; Wei Shou 魏收, *Weishu* 魏書 (Taipei: Dingwen shuju, 1980), *juan* 7b, 165.
47. Wei Shou, *Weishu*, *juan* 9, 143–144.
48. Wei Shou, *Weishu*, *juan* 9, 143–144.

49. Sun Xidan, *Liji jijie*, juan 20, 560. See also Wang Pu 王溥, *Tang huiyao* 唐會要 (Kyoto: Chubun Shuppansha, 1978), *juan* 35, 636.
50. Pan Xiang, ed., *Qufu xian zhi*, juan 4, 7a.
51. Liu Xu, *Jiu Tangshu*, juan 189a, 4940.
52. Liu Xu, *Jiu Tangshu*, juan 24, 916.
53. Ouyang Xiu and Song Qi, *Xin Tangshu*, juan 15, 373.
54. Wang Pu, *Tang huiyao*, juan 35, 635–636.
55. The title "sage," applied to the Duke of Zhou, meant his extraordinary achievements. For example, Ban Gu, *Hanshu*, juan 77, 3262, calls him *shangsheng* (上聖). Fan Ye, *Hou Hanshu*, juan 40a, 1330–1331, calls him *xiansheng* (先聖); and in *juan* 29, 1012, calls him *zhisheng* (至聖). Fang Xuanling, *Jinshu*, juan 47, 1325, calls him *shengren* (聖人); and in *juan* 99, 2586, calls him *dasheng* (大聖). Shen Yue 沈約, *Songshu* 宋書 (Taipei: Dingwen shuju, 1980), *juan* 68, 1796, calls him *shangsheng* (上聖).
56. Ouyang Xiu and Song Qi, *Xin Tangshu*, juan 15, 374.
57. Ouyang Xiu and Song Qi, *Xin Tangshu*, juan 15, 374.
58. Liao Ping 廖平, *Guxue kao* 古學考 (Taipei: Taiwan Kaiming shudian, 1969), 30.
59. Pi Xirui 皮錫瑞, preface, "*Zixu*" 自序, in *Jingxue tonglun* 經學通論, in *Xuxiu sikuquanshu* 續修四庫全書 (1875; repr., Shanghai: Shanghai guji chubanshe, 1995), vol. 180, 1a–1b.
60. Liu Xu, *Jiu Tangshu*, juan 24, 918; Du You, *Tongdian*, juan 53, 1481; Ouyang Xiu and Song Qi, *Xin Tangshu*, juan 15, 374; Wang Pu, *Tang huiyao*, juan 35, 636.
61. Wang Pu, *Tang huiyao*, juan 35, 636.
62. Emperor Wen 文 of Northern Zhou (Taizu 北周太祖, 507–556) announced a policy of disregarding institutions of the Wei and Jin dynasties and returning to the Duke of Zhou as the standard; however, his descendants returned to promoting the Confucius temple. See Linghu Defen 令狐德棻, *Zhoushu* 周書 (Taipei: Dingwen shuju, 1980), *juan* 7, 123, and *juan* 45, 806.
63. Wang Pu, *Tang huiyao*, juan 35, 637.
64. Wei Zheng 魏徵, *Suishu* 隋書 (Taipei: Dingwen shuju, 1980), *juan* 9, 180–181.
65. Wei Zheng, *Suishu*, juan 7, 127. See also Lei Wen 雷聞, *Jiaomiao zhiwai: Sui Tang guojia jisi yu zongjiao* 郊廟之外：隋唐國家祭祀與宗教 (Beijing: Joint Publishing, 2009), 68–74.
66. See Wei Zheng, *Suishu*, juan 6, 117; Kaneko Shuichi 金子修一, "Toudai no daishi, chūshi, shoushi ni tsuite" 唐代の大祀・中祀・小祀について, *Kouchi daigaku gakujutsu kenkyū houkoku* 高知大學學術研究報告, *Jimbun kagaku* 人文科學 25, no. 2 (1976): 13–19; and Zhu Yi 朱溢, "Tang zhi BeiSong shiqi de dasi, zhongsi he xiaosi" 唐至北宋時期的大祀、中祀和小祀, *Tsing Hua Journal of Chinese Studies* (Hsinchu) 清華學報 new series 39, no. 2 (2009): 287–324.

Gao Mingshi differs about some of Kaneko Shuichi's content; see Gao Mingshi, *Zhongguo chuantong zhengzhi yu jiaoyu* 中國傳統政治與教育 (Taipei: Wenjin chubanshe, 2003), 248–251.

67. Li Linfu 李林甫, *Tang liudian* 唐六典 (Beijing: Zhonghua, 1992), *juan* 4, 120. See also Wang Jing 王涇, *DaTang jiaosi lu* 大唐郊祀錄 (first published by Qian Xizuo 錢熙祚, Qian Peirang 錢培讓, and Qian Peijie 錢培杰 during the Qing Daoguang 道光 era, 1821–1850), in *Baibu congshu jicheng*, *Zhihai congshu* 百部叢書集成·指海叢書, vol. 7 (Taipei: Yiwen yinshuguan, 1966), *juan* 1, 2a–2b.
68. Li Linfu, *Tang liudian*, *juan* 4, 120. See also Xiao Song, *DaTang Kaiyuan li*, *juan* 1, 1a–1b.
69. Wang Jing, *DaTang jiaosi lu*, *juan* 10, 14a.
70. Liu Xu, *Jiu Tangshu*, *juan* 8, 196–197.
71. Du You, *Tongdian*, *juan* 53, 1484.
72. See Jin Zheng 金諍, *Keju zhidu yu Zhongguo wenhua* 科舉制度與中國文化 (Shanghai: Shanghai Renmin chubanshe, 1990).
73. Ouyang Xiu and Song Qi, *Xin Tangshu*, *juan* 15, 376–377, 380.
74. Han Yu 韓愈, *Han Changli wenji xiaozhu* 韓昌黎文集校注 (Taipei: Huazheng shuju, 1975), *juan* 7, 283.
75. Du You, *Tongdian*, *juan* 53, 1484.
76. Wang Jing, *DaTang jiaosi lu*, *juan* 10, 17a–23b.
77. Dong Lun 董倫, Li Jinglong 李景隆, and Yao Guangxiao 姚廣孝, *Ming Taizu shilu* 明太祖實錄, in *Ming shilu* 明實錄, ed. Huang Chang-chien 黃彰健 (Taipei: Institute of History and Philology, Academia Sinica, 1966), *juan* 183, 3a. For a detailed analysis, see Huang Chin-shing, "The Rise and Demise of the Martial Temple, Seventh to Fourteenth Centuries: A Political–Cultural Analysis" 武廟的崛起與衰微（七迄十四世紀）：一個政治文化的考察, in *Sages and Saints: Collected Essays on History and Religions* 聖賢與聖徒：歷史與宗教論文集 (Taipei: Asian Culture Press, 2001), 181–227.
78. Tuo Tuo 脫脫, *Songshi* 宋史 (Taipei: Dingwen shuju, 1978), *juan* 29, 546. See also Kong Jifen, *Queli wenxian kao*, *juan* 14, 491a.
79. Tuo Tuo, *Songshi*, *juan* 486, 14024–14025.
80. Tuo Tuo, *Songshi*, *juan* 105, 2548.
81. Tuo Tuo, *Songshi*, 2549–2550. For sources (which wrongly state the date as 1107 or 1105 and exhibit confusion regarding the robes), see Kong Chuan, *Dongjia zaji*, *juan* 1, 28b; and Kong Yuancuo, "Chongning sinian bayue" 崇寧四年八月, in *Kongshi zuting guangji* 孔氏祖庭廣記, *juan* 3, 28.
82. Anonymous 不著撰人, *DaJin jili* 大金集禮, in *Jingyin Wenyuange sikuquanshu*, vol. 648, *juan* 36, 2a–2b.
83. Ouyang Xiu, "Xiangzhou Guchengxian fuzimiao ji" 襄州穀城縣夫子廟記, in *Ouyang Xiu quanji* 歐陽修全集 (Taipei: Shijie shuju, 1961), 273.

84. Wang Anshi 王安石, "Fanchangxian xueji" 繁昌縣學記, in *Linchuan xiansheng wenji* 臨川先生文集 (Taipei: Huazheng shuju, 1975), *juan* 82, 863.
85. Wang Anshi, "Fanchangxian xueji," 870; and Yuan Zheng 袁征, "Cong Kongmiao zhidu kan Songdai Ruxue de bianhua" 從孔廟制度看宋代儒學的變化, in *Songshi yanjiu lunwenji* 宋史研究論文集, ed. Deng Guangming 鄧廣銘 and Wang Yunhai 王雲海 (Kaifeng: Henan University Press, 1993), 490–509. It is interesting to observe the shift from "temple records" (*miaoji* 廟記) to "school records" (*xueji* 學記) before and after the minor reform of the Qingli 慶曆 reign period, around 1043.
86. Ma Duanlin 馬端臨, *Wenxian tongkao* 文獻通考 (Shanghai: Commercial Press, 1936), in *Wanyou wenku shitongben* 萬有文庫十通本 (Beijing: Zhonghua, 1986), *juan* 43, *kao* 考 411.
87. *Ming Taizu shilu*, *juan* 30, 5b–6a.
88. Zhang Tingyu 張廷玉, *Mingshi* 明史 (Taipei: Dingwen shuju, 1980), *juan* 50, 1297.
89. For a detailed analysis, see Huang Chin-shing, "The Cultural Politics of Autocracy: The Confucius Temple and Ming Despotism, 1368–1530" 道統與治統之間：從明嘉靖九年 (1530) 孔廟改制論皇權與祭祀禮儀, in *Entering the Master's Sanctuary* (Asian Culture Press), 148–155. See also Song Lian 宋濂, "Hongwu sanshinian yanshenggong Kong Kejian shendao bei" 洪武三十年衍聖公孔克堅神道碑, in *Shitou shang de Rujia wenxian: Qufu beiwen lu*, 1:365–368.
90. Zhang Tingyu, *Mingshi*, *juan* 139, "Qian Tang zhuan" 錢唐傳, 3981. For differences in dating, see Huang Chin-shing, "Symbolic Expansion," as well as *Ming Taizu shilu*, *juan* 144, 2a; Qin Huitian, *Wuli tongkao*, *juan* 120, 1a; and Wang Qi 王圻, *Xu wenxian tongkao* 續文獻通考, *juan* 57, 7b–8a (first published in 1603; held by the Institute of History and Philology, Academia Sinica).
91. *Ming Taizu shilu*, *juan* 30, 1a–4b, and *juan* 38, 1a–10a.
92. Xu Yikui 徐一夔, *DaMing jili* 大明集禮, in *Jingyin Wenyuange sikuquanshu*, vols. 649–650, *juan* 16, 20a. Confucius quote is from *Analects* 2:24, trans. James Legge, in *The Chinese Classics*, available from Chinese Text Project, https://ctext.org/analects.
93. Wang Qi, *Xu wenxian tongkao*, *juan* 57, 11b; and Sun Chengze 孫承澤, *Chunmingmeng yulu* 春明夢餘錄 (Hong Kong: Longmen shuju, 1965), *juan* 21, 36b. *Mencius* 4b:31 translation modified from Legge, *Chinese Classics*.
94. *Ming Taizu shilu*, *juan* 144, 2a; and Ming Taizu 明太祖, "Ji Kong Xixue wen" 祭孔希學文, in *Ming Taizu wenji* 明太祖文集, ed. Yao Shiguan 姚士觀 and Shen Fu 沈鈇, in *Jingyin Wenyuange sikuquanshu*, vol. 1223, *juan* 18, 14a.
95. For Guo Wei's story, see *Zhoushu* 周書, in *Jiu Wudaishi* 舊五代史, ed. Xue Juzheng 薛居正 (Taipei: Dingwen shuju, 1980), *juan* 112, 1482. For Ming

Taizu, see Pang Zhonglu 龐鍾璐, *Wenmiao sidian kao* 文廟祀典考 (1877; repr., Taipei: Zhongguo liyue xuehui, 1977), *juan* 4, 4b.

96. See Huang Chin-shing, "Cultural Politics" (Asian Culture Press), 138–139.
97. Du You, *Tongdian, juan* 53, 1481–1483; Qiu Jun 丘濬, *Daxue yanyi bu* 大學衍義補, in *Jingyin Wenyuange sikuquanshu*, vols. 712–713, *juan* 65, 14b.
98. Liu Xu, *Jiu Tangshu, juan* 21, 825; and *juan* 24, 911.
99. See Zhu Yi, "Tang dao BeiSong shiqi de daji, zhongji he xiaoji," 292.
100. Liu Xu, *Jiu Tangshu, juan* 24, 921, 923.
101. Zhang Tingyu, *Mingshi, juan* 50, 1298.
102. *Ming Taizu shilu, juan* 53, 1b–2a. On Emperor Taizu's disregard for the military temple, see *Ming Taizu shilu, juan* 183, 3a.
103. Ming Shizong 明世宗, "Yuzhi Kongzi sidian shuo" 御製孔子祀典說, in Li Zhizao 李之藻, *Pangong liyue shu* 頖宮禮樂疏, in *Jingyin Wenyuange sikuquanshu*, vol. 651, *juan* 1, 55a–56a.
104. Qing Shizong 清世宗, *Yongzheng zhupi yuzhi* 雍正硃批諭旨, ed. E'ertai 鄂爾泰 (Taipei: Wenhai chubanshe, 1965), 4120.
105. Qing Shizong, "Yongzheng banian yuzhi zhongxiu Queli shengmiao bei" 雍正八年御製重修闕里聖廟碑, in *Shitou shang de Rujia wenxian: Qufu beiwen lu*, 2:861–864.
106. Zhao Erxun 趙爾巽, *Qingshi gao* 清史稿, ed. Qi Gong 啟功 (Beijing: Zhonghua, 1994), *juan* 84, 2537–2538; and *juan* 24, 957.
107. Cao Yuanyong 曹元用, "Qian guan ji Queli miao bei" 遣官祭闕里廟碑, quoted in Kong Zhencong, *Queli zhi, juan* 10, 40b.
108. See Zhuang Chao 莊綽, *Jile bian* 雞肋編, ed. Xiao Luyang 蕭魯陽 (Beijing: Zhonghua, 1983), *juan* 2, 76.
109. Pang Zhonglu, *Wenmiao sidian kao, juan* 3, 14b. For an example of this praise of Confucius, see Tuo Tuo, *Jinshi* 金史 (Taipei: Dingwen shuju, 1980), *juan* 4, 76–77.
110. Lü Yuanshan 呂元善, *Shengmen zhi* 聖門志, in *Congshu jicheng chubian*, vols. 3318–3321, *juan* 4, 273.
111. Song Lian, *Yuanshi* 元史 (Taipei: Dingwen shuju, 1980), *juan* 2, 484, and *juan* 76, 1892, gives date of 1308, but the original source gives seventh month of 1307. See Song Shou 宋綬 and Song Minqiu 宋敏求, *Song dazhaoling ji* 宋大詔令集, ed. Si Yizu 司義祖 (Beijing: Zhonghua, 1962), *juan* 156, "Zhuishi yuan sheng Wenxuanwang zhao" 追謚元聖文宣王詔, 583. The Northern Song, in 1008, had designated Confucius as Yuan sheng Wenxuanwang 元聖文宣王 (First King of Sageliness and Exalted Culture).
112. Zhang Dai 張岱, "Kongmiao kuai" 孔廟檜, in *Tao'an mengyi* 陶菴夢憶, in *Meihua wenxue mingzhu congkan* 美化文學名著叢刊, ed. Zhu Jianmang 朱劍芒 (Shanghai: Shijie shuju, 1947), 10.

113. Tuo Tuo, *Liaoshi* 遼史 (Taipei: Dingwen shuju, 1980), *juan* 72, 1209; *juan* 1, 12–13; *juan* 2, 15.
114. Liu Xu, *Jiu Tangshu*, *juan* 24, 917–918.
115. Lei Wen, *Jiaomiao zhiwai*, 246–250.
116. Wen Yanbo 文彥博, *Lugong wenji* 潞公文集, in *Sikuquanshu zhenben*, liuji 四庫全書珍本·六集 (Taipei: Commercial Press, 1976), vols. 245–246, *juan* 12, "Jiangzhou yichengxian xinxiu zhisheng Wenxuanwang miao bei ji" 絳州翼城縣新修至聖文宣王廟碑記, 1a–1b.
117. On the development of prefectural and county local gazetteers (*tujing* 圖經), see Cang Xiuliang 倉修良 and Chen Yangguang 陳仰光, "Cong Dunhuang tujing canjuan kan Sui Tang Wudai tujing fazhan" 從敦煌圖經殘卷看隋唐五代圖經發展, *Wenshi* 文史 55 (2001): 117–139.
118. Li Xinchuan 李心傳, *Jianyan yilai jinian yaolu* 建炎以來繫年要錄 (Commercial Press), in *Guoxue jiben congshuben* (Beijing: Zhonghua, 1988), *juan* 152, 2454.
119. Zhang Xiaoxiang 張孝祥, *Yuhu jushi wenji* 于湖居士文集, ed. Xu Peng 徐鵬 (Shanghai: Shanghai guji chubanshe, 1980), *juan* 27, "Xianshengmiao wen" 先聖廟文, 272.
120. Zhu Xi 朱熹, *Zhuzi wenji* 朱子文集, ed. Chen Junmin 陳俊民 (Taipei: Defu wenjiao jijinhui, 2000), *juan* 78, "Quzhou jiangshan xueji" 衢州江山學記, 3894–3895.
121. Zhu Xi, *Zhuzi wenji*, bieji 別集, *juan* 7, "Xiangyin shecai er xianshi zhuwen" 鄉飲舍菜二先師祝文, 5259; *juan* 86, "Nankang ye xiansheng wen" 南康謁先聖文, 4250; *juan* 86, "Zhangzhou ye xiansheng wen" 漳州謁先聖文, 426; and *juan* 86, "Ci xiansheng wen" 辭先聖文, 4249.
122. On ritual reforms during the Jin dynasty, see Kong Yuancuo, *Kongshi zuting guangji*, *juan* 3, "Tiande chunian" 天德初年, 30. On the Yuan, see Lü Yuanshan, *Shengmen zhi*, *juan* 4, 273. For Qin Huitian's correction, see Qin Huitian, *Wuli tongkao*, *juan* 119, 6b.
123. Yang Qiyuan 楊起元, *Taishi Yang Fusuo xiansheng zhengxuebian* 太史楊復所先生證學編 (in *Sikuquanshu cunmu congshu*, zibu 四庫全書存目叢書·子部 (She Yongning 佘永寧, 1617; repr., Tainan: Zhuangyan wenhua gongsi, 1995), vol. 90, *juan* 3, 9b.
124. Fan Ye, *Hou Hanshu*, *juan* 2, 118.
125. Wang Pu, *Tang Huiyao*, *juan* 35, 636.
126. For a detailed discussion of the sacrificial system at Confucius temples, see Huang Chin-shing, "Knowledge and Belief: Confucian Canonization and the Confucian Conception of Orthodoxy" 學術與信仰：論孔廟從祀制與儒家道統意識, *New History* 新史學 5, no. 2 (June 1994): 1–82. Reprinted in Huang Chin-shing, *Entering the Master's Sanctuary*, (Asian Culture Press), 217–311.
127. Liu Xu, *Jiu Tangshu*, *juan* 24, 919; and Tuo Tuo, *Songshi*, *juan* 105, 2553–2554. Both sources give the date Kaiyuan 26 (739); however, the *Xin Tangshu* and

the *Wudai huiyao* give Kaiyuan 5 (717). See Ouyang Xiu, *Xin Tangshu*, *juan* 44, 1164; and Wang Pu 王溥, *Wudai huiyao* 五代會要 (Taipei: Jiusi chubanshe, 1978), *juan* 8, 127.

128. Li Dongyang 李東陽, *Ming Huidian* 明會典, ed. Shen Shixing 申時行 (Beijing: Zhonghua, 1989), *juan* 91, 520.

129. Zhang Tingyu, *Mingshi*, *juan* 67, 1641; and Pang Zhonglu, *Wenmiao sidian kao*, *juan* 5, 25b.

130. Chen Kuo-tung 陳國棟, "Lamenting in the Confucius Temple and Burning of the Confucian Garments: Two Social Gestures of the Licentiates in the Seventeenth Century" 哭廟與焚儒服：明末清初生員層的社會性動作, *New History* 3, no. 1 (March 1992): 69–94.

131. Du You, *Tongdian*, *juan* 55, 1536.

132. Tuo Tuo, *Songshi*, *juan* 102, 2498.

133. Ma Duanlin, *Wenxian tongkao*, *juan* 89, *kao* 考 809–817.

134. Zhang Tingyu, *Mingshi*, *juan* 49, 1276–1277.

135. Pang Zhonglu, *Wenmiao sidian kao*, *juan* 4, 1b.

136. Song Lian, *Yuanshi*, *juan* 76, 1899.

137. Zhao Erxun, *Qingshi gao*, *juan* 82, 2500–2501.

138. Sun Xidan, *Liji jijie*, *juan* 12, 333.

139. Qing Shengzu 清聖祖, "Jiaomie ga'erdan gaoji xianshi Kongzi wen" 剿滅噶爾丹告祭先師孔子文, in *Shengzu Renhuangdi yuzhiwen dier ji* 聖祖仁皇帝御製文第二集, ed. Zhang Yushu 張玉書 and Yunlu 允祿, in *Jingyin Wenyuange sikuquanshu*, vol. 1298, *juan* 41, 8a–9a.

140. Qing Shizong, "Pingding Qinghai gaocheng taixue beiwen" 平定青海告成太學碑文, in *Shizong Xianhuangdi yuzhi wenji* 世宗憲皇帝御製文集, in *Jingyin Wenyuange sikuquanshu*, vol. 1300, *juan* 14, 5a–8b.

141. Qing Gaozong 清高宗, *Yuzhi wenji, chuji* 御製文集·初集, ed. Yu Minzhong 于敏中, in *Jingyin Wenyuange sikuquanshu*, vol. 1301, *juan* 17, "Pingding Jinchuan gaocheng taixue beiwen" 平定金川告成太學碑文, 12b–16a; *juan* 19, "Pingding Zhunga'er gaocheng taixue beiwen" 平定準噶爾告成太學碑文, 1a–6b; *juan* 20, "Pingding Huibu gaocheng taixue beiwen" 平定回部告成太學碑文, 5b–11b.

142. *Jingyin Wenyuange sikuquanshu*, vol. 1301, *juan* 19, "Pingding Zhunga'er gaocheng taixue beiwen," 4b.

143. Ma Fu 馬浮, "Shaoxingxian zhongxiu wenmiao ji" 紹興縣重修文廟記, *Huaguo* 華國 1, no. 4 (1923): 1.

144. Wei Yuan 魏源, *Sheng wu ji* 聖武記, in *Wei Yuan quanji* 魏源全集, ed. Wei Yuan quanji weiyuanhui 魏源全集編委會 (Changsha: Yulue shushe, 2004), vol. 3, *juan* 3, "Kangxi qinzheng Zhunga'er ji" 康熙親征準噶爾記, 118.

145. Anthony Giddens, *The Constitution of Society: Outline of the Theory of Structuration* (Berkeley: University of California Press, 1986). Beverley J. Gibbs

explains, "Giddens argues that just as an individual's autonomy is influenced by structure, structures are maintained and adapted through the exercise of agency. The interface at which an actor meets a structure is termed 'structuration.'" See Gibbs, "Structuration Theory," *Encyclopædia Britannica*, August 21, 2017, https://www.britannica.com/topic/structuration-theory.

146. Wei Shou, *Weishu*, juan 7a, 136.
147. Yuwen Maozhao 宇文懋昭, *Qinding zhongding daJin guozhi* 欽定重訂大金國志, ed. Ji Yun 紀昀, in *Jingyin Wenyuange sikuquanshu*, vol. 383, juan 18, 6a.
148. Wei Shou, *Weishu*, juan 7a, 136.
149. Ming Taizu, "Shi Dao lun" 釋道論, *Ming Taizu wenji*, juan 10, 15a–15b.
150. Tuo Tuo, *Songshi*, juan 351, 11101.
151. Yuan Jue 袁桷, *Qingrong jushi ji* 清容居士集, in *Sibu congkan chubian, suoben* 四部叢刊初編·縮本 (Taipei: Commercial Press, 1965), vols. 295–297, juan 35, 516. This edict reiterated one made by Kublai Khan (Yuan Shizong); see Anonymous, *Miaoxue dianli*, juan 1, 12, and juan 2, 41–42.
152. Zhu Guozhen 朱國禎, *Yong chuang xiaopin* 湧幢小品, in *Biji xiaoshuo daguan* 筆記小說大觀 (Taipei: Xinxing shuju, 1984), vol. 22.7, juan 19, 3a.
153. Zhang Dai, "Kongmiao kuai" 孔廟檜, in *Tao'an mengyi*, 9. Such difficulty of access continued. For instance, in 1912, a visitor to the Confucius temple in Qufu required a guide with keys to unlock every chamber. See Jiang Weiqiao 蔣維喬, "Qufu jiyou" 曲阜紀遊, in *Xin youji huikan xubian* 新遊記彙刊續編, ed. Yao Zhuxuan 姚祝萱 (Shanghai: Chung Hwa, 1925), vol. 1, juan 7, 20.
154. Anonymous, "Yue bao ji huisheng eyan yize shuai shu qi hou" 閱報紀毀聖訛言一則率書其後, in *Shen Bao* 申報 9022 (1898.05.29), section 1.
155. Kang Youwei 康有為, "Liang Yue Guangren shantang shengxuehui yuanqi" 兩粵廣仁善堂聖學會緣起 (May 17, 1897), in *Kang Youwei quanji* 康有為全集, ed. Jiang Yihua 姜義華 and Wu Genliang 吳根樑 (Shanghai: Shanghai guji chubanshe, 1990), 2:621.
156. See Huang Chin-shing, "On the Secular Character of Confucianism: A Discussion Beginning from Li Fu's 'Original Teachings'" 論儒教的俗世性格：從李紱的〈原教〉談起, *Journal of Intellectual History* 思想史 1 (September 2013): 59–84. Article also appears in Huang Chin-shing, *From Virtue to Morality: The Transformation of Moral Consciousness during the Late Qing and Early Republic Era* 從理學到倫理學：清末民初道德意識的轉化 (Beijing: Zhonghua, 2014), 312–340; not included in the Asian Culture Press edition.
157. Tuo Tuo, *Jinshi*, juan 10, 234.
158. C. K. Yang, *Religion in Chinese Society* (Berkeley: University of California Press, 1961), chapters 10 and 12.
159. Ming Shizong, "Yuzhi Kongzi sidian shuo," in *Pangong liyue shu*, juan 1, 55a.

160. Zhang Tingyu, *Mingshi, juan* 50, 1297; Zhao Erxun, *Qingshi gao*, ed. Qi Gong, *juan* 84, 2536; Pang Zhonglu, *Wenmiao sidian kao, juan* 1, 16a, and 29b; *juan* 4, 6a.
161. For instance, an executive order of the Taiwan provincial government, dated November 21, 1966, expressed concern that the worship of Confucius in diverse local shrines and temples would bring confusion to the state's Confucius temple rites; therefore, it forbade their use of the title "Confucian temple." See "Zhengling" 政令, *Wushiwu nian dongzi di sishisi qi* 五十五年冬字第四十四期 44 (November 24, 1966), in *Taiwan sheng zhengfu gongbao* 臺灣省政府公報 (Nantou: Taiwan Provincial Government), 2.
162. Zhipan 志磐, *Fozu tongji* 佛祖統紀, *juan* 46, in *Taisho Shinshu Daizokyo* 大正新修大藏經 (Taipei: Xinwenfeng chuban gongsi, 1983), vol. 49, 419a.
163. Zhou Mi 周密, *Qidong yeyu* 齊東野語, ed. Zhang Maopeng 張茂鵬 (Beijing: Zhonghua, 1983), *juan* 12, "Sanjiao tu zan" 三教圖贊, 222.
164. Xu Ke 徐珂, *Qing bai leichao* 清稗類鈔 (Taipei: Commercial Press, 1966), *juan* 15, zongjiao lei 宗教類 (*bai* 稗 37), 3.
165. Ironically, this promotion of Confucian rites was the Guangxu Emperor's gift to the empress dowager. Chen Baochen 陳寶琛, *DaQing Dezong Jinghuangdi (Guangxu) shilu* 大清德宗景 (光緒) 皇帝實錄 (Taipei: Xinwenfeng chuban gongsi, 1978), *juan* 566, 12.
166. Kang Youwei, "Zhi Beijing Kongjiaohui dian" 致北京孔教會電, in *Kang Youwei zhenglun ji* 康有為政論集, ed. Tang Zhijun 湯志鈞 (Beijing: Zhonghua, 1981), 2:921.

2. Confucianism as a Religion

The Chinese-language version of this chapter was first published in *Asian Studies* 亞洲研究 (Hong Kong) 23 (1997): 184–233; and in Huang Chin-shing, *Sages and Saints: Collected Essays on History and Religions* 聖賢與聖徒：歷史與宗教論文集 (Taipei: Asian Culture Press, 2001, 2004), 49–87. It was also reprinted in You Zi'an 游子安, ed., *Zhongguo zongjiao xinyang: Zhongguo wenhua zhongxin jiangzuo xilie* 中國宗教信仰：中國文化中心講座系列 (Hong Kong: City University of Hong Kong Press, 2006); and in Chen Ming 陳明, ed., *Rujiao xinlun* 儒教新論 (Guiyang: Guizhou Renmin chubanshe, 2010), 43–63. A Japanese-language version appeared as "Shūkyō to shite no jukyō: hikaku shūkyō niyoru shohoteki kentou 宗教としての儒教：比較宗教による初步的檢討," in *Shūkyō to shite no jukyō* 宗教としての儒教, ed. Okuzaki Hiroshi 奧崎裕司 and Richard Shek 石漢椿 (Tokyo: Kyukoshoin, 2011), 74–110.

1. Matteo Ricci 利瑪竇, *Tianzhu shiyi* 天主實義, *juan* 1, 12a. Published in the Chongzhen 崇禎 reign of the Ming dynasty (1628–1644).

2. Zhao Erxun 趙爾巽, *Qingshi gao* 清史稿, ed. Qi Gong 啟功 (Beijing: Zhonghua, 1994), *juan* 9, 311.
3. On the Confucian cult movement in Southeast Asia (excluding Vietnam and Indonesia), see Yan Qinghuang 顏清湟, "1899–1911 nian Xinjiapo he Malaiya de Kongjiao fuxing yundong" 1899–1911 年新加坡和馬來亞的孔教復興運動, in *Guowai Zhongguo jindaishi yanjiu* 國外中國近代史研究 (Beijing: China Social Sciences Press, 1985), 8:215–46.
4. Liang Qichao 梁啟超, *Qingdai xueshu gailun* 清代學術概論, in *Yinbingshi Zhuanji* 飲冰室專集, in *Yinbingshi heji* 飲冰室合集 (Shanghai: Chung Hwa, 1936), vol. 9, sec. 26, 63. On early participation in the Confucius cult, see *Yi jiao congbian* 翼教叢編, ed. Su Yu 蘇輿 (Taipei: Institute of Chinese Literature and Philosophy, Academia Sinica, 2005).
5. Deng Haoran 鄧浩然, "Yinshu yuanqi zhi er" 印書緣起之二, in *Gaige Qufu lin miao banfa boyi* 改革曲阜林廟辦法駁議, ed. Chen Huanzhang 陳煥章, in *Zun Kong congshu* 尊孔叢書 (Kowloon: Yiqiang yinshuachang, 1963), 4.
6. Liang Qichao, "Nanhai Kang xiansheng zhuan" 南海康先生傳 (1901), in *Yinbingshi wenji* 飲冰室文集 (Taipei: Chung Hwa, 1970), vol. 2, *juan* 6, 86.
7. Kang Youwei 康有為, "Kongjiaohui xu er" 孔教會序二 (October 7, 1912), in *Kang Nanhai zhengshi wenxuan (1898–1927)* 康南海政史文選, ed. Shen Maojun 沈茂駿 (Guangzhou: Guangdong Higher Education Press, 1993), 118.
8. Chen Huanzhang 陳煥章, *Kongjiao lun* 孔教論, in *Minguo congshu* 民國叢書 (Kongjiaohui and Shanghai: Commercial Press, 1913; repr., Shanghai: Shanghai shudian, 1992), series 4, no. 2, 31.
9. Kang Youwei, "Kongjiaohui xu er," 116.
10. Liang Qichao, "Baojiao fei suoyi zun Kong lun" 保教非所以尊孔論 (1902), in *Yinbingshi wenji*, vol. 2, *juan* 9, 53.
11. See, for example, Kang Youwei, "Kongjiaohui xu er," 117–118; and Chen Huanzhang, *Kongjiao lun*, 1–4.
12. Kang Youwei called Confucius "the religious founder of the great earth" (大地教主) and "the religious founder for ten thousand generations" (萬世教主). See Kang Youwei, *Kongzi gaizhi kao* 孔子改制考 (Beijing: Zhonghua, 1988), 7; and *juan* 7, 165.
13. Chen Huanzhang, *Kongjiao lun*, 61.
14. Kang Youwei, "Yi Kongjiao wei guojiao pei tian yi" 以孔教為國教配天議 (April 1913), in *Kang Nanhai zhengshi wenxuan*, 129–134.
15. See, for example, Chen Duxiu 陳獨秀, "Bo Kang Youwei zhi zongtong zongli shu" 駁康有為致總統總理書 (October 1, 1916). See also *Duxiu wencun* 獨秀文存 (Shanghai: Yadong tushuguan 上海亞東圖書館, 1922; repr., Hefei: Anhui Renmin chubanshe, 1987), 1:68–72.
16. Liang Qichao, "Nanhai Kang xiansheng zhuan," in *Yinbingshi wenji*, vol. 2, *juan* 6, 67. See also Liang Qichao, "Fu youren lun baojiao shu" 復友人論保教書

(1897) and "Lun Zhina zongjiao gaige" 論支那宗教改革 (1899), in *Yinbingshi wenji*, vol. 1, *juan* 3, 9–11, 55–61.

17. Liang Qichao, "Baojiao fei suoyi zun Kong lun," in *Yinbingshi wenji*, vol. 2, *juan* 9, 52. For his letters with Yan Fu 嚴復 (1853–1921), beginning from 1896, see Liang Qichao, "Yu Yan Youling xiansheng shu" 與嚴幼陵先生書, in *Yinbingshi wenji*, vol. 1, *juan* 1, 106–111. On Yan Fu's perspective, see "You ru san bao" 有如三保 (June 3–4, 1898) and "Baojiao yu yi" 保教餘義 (June 7–8, 1898), in *Yan Jidao wenchao* 嚴幾道文鈔 (Shanghai Guohua shuju, 1922; repr., Taipei: Shijie shuju, 1971), *juan* 2, 1a–5a, 8a–10b.

18. Liang Qichao, "Baojiao fei suoyi zun Kong lun," in *Yinbingshi wenji*, vol. 2, *juan* 9, 52.

19. Zhang Taiyan 章太炎, "Bo jianli Kongjiao yi 駁建立孔教議," in *Taiyan wenlu chubian* 太炎文錄初編, in *Zhang Taiyan quanji* 章太炎全集 (Shanghai: Shanghai Renmin chubanshe, 1985), 4:197. See also Zhang Taiyan, "Rushu zhenlun ji you fan Kongjiao zhi guandian" 儒術真論即有反孔教之觀點 (1899), in *Zhang Taiyan zhenglun xuanji* 章太炎政論選集, ed. Tang Zhijun 湯志鈞 (Beijing: Zhonghua, 1977), 1:118–125.

20. Zhang Taiyan, "Bo jianli Kongjiao yi," 4:197.

21. Hu Shi 胡適, "Wu Yu wenlu xu" 吳虞文錄序 (June 16, 1921), in *Hu Shi wencun* 胡適文存 (Taipei: Far East, 1953), vol. 1, *juan* 4, 794–797.

22. Chen Duxiu, "Kongzi zhi dao yu xiandai shenghuo" 孔子之道與現代生活 (December 1, 1916), in *Duxiu wencun*, 1:80–81. See also Chen Duxiu, "Zai lun Kongjiao wenti" 再論孔教問題 (January 1, 1917), "Fupi yu zun Kong" 復辟與尊孔 (August 1, 1917), and "Da Wu Youling" 答吳又陵 (January 1, 1917), in *Duxiu wencun*, 1:91–93, 111–116; 3:646. For further details, see Tse-tsung Chow, "The Anti-Confucian Movement in Early Republican China," in *The Confucian Persuasion*, ed. Arthur F. Wright (Stanford, Calif.: Stanford University Press, 1960), 288–312. On Liang Qichao's 1913 support for the cult of Confucius, but with freedom of religions, see Liang Qichao, "Jinbudang ni Zhonghuaminguo xianfa caoan" 進步黨擬中華民國憲法草案 (1913), in *Yinbingshi wenji*, vol. 6, *juan* 30, 62. For his opposition to the cult of Confucius in 1915, see Liang Qichao, "Kongzi jiaoyi shiji biyi yu jinri guomin zhe he zai yu changming zhi qi dao he you" 孔子教義實際裨益於今日國民者何在欲昌明之其道何由 (1915), in *Yinbingshi wenji*, vol. 6, *juan* 33, 60–67.

23. Wu Yu 吳虞, "Jiazu zhidu wei zhuanzhi zhuyi zhi genju lun" 家族制度為專制主義之根據論, "Chiren yu lijiao" 吃人與禮教, in *Wu Yu wenlu* 吳虞文錄, in *Minguo congshu* (Yadong tushuguan, 1927; repr., Shanghai: Shanghai shudian, 1992), series 2, no. 96, 1:1–13, 63–72.

24. Cai Yuanpei 蔡元培, "Zai xinjiaoziyouhui zhi yanshuo" 在信教自由會之演說 (January 1917), in *Cai Yuanpei wenji* 蔡元培文集, ed. Gao Pingshu 高平叔 (Taipei: Jinxiu chuban shiye gufen youxian gongsi, 1995), *juan* 5, "Zhexue" 哲學, 298.

25. Cai Yuanpei, "Zai xinjiaoziyouhui zhi yanshuo," 299.
26. Chen Duxiu, "Zai lun Kongjiao wenti," 1:91.
27. Cai Yuanpei, "Yi meiyu dai zongjiao shuo" 以美育代宗教說 (August 1917), in *Cai Yuanpei wenji, juan* 2, "Jiaoyu shang" 教育上, 378.
28. Chen Huanzhang, *Kongjiao lun*, 2–3, 93; Chen Duxiu, "Bo Kang Youwei zhi zongtong zongli shu," 1:69; Cai Yuanpei, "Zai xinjiaoziyouhui zhi yanshuo," 299.
29. Kang Youwei, "Kongjiaohui xu er," 115–116; Liang Qichao, "Baojiao fei suoyi zun Kong lun," in *Yinbingshi wenji*, vol. 2, *juan* 9, 53; Chen Duxiu, "Bo Kang Youwei zhi zongtong zongli shu," 1:69–70.
30. See Miyakawa Hisayuki 宮川尚志, "Jukyō no shūkyōteki seikaku" 儒教の宗教的性格, *Shūkyō kenkyū* 宗教研究 38, no. 1 (January 1965): 1–24.
31. C. K. Yang, *Religion in Chinese Society: A Study of Contemporary Social Functions of Religion and Some of Their Historical Factors* (Berkeley: University of California Press, 1961), 26–27, and chap. 10.
32. Mou Zhongjian 牟鍾鑒, *Zhongguo zongjiao yu wenhua* 中國宗教與文化 (Taipei: Tangshan, 1995), 7, 139.
33. Émile Durkheim, *The Elementary Forms of Religious Life*, trans. Karen E. Fields (New York: Free Press, 1995), chap. 1.
34. Heinrich von Stietencron, "Hindu Religious Traditions and the Concept of 'Religion': Consequences of Cross-Cultural Research," 4th Gonda Lecture (1996), *International Institute for Asian Studies Newsletter* 11 (1997): 18.
35. Kang Youwei, "Kongzi wei zhifa zhi wang kao" 孔子為制法之王考, *Kongzi gaizhi kao, juan* 8. *Chenwei* were the unorthodox but popular interpretations of Confucian classics in the Han period.
36. Zhang Taiyan, "Bo jianli Kongjiao yi," 4:196–198.
37. For modern scholars' perceptions of Confucius during the Han, see Gu Jiegang 顧頡剛, "Chunqiu shi de Kongzi he Handai de Kongzi" 春秋時的孔子和漢代的孔子 (October 3, 1926), in *Gushi bian* 古史辨, ed. Gu Jiegang, in *Minguo congshu* (Pushe 樸社, 1930; repr., Shanghai: Shanghai shudian, 1992), series 4, no. 66, 2:131–139. See also Zhou Yutong 周予同, "Weichen zhong de Kongsheng yu tade mentu" 緯讖中的孔聖與他的門徒, in *Zhou Yutong jingxueshi lunzhu xuanji* 周予同經學史論著選集, ed. Zhu Weizheng 朱維錚 (Shanghai: Shanghai Renmin chubanshe, 1983), 292–321.
38. Fan Ye 范曄, "Zhi di ba jisi zhong" 志第八祭祀中, *Hou Hanshu* 後漢書 (Taipei: Dingwen shuju, 1983), 3188.
39. Fan Ye, *Hou Hanshu juan* 7, 313–317.
40. Liu Zhen 劉珍, *Dongguan Han ji jiaozhu* 東觀漢記校注, ed. Wu Shuping 吳樹平 (Zhengzhou: Zhongzhou guji chubanshe, 1987), *juan* 3, 126.
41. Fan Ye, "Zhi di ba jisi zhong," *Hou Hanshu*, 3188.
42. Ren Jiyu 任繼愈, *Zhongguo Daojiao shi* 中國道教史 (Shanghai: Shanghai Renmin chubanshe, 1990), 12–15.

43. Fan Ye, *Hou Hanshu*, juan 7, 320.
44. On the entry of Buddhism into China, see Tang Yongtong 湯用彤, *Han Wei liang Jin Nanbeichao Fojiao shi* 漢魏兩晉南北朝佛教史 (Beijing: Zhonghua, 1955), chaps. 4–6.
45. Fan Ye, *Hou Hanshu*, juan 42, 1428.
46. Fan Ye, *Hou Hanshu*, juan 30b, 1082.
47. Tang Yongtong, "Handai Fofa zhi liubu" 漢代佛法之流布, in *Han Wei liang Jin Nanbeichao Fojiao shi*, 56.
48. Wang Xianqian 王先謙, *Hou Hanshu jijie* 後漢書集解 (Taipei: Yiwen yinshuguan, 1951), juan 7, 13b–14a.
49. Daoxuan 道宣, *Ji gujin Fo Dao lunheng* 集古今佛道論衡, juan 2, in *Taisho Shinshu Daizokyo* 大正新修大藏經 [*Taishozo* 大正藏] (1924–1934; repr., Taipei: Xinwenfeng chuban gongsi, 1983), vol. 52, 373c.
50. Daoxuan, *Ji gujin Fo Dao lunheng*, vol. 52, 373c.
51. Hong Gua 洪适, *Li shi* 隸釋 (Hongshi Himuzhai 洪氏晦木齋; repr., Beijing: Zhonghua, 1985), juan 1, 15a–15b, 18a–18b.
52. Hong Gua, *Li shi*, 26b.
53. Hong Gua, *Li shi*, 27b–28a. See also Huang Chin-shing, "Power and Belief: The Shaping of a National Cult, Worship in the Confucian Temple in Imperial China 權力與信仰：孔廟祭祀制度的形成," in *Entering the Master's Sanctuary: Power, Belief and Legitimacy in Traditional China* 優入聖域：權力、信仰與正當性 (Taipei: Asian Culture Press, 1994), 163–216.
54. Chen Pan 陳槃, "A Revision of 'An Explanation of Zhong Huang's Annotations in *The Canon of Filial Piety*'" 孝經中黃讖解題改寫本, *Bulletin of the Institute of History and Philology, Academia Sinica* 中央研究院歷史語言研究所集刊 59, no. 4 (December 1988): 891–897.
55. Chen Shou 陳壽, *Sanguo zhi* 三國志 (Taipei: Dingwen shuju, 1983), juan 1, 32.
56. Although scholars debate the dating of *Mouzi lihuo lun* 理惑論, the range of possible dates does not affect my presentation of its overall influence.
57. Mouzi, *Mouzi lihuo lun*, in Sengyou 僧祐, *Hong ming ji* 弘明集, juan, 1, in *Taishozo*, vol. 52, 1b.
58. Mouzi, *Mouzi lihuo lun*, vol. 52, 3b, 5b.
59. Mouzi, *Mouzi lihuo lun*, vol. 52, 2a, 2c.
60. Wang Ming 王明, "Zhishan chuxie lingren shoudao jiewen di yibaiba" 致善除邪令人受道戒文第一百八, in *Taipingjing hejiao* 太平經合校 (Beijing: Zhonghua, 1960), juan 71, 289.
61. "Sage" was the highest standard in Confucianism. In the *Analects*, Confucius said, "The sage and the man of perfect virtue—how dare I rank myself with them?" and "A sage it is not mine to see; could I see a man of real talent and virtue? That would satisfy me." Likewise, Confucius often praised his

disciple Yan Hui as a worthy: "An admirable worthy indeed was Hui!" See Zhu Xi 朱熹, *Lunyu jizhu* 論語集注, in *Sishu zhangju jizhu* 四書章句集注 (Beijing: Zhonghua, 1983), *juan* 4, 99, 101; *juan* 3, 87.

62. Wang Ming, *Baopuzi neipian jiaoshi* 抱朴子內篇校釋 (Beijing: Zhonghua, 1988), *juan* 7, "Sai nan" 塞難, 138. *juan* 10, "Ming ben" 明本, 184–185.

63. In addition to *Laozi huahu jing* 老子化胡經, similar content appears in *Laojun bianhua wuji jing* 老君變化無極經 and *Laozi bianhua jing* 老子變化經. See *Daocang tiyao* 道藏提要, ed. Ren Jiyu 任繼愈 (Beijing: China Social Sciences Press, 1995), 943; and Xiang Mai 祥邁, *Bianwei lu* 辯偽錄, *juan* 2, in *Taishozo*, vol. 52, 764b.

64. Dao'an 道安, *Er jiao lun* 二教論, in Daoxuan, *Guang hong ming ji* 廣弘明集, *juan* 8, in *Taishozo*, vol. 52, 140a.

65. Xiao Yan 蕭衍 (Emperor Wu of the Liang dynasty 梁武帝), "She shi Lilao Daofa zhao" 捨事李老道法詔, in *Guang hong ming ji*, *juan* 4, in *Taishozo*, vol. 52, 112a–112b.

66. Chen Shan 陳善, *Men shi xinhua* 捫蝨新話, in *Congshu jicheng chubian* 叢書集成初編 (Baoyantang miji 寶顏堂祕笈; repr., Shanghai: Commercial Press, 1939), vols. 310–311, *juan* 2, "Kongzi Laozi jie shi pusa" 孔子老子皆是菩薩, 18.

67. Wang Ming, *Baopuzi neipian jiaoshi*, *juan* 7, 138.

68. Bian Shao 邊韶, "Laozi ming 老子銘," in *Quan shanggu sandai Qin Han Sanguo Liuchao wen* 全上古三代秦漢三國六朝文, ed. Yan Kejun 嚴可均 (Taipei: Hongye shuju, 1975), *juan* 62, 3b.

69. Zhiqian 支謙, trans., *Fo shuo taizi ruiying benqi jing* 佛說太子瑞應本起經, *juan* 1, in *Taishozo*, vol. 3, 473b.

70. Ge Hong 葛洪, *Shenxian zhuan* 神仙傳, in *Daocang jinghua lu* 道藏精華錄, ed. Shouyizi 守一子 (Hangzhou: Zhejiang guji chubanshe, 1989), *juan* 1, 1b. See also Robert Ford Campany, *To Live as Long as Heaven and Earth: A Translation and Study of Ge Hong's Traditions of Divine Transcendents* (Berkeley: University of California Press, 2002).

71. Zhen Luan 甄鸞, "Xiao dao lun" 笑道論, in *Guang hong ming ji*, *juan* 9, in *Taishozo*, vol. 52, 144c.

72. Liu Yiqing 劉義慶, *Shi shuo xin yu jiaojian* 世說新語校箋, commentary by Liu Xiaobiao 劉孝標 and Yang Yong 楊勇 (Taipei: Minglun chubanshe, 1970), 361.

73. Dao'an, *Er jiao lun*, in *Taishozo*, vol. 52, 138b.

74. See, for example, Tang Taizong, "Ling daoshi zai seng qian zhao" 令道士在僧前詔, in *Guang hong ming ji*, *juan* 25, in *Taishozo*, vol. 52, 283c. Compare with Wu Zetian's 武則天 691 edict, in Liu Xu 劉昫, *Jiu Tangshu* 舊唐書 (Taipei: Dingwen shuju, 1981), *juan* 6, 121.

75. Daoxuan, "Zhou mie Fofa ji dao su yishi" 周滅佛法集道俗議事, in *Guang hong ming ji*, *juan* 8, in *Taishozo*, vol. 52, 136a.

76. Linghu Defen 令狐德棻, *Zhoushu* 周書 (Taipei: Dingwen shuju, 1980), *juan* 5, 83, 85.
77. *Guang hong ming ji* and *Ji gujin Fo Dao lunheng* include these edicts.
78. Wang Dang 王讜, *Tang yulin jiaozheng* 唐語林校證, ed. Zhou Xunchu 周勛初 (Beijing: Zhonghua, 1987), *juan* 6, 519. According to Buddhist texts, around the center of the world are four other continents; China is located on one of these, named Jambudvīpa. See *Da loutan jing* 大樓炭經, *juan* 1, in *Taishozo*, vol. 1, 277.
79. See Du You 杜佑, *Tongdian* 通典, ed. Wang Wenjin 王文錦 (Beijing: Zhonghua, 1988), *juan* 53, 1478, 1481.
80. Bai Juyi 白居易, "Sanjiao lun heng" 三教論衡, in *Bai Juyi ji jianjiao* 白居易集箋校, commentary by Zhu Jincheng 朱金城 (Shanghai: Shanghai guji chubanshe, 1988), *juan* 68, 3682–3683.
81. Mandated by Qing Renzong 清仁宗 (Jiaqing 嘉慶 emperor, r. 1796–1820). *Qin ding quan Tang wen* 欽定全唐文, ed. Dong Gao 董誥 (Taipei: Datong shuju, 1979), *juan* 309–313.
82. Bai Juyi, "Sanjiao lunheng," in *Bai Juyi ji jianjiao*, *juan* 68, 3673–3683.
83. Dao'an, *Er jiao lun*, in *Taishozo*, vol. 52, 136c.
84. Huang Zongxi 黃宗羲, "Yuzhang xuean" 豫章學案, in *Song Yuan xuean* 宋元學案 (Beijing: Zhonghua, 1986), *juan* 39, 1273. This essay is the selection of Luo Congyan 羅從彥 (1072–1135), "Zun Yao lu" 遵堯錄.
85. Yelü Chucai 耶律楚材, "Jiyong zhi shilang" 寄用之侍郎, in *Zhanran jushi wenji* 湛然居士文集, in *Sibu congkan chubian,* ji bu 四部叢刊初編・集部 (Shanghai: Hanfenlou 涵芬樓; repr., Shanghai: Shanghai shudian, 1989), vol. 223, *juan* 6, 15a.
86. Zhipan 志磐, *Fozu tongji* 佛祖統紀, *juan* 47, in *Taishozo*, vol. 49, 430a.
87. Tang Zhen 唐甄, *Qian shu* 潛書 (Beijing: Zhonghua, 1984), *juan* 1a, "Xing gong" 性功, 22.
88. Zhipan, *Fozu tongji*, *juan* 47, in *Taishozo*, vol. 49, 429c–430a.
89. Tang Zhen, *Qian shu*, *juan* 1a, "Xing gong," 22.
90. Wei Zheng 魏徵, *Suishu* 隋書 (Taipei: Dingwen, 1980), *juan* 77, 1754.
91. Tao Zongyi 陶宗儀, *Nancun chuo geng lu* 南村輟耕錄 (Beijing: Zhonghua, 1980), *juan* 5, 57, "San jiao" 三教.
92. Xiang Mai, *Bianwei lu*, *juan* 3, in *Taishozo*, vol. 52, 770c.
93. See Cai Meibiao 蔡美彪 et al., eds., *Zhongguo lishi dacidian: Liao Xia Jin Yuan shi juan* 中國歷史大辭典・遼夏金元史卷 (Shanghai: Shanghai Lexicographical Publishing, 1986), 314, 334, and 478.
94. Song Lian 宋濂, *Yuanshi* 元史 (Taipei: Dingwen shuju, 1980), *juan* 163, 3824–3825.
95. Tao Zongyi, *Nancun chuo geng lu*, *juan* 2, 22, "Shou Kongzi jie" 受孔子戒.
96. Song Lian, *Yuanshi*, *juan* 183, 4222.

97. Xia Jingqu 夏敬渠, *Yesou pu yan* 野叟曝言 (Taipei: Shijie shuju, 1962), chap. 154.
98. "Zhang Daoling qi shi Zhao Sheng" 張道陵七試趙昇, in *Gujin xiaoshuo* 古今小說, ed. Feng Menglong, in *Guben xiaoshuo congkan* 古本小說叢刊 (Beijing: Zhonghua, 1990), vol. 31, 1–4, *juan* 13, 1a.
99. Xu Ke 徐珂, "Qing huihuijiao" 青回回教, in *Qing bai leichao* 清稗類鈔 [Qing Petty Matters Anthology] (Taipei: Commercial Press, 1966), *juan* 15, 40. See also "Zhongjian Qingzhensi ji" 重建清真寺記, in Chen Yuan 陳垣, "Kaifeng Yisileyejiao kao" 開封一賜樂業教考, in *Chen Yuan shixue lunzhu xuan* 陳垣史學論著選, ed. Wu Ze 吳澤 (Shanghai: Shanghai Renmin chubanshe, 1981), 67–68. The Three Pure Ones (三清), or three founding masters, are Yuanshi *tianzun* 元始天尊, Lingbao *tianzun* 靈寶天尊, and Daode *tianzun* 道德天尊.
100. Yang Yongchang 楊永昌, "Zhongguo Qingzhensi mingcheng de youlai ji qi yange" 中國清真寺名稱的由來及其沿革, in *Mantan Qingzhensi* 漫談清真寺 (Yinchuan: Ningxia Renmin chubanshe, 1981), 1. Chen Yuan, "Kaifeng yisileyejiao kao," 77, says that *Yisileye* 一賜樂業 or *Yishilie* 以色列 means "Israel."
101. Sun Chuo 孫綽, *Yu dao lun* 喻道論, in *Hong ming ji*, *juan* 3, in *Taishozo*, vol. 52, 17a.
102. For Tang Taizong's statement about the descent of the House of Li from Laozi, in 637, see Wu Yun 吳雲, ed., *Tang Taizong ji* 唐太宗集 (Xian: Shaanxi Renmin chubanshe), 318.
103. Wang Qinruo 王欽若, ed., *Cefu yuangui* 冊府元龜 (Taipei: Chung Hwa, 1972), *juan* 50, 3a.
104. Luo Xianglin 羅香林, "Tangdai sanjiao jianglun kao" 唐代三教講論考, *Journal of Oriental Studies* 東方文化 1, no. 1 (January 1954): 85–97.
105. Zhang Jiuling 張九齡, "He lun sanjiao zhuang 賀論三教狀," in *Qujiang ji* 曲江集 (Guangzhou: Guangdong Renmin chubanshe, 1986), 558. See also Jao Tsung-i 饒宗頤, "Sanjiao lun yu Song Jin xueshu" 三教論與宋金學術, *Dongxi wenhua* 東西文化 11 (May 1968): 24.
106. Ming Taizu 明太祖, "Sanjiao lun" 三教論, in *Ming Taizu wenji* 明太祖文集, ed. Yao Shiguan 姚士觀 and Shen Fu 沈鈇, in *Jingyin Wenyuange sikuquanshu* 景印文淵閣四庫全書 (Taipei: Commercial Press, 1983), vol. 1223, *juan* 10, 18b.
107. As cited in Jao Tsung-i, "Sanjiao lun yu Song Jin xueshu," 32.
108. Yongrong 永瑢 and Ji Yun 紀昀, *Qin ding sikuquanshu zongmu tiyao* 欽定四庫全書總目提要, in *Jingyin Wenyuange sikuquanshu*, vol. 1–5, *juan* 132, 12a.
109. Chen Zhong-yu 陳衷瑜, ed., *Linzi benxing shilu* 林子本行實錄 (Jinjiang: Shangyang shuyuan, 1939), 14b.
110. Pan Jingruo 潘鏡若, ed. *Sanjiao kaimi guizheng yanyi* 三教開迷歸正演義, in *Guben xiaoshuo jicheng* 古本小說集成 (Shanghai: Shanghai guji chubanshe, 1990), *juan* 1, 6a.

111. Xu Ke, *Qing bai leichao, juan* 15, "Zongjiao lei" 宗教類 (*bai* 稗 37), "Henan you sanjiaotang" 河南有三教堂, 3. See also Shigematsu Toshiaki 重松俊章, "Shina sankyo shi jo no jakkan no mondai" 支那三教史上の若干の問題, *Shien* 21 (1939): 143–152.
112. Zhipan, *Fozu tongji, juan* 46, in *Taishozo*, vol. 49, 419a.
113. Zhou Mi 周密, *Qidong yeyu* 齊東野語, ed. Zhang Maopeng 張茂鵬 (Beijing: Zhonghua, 1983), *juan* 12, 222.
114. Xiang Mai, *Bianwei lu, juan* 2, in *Taishozo*, vol. 52, 763b; Cao An 曹安, *Lanyan zhangyu* 讕言長語, in *Baoyantang miji* 寶顏堂祕笈, ed. Chen Jiru 陳繼儒 (Shanghai: Wenming shuju, 1922), vol. 36, *juan* 1, 5b.
115. Sun Fu 孫復, "Ruru" 儒辱, in *Sun Mingfu xiaoji* 孫明復小集, in *Jingyin Wenyuange sikuquanshu*, vol. 1090, 37b.
116. *Xinbian lianxiang soushenguangji* 新編連相搜神廣記 (published in the Yuan dynasty), in *Huitu sanjiao yuanliu soushen daquan* 繪圖三教源流搜神大全 (Shanghai: Shanghai guji chubanshe, 1990), appendix (*fulu* 附錄).
117. Yelü Chucai, *Zhanran jushi wenji, juan* 3, 6a; Lin Guoping 林國平, *Lin Zhao'en yu sanyijiao* 林兆恩與三一教 (Fuzhou: Fujian Renmin chubanshe, 1992).
118. See Allen John Young (林樂知, 1836–1907), "Xiao bian mingjiao lun" 消變明教論, in *Zhongguo sixiang baoku* 中國思想寶庫 (Beijing: Zhongguo guangbo dianshi chubanshe, 1990), 186.
119. Okamatsu Santaro 岡松參太郎, *Linshi Taiwan jiuguan diaochahui diyi bu diaocha disan hui baogaoshu, Taiwan sifa* 臨時臺灣舊慣調查會第一部調查第三回報告書・臺灣私法, trans. Chen Jintian 陳金田 (Nantou: Taiwan sheng wenxian weiyuanhui, 1990), *juan* 2, 170.
120. On the religions of other cultures, see Wilfred Cantwell Smith, *The Meaning and End of Religion* (Minneapolis, Minn.: Fortress, 1991), chap. 3.
121. Lin Zhao'en 林兆恩, *Linzi quanji* 林子全集, in *Sikuquanshu cunmu congshu*, zibu 四庫全書存目叢書・子部 (Ming Chongzhen era, 1628–1644; repr., Tainan: Zhuangyan wenhua shiye youxian gongsi, 1995), vol. 91–92, *juan* 10, "Zong Kong zhi ru" 宗孔之儒, 1a.
122. Lin Zhao'en, *Linzi quanji, juan* 6, 1b.
123. Ming Taizu, "Sanjiao lun," *juan* 10, 17a–17b, 18b.
124. Max Weber, *Economy and Society: An Outline of Interpretive Sociology*, ed. Guenther Roth and Claus Wittich (Berkeley: University of California Press, 1978), 399.
125. Paul Tillich, *Dynamics of Faith* (New York: Harper & Row, 1957).
126. Chen Duxiu, "Zai lun Kongjiao wenti," 1, no. 94.
127. See Yazi 亞子 and Liangzi 良子, *Kongfu da jienan* 孔府大劫難 (Hong Kong: Tiandi tushu gongsi, 1992).
128. In the Yan Yuan chapter of the *Analects*, Confucius said: "Yen Yuan asked about perfect virtue. The Master said, 'To subdue one's self and return to

propriety, is perfect virtue. If a man can for one day subdue himself and return to propriety, all under heaven will ascribe perfect virtue to him. Is the practice of perfect virtue from a man himself, or is it from others?'" James Legge, trans., *The Chinese Classics* (Oxford: Clarendon, 1893; repr., Taipei: SMC, 1991), vol. 1, 250. Also see Zhu Xi, *Lunyu jizhu, juan* 6, 131.

3. Sages and Saints

The Chinese-language version of this chapter was first published as "Sages and Saints: A Comparison between Confucianism and Christianity in Terms of Canonization" "聖賢"與"聖徒": 儒教從祀制與基督教封聖制的比較, in the *Bulletin of the Institute of History and Philology, Academia Sinica* 中央研究院歷史語言研究所集刊 71, no. 3 (September 2000): 509–561; and in Huang Chin-shing, *Sages and Saints: Collected Essays on History and Religions* 聖賢與聖徒: 歷史與宗教論文集 (Taipei: Asian Culture Press, 2001), 89–179; or (Beijing: Peking University Press, 2005), 144–204.

1. See Huang Chin-shing, "Knowledge and Belief: Confucian Canonization and the Confucian Conception of Orthodoxy" 學術與信仰: 論孔廟從祀制與儒家道統意識, in *Entering the Master's Sanctuary: Power, Belief and Legitimacy in Traditional China* 優入聖域: 權力、信仰與正當性 (Taipei: Asia Culture Press, 1994), 217–311.
2. On saints as exemplars in Christianity, see Peter Brown, "The Saint as Exemplar in Late Antiquity," in *Saints and Virtues*, ed. John Stratton Hawley (Berkeley: University of California Press, 1987), 3–14.
3. Rodney L. Taylor, "The Sage as Saint," in *Sainthood: Its Manifestations in World Religions*, ed. Richard Kieckhefer and George D. Bond (Berkeley: University of California Press, 1988), 218–242.
4. Fan Ye 范曄, *Hou Hanshu* 後漢書 (Taipei: Dingwen shuju, 1983), *juan* 2, 118; *juan* 3, 150; and *juan* 5, 238.
5. Wang Pu 王溥, *Tang huiyao* 唐會要 (Kyoto: Chubun shuppansha, 1978), *juan* 35, 636.
6. For a detailed analysis, see Huang Chin-shing, "Knowledge and Belief" (Asian Culture Press), 217–311.
7. For example, in the New Testament, 1 Corinthians 1:1–2: "Paul, called by the will of God to be an apostle of Christ Jesus, and our brother Sosthenes, To the church of God that is in Corinth, to those sanctified in Christ Jesus, called to be saints . . ." (English Standard Version).
8. "The Martyrdom of St. Polycarp: Bishop of Smyrna," in *Medieval Saints: A Reader*, ed. Mary-Ann Stouck (Peterborough: Broadview, 1998), 3–9; and

David Hugh Farmer, *The Oxford Dictionary of Saints* (Oxford: Oxford University Press, 1992), xviii, 405.

9. Peter Brown, *Society and the Holy in Late Antiquity* (Berkeley: University of California Press, 1982), 245.
10. Xu Song 許嵩, *Jiankang shilu* 建康實錄 (Beijing: Zhonghua, 1986), *juan* 9, 283.
11. See Huang Chin-shing, "Power and Belief: The Shaping of a National Cult, Worship of the Confucian Temple in Imperial China" 權力與信仰：孔廟祭祀制度的形成, in *Entering the Master's Sanctuary: Power, Belief and Legitimacy in Traditional China* 優入聖域：權力、信仰與正當性 (Taipei: Asian Culture Press), 195–203
12. Chen Shou 陳壽, *Sanguo zhi* 三國志 (Taipei: Dingwen shuju, 1983), *juan* 2, 78.
13. Pan Xiang 潘相, ed., *Qufu xianzhi* 曲阜縣志 (1774; repr., Taipei: Taiwan Xuesheng shuju, 1968), *juan* 21, 11b.
14. Ouyang Xiu 歐陽修 and Song Qi 宋祁, *Xin Tangshu* 新唐書 (Taipei: Dingwen shuju, 1981), *juan* 15, 373.
15. Liu Yuxi 劉禹錫, *Liu Yuxi ji* 劉禹錫集 (Shanghai: Shanghai Renmin chubanshe, 1975), *juan* 20, 184.
16. Lü Yuanshan 呂元善, *Shengmen zhi* 聖門志, in *Congshu jicheng chubian* 叢書集成初編 (Shanghai: Commercial Press, 1936), vols. 3318–3321, *juan* 1a, 18.
17. Wang Shizhen 王世貞, *Yanzhou shanren sibu gao* 弇州山人四部稿 (Taipei: Weiwen tushu gongsi, 1976), *juan* 115, 2a. Originally published by Shijingtang 世經堂 during the Wanli reign of the Ming dynasty (1573–1620).
18. Sun Chengze 孫承澤, *Tianfu Guangji* 天府廣記 (Beijing: Tianjing chubanshe, 1962), *juan* 9, 88–89.
19. *Shizong shilu* 明世宗實錄, in *Ming shilu* 明實錄, ed. Huang Chang-chien 黃彰健 (Taipei: Institute of History and Philology, Academia Sinica, 1966), *juan* 235, 2a.
20. *Muzong shilu* 明穆宗實錄, in *Ming shilu* 明實錄, *juan* 61, 5b–6a.
21. Wang Shizhen, *Yanzhou shanren sibu gao*, *juan* 115, 2a.
22. For instance, persuaded by Ambrose (c. 340–397), the bishop of Milan, Augustine's mother ceased to participate in the local African customs regarding saints. See Augustine, *Confessions*, trans. F. J. Sheed (Indianapolis: Hackett, 1993), 88–89.
23. Peter Brown, *The Cult of the Saints: Its Rise and Function in Latin Christianity* (Chicago: University of Chicago Press, 1981), chaps. 1–2.
24. Richard Kieckhefer, "Imitators of Christ: Sainthood in the Christian Tradition," in *Sainthood: Its Manifestations in World Religions*, ed. Richard Kieckhefer and George D. Bond (Berkeley: University of California Press, 1988), 25–29.

25. Pierre Delooz, "Toward a Sociological Study of Canonized Sainthood," in *Saints and Their Cults: Studies in Religious Sociology, Folklore, and History*, ed. Stephen Wilson (Cambridge: Cambridge University Press, 1983), 194.
26. Eric Waldram Kemp, *Canonization and Authority in the Western Church* (London: Oxford University Press, 1948), 143.
27. André Vauchez, *Sainthood in the Later Middle Ages*, trans. Jean Birrell (Cambridge: Cambridge University Press, 1997), chaps. 2–4.
28. Vauchez, *Sainthood*, chap. 5.
29. In 1330, the Yuan bestowed upon Father Kong the title of King Who Awakened the Sage (*Qishengwang* 啟聖王); see Song Lian 宋濂, *Yuanshi* 元史 (Taipei: Dingwen shuju, 1980), *juan* 76, 1892–1893. In 1530, the Ming decided to build his ancestral shrine (*Qisheng ci* 啟聖祠); see Zhang Tingyu 張廷玉, *Mingshi* 明史 (Taipei: Dingwen shuju, 1980), *juan* 50, 1296–1300. In 1732, the Qing changed the name to the Ancestral Shrine for Worshipping the Sage (*Congsheng ci* 崇聖祠); see Pang Zhonglu 龐鍾璐, *Wenmiao sidian kao* 文廟祀典考 (1877; repr., Taipei: Zhongguo liyue xuehui, 1977), *juan* 1, 7a–8a.
30. Alban Butler, *Butler's Lives of the Saints*, ed. Michael Walsh (San Francisco: Harper Collins, 1991), 249–251; Richard P. McBrien, *Catholicism* (San Francisco: Harper Collins, 1994), 1111; Jaroslav Pelikan, *Mary through the Centuries: Her Place in the History of Culture* (New Haven, Conn.: Yale University Press, 1996).
31. Farmer, *Oxford Dictionary of Saints*, 389.
32. For differences in early sources regarding the seventy-two, see Huang Chin-shing, "Knowledge and Belief," 236–241. Regarding differences about the apostles, see Hans Dieter Betz, "Apostles," in *The Encyclopedia of Religion*, ed. Mircea Eliade (New York: Simon & Schuster Macmillan, 1995), 1:356–59; and Robert Eisenman, *James, the Brother of Jesus: The Key to Unlocking the Secrets of Early Christianity and the Dead Sea Scrolls* (New York: Viking Penguin, 1996).
33. Sima Qian 司馬遷, *Shiji* 史記 (Beijing: Zhonghua, 1982), *juan* 47, 1947, 1938.
34. Du You 杜佑, *Tongdian* 通典, ed. Wang Wenjin 王文錦 (Beijing: Zhonghua, 1988), *juan* 53, 1480.
35. Wang Pu, *Tang huiyao*, *juan* 35, 636.
36. Chen Yin-ke 陳寅恪, *Tangdai zhengzhi shi shulun gao, shang pian* 唐代政治史述論稿·上篇, in *Chen Yin-ke xiansheng wenji* 陳寅恪先生文集 (Taipei: Liren shuju, 1981), vol. 3.
37. The School of New Learning was Wang Anshi's faction, which dominated the Confucius temple until 1241. In 1241, the Song emperor Lizong removed Wang Anshi's spirit tablet from the temple and enshrined Zhu Xi and his five philosophical predecessors from the Northern Song. Although these men were originally within a much broader fellowship of Daoxue (School of the Way) Confucians, Zhu Xi's efforts to impose a "pure Confucian" standard

on Daoxue gradually triumphed in the late Song and Yuan. A different strand within Daoxue, contesting Zhu Xi dominance during the Ming, culminated with Wang Yangming. See Huang Chin-shing, "Knowledge and Belief" (Asian Culture Press), 241–285. On Daoxue and distinctions about Song and Yuan Confucianism, see Hoyt Cleveland Tillman, "A New Direction in Confucian Scholarship: Approaches to Examining the Differences between Neo-Confucianism and Tao-hsueh," *Philosophy East and West* 42, no. 3 (1992): 455–474; also Tillman, "The Uses of Neo-Confucianism, Revisited: A Reply to Professor de Bary," *Philosophy East and West* 44, no. 1 (1994): 135–142.

38. See Butler, *Butler's Lives of the Saints*, 28–30, 266–269; Jacobus de Voragine, *The Golden Legend: Readings on the Saints*, trans. William Granger Ryan (Princeton, N.J.: Princeton University Press, 1993), 2:116–132; Peter Brown, *Augustine of Hippo: A Biography* (Berkeley: University of California Press, 1969), 433; and Anthony Kenny, *Aquinas on Mind* (London: Routledge, 1994), 11.
39. Vauchez, *Sainthood in the Later Middle Ages*, 397–403.
40. Qu Jiusi 瞿九思, *Kongmiao liyue kao* 孔廟禮樂考, *juan* 5, 33a–33b. Originally published during the Wanli reign of the Ming dynasty.
41. Qu Jiusi, *Kongmiao liyue kao*, *juan* 5, 46a.
42. Wen Tianxiang 文天祥 (1236–1283), in 1843; Lu Xiufu 陸秀夫 (1236–1279), in 1859; Fang Xiaoru 方孝孺 (1357–1402), in 1863; Liu Zongzhou 劉宗周 (1578–1645), in 1822; and Huang Daozhou 黃道周 (1585–1646), in 1825.
43. Kemp, *Canonization and Authority*, 7–8.
44. J. H. W. G. Liebeschuetz, *Continuity and Change in Roman Religion* (Oxford: Oxford University Press, 1979), 277–304; Jacob Burckhardt, *The Age of Constantine the Great*, trans. Moses Hadas (Berkeley: University of California Press, 1949), chap. 9; and Ramsay MacMullen, *Christianizing the Roman Empire (A.D. 100–400)* (New Haven, Conn.: Yale University Press, 1984), chap. 10.
45. H. Thurston, "Saints and Martyrs," in *Encyclopaedia of Religion and Ethics*, ed. James Hastings (New York: Charles Scribner's Sons; and Edinburgh: T. & T. Clark, 1924–1927), 11:51–59.
46. Peter Brown, "The Rise and Function of the Holy Man in Late Antiquity" and "Town, Village, and Holy Man: The Case of Syria," in *Society and the Holy in Late Antiquity* (Berkeley: University of California Press, 1982), 103–165.
47. Farmer, *Oxford Dictionary of Saints*, 211–218; Nicolas Cheetham, *A History of the Popes* (New York: Dorset, 1982).
48. Farmer, *Oxford Dictionary of Saints*, 45–46, 113–134, 185–188.
49. Vauchez, *Sainthood in the Later Middle Ages*, 397–412.
50. What "miracle" means in Christianity is in sharp contrast to the definition in Confucianism, Islam, or Buddhism; see Manabu Waida, "Miracles," in

The Encyclopedia of Religion, ed. Mircea Eliade (New York: Simon & Schuster Macmillan, 1995), 9:541–548.

51. For examples, see Mark 1:40–45, 8:22–26, 9:29–31; Luke, 4:39.
52. Acts, 3:6–8, 14:8–13, 16:18.
53. Ronald C. Finucane, *Miracles and Pilgrims: Popular Beliefs in Medieval England* (Totowa, N.J.: Rowman and Littlefield, 1977), 11.
54. Kemp, *Canonization and Authority*, 104–105; Paul Elie, "The Patron Saint of Paradox," *New York Times Magazine* (November 8, 1998): 44.
55. Zhu Xi 朱熹, *Lunyu jizhu* 論語集注, in *Sishu zhangju jizhu* 四書章句集注 (Beijing: Zhonghua, 1983), *juan* 4, 98; and *Zhongyong zhangju* 中庸章句, 21.
56. Kong Chuan 孔傳, *Dongjia zaji* 東家雜記, in *Congshu jicheng chubian* 叢書集成初編 (Shanghai: Commercial Press, 1936), vol. 3315, *juan* 1, 11–12; and Hong Mai 洪邁 ed., *Yijian san zhi* 夷堅三志, in *Yijian zhi* 夷堅志 (Taipei: Mingwen shuju, 1982), *juan* 6, 1382–1383.
57. Donald Attwater with Catherine Rachel John, *Penguin Dictionary of Saints* (London: Penguin, 1995), 5, 16.
58. Han Yu 韓愈, *Han Changli wenji xiaozhu* 韓昌黎文集校注 (Taipei: Huazheng shuju, 1975), *juan* 7, 283.
59. Kong Jifen 孔繼汾, *Queli wenxian kao* 闕里文獻考 (1762), *juan* 33, 30a–30b.
60. Cheng Minzheng 程敏政, *Huangdun wenji* 篁墩文集, in *Jingyin Wenyuange sikuquanshu* 景印文淵閣四庫全書 (Taipei: Commercial Press, 1983–1986), vols. 1252–1253, *juan* 10, 3a.
61. See Qiu Jun 丘濬, *Daxue yanyi bu* 大學衍義補, in *Jingyin Wenyuange sikuquanshu* 景印文淵閣四庫全書 (Taipei: Commercial Press, 1983–1986), vols. 712–713, *juan* 66, 16a; Hu Yitang 胡亦堂 and Xie Yuanzhong 謝元鍾 eds., *Linchuan xian zhi* 臨川縣志 (Taipei: Chengwen chubanshe, 1989), *juan* 9, 2b–4b.
62. Cheng Minzheng, *Huangdun wenji*, *juan* 10, 3a–3b.
63. Alain Erlande-Brandenburg, *Notre-Dame de Paris*, trans. John Goodman (New York: Abrams, 1997); Erlande-Brandenburg, *Saint-Denis' Basilica*, trans. Angela Moyon (Rennes: Ouest-France, 1984).
64. Sima Qian, *Shiji*, *juan* 67, 2185–2126; Chen Shike 陳士珂, ed., *Kongzi jiayu shuzheng* 孔子家語疏證 (Taipei: Commercial Press, 1976), *juan* 9, 221–233.
65. See Huang Chin-shing, "Knowledge and Belief" (Asian Culture Press), 236–240.
66. Zhu Xi, *Lunyu jizhu*, *juan* 8, 168; *juan* 4, 94.
67. On the *shi* class, see Yu Yingshi 余英時, "Gudai zhishi jieceng de xingqi yu fazhan" 古代知識階層的興起與發展, in *Zhongguo zhishi jieceng shilun: Gudai pian* 中國知識階層史論·古代篇 (Taipei: Linking, 1980), 22.
68. For details of my computation of percentages and other methodology, see Huang Chin-shing, *Sages and Saints*, 116–121.

69. Saint Augustine, *The City of God*, trans. Marcus Dods (Chicago: Encyclopaedia Britannica, 1952), books 11–18.
70. Harold J. Berman and John Witte Jr., "Church and State," in *Encyclopedia of Religion*, ed. Mircea Eliade (New York: Simon & Schuster Macmillan, 1995), 3:489–495.
71. Xiao Song 蕭嵩, *DaTang Kaiyuan li* 大唐開元禮, in *Jingyin Wenyuange sikuquanshu* 景印文淵閣四庫全書 (Taipei: Commercial Press, 1983), vol. 646, *juan* 1, 11b–12a; *juan* 54, 1a; *juan* 69, 1a; and *juan* 72, 1a; Du You, *Tongdian*, *juan* 53, 1475; Li Zhizao 李之藻, *Pangong liyue shu* 頖宮禮樂疏, in *Jingyin Wenyuange sikuquanshu*, vol. 651, *juan* 3, 1a–4a.
72. Donald Weinstein and Rudolph Bell, *Saints & Society: The Two Worlds of Western Christendom, 1000–1700* (Chicago: University of Chicago Press, 1982), 197. See also André Vauchez, "The Saint," in *The Medieval World*, ed. Jacques Le Goff, trans. Lydia G. Cochrane (London: Collins & Brown, 1990), 326–327.
73. Weinstein and Bell, *Saints & Society*, 199.
74. Weinstein and Bell, *Saints & Society*, 220, 204.
75. Kong Jifen, *Queli wenxian kao*, *juan* 14, 36a.
76. Pang Zhonglu, *Wenmiao sidian kao*, *juan* 5, 9b–27b.
77. Zhang Taiyan 章太炎, "Bo jianli kongjiao yi" 駁建立孔教議, in *Zhang Taiyan quanji* 章太炎全集 (Shanghai: Shanghai Renmin chubanshe, 1985), 4:195.
78. Yuan Jue 袁桷, *Qingrong jushi ji* 清容居士集, in *Sibu congkan chubian*, suoben 四部叢刊初編·縮本 (Taipei: Commercial Press, 1965), vol. 295–297, *juan* 35, 516.
79. Anonymous, *Miaoxue dianli* 廟學典禮, ed. Wang Ting 王頲 (Hangzhou: Zhejiang guji chubanshe, 1992), *juan* 1, 12; and *juan* 2, 12, 36, 41.
80. Guilio Aleni 艾儒略, *Zhi fangwai ji jiaoshi* 職方外紀校釋, ed. Xie Fang 謝方 (Beijing: Zhonghua, 1996), *juan* 2, 70–71.
81. Chen Kuo-tung 陳國棟, "Lamenting in the Confucius Temple and Burning of the Confucian Garments: Two Social Gestures of the Licentiates in the Seventeenth Century" 哭廟與焚儒服──明末清初生員層的社會性動作, *New History* 新史學 3, no. 1 (March 1992): 69–94.
82. "A List of Patron Saints," in Butler, *Butler's Lives of the Saints*, 439–440; Elizabeth Hallam, *Saints: Who They Are and How They Help You* (New York: Simon & Schuster, 1994).
83. Li Qiao 李喬, *Zhongguo hangyeshen chongbai* 中國行業神崇拜 (Beijing: Zhongguo huaqiao chuban gongsi, 1990), 25.
84. J. A. MacCulloch and Vincent A. Smith, "Relics," in *Encyclopedia of Religion and Ethics*, ed. James Hastings (New York: Charles Scribner's Sons; and Edinburgh: T. & T. Clark, 1924–1927), 10:650–662.
85. Brown, *Cult of the Saints*, chap. 2.

86. During this period, the most popular saints included Saint Timothy (c. 17–c. 97), Saint Andrew (d. c. 60), and Saint Luke (d. c. 84). See Kenneth L. Woodward, *Making Saints: How the Catholic Church Determines Who Becomes a Saint, Who Doesn't, and Why* (New York: Simon & Schuster, 1996), 63.
87. Quoted in Finucane, *Miracles and Pilgrims*, 25.
88. Mary Lee Nolan and Sidney Nolan, *Christian Pilgrimage in Modern Western Europe* (Chapel Hill: University of North Carolina Press, 1989), 116–117.
89. MacCulloch and Smith, "Relics," 10:653.
90. Patrick J. Geary, "The Ninth-Century Relic Trade: A Response to Popular Piety?," in *Living with the Dead in the Middle Ages* (Ithaca, N.Y.: Cornell University Press, 1994), 183–186. On the origin of the Eucharist, see Matthew 26:26–29.
91. Lionel Rothkrug, "Popular Religion and Holy Shrines," in *Religion and the People, 800–1700*, ed. James Obelkevich (Chapel Hill: University of North Carolina Press, 1979), 20–86.
92. Patrick J. Geary, "Sacred Commodities: The Circulation of Medieval Relics," in *Living with the Dead in the Middle Ages* (Ithaca, N.Y.: Cornell University Press, 1994), 194–218.
93. Aron Gurevich, "Peasants and Saints," in *Medieval Popular Culture: Problems of Belief and Perception*, trans. János M. Bak and Paul A. Hollingsworth (Cambridge: Cambridge University Press, 1993), 39–41.
94. Quoted in MacCulloch and Smith, "Relics," 10:654.
95. Zhu Xi, *Lunyu jizhu*, juan 4, 103.
96. Xing Bing 邢昺, *Xiaojing zhushu* 孝經注疏, *Shisanjing zhushu* edition 十三經注疏本 (Taipei: Yiwen yinshuguan, 2001), *juan* 1, 3a.
97. Sima Qian, *Shiji*, juan 47, 1945–1946. Also see Huang Chin-shing, "Power and Belief" (Asian Culture Press), 168–171.
98. Zhu Xi, *Lunyu jizhu*, juan 6, 125.
99. Sun Xidan 孫希旦, *Liji jijie* 禮記集解, ed. Shen Xiaohuan 沈嘯寰 and Wang Xingxian 王星賢 (Beijing: Zhonghua, 1989), *juan* 11, "Tang Gong" 檀弓下, 294.
100. Sun Xidan *Liji jijie*, juan 26, "Jiao Te Sheng" 郊特牲, 714.
101. Wang Xianqian 王先謙, *Xunzi jijie* 荀子集解 (Beijing: Zhonghua, 1988), *juan* 13, 371.
102. Lü Simian 呂思勉, *Du shi zhaji* 讀史札記 (Taipei: Muduo chubanshe, 1983), "Mu ji" 墓祭, 275–277.
103. Kong Yingda 孔穎達, *Chunqiu Zuozhuan zhengyi* 春秋左傳正義 (*Shisanjing zhushu* edition), *juan* 44, 13b.
104. Ying-shih Yü, "'O Soul, Come Back!' A Study in the Changing Conception of the Soul and Afterlife in Pre-Buddhist China," *Harvard Journal of Asiatic Studies* 47, no. 2 (December 1987): 363–395; Tu Cheng-sheng 杜正勝,

"Xingti, Jingqi yu hunpo: Zhongguo chuantong dui 'ren' renshi de xingcheng" 形體、精氣與魂魄：中國傳統對「人」認識的形成, *New History* 2, no. 3 (September 1991): 1–65.

105. Ernst Kitzinger, *Byzantine Art in the Making: Main Lines of Stylistic Development in Mediterranean Art, 3rd–7th Century* (Cambridge, Mass.: Harvard University Press, 1980), 20–21; and John Lowden, *Early Christian & Byzantine Art* (London: Phaidon, 1998), 25–32.

106. Thomas F. Mathews, *The Clash of Gods: A Reinterpretation of Early Christian Art* (Princeton, N.J.: Princeton University Press, 1993), 4.

107. Johan Huizinga, *The Autumn of the Middle Ages*, trans. Rodney J. Payton and Ulrich Mammitzsch (Chicago: University of Chicago Press, 1996), 189–190.

108. See examples in Liu Yiqing 劉義慶, *Shi shuo xin yu jiaojian* 世說新語校箋, commentary by Liu Xiaobiao 劉孝標 and Yang Yong 楊勇 (Taipei: Minglun chubanshe, 1970), 662; and Wei Zheng 魏徵, *Suishu* 隋書 (Taipei: Dingwen shuju, 1980), *juan* 73, 1676.

109. Ban Gu 班固, *Hanshu* 漢書 (Taipei: Dingwen shuju, 1987), *juan* 30, 1716–1717.

110. Zhu Yizun 朱彝尊, *Pushuting ji* 曝書亭集 (Taipei: Shijie shuju, 1964), *juan* 56, 651. Also see Shi Zhecun 施蟄存, *Shuijingzhu bei lu* 水經注碑錄 (Tianjin: Tianjin guji chubanshe, 1987), *juan* 10, 387–400.

111. Fan Ye, *Hou Hanshu, juan* 60b, 1998.

112. He Suiliang 賀遂亮, "Yizhou xueguan miaotang ji" 益州學館廟堂記, in *Baqiongshi jinshi buzheng* 八瓊室金石補正, ed. Lu Zengxiang 陸增祥, in *Shike shiliao xinbian* 石刻史料新編 (Wuxing 吳興: Liushi xigulou 劉氏希古樓, 1924; repr., Taipei: Xinwenfeng chuban gongsi, 1977), *juan* 35, 1a–1b.

113. Li Daoyuan 酈道元, Yang Shoujing 楊守敬, and Xiong Huizhen 熊會貞, *Shuijing zhushu* 水經注疏 (Nanjing: Jiangsu guji chubanshe, 1989), *juan* 8, 777–778. Also see Hsing I-tien 邢義田, "Handai Kongzi jian Laozi huaxiang de goucheng ji qi zai shehui, sixiangshi shang de yiyi" 漢代孔子見老子畫像的構成及其在社會、思想史上的意義 (unpublished).

114. Hong Gua 洪适, *Li shi* 隸釋 (Hongshi Huimuzhai 洪氏晦木齋; repr., Beijing: Zhonghua, 1985), *juan* 1, 24b–25a.

115. Chen Dengyuan 陳登原, *Guoshi jiuwen* 國史舊聞 (Taipei: Mingwen shuju, 1984), 1:365.

116. Li Daoyuan, *Shuijing zhushu, juan* 25, 2110. My supposition was confirmed when I later obtained a rubbing from the Confucius temple. See Gong Yanxing 宮衍興 and Wang Zhengyu 王政玉, *Kongmiao zhushen kao* 孔廟諸神考 (Jinan: Shandong Friendship, 1994), 219.

117. Yang Xuanzhi 楊衒之, *Luoyang qielanji xiaozhu* 洛陽伽藍記校注, ed. Fan Xiangyong 范祥雍 (Taipei: Huazheng shuju, 1980), *juan* 1, 1.

118. Fang Xuanling 房玄齡, *Jinshu* 晉書 (Taipei: Dingwen shuju, 1987), *juan* 55, 1510.
119. Kong Yuancuo 孔元措, *Kongshi zuting guangji* 孔氏祖庭廣記, in *Congshu jicheng chubian* 叢書集成初編 (Shanghai: Commercial Press, 1936), 3316–3317, *juan* 10, 118. On the ten disciples, see Zhu Xi, *Lunyu jizhu*, *juan* 6, 123.
120. Wang Pu, *Tang huiyao*, *juan* 35, 637–639.
121. Zhu Jincheng 朱金城, *Bai Juyi ji jianjiao* 白居易集箋校 (Shanghai: Shanghai guji chubanshe, 1988), *juan* 65, 3545; Jin Shen 金申, *Zhongguo lidai jinian Foxiang tudian* 中國歷代紀年佛像圖典 (Beijing: Cultural Relics Press, 1994); and Jin Shen, *Fojiao diaosu mingpin tulu* 佛教雕塑名品圖錄 (Beijing: Beijing gongyi meishu chubanshe, 1995).
122. Qiu Jun, *Daxue yanyi bu*, *juan* 65, 12a.
123. Zhao Yi 趙翼, *Gai yu congkao* 陔餘叢考 (Taipei: Shijie shuju, 1960), *juan* 32, 21a–21b.
124. Su Shi 蘇軾, *Su Shi wenji* 蘇軾文集, ed. Kong Fanli 孔凡禮 (Beijing: Zhonghua, 1992), *juan* 7, 203. "Gui zuo bai shuo" 跪坐拜說 is also called "Bailu lidian suxiang shuo" 白鹿禮殿塑像說. See Qin Huitian 秦蕙田, *Wuli tongkao* 五禮通考 (Weijingwo 味經窩; repr., Taoyuan: Shenghuan tushu gongsi, 1994), *juan* 118, 29b; Zhu Xi, "Gui zuo bai shuo" 跪坐拜說, in *Zhuzi Daquan* 朱子大全, in *Sibu beiyao*, zibu 四部備要·子部 (Taipei: Taiwan Chung Hwa, 1965), *juan* 68, 1a–2b (originally published during the Ming dynasty by Mr. Hu 胡氏); and Zhu Xi, *Zhuzi yulei* 朱子語類, ed. Li Jingde 黎靖德 (Beijing: Zhonghua, 1986), *juan* 3, 52.
125. Song Lian, *Songxueshi quanji* 宋學士全集, in *Congshu jicheng chubian* 叢書集成初編 (Shanghai: Commercial Press, 1939), vols. 2110–2133, *juan* 28, 1019–1022.
126. Song Na 宋訥, *Xi yin wengao* 西隱文稿 (Taipei: Wenhai chubanshe, 1970), *juan* 7, 388. Also see Huang Chin-shing, "On Iconoclasm and the Cult of 'Sage-Master'" 毀像與聖師祭, *Continent Magazine* 大陸雜誌 99, no. 5 (November 1999): 1–8.
127. Shen Defu 沈德符, *Wanli yehuo bian* 萬曆野獲編 (Beijing: Zhonghua, 1980), *juan* 14, 361; Zhu Guozhen 朱國禎, *Yong chuang xiaopin* 湧幢小品, in *Biji xiaoshuo daguan* 筆記小說大觀 (Taipei: Xinxing shuju, 1984), vol. 22.7, *juan* 16, 1b.
128. *Ming Shizong shilu*, *juan* 119, 4a, 6a.
129. Li Guan 黎貫, "Lun Kongzi sidian shu" 論孔子祀典疏, in *Guangdong wenzheng* 廣東文徵, ed. Jiang Maosen 江茂森 (Hong Kong: Chu Hai College, 1973), *juan* 6, 209.
130. Zhu Guozhen, *Yong chuang xiaopin*, *juan* 16, 4b; and Gu Yanwu 顧炎武, *Yuan chaoben Rizhi lu* 原抄本日知錄 (Taipei: Minglun chubanshe), *juan* 18, 429.

131. Quoted by Fei Mi 費密, *Hong dao shu* 弘道書, in *Feishi yishu* 費氏遺書 (Yilantang 怡蘭堂, 1919), *juan* 2, 3a.
132. Shen Defu, *Wanli yehuo bian*, "Buyi" 補遺, *juan* 1, 812.
133. Yazi 亞子 and Liangzi 良子, *Kongfu da jienan* 孔府大劫難 (Hong Kong: Tiandi tushu gongsi, 1992), 139–60.
134. Zhu Xi, *Mengzi jizhu* 孟子集注, in *Sishu zhangju jizhu* 四書章句集注 (Beijing: Zhonghua, 1983), *juan* 11, 336, utilized and changed to pinyin in D. C. Lau, trans., *Mencius* (London: Penguin, 1970), 169.
135. Quoted in Jaroslav Pelikan, *Imago Dei: The Byzantine Apologia for Icons* (Princeton, N.J.: Princeton University Press, 1990), 1–2.
136. See *Jidujiao wenhua* 基督教文化, ed. Zhang Zhijiang 張治江 and Li Fangyuan 李芳園 (Changchun: Changchun chubanshe, 1992), 75–86.
137. Sister Charles Murray, "Art and the Early Church," in *Art, Archaeology, and Architecture of Early Christianity*, ed. Paul Corby Finney (New York: Garland, 1993), 303–345.
138. David Freedberg, *The Power of Images: Studies in the History and Theory of Response* (Chicago: University of Chicago Press, 1989), 97.
139. Mathews, *Clash of Gods*, chap. 1; Ernst Kitzinger, *Early Medieval Art in the British Museum* (London: British Museum, 1963), 1–35.
140. Freedberg, *Power of Images*, 398.
141. Peter Brown, "A Dark Age Crisis: Aspects of the Iconoclastic Controversy," in *Society and the Holy in Late Antiquity* (Berkeley: University of California Press, 1982), 251–301.
142. George Ostrogorsky, *History of the Byzantine State*, trans. Joan Hussey (New Brunswick, N.J.: Rutgers University Press, 1957), chap. 3.
143. Pelikan, *Imago Dei*, 182.
144. Ostrogorsky, *History of the Byzantine State*, 146–147.
145. A. H. M. Jones, *The Later Roman Empire, 284–602: A Social, Economic, and Administrative Survey* (Norman: University of Oklahoma Press, 1964), 2:957–964; Keith Thomas, *Religion and the Decline of Magic: Studies in Popular Beliefs in Sixteenth- and Seventeenth-Century England* (New York: Charles Scribner's Sons, 1971), 25–50.
146. MacCulloch and Smith, "Relics," 10:653–656.
147. Carlos M. N. Eire, *War against the Idols: The Reformation of Worship from Erasmus to Calvin* (Cambridge: Cambridge University Press, 1989), 45.
148. Martin Luther, "The Freedom of a Christian," in *Luther: Selected Political Writings*, ed. J. M. Porter (Philadelphia: Fortress, 1974), 25–35.
149. Sergiusz Michalski, *The Reformation and the Visual Arts: The Protestant Image Question in Western and Eastern Europe* (London: Routledge, 1993), 18–36.
150. Ernst Troeltsch, *The Social Teaching of the Christian Churches*, trans. Olive Wyon (Louisville, Ky.: Westminster/John Knox Press, 1992), 3:576–81.

151. John Calvin, *Jidujiao yaoyi* 基督教要義 [*Institutes of the Christian Religion*], ed. J. T. McNeill, trans. Xu Qingyu 徐慶譽 and Xie Bingde 謝秉德 (Hong Kong: Jidujiao fuqiao chubanshe, Jinling shenxueyuan tuoshi bu, 1995), series 1, 1:58–66.
152. English translation modified from Henry Beveridge, trans., *Institutes of the Christian Religion* (Christian Classics Ethereal Library, 1845).
153. See Eire, *War against the Idols*, 1–11.
154. Finucane, *Miracles and Pilgrims*, 204.
155. Victor Turner and Edith Turner, *Image and Pilgrimage in Christian Culture: Anthropological Perspectives* (New York: Columbia University Press, 1978), 143–144.
156. Edward Gibbon, *The Decline and Fall of the Roman Empire* (Chicago: Encyclopaedia Britannica, 1952), 1:464–467; Immanuel Kant, *Religion within the Limits of Reason Alone*, trans. Theodore M. Greene and Hoyt H. Hudson (New York: Harper & Row, 1960), 79–86; Max Weber, *The Protestant Ethic and the Spirit of Capitalism*, trans. Talcott Parsons (New York: Charles Scribner's Sons, 1958).
157. Takezoe Koko 竹添光鴻, *Saden Kaisen* (*Zuozhuan huijian*) 左傳會箋 (Seisei shohku 井井書屋, 1903; repr., Taipei: Guangwen shuju, 1968), *juan* 5, 69.
158. I borrow the metaphor of family resemblances from Ludwig Wittgenstein, *Philosophical Investigations*, trans. G. E. M. Anscombe (New York: Macmillan, 1968), 32.
159. Max Weber, *The Religion of China: Confucianism and Taoism*, trans. Hans H. Gerth (New York: Macmillan, 1964), chap. 5.
160. Zhu Xi, *Zhuzi yulei, juan* 3, 52.
161. Ye Sheng 葉盛, *Shui dong riji* 水東日記 (Beijing: Zhonghua, 1980), *juan* 19, 191.
162. Pang Zhonglu, *Wenmiao sidian kao, juan* 1, 12b.
163. On Qing censorship and control, see *Qingdai wenziyu dang* 清代文字獄檔, ed. Beiping gugongbowuyuan wenxiangguan 北平故宮博物院文獻館 (1934; repr., Taipei: Huawen shuju, 1969), vol. 6; and Kong Demao 孔德懋, *Kongfu neizhai yishi: Kongzi houyi de huiyi* 孔府內宅軼事：孔子後裔的回憶 (Tianjin: Shanxi Renmin chubanshe, 1982), 30–32.
164. For example, Zhu Xi, *Zhuzi daquan, juan* 86; Ye Shi 葉適, *Ye Shi ji* 葉適集 (Beijing: Zhonghua, 1983), *juan* 26, 535–537; Xue Xuan 薛瑄, *Xue Xuan quanji* 薛瑄全集 (Taiyuan: Shanxi Renmin chubanshe, 1990), vol. l, *juan* 21, 892–897.
165. Sima Qian, *Shiji, juan* 47, 1945–1946.
166. Lu Yuanshan, *Shengmen zhi, juan* 4, 273.
167. Yang Qiyuan 楊起元, *Taishi Yang Fusuo xiansheng zhengxue bian* 太史楊復所先生證學編, in *Sikuquanshu cunmu congshu*, zibu 四庫全書存目叢書•子部 (She

Yongning 余永寧, 1617; repr., Tainan: Zhuangyan wenhua gongsi, 1995), vol. 90, *juan* 3, 9b.

168. Liu Xu 劉昫, *Jiu Tangshu* 舊唐書 (Taipei: Dingwen shuju, 1981), *juan* 24, 919; Tuo Tuo 脫脫, *Songshi* 宋史 (Taipei: Dingwen shuju, 1978), *juan* 105, 2553–2554.
169. Li Dongyang 李東陽, *Ming huidian* 明會典, ed. Shen Shixing 申時行 (Beijing: Zhonghua, 1989), *juan* 91, 520; Zhang Tingyu, *Mingshi, juan* 67, 1641; Pang Zhonglu, *Wenmiao sidian kao, juan* 5, 25b.
170. Qin Huitian, *Wuli tongkao, juan* 117, 1b.
171. Hippolyte Delehaye, *The Legends of the Saints*, trans. Donald Attwater (Dublin: Four Courts, 1998), 138–139.
172. See C. K. Yang, *Religion in Chinese Society: A Study of Contemporary Social Functions of Religion and Some of Their Historical Factors* (Berkeley: University of California Press, 1961), 145–146; Qin Huitian, *Wuli tongkao, juan* 117, 13a–25a.
173. Pang Zhonglu, *Wenmiao sidian kao, juan* 1, 11b–12a.
174. Liang Qichao 梁啟超, "Bianfa tongyi" 變法通議, in *Yinbingshi wenji* 飲冰室文集 (Taipei: Chung Hwa, 1970), vol. 1, *juan* 1, 49.
175. Ye Dehui 葉德輝, "Ye libu yu Liu Xianduan Huang Yuwen liang sheng shu" 葉吏部與劉先端黃郁文兩生書, in *Yi jiao congbian* 翼教叢編, ed. Su Yu 蘇輿 (Taipei: Institute of Chinese Literature and Philosophy, Academia Sinica, 2005), *juan* 6, 344.
176. Lu Xun 魯迅, "Zai xiandai Zhongguo de Kongfuzi" 在現代中國的孔夫子 (April 29, 1935), *Qiejieting zawen erji* 且介亭雜文二集, in *Lu Xun quanji* 魯迅全集 (Taipei: Tangshan chubanshe, 1989), 8:102.
177. Ostrogorsky, *History of the Byzantine State*, 144ff.; Finucane, *Miracles and Pilgrims*, chap. 12; Eire, *War against the Idols*, chap. 8.
178. For example, John Paul II enshrined more saints than any pope in the twentieth century, and many believers clamor for sainthood for Mother Teresa. See Brendan Koerner, "Saint Makers," *U.S. News and World Report* (January 11, 1999): 54; and Meenakshi Ganguly, "The Road to Sainthood," *Time* (May 17, 1999): 21.

4. The Cultural Politics of Autocracy

This chapter originally appeared under the same title in a translation by Curtis Dean Smith and Thomas A. Wilson in *On Sacred Grounds: Culture, Society, Politics, and the Formation of the Cult of Confucius*, ed. Thomas A. Wilson (Cambridge, Mass.: Harvard University Press, 2002), 267–296.

1. Zhang Tingyu 張廷玉, *Mingshi* 明史 (Taipei: Dingwen shuju, 1980), *juan* 17, 219.
2. Zhang Tingyu, *Mingshi*, *juan* 191, 5078.
3. Mao Qiling 毛奇齡, "Bianding Jiajing daliyi" 辨定嘉靖大禮議, in *Longwei mishu* 龍威秘書, ed. Ma Junliang 馬駿良 (N.P., n.d.).
4. Zhang Tingyu, *Mingshi*, *juan* 17, 220–222.
5. Zhang Tingyu, *Mingshi*, *juan* 196, 5178.
6. *Shizong shilu* 明世宗實錄, in *Ming shilu* 明實錄, ed. Huang Chang-chien 黃彰健 (Taipei: Institute of History and Philology, Academia Sinica, 1966), *juan* 109, 120.
7. Pang Zhonglu 龐鍾璐, *Wenmiao sidian kao* 文廟祀典考 (1877; repr., Taipei: Zhongguo liyue xuehui, 1977), *juan* 4, 11b–13b.
8. Zhang Cong 張璁, *Yudui lu* 諭對錄, in *Sikuquanshu cunmu congshu, shibu* 四庫全書存目叢書·史部 (Baolunlou 寶綸樓, 1609; repr., Tainan: Zhuangyan wenhua shiye gongsi, 1996), vol. 57, *juan* 22, 1b; and *Luoshan zoushu* 羅山奏疏 (1577), *juan* 6, 1a.
9. *Shizong shilu*, *juan* 119, 3a–4a. Due to the length of Zhang Cong's original memorial, I use the abstracted version found in the *Ming shilu*.
10. According to the order of sacrifices in the Confucius temple, beside Confucius as the supreme sage were the four correlates and ten savants or wise men, established in the main hall, and the former worthies and scholars, who received sacrifice, in the side cloisters.
11. The statement "Although the son be equal to a sage, he should not take precedence over his father" originates in the *Zuo Commentary of the Spring and Autumn Annals* 春秋左氏傳. See Hong Liangji 洪亮吉, *Chunqiu Zuozhuan gu* 春秋左傳詁 (Beijing: Zhonghua, 1987), *juan* 9, 354. It was adopted by Fang Xianfu 方獻夫 as a metaphor for the lord–subject relationship during the Great Rites Controversy, and Shizong took a liking to this phrase.
12. Zhang Cong, *Yudui lu*, *juan* 22, 15b, 17a.
13. *Shizong shilu*, *juan* 119, 4a. For the original annotation, see Zhang Cong, *Yudui lu*, *juan* 22, 1b–15a.
14. Quoted in Zhang Cong, *Yudui lu*, *juan* 22, 3a.
15. Qiu Jun 丘濬, *Daxue yanyi bu* 大學衍義補, in *Jingyin Wenyuange sikuquanshu* 景印文淵閣四庫全書 (Taipei: Commercial Press, 1983), vol. 712–713, *juan* 65, 6b–7a.
16. Qiu Jun 丘濬, *Daxue yanyi bu*, *juan* 65, 11a–14a.
17. Shen Defu 沈德符, *Wanli yehuo bian* 萬曆野獲編 (Beijing: Zhonghua, 1980), *juan* 14, 361.
18. Zhang Tingyu, *Mingshi*, *juan* 50, 1297–1298.
19. Cheng Minzheng 程敏政, *Huangdun wenji* 篁墩文集, in *Jingyin Wenyuange sikuquanshu* 景印文淵閣四庫全書 (Taipei: Commercial Press, 1983), vol. 1252–1253, *juan* 10, 4a–10b.

20. See Huang Chin-shing, "Knowledge and Belief: Confucian Canonization and the Confucian Conception of Orthodoxy" 學術與信仰：論孔廟從祀制與儒家道統意識, *New History* 新史學 5, no. 2 (June 1994): 1–82.
21. Gui E 桂萼, *Gui Wenxiang gong zouyi* 桂文襄公奏議 (1762), *juan* 8, 17a–20b; Ouyang Xiu 歐陽修, *Ouyang Xiu quanji* 歐陽修全集 (Taipei: Shijie shuju, 1961), 977–995. Ouyang Xiu's opinions were counter to those of Sima Guang 司馬光. For background on the Puyuan debate's connection with Ouyang Xiu's enshrinement in the Confucius temple, see Gu Yanwu 顧炎武, *Yuan chaoben Rizhi lu* 原抄本日知錄 (Taipei: Minglun chubanshe, 1971), *juan* 18, 432. Much earlier, Xu Xuemo 徐學謨 (1522–1594) had said that Shizong wished to enshrine Ouyang Xiu in the temple because his position in the Puyuan debates "was in accordance with the sages' thoughts." Xu Xuemo, *Shimiao shi yulu* 世廟識餘錄 (Taipei: Guofeng chubanshe, 1965), *juan* 4, 5a. Shizong's mention of Ouyang Xiu shows that Xu's and Gu's claims are not baseless; see Zhang Cong, *Yudui lu*, *juan* 22, 26a.
22. This position first originated with Xie Duo and was used later by Zhang Cong; see Zhang Tingyu, *Mingshi*, *juan* 163, 4432; *juan* 50, 1298–1300.
23. Hong Mai 洪邁, *Rongzhai suibi* 容齋隨筆 (Shanghai: Shanghai guji chubanshe, 1978), *juan* 22, 26a; Xiong He 熊鉌, *Xiong Wuxuan xiansheng wenji* 熊勿軒先生文集 (Shanghai: Commercial Press, 1936), *juan* 4, 52.
24. Cheng Minzheng, *Huangdun wenji*, *juan* 10, 10b–12a.
25. Shen Defu, "Buyi" 補遺, in *Wanli yehuo bian* 萬曆野獲編, *juan* 2, 854; Jiao Hong 焦竑, *Yutang congyu* 玉堂叢語 (Beijing: Zhonghua, 1981), *juan* 3, 93.
26. Xu Xuemo, *Shimiao shi yulu*, *juan* 6, 19b.
27. Li Guan 黎貫, "Lun Kongzi sidian shu" 論孔子祀典疏, in *Guangdong wenzheng* 廣東文徵, ed. Jiang Maosen 江茂森 (Hong Kong: Chu Hai College, 1973), *juan* 6, 209.
28. Xu Xuemo, *Shimiao shi yulu*, *juan* 6, 19b–20a. Xu criticized Zhang Cong: "This is also just remnants of [his] ingratiating [himself] by debating over rituals." Erudites such as Qu Jiusi 瞿九思, when considering the reorganization of the institution of the Confucius temple in the Wanli era (1573–1620), were unable to make sense of the Shrine for Giving Birth to the Sage: "No one refers to the Duke Who Gave Birth to the Sage. Shizong called the four correlates 'sages,' and the ten correlates in the side halls 'worthies,' all of which are not noble titles. Only the Duke Who Gave Birth to the Sage has noble status. Perhaps the emperor felt this statute to be too lofty and so did not discuss it. Perhaps this was not an omission." Qu Jiusi 瞿九思, *Kongmiao liyue kao* 孔廟禮樂考, *juan* 10, 47b. Published in the Wanli reign of the Ming dynasty.
29. Gu Yanwu, *Yuan chaoben Rizhi lu*, *juan* 18, 429. See also Shao Changheng 邵長蘅 (1637–1713), *Qingmen lugao* 青門簏稾, in *Changzhou xianzhe yishu* 常州

先哲遺書, ed. Sheng Xuanhuai 盛宣懷, in *Yuanke jingyin congshu jicheng sanbian* 原刻景印叢書集成三編 (Taipei: Yiwen yinshuguan, 1960), juan 10, 10a. Shao suggested reinstalling Confucius's sculpture during the early Qing.

30. Yu Zhengxie 俞正燮, *Guisi cungao* 癸巳存稿 (Taipei: Commercial Press, 1971), juan 9, 256.
31. Xu Jie 徐階, *Shijingtang ji* 世經堂集 (1681), juan 6, 41a–41b.
32. Xu Jie 徐階, *Shijingtang ji*, juan 6, 41b.
33. Shen Defu, *Wanli yehuo bian*, juan 14, 361–362.
34. See Li Zhizao 李之藻, *Pangong liyue shu* 頖宮禮樂疏, in *Jingyin Wenyuange sikuquanshu* 景印文淵閣四庫全書 (Taipei: Commercial Press, 1983), vol. 651, juan 1, 42b.
35. Zhang Cong, *Luoshan zoushu*, juan 6, 29a.
36. Zhang Cong, *Luoshan zoushu*, juan 6, 30a.
37. Zhang Tingyu, *Mingshi*, juan 50, 1297.
38. The title King Who Gave Birth to the Sage (*Qisheng wang* 啟聖王) had been bestowed on Shulaing He during the Yuan dynasty, in 1330. Song Lian 宋濂, *Yuanshi* 元史 (Taipei: Dingwen shuju, 1980), juan 76, 1892–1893.
39. Zhang Cong, *Luoshan zoushu*, juan 6, 30a.
40. At the urging of Senior Messenger Xue Kan 薛侃, Lu Jiuyuan 陸九淵 (1139–1193) was included among those who received sacrifices. Zhang Tingyu, *Mingshi*, juan 50, 1300.
41. Zhang Tingyu, *Mingshi*, juan 191, 5068.
42. Zhang Tingyu, *Mingshi*, juan 208, 5499.
43. For complete versions of these essays, see Zhu Silan 朱絲欄, ed., *Jiajing sidain kao* 嘉靖祀典考 (Taipei: Institute of History and Philology, Academia Sinica, n.d.), which also includes edited versions of these sources on the temple.
44. *Shizong shilu*, juan 119, 6a.
45. Li Guan, "Lun Kongzi sidian shu," in *Guangdong wenzheng*, juan 6, 209.
46. Zhang Cong, *Luoshan zoushu*, juan 6, 4b–25a.
47. Zhang Cong, *Yudui lu*, juan 22, 26b–27a.
48. *Shizong shilu*, juan 109, 4a.
49. Zhu Xi 朱熹, *Lunyu jizhu* 論語集注, in *Sishu zhangju jizhu* 四書章句集注 (Beijing: Zhonghua, 1983), juan 8, 171.
50. Ming Shizong, "Zheng Kongzi sidian shuo," in Zhu Silan, *Jiajing sidain kao*, juan 5.
51. Ming Shizong, "Zheng Kongzi sidian shuo," juan 5.
52. Ming Shizong, "Zheng Kongzi sidian shenji," in Zhu Silan, *Jiajing sidain kao*, juan 5.
53. Kong Zhencong 孔貞叢, ed., *Queli zhi* 闕里志, juan 11, 17a–18a. Published in the Wanli reign of the Ming dynasty (1573–1620).

54. Zhu Yizun 朱彝尊, *Pushuting ji* 曝書亭集 (Taipei: Shijie shuju, 1964), *juan* 60, 697.
55. *Shizong shilu, juan* 109, 11a–11b.
56. Shen Defu, *Wanli yehuo bian, juan* 14, 360.
57. Zhang Tingyu, *Mingshi, juan* 208, 5502; see also *Shizong shilu, juan* 119, 8b.
58. Feng Qi 馮琦 ed., *Songshi jishi benmo* 宋史紀事本末 (Beijing: Zhonghua, 1955), *juan* 1, 248–257.
59. *Ming Shizong shilu*, "Zheng Kongzi sidian shuo," in Zhu Silan, *Jiajing sidain kao, juan* 5.
60. *Ming Shizong shilu, juan* 5.
61. *Ming Shizong shilu, juan* 5.
62. *Ming Shizong shilu, juan* 5.
63. *Ming Shizong shilu, juan* 5.
64. Zhang Tingyu, *Mingshi, juan* 197, 5223.
65. Ming Shizong, "Fenjiao huiyi diyi shu 分郊會議第一疏" and "Zheng Kongzi sidian shenji," in Zhu Silan, *Jiajing sidain kao, juan* 1, *juan* 5.
66. *Taizu shilu* 明太祖實錄, in *Ming shilu*, ed. Huang Chang-chien 黃彰健 (Taipei: Institute of History and Philology, Academia Sinica, 1966), *juan* 30, 5b–6a.
67. The discontinuation of sacrifices to Confucius throughout the empire in 1369 is not mentioned in the "Treatise on Rites" ("Lizhi" 禮志) or "Taizu's Basic Annals" ("Taizu benji" 太祖本紀) in the *Ming History*, nor is it mentioned in the *Ming Veritable Records* (*Ming shilu* 明實錄), probably because later official historians concealed these facts for Taizu's sake. This information can be found only in Qian Tang's 錢唐 biography in the *Ming History*. See Zhang Tingyu, *Mingshi, juan* 39, 3981. Qin Huitian 秦蕙田 (1702–1764) mistakenly quotes Wang Qi 王圻, *Xu wenxian tongkao* 續文獻通考, which dates this edict to May 29, 1369 (Hongwu 2/4/23). In fact, it should be on June 5, 1382 (15/4/23). See *Taizu shilu, juan* 144, 2a; Qin Huitian, *Wuli tongkao* 五禮通考 (Weijingwo 味經窩; repr., Taoyuan: Shenghuan tushu gongsi, 1994), *juan* 120, 1b–2a; and Wang Qi, *Xu wenxian tongkao* (1603; held by the Institute of History and Philology, Academia Sinica), *juan* 57, 7b–8a.
68. Xu Yikui 徐一夔, *DaMing jili* 大明集禮, in *Jingyin Wenyuange sikuquanshu* 景印文淵閣四庫全書 (Taipei: Commercial Press, 1983), vol. 649–650, *juan* 16, 20a. *DaMing jili* was completed in the third month of 1370 and it includes "Zhiji Qufu Kongzi yuzhi zhuwen" 致祭曲阜孔子御製祝文 (1369).
69. *Taizu shilu, juan* 30, 1a–4b; *juan* 38, 1a–10a.
70. Zhang Tingyu, *Mingshi, juan* 139, 3981–3982. The Three August Ones (*san huang* 三皇) refers to cultural heroes of remote antiquity whose legendary accomplishments at the beginning of the mythological era are credited with the foundation of Chinese civilization. Fuxi 伏羲 apprehended the patterns

of the heavens and earth, drew the eight trigrams, domesticated the animals, and ruled as the Son of Heaven with the power of wood; Shennong 神農, the Divine Farmer, taught the people how to domesticate the five grains and ruled with the power of fire; and Huangdi 黃帝, the Yellow Emperor, ruled with the power of earth.

71. *Taizu shilu*, juan 67, 7a. See also Deng Qiu 鄧球, *HuangMing yonghua leibian* 皇明詠化類編, juan 72, 12b; published in the Ming dynasty Longqing 隆慶 era (1567–1572). Song Lian's treatise can be found in Li Zhizao, *Pangong liyue shu*, juan 1, 42a–44b. Yu Zhengxie (*Guisi cungao*, juan 9, 256) and Shao Changheng (*Qingmen lugao*, juan 10, 9b) say that Song Lian was exiled due to his request to destroy the statues. The histories are inaccurate. In "DaMing Chijian taixue bei" 大明勅建太學碑 (Plaque for the Building of the National University by Imperial Order), Song Na 宋訥 clearly records, "From the time of Confucius, statues were not made for [the imperial temple; rather] spirit tablets were used in the sacrifice. This changed after many centuries of barbarian customs." Song Na, *Xi yin wengao* 西隱文稿 (Taipei: Wenhai chubanshe, 1970), juan 7, 388. Obviously, Taizu had no objection to eliminating the statues.
72. *Kongfu dang'an xuanbian* 孔府檔案選編 (Beijing: Zhonghua, 1982), juan 1, 17. Taizu mistook Gaozong for Gaozu.
73. Ye Sheng 葉盛, *Shuitong riji* 水東日記 (Beijing: Zhonghua, 1980), juan 19, 188; *Taizu shilu*, juan 31, 8b. These two records are more colloquial and are certainly original documents.
74. Zhang Tingyu, *Mingshi*, juan 139, 3982.
75. Wang Qi, *Xu wenxian tongkao*, juan 57, 11b. See also Sun Chengze 孫承澤, *Chunmingmeng yulu* 春明夢餘錄 (Hong Kong: Longmen shuju, 1965), juan 21, 36b.
76. *Taizu shilu*, juan 144, 2a.
77. For more on the Hu Weiyong case, see Zhang Tingyu, *Mingshi*, juan 308, 7906.
78. Qu Jiusi, *Kongmiao liyue kao*, juan 1, 20a.
79. *Taizu shilu*, juan 53, 1b–2a.
80. Song Lian, *Yuan shi*, juan 76, 1902.
81. *Taizu shilu*, juan 62, 3b–4a.
82. *Taizu shilu*, juan 64, 2b–3b.
83. *Taizu shilu*, juan 188, 5b–6a.
84. Li Dongyang 李東陽, *Ming huidian* 明會典, ed. Shen Shixing 申時行 (Beijing: Zhonghua, 1989), juan 91, 517–520.
85. Ouyang Xiu and Song Qi 宋祁, *Xin Tangshu* 新唐書 (Taipei: Dingwen shuju, 1981), juan 15, 377.

86. Du You 杜佑, *Tongdian* 通典, ed. Wang Wenjin 王文錦 (Beijing: Zhonghua, 1988), *juan* 53, 1484.
87. For more on the evolution of the differences between the temple of culture and the martial temple, see Tao Xisheng 陶希聖, "Wumiao zhi zhengzhi shehui de yanbian" 武廟之政治社會的演變, *Shihuo yuekan* 食貨月刊 2, no. 5 (August 1972): 1–19.
88. Qin Huitian, *Wuli tongkao*, *juan* 120, 18a.
89. *Taizu shilu*, *juan* 183, 3a.
90. *Taizu shilu*, *juan* 189, 1a.
91. Wu Chen 吳沈, "Kongzi feng wang bian" 孔子封王辯, in *Queli zhi*, ed. Kong Zhencong, *juan* 11, 63a–63b. Wu Chen entered government service in 1379 as a Confucian scholar and was liked by Taizu. "Kongzi feng wang bian" may have been written because Taizu retained Confucius's title of king, whereas the titles of all other spirits were stripped in 1370. For more about Wu Chen, see Fu Weilin 傅維麟, *Mingshu* 明書 (Taipei: Huazheng shuju, 1974), *juan* 17, 6b–7b; and Guo Tingxun 過庭訓, *Ben chao fensheng renwu kao* 本朝分省人物考 (Taipei: Chengwen chubanshe, 1971), *juan* 52, 23a–25a.
92. Ming Shizong, "Zheng Kongzi sidian shuo," in *Jiajing sidain kao* 嘉靖祀典考, ed. Zhu Silan (Taipei: Institute of History and Philology, Academia Sinica, n.d.), *juan* 5.
93. Kong Zhencong, *Queli zhi*, *juan* 11, 63a.
94. *Shizong shilu*, *juan* 119, 8a.
95. *Shizong shilu*, *juan* 120, 6b; Li Dongyang, *DaMing huidian*, *juan* 91, 16a–18b. The Qing Emperor Kangxi 清康熙帝 (r. 1661–1722) based the Hall of the Transmission of the Mind/Heart (*Chuan xin dian* 傳心殿) on this scheme, but the ideas behind these two temples were completely different. See Huang Chin-shing, "An Investigation of Early Ch'ing Political Attitudes: The Politicization of Confucian Orthodoxy" 清初政權意識型態之探究：政治化的道統觀, *Bulletin of the Institute of History and Philology, Academia Sinica* 中央研究院歷史語研究所集刊 58, no. 1 (March 1987): 105–132.
96. Xiong He, *Xiong Wuxuan xiansheng wenji*, *juan* 4, 55; Song Lian, "Kongzi miaotang yi" 孔子廟堂議, in Li Zhizao, *Pangong liyue shu*, *juan* 1, 44a–44b.
97. Xiong He added, "If Confucius did indeed actually unite the laws and regulations of the ancestors, complete the great accomplishments of the sages, and is then offered sacrifices by everyone throughout all the ages, from the Son of Heaven down to the villages, at the spring and autumn sacrifices, the Son of Heaven must personally bow and complete all matters." Xiong He, *Xiong Wuxuan xiansheng wenji*, *juan* 4, 55.
98. Fei Mi 費密, *Hong dao shu* 弘道書, in *Feishi yishu* 費氏遺書 (Yilantang 怡蘭堂, 1919), *juan* 2, 7a. Fei also said that for Shizong to change Confucius's title to

Great Sage and Former Master was incongruous and extremely defaming (*juan* 2, 6b).

99. Zhang Cong, *Yudui lu*, *juan* 23, 9a–9b.
100. Lü Kun 呂坤, *Shenyin yu* 呻吟語 (Taipei: Hanjing wenhua shiye gongsi, 1981), *juan* 1, 4a–12a.
101. As Qian Mu 錢穆 observed on his visit to the Confucius temple in Qufu, most of the steles dedicated to Confucius were set up by alien rulers. Qian Mu, "Shiyou zayi" 師友雜憶 [Recollections of Teachers and Friends], *China Monthly* 中國人月刊 2, no. 5 (May 1980): 59. According to Kong Jifen, there are thirteen stele pavilions (*beiting* 碑亭) in the Confucius temple; nine were built by three Qing rulers. He also confirms that no new buildings "could be added, since our [Qing] dynasty has enlarged [the temple] to such an extent." Kong Jifen, 孔繼汾 *Queli wenxian kao* 闕里文獻考 (1762), in *Ru Cang* 儒藏 (Chengdou: Sichuan daxue chubanshe, 2005), *juan* 12, 1b; *juan* 11, 1a.

5. Xunzi

1. Huang Chin-shing 黃進興, *Entering the Master's Sanctuary: Power, Belief and Legitimacy in Traditional China* 優入聖域：權力、信仰與正當性 (Taipei: Asian Culture Press, 2003), chap. 7, 324.
2. See Huang Chin-shing, "Knowledge and Belief: Confucian Canonization and the Confucian Conception of Orthodoxy" 學術與信仰：論孔廟從祀制與儒家道統意識, in *Entering the Master's Sanctuary*, 295–297.
3. Ma Duanlin 馬端臨, *Wenxian tongkao* 文獻通考 (Shanghai: Commercial Press, 1936), in *Wanyou wenku shitongben* 萬有文庫十通本 (Beijing: Zhonghua, 1986), *juan* 44, *kao* 考 413.
4. Zhu Xi 朱熹, *Mengzi jizhu* 孟子集注, in *Sishu zhangju jizhu* 四書章句集注 (Beijing: Zhonghua, 1983), *juan* 6, 273; D. C. Lau, trans., *Mencius* (London: Penguin, 1970), 115.
5. Zhu Xi, *Mengzi jizhu*, *juan* 6, 273; Lau, *Mencius*, 114–115.
6. Yang Xiong 揚雄, *Fayan zhu* 法言注 (Beijing: Zhonghua, 1992), *juan* 2, 45.
7. Han Yu 韓愈, *Han Changli wenji jiaozhu* 韓昌黎文集校注 (Taipei: Huazheng shuju, 1975), *juan* 3, 126.
8. John Knoblock, trans., *Xunzi: A Translation and Study of the Complete Works* (Stanford, Calif.: Stanford University Press, 1988), 224. See also Wang Xianqian 王先謙, *Xunzi jijie* 荀子集解 (Beijing: Zhonghua, 1988), book 1, *juan* 3, 94.
9. On Mencius, see Zhu Xi, "Gaozi" 告子, in *Mengzi jizhu*. On Xunzi, see Wang Xianqian, "Xing e pian" 性惡篇, in *Xunzi jijie*. On Yang Xiong, see Yang

Xiong, "Xiu shen" 修身, in *Fayan zhu*. On Han Yu, see "Yuan xing" 原性, in *Han Changli wenji jiaozhu*.

10. Yang Jing 楊倞, "Xunzi xu" 荀子序, in Wang Xianqian, *Xunzi jijie*, book 1, 51.
11. Wang Zhong 汪中, "Xun Qingzi tonglun" 荀卿子通論, in *Wang Zhong ji* 汪中集 (Taipei: Institute of Chinese Literature and Philosophy, Academia Sinica, 2000), *juan* 4, 119.
12. Sima Qian 司馬遷, *Shiji* 史記 (Beijing: Zhonghua, 1982), *juan* 85, 2510; Yang Hsien-yi and Gladys Yang, trans., *Records of the Historian* (Hong Kong: Commercial Press, 1975), 155.
13. Sima Qian, *Shiji*, *juan* 74, "Mengzi Xun Qing liezhuan" 孟子荀卿列傳.
14. Liu Xiang 劉向, "Xun Qing shulu" 荀卿書錄, in Wang Xianqian, *Xunzi jijie*, *juan* 20, 559.
15. Zhao Qi 趙歧, "Mengzi tici" 孟子題辭, in Jiao Xun 焦循, *Mengzi zhengyi* 孟子正義 (Beijing: Zhonghua, 1987), *juan* 1, 17.
16. Zhu Yizun 朱彝尊, *Jingyi kao* 經義考 (Taipei: Institute of Chinese Literature and Philosophy, Academia Sinica, 1997), vol. 7, *juan* 232, 124–131; also see Jiao Xun, *Mengzi zhengyi* (Beijing: Zhonghua, 1987), *juan* 1, 19.
17. Xu Gan 徐幹, *Zhong lun* 中論, in *Zhongguo zixue mingzhe jicheng, zhenben chubian* 中國子學名著集成・珍本初編 (Cheng Rong 程榮, Han Wei congshu ben 漢魏叢書本, Ming dynasty; repr., Taipei: Zhongguo zixue mingzhe jicheng bianyin jijinhui, 1978), Rujia zibu 儒家子部, vol. 30, *juan* 1, "Xu" 序.
18. Su Shi 蘇軾, "Chaozhou Han Wengong miao bei" 潮州韓文公廟碑, in *Su Shi wenji* 蘇軾文集, ed. Kong Fanli 孔凡禮 (Beijing: Zhonghua, 1992), *juan* 17, 509.
19. Han Yu, "Chuzhou Kongzi miao bei" 處州孔子廟碑, in *Han Yu quanji jiaozhu* 韓愈全集校注, ed. Qu Shouyuan 屈守元 and Chang Sichun 常思春 (Chengdu: Sichuan daxue chubanshe, 1996), 5:2430; Wang Pu 王溥, *Tang huiyao* 唐會要 (Kyoto: Chubun shuppansha, 1978), *juan* 35, 639. Regarding the Shrine to the Five Worthies, see Kong Daofu 孔道輔, "Wuxiantang ji" 五賢堂記, in Kong Zhencong 孔貞叢, ed., *Queli zhi* 闕里志, *juan* 12, 43a–44b; published in the Wanli reign of the Ming dynasty (1573–1620). See also Sun Fu 孫復, "Ruru" 儒辱, in *Sun Mingfu xiaoji* 孫明復小集, in *Jingyin Wenyuange sikuquanshu* 景印文淵閣四庫全書 (Taipei: Commercial Press, 1983), vol. 1090, 29a–30b; and Shi Jie 石介, *Culai Shi xiansheng wenji* 徂徠石先生文集 (Beijing: Zhonghua, 1984), *juan* 7, 79.
20. Han Yu, "Yuan dao" 原道, in *Han Yu quanji jiaozhu* 韓愈全集校注, ed. Qu Shouyuan 屈守元 and Chang Sichun 常思春 (Chengdu: Sichuan daxue chubanshe, 1996), 5:2665.
21. Han Yu, "Du Xun" 讀荀, in *Han Yu quanji jiaozhu* 韓愈全集校注, ed. Qu Shouyuan 屈守元 and Chang Sichun 常思春 (Chengdu: Sichuan daxue chubanshe, 1996), 5:2717.

22. Han Yu, "Jinxue jie" 進學解, in *Han Yu quanji jiaozhu* 韓愈全集校注, ed. Qu Shouyuan 屈守元 and Chang Sichun 常思春 (Chengdu: Sichuan daxue chubanshe, 1996), 4:1910.
23. Han Yu, "Song Meng Dongye xu" 送孟東野序, in *Han Yu quanji jiaozhu* 韓愈全集校注, ed. Qu Shouyuan 屈守元 and Chang Sichun 常思春 (Chengdu: Sichuan daxue chubanshe, 1996), 3:1464.
24. For more discussion of enshrinement during the Northern Song, see Huang Chin-shing, "Knowledge and Belief," in *Entering the Master's Sanctuary*, 241–261.
25. Song Lian 宋濂, *Yuanshi* 元史 (Taipei: Dingwen shuju, 1980), *juan* 76, 892–983. On *Mencius* commentator Zhao Qi's unsuccessful advocacy for declaring Mencius the second sage, see Jiao Xun 焦循, *Mengzi zhengyi* 孟子正義 (Beijing: Zhonghua, 1987), *juan* 1, 13.
26. Cheng Hao 程顥 and Cheng Yi 程頤, *Er Cheng ji* 二程集 (Taipei: Liren shuju, 1982), *juan* 19, 255.
27. Zhang Lei 張耒, *Zhang Lei ji* 張耒集 (Beijing: Zhonghua, 1990), *juan* 1, 667.
28. Zhu Xi, *Zhuzi yulei* 朱子語類, ed. Li Jingde 黎靖德 (Taipei: Huashi chubanshe, 1987), *juan* 137, 3254.
29. Cheng Hao and Cheng Yi, *Waishu* 外書, in *Er Cheng ji*, *juan* 10, 403.
30. *Taizu shilu* 太祖實錄, in *Ming shilu* 明實錄, ed. Huang Chang-chien 黃彰健 (Taipei: Institute of History and Philology, Academia Sinica, 1984), *juan* 245, 2a.
31. Cheng Hao and Cheng Yi, *Waishu*, *juan* 10, 403.
32. Zhu Xi, *Zhuzi yulei*, *juan* 137, 3255.
33. Li Yuangang 李元綱, *Shengmen shiye tu* 聖門事業圖, Song text in *Baichuan xuehai* 百川學海, Chinese Text Project, https://ctext.org, 1001.
34. Cheng Minzheng 程敏政, *Huangdun wenji* 篁墩文集, in *Jingyin Wenyuange sikuquanshu* 景印文淵閣四庫全書 (Taipei: Commercial Press, 1983), vol. 1252–1253, *juan* 10, 3a.
35. Qu Jiusi 瞿九思, *Kongmiao liyue kao* 孔廟禮樂考, *juan* 5, 45b; published in the Wanli reign of the Ming dynasty.
36. Xiong He 熊鉌, *Xiong Wuxuan xiansheng wenji* 熊勿軒先生文集 (Shanghai: Commercial Press, 1936), *juan* 4, 51.
37. Xiong He, *Xiong Wuxuan xiansheng wenji*, *juan* 3, 34.
38. Song Lian, *Song Lian quanji* 宋濂全集 (Hangzhou: Zhejiang guji chubanshe), vol. 1, *juan* 2, 20.
39. Wang Yi 王禕, *Wang Zhongwengong ji* 王忠文公集, in *Congshu jicheng chubian* 叢書集成初編 (Shanghai: Shanghai Commercial Press, 1939), series vol. 2421–2428, vol. 5, *juan* 12, "Kongzi miaoting congsi yi" 孔子廟庭從祀議, 303–306.
40. Cheng Minzheng, *Huangdun wenji*, *juan* 10, 8b.

41. Zhang Jiugong 張九功, "Qing congsi Kongting shu" 請從祀孔庭疏 and "Bibu mingjiao shu" 裨補名教疏, in *Xue Wenqinggong hang shilu* 薛文清公行實錄, in Xue Xuan 薛瑄, *Xue Xuan quanji* 薛瑄全集 (Taiyuan: Shanxi Renmin chubanshe, 1990), *juan* 2, 1628–1629.
42. Sima Qian, *Shiji*, *juan* 87, "Li Si liezhuan" 李斯列傳, 2539.
43. Lu Guimeng 陸龜蒙, "Da Ru ping" 大儒評, in *Qin ding quan Tang wen* 欽定全唐文, ed. Dong Gao 董誥 (Taipei: Datong shuju, 1979), vol. 17, *juan* 801, 11a; mandated by Qing Renzong 清仁宗 (Emperor Jiaqing 嘉慶), r. 1796–1820.
44. Su Shi, *Su Shi wenji*, *juan* 4, 101.
45. Zhang Cong 張璁, *Yudui lu* 諭對錄, in *Sikuquanshu cunmu congshu, shibu* 四庫全書存目叢書·史部 (Baolunlou 寶綸樓, 1609; repr., Tainan: Zhuangyan wenhua shiye gongsi, 1996), vol. 57, *juan* 22, 12a. Also see *Taizu shilu*, *juan* 245, 2a.
46. Hu Juren 胡居仁, *Ju ye lu* 居業錄, and Luo Qinshun 羅欽順, *Kun zhi ji* 困知記, in *Congshu jicheng xinbian* 叢書集成新編 (Zhengyi tang quanshu 正誼堂全書; repr., Taipei: Xinwenfeng chuban gongsi, 1985), "Zhexue lei" 哲學類, vol. 23, *juan* 1, 6; *juan* 4, 37.
47. For an analysis of the 1530 changes in the Confucius temple institution, see Huang Chin-shing, "Between Orthodoxy and Legitimacy: Reflections from the Debates on Ritual Reforms of the Confucius temple in 1530" 道統與治統之間：從明嘉靖九年孔廟改制論皇權與祭祀禮儀, in *Entering the Master's Sanctuary*, 125–163.
48. See, for instance, Fang Bao's 方苞 (1668–1749) famous *Shanding Xunzi* 刪定荀子, in Yan Lingfeng 嚴靈峰, ed., *Wuqiubeizhai Xunzi jicheng* 無求備齋荀子集成 (Taipei: Cheng Wen, 1977), vol. 28.
49. Gui Youguang 歸有光, *Zhenchuan xiansheng ji* 震川先生集 (Taipei: Yuanliu chubanshe, 1983), *juan* 1, 20.
50. Li Zhi 李贄, *Cang shu* 藏書 (Taipei: Xuesheng shuju, 1974), "Ruchen zhuan" 儒臣傳, *juan* 32, 519.
51. See Wang Xianqian, "Kaozheng shang" 考證上, in *Xunzi jijie*, 4–20. Some have counted books explicating Xunzi during the Tang and through the Ming and listed only seven, but there were more than twenty-five during the Qing. Figures are cited by Guo Zhikun 郭志坤, *Xunxue lungao* 荀學論稿 (Shanghai: Joint Publishing, 1990), 306.
52. Such critics include, for instance, Fang Bao, *Shanding Xunzi*. Also see Huang Shengmin 黃聖旻, "Wang Xianqian 'Xunzi jijie' yanjiu" 王先謙〈荀子集解〉研究 (master's thesis, National Cheng Kung University, 1997), 40–41.
53. Wang Zhong, "Xun Qingzi tonglun," *juan* 4, 117, 119.
54. On the rise of the study of ritual in modern China, see Chow Kai-wing, *The Rise of Confucian Ritualism in Late Imperial China* (Taipei: SMC, 1996); and

Chang So-an 張壽安, *Yi Li dai Li* 以禮代理 (Taipei: Institute of Modern History, Academia Sinica, 1994).

55. Ling Tingkan 凌廷堪, *Jiaoli tang wenji* 校禮堂文集, in *Xuxiu siku quanshu* 續修四庫全書 (Zhang Qijin 張其錦, 1813; repr., Shanghai: Shanghai guji chubanshe, 1995), vol. 1480, *juan* 10, "Xun Qing song" 荀卿頌, 1b–2b.
56. Wang Xianqian, *Xunzi jijie*, "Xu" 序, 1.
57. Kang Youwei 康有為, *Wanmu caotang koushuo* 萬木草堂口說, in *Kang Youwei xueshu zhuzuo xuan* 康有為學術著作選, ed. Lou Yulie 樓宇烈 (Beijing: Zhonghua, 1988), 184.
58. Yan Ruoqu 閻若璩, *Shangshu guwen shuzheng* 尚書古文疏證, in *Jingyin Wenyuange sikuquanshu*, vol. 66, *juan* 8, 86b–87a. Li Zhi criticized Song Confucians for blaming Xunzi for Li Si's despicable actions as chancellor of Qin; see Li Zhi, *Fen shu* 焚書, in *Fen shu / Xu fen shu* 焚書／續焚書 (Taipei: Hanjing wenhua gongsi, 1984), *juan* 5, 218.
59. Yao Chen 姚諶, "Ni shang Xun Qingzi congsi yi" 擬上荀卿子從祀議, in Shen Cuifen 沈粹芬, ed., *Qing wen hui* 清文匯 (Beijing: Beijing chubanshe, 1996), vol. 3, *juan* 11, 8b.
60. Yan Kejun 嚴可均, *Tieqiao mangao* 鐵橋漫稿, in *Congshu jicheng xubian* 叢書集成續編 (Xinjuzhai congshu 心矩齋叢書; repr., Taipei: Xinwenfeng chuban gongsi, 1989), "Wenxue lei" 文學類, vol. 158, *juan* 3, "Xunzi dang congsi yi" 荀子當從祀議, 2b–3a.
61. Qian Daxin 錢大昕, *Qianyantang ji* 潛研堂集 (Shanghai: Shanghai guji chubanshe, 1986), *juan* 27, "Ba Xunzi" 跋荀子, 475–476. On Zhu Xi's discussion of "physical nature" (*qizhi zhi xing* 氣質之性), see Zhu Xi, *Zhuzi yulei*, *juan* 4, 69–78.
62. Yan Kejun, *Tieqiao mangao*, *juan* 3, "Xunzi dang congsi yi," 3b.
63. Yao Chen, "Ni shang Xun Qingzi congsi yi," 8a–8b.
64. Yongrong 永瑢 and Ji Yun 紀昀, *Siku quanshu zongmu tiyao* 四庫全書總目提要, Wuyingdian 武英殿 edition (Taipei: Commercial Press, 1983), *juan* 91, 6b.
65. In his book *Orthodox Learning* 學統, with preface dated 1685, Xiong Cilu 熊賜履 (1635–1709) had already placed Xunzi under the categories of "mixed learning" and "heterodox learning," which were far inferior to the category of "orthodox learning." See Xiong Cilu 熊賜履, *Xuetong* 學統, in *Congshu jicheng xinbian* (Xinwenfeng chuban gongsi, 1985), Shidi lei 史地類, vols. 99–100, *juan* 43, 553–557; published in Hubei congshu 湖北叢書.
66. Xu Shichang 徐世昌, "Wang Xixun zhuan" 汪喜荀傳, in *Wang Xisun zhuzuoji* 汪喜孫著作集, ed. Yang Jinlong 楊晉龍 (Taipei: Institute of Chinese Literature and Philosophy, Academia Sinica, 2003), 3:1318–1319.
67. Ma Jigao 馬積高, *Xunxue yuanliu* 荀學源流 (Shanghai: Shanghai guji chubanshe, 2000), 327–328.

68. Pang Zhonglu 龐鍾璐, *Wenmiao sidian kao* 文廟祀典考 (1877; repr., Taipei: Zhongguo liyue xuehui, 1977), *juan* 48, 1a–1b.
69. Liang Qichao 梁啟超, "Lun Zhina zongjiao gaige" 論支那宗教改革, in *Yinbingshi wenji* 飲冰室文集 (Taipei: Chung Hwa, 1970), vol. 1, *juan* 3, 57.
70. Liang Qichao, "Wang you Xia Suiqing xiansheng" 亡友夏穗卿先生, in *Yinbingshi wenji* 飲冰室文集 (Taipei: Chung Hwa, 1970), vol. 8, *juan* 44a, 21.
71. Liang Qichao, "Lun Zhongguo xueshu sixiang bianqian zhi dashi" 論中國學術思想變遷之大勢, in *Yinbingshi wenji* 飲冰室文集 (Taipei: Chung Hwa, 1970), vol. 2, *juan* 7, 16.
72. Liang Qichao, "Lun Zhina zongjiao gaige," vol. 1, *juan* 3, 57.
73. Tan Sitong 譚嗣同, *Tan Sitong quanji* 譚嗣同全集, ed. Cai Shangsi 蔡尚思 (Beijing: Zhonghua, 1981), "Renxue" 仁學, 2:337.
74. Liang Qichao, "Nanhai Kang xiansheng zhuan" 南海康先生傳, in *Yinbingshi wenji* 飲冰室文集 (Taipei: Chung Hwa, 1970), vol. 1, 68–69. See also *Qingdai xueshu gailun* 清代學術概論 (Beijing: Dongfang chubanshe, 1996), 76. However, when he wrote *Moral Education Reflections* 德育鑑, in 1905, Liang had revised his opinion to "Xunzi is certainly the orthodox transmission of Confucius, and the Song and Ming Confucian discussions of the heart-mind and nourishing the heart-mind are probably not extraneous to it." See Liang Qichao, *Deyu jian* 德育鑑, in *Yinbingshi zhuanji* 飲冰室專集, in *Yinbingshi heji* 飲冰室合集 (Shanghai: Chung Hwa, 1936), vol. 6, *juan* 26, 48.
75. Hu Shi 胡適, *Zhongguo zhexue shi dagang, juan shang* 中國哲學史大綱·卷上 (Taipei: Liren shuju, 1982), 311, 395.
76. Wu Yu 吳虞, "Du Xunzi shuhou" 讀荀子書後, in *Wu Yu wenlu* 吳虞文錄, in *Minguo congshu* 民國叢書 (Yadong tushuguan 亞東圖書館, 1927; repr., Shanghai: Shanghai shudian, 1992), series 2, no. 96, 2:12.
77. Liang Qichao, "Du Mengzi jieshuo" 讀孟子界說, in *Yinbingshi wenji* 飲冰室文集 (Taipei: Chung Hwa, 1970), vol. 1, *juan* 3, 17–21; Hu Shih, *Zhongguo zhexue shi dagang*, 1:300, 394.
78. Zhang Taiyan 章太炎, "Ding Kong" 訂孔, in *Zhang Taiyan zhenglun xuanji* 章太炎政論選集, ed. Tang Zhijun 湯志鈞 (Beijing: Zhonghua, 1977), 1:180. In another essay on later sages, Zhang Taiyan even remarked, "Being similar to Xun Qing is being similar to Confucius; differing from Xun Qing is also differing from Confucius." Zhang Taiyan, "Hou sheng" 後聖, *Zhang Taiyan zhenglun xuanji*, 1:39.
79. In 1919, the Beiyang (Northern) government in Beijing carried out the rites at the Confucius temple and enshrined Yan Yuan and Li Gong.
80. Wu Yu, *Wu Yu wenlu*, 2:10.
81. Qian Mu 錢穆, *Zhongguo xueshu sixiang shi luncong* 中國學術思想史論叢 (Taipei: Dongda tushu gongsi, 1980), 2:241.

82. Mou Zongsan 牟宗三, *Xinti yu xingti* 心體與性體 (Taipei: Zhengzhong shuju, 1996), 7, 13, 96–97. Professor Mou also concluded, "Mencius and others ... are adequate to represent the orthodox line of the Confucian tradition; but Xunzi does not participate in the intrinsic character of the development of the essential essence of the tradition of Confucian teachings."
83. Chen Duxiu 陳獨秀, "Zailun Kongjiao wenti" 再論孔教問題 (January 1, 1917), in *Duxiu wencun* 獨秀文存 (Shanghai Yadong Library 上海亞東圖書館, 1922; repr., Hefei: Anhui Renmin chubanshe, 1987), 1:133–134.
84. I should acknowledge that, during the Cultural Revolution's clamor to "Criticize Confucius and Promote the Qin," Xun was praised because of his connections to Li Si and Han Fei. Nevertheless, Confucius temples overall were hit with unprecedented destruction.
85. Xiong He, *Xiong Wuxuan xiansheng wenji*, juan 4, 48.
86. Yan Fu 嚴復, *Yan Jidao wenchao* 嚴幾道文鈔 (Shanghai Guohua, 1922; repr., Taipei: Shijie shuju, 1971), juan 1, "Yuan qiang" 原強, 6b–7a.
87. Hu Shi, "Xunzi, Xinlixue yu mingxue" 荀子、心理學與名學, in *Zhongguo zhexue shi dagang, juan shang*, 321–339.
88. Feng Youlan 馮友蘭, *Zhongguo zhexue shi* 中國哲學史, in *Sansongtang quanji* 三松堂全集 (Zhengzhou: Henan Renmin chubanshe, 1985), 2:274–278.
89. See, for example, Fang Erjia 方爾加, *Xunzi xinlun* 荀子新論 (Beijing: Zhongguo heping chubanshe, 1993), chap. 4. Fang believes it is a consensus in academic circles that Xunzi is an outstanding materialist.
90. Li Zhizao 李之藻, *Pangong liyue shu* 頖宮禮樂疏, in *Jingyin Wenyuange sikuquanshu* 景印文淵閣四庫全書 (Taipei: Commercial Press, 1983), vol. 651, juan 2, 24a.
91. Li Zhizao, *Pangong liyue shu*, juan 2, 24a.
92. Cheng Shude 程樹德, *Lunyu jishi* 論語集釋 (Beijing: Zhonghua, 1990), juan 24, 817; translation adapted from James Legge, *The Chinese Classics* (Oxford: Clarendon Press, 1893; repr., Taipei: SMC, 1991), 1:250.
93. Jiao Xun, *Mengzi zhengyi*, juan 23, 786; Lau, *Mencius*, 167.
94. Jiao Xun, *Mengzi zhengyi*, juan 27, 927; Lau, *Mencius*, 189.
95. Wang Xianqian, *Xunzi jijie*, juan 1, 11.
96. Cheng Shude, *Lunyu jishi*, juan 4, 103; Legge, *Chinese Classics*, 1:150.
97. Zhang Xuecheng 章學誠, *Wen shi tongyi jiaozhu* 文史通義校注 (Taipei: Hanjing wenhua gongsi, 1986), juan 4, "Shuo lin" 說林, 354.
98. Kang Youwei, *Wanmu caotang koushuo*, 184.
99. Yu Yue 俞樾, *Chunzaitang zawen* 春在堂襍文, in *Chunzaitang quanshu* 春在堂全書 (Taipei: Zhongguo wenxian chubanshe, 1968), part 6, juan 7 六編七, "Gujing jingshe baji xu" 詁經精舍八集序, 5b–6a.
100. Mou Zongsan, *Xunxue dalue* 荀學大略 (Taipei: Xuesheng shuju, 1990), "Xu" 序, 193–94. Lin Yueh-hui 林月惠 of the Institute of Chinese Literature and

Philosophy reminded me that Professor Mou often repeated in class, "For hearing the Way, respect Meng Ke, and for engaging in learning, model yourself after Xun Qing."

101. Zhao Bingwen 趙秉文, *Fu shui ji* 滏水集, in *Jingyin Wenyuange sikuquanshu* 景印文淵閣四庫全書 (Taipei: Commercial Press, 1983), vol. 1190, *juan* 1, "Yuan jiao" 原教, 2b.
102. Kang Youwei, *Wanmu caotang koushuo*, 184.

6. The Disenchantment with Confucianism in Modern China

1. In addition to chapter 2, "Confucianism as a Religion," see Huang Chin-shing, "Decoding the Symbols of Confucian Temples: Remarks on the Religiosity of Confucianism" 解開孔廟祭典的符碼——兼論其宗教性, in *Wenhua yu lishi de zhuisuo: Yu Yingshih jiaoshou bazhi shouqing lunwenji* 文化與歷史的追索：余英時教授八秩壽慶論文集, ed. Hoyt Tillman (Taipei: Linking, 2009), 535–558. On public religion, see Anthony C. Yu, *State and Religion in China* (Chicago: Open Court, 2005), chap. 3. Our usage of public religion is quite different from its usage by Western scholars focused on Western religions, such as, for example, José Casanova, "Public Religions Revisited," in *Religion: Beyond a Concept*, ed. Hent de Vries (New York: Fordham University Press, 2008), 101–119.
2. Qin Huitian 秦蕙田, *Wuli tongkao* 五禮通考 (Weijingwo 味經窩; repr., Taoyuan: Shenghuan tushu gongsi, 1994), *juan* 117, 1b.
3. Yan Fu 嚴復, "Baojiao yuyi" 保教餘義 (June 7–8, 1898), in *Yan Fu wenji biannian (1)* 嚴復文集編年(一), in *Yan Fu heji* 嚴復合集, ed. Lin Zaijue 林載爵 (Taipei: C. F. Koo Foundation, 1998), 1:157.
4. Kang Youwei 康有為, "Liang Yue guangrenshantang shengxuehui yuanqi" 兩粵廣仁善堂聖學會緣起, in *Kang Youwei quanji* 康有為全集, ed. Jiang Yihua 姜義華 and Wu Genliang 吳根樑 (Shanghai: Shanghai guji chubanshe, 1990), 2:621. The term "Confucius cult" is in this context highlights Kang Youwei's proposed reformation of Confucianism, which was inspired by observations of the civic impact of Christianity.
5. Tuo Tuo 脫脫, *Songshi* 宋史 (Taipei: Dingwen shuju, 1978), *juan* 351, 11101.
6. Yuan Jue 袁桷, *Qingrong jushi ji* 清容居士集, in *Sibu congkan chubian, suoben* 四部叢刊初編·縮本 (Taipei: Commercial Press, 1965), vols. 295–297, *juan* 35, 516. See also Anonymous 佚名, *Miaoxue dianli* 廟學典禮, ed. Wang Ting 王頲 (Hangzhou: Zhejiang guji chubanshe, 1992), *juan* 1, 12; *juan* 2, 41–42.

7. Zhu Guozhen 朱國禎, *Yong chuang xiaopin* 湧幢小品, in *Biji xiaoshuo daguan* 筆記小說大觀 (Taipei: Xinxing shuju, 1984), vol. 22, no. 7, *juan* 19, 3a.
8. Zhang Dai 張岱, "Kongmiao kuai" 孔廟檜, in *Tao'an mengyi* 陶菴夢憶, in *Meihua wenxue mingzhu congkan* 美化文學名著叢刊, ed. Zhu Jianmang 朱劍芒 (Shanghai: Shijie shuju, 1947), 9. The situation did not change even in the early republican era. See Jiang Weiqiao 蔣維喬, "Qufu jiyou 曲阜紀遊," in *Xin youji huikan xubian* 新遊記彙刊續編, ed. Yao Zhuxuan 姚祝萱 (Shanghai: Chung Hwa, 1925), vol. 1, *juan* 7, 20.
9. Anonymous, "Yue bao ji huisheng eyan yize shuai shu qi hou" 閱報紀毀聖訛言一則率書其後, in *Shen bao* 申報 9022 (May 29, 1898) 光緒二十四年四月初十日, section 1.
10. Tan Sitong 譚嗣同, *Renxue* 仁學, in *Tan Sitong quanji* 譚嗣同全集, ed. Cai Shangsi 蔡尚思 (Beijing: Zhonghua, 1981), 2:353.
11. Liang Qichao 梁啟超, "Bianfa tongyi" 變法通議, in *Yinbingshi wenji* 飲冰室文集 (Taipei: Chung Hwa, 1970), vol. 1, *juan* 1, 49.
12. Zhang Cong 張璁, *Yudui lu* 諭對錄, in *Sikuquanshu cunmu congshu, shibu* 四庫全書存目叢書・史部 (Baolunlou 寶綸樓, 1609; repr., Tainan: Zhuangyan wenhua shiye gongsi, 1996), vol. 57, *juan* 22, 24b.
13. Liang Qichao, "Nanhai Kang xiansheng zhuan" 南海康先生傳, in *Yinbingshi wenji*, vol. 2, *juan* 6, 67.
14. On the turns in the term "religion" in modern Chinese history, see Chen Hsi-yuan 陳熙遠, "'Zongjiao/Religion': A Keyword in the Cultural History of Modern China" 「宗教」：一個中國近代文化史上的關鍵詞, *New History* 13, no. 4 (December 2002): 37–66.
15. Kang Youwei, *Kang Youwei zhenglun ji* 康有為政論集, ed. Tang Zhijun 湯志鈞 (Beijing: Zhonghua, 1981), 1:13.
16. Kang Youwei, "Shang Qingdi dier shu" 上清帝第二書 (1895), in *Kang Youwei quanji*, 2:97.
17. Kang Youwei, "Liang Yue guangrenshantang shengxuehui yuanqi," in *Kang Youwei quanji*, 2:620.
18. Song Shu 宋恕, "Liuzi kezhai beiyi (chugao)" 六字課齋卑議（初稿）, in *Song Shu ji* 宋恕集, ed. Hu Zhusheng 胡珠生 (Beijing: Zhonghua, 1993), 1:2.
19. Song Shu, "Liuzi kezhai beiyi (chugao)," 1:36.
20. Song Shu, "Liuzi kezhai beiyi (chugao)," 1:36.
21. Ouyang Xiu 歐陽修 and Song Qi 宋祁, *Xin Tangshu* 新唐書 (Taipei: Dingwen shuju, 1981), *juan* 15, 373.
22. Song Shu, "Shu Zhou Huanshu *Dajian suwang jiaohui yi* hou" 書周煥樞《大建素王教會議》後, in *Song Shu ji*, 1:283.
23. Ye Dehui 葉德輝, "Ye libu yu Nanxuehui Pi Lumen xiaolian shu" 葉吏部與南學會皮鹿門孝廉書, in *Yi jiao congbian* 翼教叢編, ed. Su Yu 蘇輿 (Taipei:

Institute of Chinese Literature and Philosophy, Academia Sinica, 2005), *juan* 6, 351.
24. Feng Youlan 馮友蘭, "Kongzi zai Zhongguo lishi zhong zhi diwei" 孔子在中國歷史中之地位 (1927), in *Sansongtang xueshu wenji* 三松堂學術文集 (Beijing: Peking University Press, 1984), 131.
25. Ye Dehui, "Ye libu yu Liu Xianduan Huang Yuwen liang sheng shu" 葉吏部與劉先端黃郁文兩生書, in *Yi jiao congbian, juan* 6, 344.
26. Kang Youwei, *Kongzi gaizhi kao* 孔子改制考, in *Kang Youwei quanji*, 3:284.
27. See Kang Youwei, "Qing shangding jiaoan falu, lizheng keju wenti, ting tianxia xiangyi zengshe wenmiao, bing cheng *Kongzi gaizhi kao*, yi zun shengshi bao dajiao jue huo meng zhe" 請商定教案法律,釐正科舉文體,聽天下鄉邑增設文廟,並呈《孔子改制考》,以尊聖師保大教絕禍萌折, in *Kang Youwei zaoqi yigao shuping* 康有為早期遺稿述評, ed. Huang Mingtong 黃明同 and Wu Xizhao 吳熙釗 (Guangzhou: Sun Yat-sen University Press, 1988), 287–292. The earliest to discover a problem with the text of this memorandum was Huang Chang-chien 黃彰健, "Kang Youwei 'Wuxu zougao' bianwei" 康有為「戊戌奏稿」辨偽, in *Wuxu bianfa shi yanjiu* 戊戌變法史研究 (Taipei: Institute of History and Philology, Academia Sinica, 1970), 555–557.
28. Kang Youwei, "Yi Kongjiao wei guojiao pei tian yi" 以孔教為國教配天議 (April 1913), in *Kang Youwei zhenglun ji*, 2:842–859.
29. Liang Qichao, "Baojiao fei suoyi zun Kong lun" 保教非所以尊孔論, in *Yinbingshi wenji*, vol. 2, juan 9, 53.
30. Ding Wenjiang 丁文江, *Liang Rengong nianpu changbian chugao* 梁任公年譜長編初稿 (Taipei: Shijie shuju, 1972), 53.
31. The signed petition, "Qing lianming shangshu chaban shengxiang bei hui gongqi" 請聯名上書查辦像被毀公啟, is quoted from Lin Keguang 林克光, *Gexin pai juren Kang Youwei* 革新派巨人康有為 (Beijing: China Renmin University Press, 1998), 207. After German troops entered Mo County in the first month of the year, they demolished the statue of Confucius and dug the eyeballs out of Zilu's statue. Out of fear, local officials tried to keep the matter secret; however, when news got to Beijing, the literati vigorously expressed their righteous indignation.
32. Kang Youwei, "Qing zun Kongsheng wei guojiao li jiaobu jiaohui yi Kongzi jinian er fei yinsi zhe" 請尊孔聖為國教立教部教會以孔子紀年而廢淫祀折 (1898), in *Kang Youwei zhenglun ji*, 1:279–280.
33. Quoted in Huang Mingtong and Wu Xizhao, eds., *Kang Youwei zaoqi yigao shuping* (Guangzhou: Sun Yat-sen University Press, 1988), 290.
34. Kang Youwei, "Qing zun Kongsheng," 1:282–283.
35. Kang Youwei, "Qing zun Kongsheng," 1:280.
36. Kang Youwei, "Qing zun Kongsheng," 1:279.

37. Quoted in Liang Yuansheng 梁元生, *Xuanni fuhai dao Nanzhou: Rujia sixiang yu zaoqi xinjiapo huaren shehui shiliao huibian* 宣尼浮海到南洲：儒家思想與早期新加坡華人社會史料彙編 (Hong Kong: Chinese University Press, 1995), "Jilong huashang chang si Kongzi" 吉隆華商倡祀孔子, 149–150.
38. Kang Youwei, "Qing zun Kongsheng," 1:281.
39. Liu Shipei 劉師培, "Lun Zhongguo gudai xintian zhi sixiang" 論中國古代信天之思想, in *Liu Shenshu yishu buyi* 劉申叔遺書補遺, ed. Wan Shiguo 萬仕國 (Yangzhou: Guangling shushe, 2008), 53.
40. Kang Youwei, "Qing zun Kongsheng," 1:281. From ancient times there were popular venerations of "Heaven, Earth, Ruler, and Teacher." See Yu Yingshi 余英時, *Qing huai Zhongguo—Yu Yingshi zixuanji* 情懷中國—余英時自選集 (Hong Kong: Cosmos, 2010), particularly, "'Tian di jun qin shi' de qiyuan" 「天地君親師」的起源, 74–80.
41. Kang Youwei, *Kang Nanhai zi bian nianpu* 康南海自編年譜 (Beijing: Zhonghua, 1992), 44. This suggestion later supplemented his original 1898 memorandum; see Huang Mingtong and Wu Xizhao, eds., *Kang Youwei zaoqi yigao shuping*, 288–289.
42. Chen Baozhen 陳寶箴, "Zou lizheng xueshu zaojiu rencai zhe" 奏釐正學術造就人才摺 (1898), in *Wuxu bianfa* 戊戌變法, ed. Zhongguoshi Xuehui 中國史學會 and Jian Bozan 翦伯贊 (Shanghai: Shenzhou guoguang she, 1955), 2:358.
43. On the historical development of Christianity, see especially Jaroslav Pelikan, "Christianity," in *The Encyclopedia of Religion*, ed. Mircea Eliade (New York: Simon & Schuster Macmillan, 1995), 3:348–362.
44. Even though Kang's former disciple Liang Qichao turned against the movement to "preserve the cult," he still acknowledge the widespread support in China for Kang's Cult of Confucius Association and its goal of establishing a state religion, sacrificial rites to heaven, and veneration of Confucius. Liang Qichao 梁啟超, *Qingdai xueshu gailun* 清代學術概論, in *Yinbingshi Zhuanji* 飲冰室專集, in *Yinbingshi heji* 飲冰室合集 (Shanghai: Chung Hwa, 1936), vol. 9, *juan* 34, section 26, 63.
45. Kang Youwei, "Shaanxi Kongjiaohui jiangyan" 陝西孔教會講演, in *Kang Youwei zhenglun ji*, 2:1107.
46. See Liang Yuansheng, *Xuanni fuhai dao Nanzhou*.
47. Kang Youwei, "Zhi Beijing Kongjiaohui dian" 致北京孔教會電, in *Kang Youwei zhenglun ji*, 2:921. See Kang's letter to the Ministry of Education, within this same volume, where he quotes Chen Huanzhang's 陳煥章 statement about destruction of temples to culture in the wake of the ministry's negation of Confucius's classics.
48. Beijing shifan daxue lishixi Zhongguo jindaishi zu 北京師範大學歷史系中國近代史組, ed., *Zhongguo jindai shi ziliao xuanbian* 中國近代史資料選編 (Beijing:

Zhonghua, 1977), 2:296–302. The Great Proletarian Cultural Revolution also destroyed Confucius temples. See Yazi 亞子 and Liangzi 良子, *Kongfu da jienan* 孔府大劫難 (Hong Kong: Tiandi tushu gongsi, 1992).

49. See Gao Pingshu 高平叔, "Note of January 19, 1912," in *Cai Yuanpei nianpu changbian* 蔡元培年譜長編 (Beijing: People's Education Press, 1998), 1:400–401.

50. Kang Youwei, "Zhonghua jiuguo lun" 中華救國論 (June 1912), in *Kang Youwei zhenglun ji*, 2:699–731.

51. People castigated Kang during the early republic; for instance, in 1921, Liang Shuming published a statement saying that he respected everyone except Kang Youwei. Liang Shuming 梁漱溟, *Dongxi wenhua ji qi zhexue* 東西文化及其哲學 (Hong Kong: Ziyou xueren she, 1960), 4, 136–137.

52. Lu Xun 魯迅, "Zai xiandai Zhongguo de Kongfuzi" 在現代中國的孔夫子 (April 29, 1935), *Qiejieting zawen erji* 且介亭雜文二集, in *Lu Xun quanji* 魯迅全集 (Taipei: Tangshan chubanshe, 1989), 8:102.

53. Chen Huanzhang 陳煥章, *Kongjiao lun* 孔教論, in *Minguo congshu* 民國叢書 (Kongjiaohui and Shanghai: Commercial Press, 1913; repr., Shanghai: Shanghai shudian, 1992), series 4, no. 2, 61–62.

54. See Gu Jiegang's 1926 lecture at Xiamen University. Gu Jiegang 顧頡剛, "Chunqiu shi de Kongzi he Handai de Kongzi" 春秋時的孔子和漢代的孔子, in *Gushi bian* 古史辨, ed. Gu Jiegang (Pushe 樸社, 1930), in *Minguo congshu* 4, no. 66 (Shanghai: Shanghai shudian, 1992), 2:138.

55. For example, the People's Republic of China generally excludes Confucianism from the category of religion. See James Miller, "The Opium of the People," in *Chinese Religions in Contemporary Societies*, ed. James Miller (Santa Barbara: ABC-Clio, 2006), 5. Moreover, what people in Taiwan call "Confucian religion" refers to the folk religion of the Cult of the Three Unified, discussed in chapter 2.

56. Ye Dehui, "Ye libu ming jiao" 葉吏部明教 and "Ye libu du xixue shufa shu hou" 葉吏部讀西學書法書後, in *Yi jiao congbian*, juan 3, 141–146; juan 4, 259.

57. Tang Zhijun 湯志鈞, ed., *Zhang Taiyan nianpu changbian* 章太炎年譜長編 (Beijing: Zhonghua, 1979), 1:38–41.

58. Liu Shipei, "Lun Kongjiao yu Zhongguo zhengzhi wushe" 論孔教與中國政治無涉 (1904), in *Liu Shipei lunxue lunzheng* 劉師培論學論政, ed. Li Miaogen 李妙根 (Shanghai: Fudan University Press, 1990), 343.

59. Liang Qichao, "Yu Yan Youling xiansheng shu" 與嚴幼陵先生書, in *Yinbingshi wenji*, vol. 1, juan 1, 109. Ding Wenjiang dates this letter to 1897; however, this is a mistake, because Yan's first letter to Liang certainly was before October 1896. See Ding Wenjiang, *Liang Rengong nianpu changbian chugao*, 42; Yan Fu, "Yu Liang Qichao shu yi" 與梁啟超書一, in *Yan Fu wenji biannian (1)*,

in *Yan Fu heji* 嚴復合集, ed. Lin Zaijue 林載爵 (Taipei: C. F. Koo Foundation, 1998), 1:104–106.

60. Huang Zunxian 黃遵憲, "Zhi Liang Qichao han" 致梁啟超函 (May 1902), in *Huang Zunxian quanji* 黃遵憲全集, ed. Chen Zheng 陳錚 (Beijing: Zhonghua, 2005), 1:426.
61. Liang Qichao, "Fu youren lun Baojiao shu" 復友人論保教書, in *Yinbingshi wenji*, vol. 1, *juan* 3, 11.
62. Kang Youwei, "Baoguohui zhangcheng" 保國會章程 (1898), in *Kang Youwei zhenglun ji*, 1:233–236. On Liang's relationship to the Association to Save the Nation, see Ding Wenjiang, *Liang Rengong nianpu changbian chugao*, 50–53.
63. Liang Qichao, "Lun Fojiao yu qunzhi zhi guanxi" 論佛教與群治之關係 (1902), in *Yinbingshi wenji*, vol. 2, *juan* 10, 45–52.
64. On Liang's obsession with saving the nation, see Huang Chin-shing, "Liang Qichao and his Ultimate Concern" 梁啟超的終極關懷, in *Entering the Master's Sanctuary: Power, Belief and Legitimacy in Traditional China* 優入聖域：權力、信仰與正當性 (Taipei: Asian Culture Press, 1994), 437–452.
65. Liang Qichao, "Fu youren lun Baojiao shu," and "Lun Zhina zongjiao gaige" 論支那宗教改革, in *Yinbingshi wenji*, vol. 1, *juan* 3, 9–11; and vol. 1, *juan* 3, 55–61.
66. Liang Qichao, "Baojiao fei suoyi zun Kong lun," in *Yinbingshi wenji*, vol. 2, *juan* 9, 52–53.
67. Huang Zunxian, "Zhi Liang Qichao han," in *Huang Zunxian quanji*, 1:426.
68. Liang Qichao, "Lun Fojiao yu qunzhi zhi guanxi," in *Yinbingshi wenji*, vol. 2, *juan* 10, 45.
69. Huang Zunxian, "Zhi Liang Qichao han," 1:427.
70. On the breakup of Liang and Kang's relationship, see Liang, "Qingdai xueshu gailun," in *Yinbingshi heji*, vol. 9, *juan* 34, 63–66.
71. Liang Qichao, "Baojiao fei suoyi zun Kong lun," 50.
72. Liang Qichao, *Xinmin shuo* 新民說, in *Yinbingshi heji*, vol. 3, *juan* 4, sec. 11, "Lun jinbu" 論進步, 59–60.
73. Liang Qichao, "Baojiao fei suoyi zun Kong lun," 52.
74. Liang Qichao, "Baojiao fei suoyi zun Kong lun," 52. See also James Legge, trans., *The Chinese Classics* (Oxford: Clarendon Press, 1893; repr., Taipei: SMC, 1991), 1:240–241, 201.
75. Kang Youwei, *Kang Youwei zhenglun ji*, 1:282.
76. Liang Qichao, "Lun Fojiao yu qunzhi zhi guanxi," in *Yinbingshi wenji*, vol. 2, *juan* 10, 45.
77. Feng Youlan, "Kongzi zai Zhongguo lishi zhong zhi diwei," in *Sansongtang xueshu wenji*, 131; Feng Youlan, *Zhongguo zhexue jianshi* 中國哲學簡史, in *Sansongtang quanji* 三松堂全集 (Zhengzhou: Henan Renmin chubanshe, 1989), 6:44.

78. Zhou Yutong 周予同, "Kongzi" 孔子 (1945), in *Zhou Yutong jingxueshi lunzhe xuanji* 周予同經學史論著選集, ed. Zhu Weizheng 朱維錚 (Shanghai: Shanghai Renmin chubanshe, 1983), 388.
79. Kang Youwei, "Yi Kongjiao wei guojiao pei tian yi," in *Kang Youwei zhenglun ji*, 2:842–849.
80. Li Dazhao 李大釗, "Wuzhuang ji Kong" 武裝祭孔 (1919), in *Li Dazhao quanji* 李大釗全集, ed. Zhu Wentong 朱文通 (Shijiazhuang: Hebei jiaoyu chubanshe, 1999), 3:345.
81. Zhang Taiyan, "Bo jianli Kongjiao yi" 駁建立孔教議, in *Taiyan wenlu chubian*, in *Zhang Taiyan quanji*, 4:197. See also Zhang Taiyan, *Zhang Taiyan zhenglun xuanji* 章太炎政論選集, ed. Tang Zhijun (Beijing: Zhonghua, 1977), 118–125.
82. Yuan Shikai 袁世凱, "Dazongtong zhi Kongshe zhuci" 大總統致孔社祝詞, *Kongshe zazhi, luyao* 孔社雜誌·錄要 (December 1913), quoted in Zhang Weibo 張衛波, *Minguo chuqi zun Kong sichao yanjiu* 民國初期尊孔思潮研究 (Beijing: Renmin jiaoyu chubanshe, 2006), 163.
83. Huang Ko-wu 黃克武, "The Debate of the Confucian State Religion during Early Republican China (1912–1917)" 民國初年孔教問題之爭論, *Bulletin of Historical Research, National Taiwan Normal University* 國立臺灣師範大學歷史學報 12 (1984): 209–210.
84. Lao Naixuan 勞乃宣, *Tongxiang Lao xiansheng (Naixuan) yigao* 桐鄉勞先生（乃宣）遺稿, in *Jindai Zhongguo shiliao congkan* 近代中國史料叢刊 (Tongxiang Lushi 桐鄉盧氏, 1927; repr., Taipei: Wenhai chubanshe, 1969), series 36, no. 357, *juan* 1, "Lun Kongjiao" 論孔教, 46a–48a.
85. Zhang Dongsun 張東蓀, "Yu zhi Kongjiao guan" 余之孔教觀, in *Minguo jingshi wenbian* 民國經世文編, in *Jindai Zhongguo shiliao congkan* (Shanghai: Jingshi wenshe, 1914; repr., Taipei: Wenhai chubanshe, 1970), series 50, no. 492–498, *juan* 12, "Zongjiao" 宗教, 9a.
86. Hu Shi 胡適, "Wu Yu wenlu xu" 吳虞文錄序 (June 16, 1921), in *Hu Shi wencun* 胡適文存 (Taipei: Far East, 1953), vol. 1, *juan* 4, 795.
87. Chen Duxiu 陳獨秀, "Kongzi zhi dao yu xiandai shenghuo" 孔子之道與現代生活, "Zai lun Kongjiao wenti" 再論孔教問題, "Fupi yu zun Kong" 復辟與尊孔, and "Da Wu Youling" 答吳又陵, in *Duxiu wencun* 獨秀文存 (Shanghai Yadong Library 上海亞東圖書館, 1922; repr., Hefei: Anhui Renmin chubanshe, 1987), 1:80–81, 91–93, 111–116; 3:646. See also Tse-tsung Chow, "The Anti-Confucian Movement in Early Republican China," in *The Confucian Persuasion*, ed. Arthur F. Wright (Stanford, Calif.: Stanford University Press, 1960), 288–312. On the 1913 provisional constitution and Liang's concern for people to have freedom to believe or not believe, see Liang Qichao, "Jinbudang ni Zhonghuaminguo xianfa caoan" 進步黨擬中華民國憲法草案, in *Yinbingshi wenji*, vol. 6, *juan* 30, 62. On his opposition in 1915 to the Confucius

cult, see Liang Qichao, "Kongzi jiaoyi shiji biyi yu jinri guomin zhe he zai yu changming zhi qi dao he you" 孔子教義實際裨益於今日國民者何在欲昌明之其道何由, in *Yinbingshi wenji*, vol. 6, *juan* 33, 60–67.

88. Wu Yu 吳虞, "Jiazu zhidu wei zhuanzhi zhuyi zhi genju lun" 家族制度為專制主義之根據論, and "Chiren yu lijiao" 吃人與禮教, in *Wu Yu wenlu* 吳虞文錄, in *Minguo congshu* (Yadong tushuguan 亞東圖書館, 1927; repr., Shanghai: Shanghai shudian, 1990), vol. 2, no. 96, 1:1–13, 63–72.

89. Cai Yuanpei 蔡元培, "Zai xinjiaoziyouhui zhi yanshuo" 在信教自由會之演說 (1917), in *Cai Yuanpei wenji* 蔡元培文集, ed. Gao Pingshu 高平叔 (Taipei: Jinxiu chuban shiye gufen youxian gongsi, 1995), *juan* 5, "Zhexue" 哲學, 298.

90. Cai Yuanpei 蔡元培, "Zai xinjiaoziyouhui zhi yanshuo," 299.

91. See Cai Yuanpei, *Zhongguo lunli xueshi* 中國倫理學史, in *Cai Yuanpei wenji*, *juan* 5, "Zhexue," 168, 192–193.

92. Feng Youlan, *Zhongguo zhexue jianshi*, in *Sansongtang quanji*, 6:288.

93. Chen Duxiu, "Zai lun Kongjiao wenti," in *Duxiu wencun*, 1:91.

94. Cai Yuanpei, "Yi meiyu dai zongjiao shuo" 以美育代宗教說, in *Cai Yuanpei wenji*, *juan* 2, "Jiaoyu shang" 教育上, 378.

95. Chen Duxiu, "Zai lun Kongjiao wenti," in *Duxiu wencun*, 1:94.

96. Chen Duxiu, "Da Yu Songhua" 答俞頌華, in *Duxiu wencun*, 3:674

97. Hu Shi, "Mingjiao" 名教, in *Hu Shi wencun*, vol. 3, *juan* 1, 40.

98. Liang Shuming, *Dongxi wenhua ji qi zhexue*, 142. Xiong Shili 熊十力 also opposed regarding Confucianism as a religion. See Guo Qiyong 郭齊勇, "Dangdai xinrujia dui Ruxue zongjiaoxing wenti de fansi" 當代新儒家對儒學宗教性問題的反思, *Zhongguo zhexueshi* 中國哲學史 (January 1999): 41.

99. Liang Shuming, *Liang Shuming quanji* 梁漱溟全集, ed. Zhongguo wenhua shuyuan xueshu weiyuanhui 中國文化書院學術委員會 (Jinan: Shandong Renmin chubanshe, 1992), *juan* 5, "Zhongguo minzu zijiu yundong zhi zuihou juewu" 中國民族自救運動之最後覺悟 (1930), 64, 71.

100. Bertrand Russell, *The Problem of China* (London: George Allen and Unwin, 1966), 34; see also 43–44, and Russell, *Why I Am Not a Christian* (London: Routledge, 2004), preface and chap. 1.

101. Liang Shuming, *Zhongguo wenhua yaoyi* 中國文化要義 (Taipei: Cheng Chung Bookstore, 1969), 106–110. See also Liang Shuming, *Liang Shuming quanji*, *juan* 5, "Zhongguo minzu zijiu yundong zhi zuihou jiaowu," 69.

102. Xiong Shili 熊十力, *Dujing shiyao* 讀經示要, in *Minguo congshu* (Nanfang yinshuguan, 1945; repr., Shanghai: Shanghai shudian, 1992), series 5, vol. 1, 135.

103. Liang Shuming, "Zhongguo minzu zijiu yundong zhi zuihou jiaowu," in *Liang Shuming quanji*, *juan* 5, 71; Feng Youlan, "Rujia duiyu hunsangjili zhi lilun" 儒家對於婚喪祭禮之理論 (1928), in *Sansongtang xueshu wenji*, 132–145.

104. He Lin 賀麟, *Dangdai Zhongguo zhexue* 當代中國哲學 (1945; repr., Chiayi: Xibu chubanshe, 1971), "Fulu: Kangzhan qinian lai zhi zhexue" 附錄：抗戰七年來之哲學, 146. See also Chow Tse-tsung, *The May Fourth Movement: Intellectual Revolution in Modern China* (Stanford, Calif.: Stanford University Press, 1967), 320–327.
105. This view is anticipated by Reginald F. Johnston (1874–1938), the mentor of the last emperor of the Qing dynasty. See Johnston, *Confucianism and Modern China* (New York: D. Appleton-Century Company, 1935), 97–99.
106. Li Dazhao, "Fei zongjiao zhe xuanyan" 非宗教者宣言 (April 4, 1922), and "Zongjiao fangai jinbu" 宗教妨礙進步 (April 9, 1922), in *Li Dazhao quanji*, 4:74.
107. Cai Yuanpei, "Yi meiyu dai zongjiao shuo," in *Cai Yuanpei wenji, juan* 2, "Jiaoyu shang," 378.
108. Cai Yuanpei, "Fei zongjiao yundong," in *Cai Yuanpei wenji, juan* 5, "Zhexue," 36.
109. Li Dazhao, "Zhenli (er)" 真理 (二), *Li Dazhao quanji*, 2:452.
110. See Liang Qichao, "Ping fei zongjiao tongmeng" 評非宗教同盟 (April 16, 1922), in *Yinbingshi wenji*, vol. 7, *juan* 38, 17–25.
111. Wing-tsit Chan, *Religious Trends in Modern China* (New York: Columbia University Press, 1953), 13. For a more recent study, see Han Hua 韓華, *Minchu Kongjiaohui yu guojiao yundong yanjiu* 民初孔教會與國教運動研究 (Beijing: Beijing tushuguan chubanshe, 2007).
112. Compare Lin Guoping 林國平, *Lin Zhao'en yu sanyijiao* 林兆恩與三一教 (Fuzhou: Fujian Renmin chubanshe, 1992), and Wang Fan-sen, "The T'ai-ku School: Sectarian Confucianism in Nineteenth-Century China" 道咸年間民間性儒家學派—太谷學派研究的回顧, *New History* 5, no. 4 (December 1994): 141–162, along with Wang Fan-sen, "The Religious Transformation of Confucianism in Late Ming and Early Qing Thought" 明末清初儒學的宗教化—以許三禮的告天之學為例, *New History* 9, no. 2 (June 1998): 89–123.
113. Chen Huanzhang, *Kongjiao lun*, 2–3, 93; Chen Duxiu, *Duxiu wencun*, 69, 645; Cai Yuanpei, "Zai xinjiaoziyouhui zhi yanshuo," in *Cai Yuanpei wenji*, 299. Cai also claimed that "state religion" (*guojiao* 國教) was not a noun.
114. Kang Youwei, "Kongjiaohui xu er" 孔教會序二, in *Kang Youwei zhenglun ji*, 2:735–736; Liang Qichao, "Baojiao fei suoyi zun Kong lun," in *Yinbingshi wenji*, vol. 2, *juan* 9, 53; Chen Duxiu, "Bo Kang Youwei zhi zongtong zongli shu" 駁康有為致總統總理書, in *Duxiu wencun*, 69–70.
115. Gu Jiegang, "Chunqiu shi de Kongzi he Handai de Kongzi," in *Gushi bian*, 2:139.
116. Fu Sinian 傅斯年, "Ping 'Chunqiu shi de Kongzi he Handai de Kongzi'" 評春秋時的孔子和漢代的孔子, in *Gushi bian*, 2:140; Lu Xun, "Zai xiandai Zhongguo de Kongfuzi," *Qiejieting zawen erji*, in *Lu Xun quanji*, 8:105.

117. Wing-tsit Chan, *Religious Trends in Modern China*, 16.
118. C. K. Yang, *Religion in Chinese Society: A Study of Contemporary Social Functions of Religion and Some of Their Historical Factors* (Berkeley: University of California Press, 1961), 26.
119. Liang Shuming, *Dongxi wenhua ji qi zhexue*, 142.
120. Liang Shuming, "Ru Fo yitong lun zhisan" 儒佛異同論之三 (1966), in *Dongfang xueshu gaiguan* 東方學術概觀 (Bashu shushe, 1986; repr., Hong Kong: Chung Hwa, 1988), 31.
121. Zhong Zhaopeng 鍾肇鵬, "Yi Ruxue dai zongjiao" 以儒學代宗教, in *Feng Youlan xueji* 馮友蘭學記, ed. Wang Zhongjiang 王中江 and Gao Xiuchang 高秀昌 (Beijing: Joint Publishing, 1995), 82–90.
122. Western religions encompass a transcendent God and involve an elaborate church organization, aspects that are not present in the Confucian religion. In the past, many people confused the specifics of Western religions with the definition of religions; however, since the last quarter of the twentieth century, Western scholars have increasingly utilized far broader and culturally neutral conceptions of religion.
123. Mou Zhongjian 牟鍾鑒, "Guanyu Zhongguo zongjiaoshi de ruogan sikao" 關於中國宗教史的若干思考, in *Zhongguo zongjiao yu wenhua* 中國宗教與文化 (Taipei: Tangshan chubanshe, 1995), 139.
124. See, for example, Tu Weiming and Mary Evelyn, eds., *Confucian Spirituality* (New York: Crossroad, 2003).
125. Mou Zongsan 牟宗三, Xu Fuguan 徐復觀, Zhang Junmai 張君勱, and Tang Junyi 唐君毅, "Wei Zhongguo wenhua jinggao shijie renshi xuanyan" 為中國文化敬告世界人士宣言, *Huanghuagang zazhi* 黃花崗雜誌 9 (May 2004): 85; 10 (August 2004): 106–116, especially 107–112; and 11 (November 2004): 72–83. First published simultaneously in *Minzhu pinglun* 民主評論 (January 1, 1958) and *Zaisheng* 再生 (January 1, 1958).
126. Mou Zongsan, "Zuowei zongjiao de rujiao" 作為宗教的儒教 (1960), *Zhongguo zhexue de tezhi* 中國哲學的特質, in *Mou Zongsan xiansheng quanji* 牟宗三先生全集 (Taipei: Cultural Foundation of the United Daily News Group, 2003), 28:107.
127. C. K. Yang, *Religion in Chinese Society*, chaps. 10 and 12.
128. For example, Kang Youwei, "Zhonghua jiu guo lun"; and Chen Huanzhang, *Kongjiao lun*, 1–4.
129. See Mou Zongsan, "Renwenzhuyi de jiben jingshen" 人文主義的基本精神 (1953), and "Kongzi yu 'renwenjiao'" 孔子與「人文教」 (1957), in *Mou Zongsan xiansheng quanji*, 9:195–203; and 24:143–146.
130. Tu Weiming 杜維明, *Lun ruxue de zongjiaoxing: dui Zhongyong de xiandai quanshi* 論儒學的宗教性：對《中庸》的現代詮釋, trans. Duan Dezhi 段德智 (Wuchang: Wuhan University Press, 1999), 136.

131. Yu Yingshi, "Qian Mu yu xinrujia" 錢穆與新儒家, in *You ji fengchui shuishang lin: Qian Mu yu jindai Zhongguo xueshu* 猶記風吹水上鱗：錢穆與近代中國學術 (Taipei: San Min, 1991), 70–89.
132. One example is Tu Weiming, *Lun ruxue de zongjiaoxing*. The original book is Tu Weiming, *Centrality and Commonality: An Essay on Confucian Religiousness* (1976; rev. ed., Albany: State University of New York Press, 1989).
133. In the terms employed by the discipline of religious studies, such reductionism transforms belief (*xinyang* 信仰) into knowledge (*zhishi* 智識).
134. Liang Shuming, *Dongxi wenhua ji qi zhexue*, 90, 140–141.
135. Zhu Xi 朱熹, *Lunyu jizhu* 論語集注, in *Sishu zhangju jizhu* 四書章句集注 (Beijing: Zhonghua, 1983), *juan* 6, 131.
136. Talal Asad, *Genealogies of Religion: Discipline and Reasons of Power in Christianity and Islam* (Baltimore, Md.: Johns Hopkins University Press, 1993), chaps. 1 and 2.

7. The Lonely Confucius Temples Across the Taiwan Straits

A Chinese-language version of this chapter was first published as "Deconstructing and Reconstructing the Confucian Temple: The Difficulties in the Transformation of Traditional Culture in Modern China," in *Contemporary Monthly* 當代 86 (June 1993): 120–133.

1. Joseph R. Levenson, *Confucian China and its Modern Fate* (Berkeley: University of California Press, 1965).
2. Yan Yuan 顏淵 asked about perfect virtue. The master replied, "To subdue one's self and return to propriety is perfect virtue. If a man can for one day subdue himself and return to propriety, all under heaven will ascribe perfect virtue to him. Is the practice of perfect virtue from a man himself, or is it from others?" Zhu Xi 朱熹, *Lunyu jizhu* 論語集注, in *Sishu zhangju jizhu* 四書章句集注 (Beijing: Zhonghua, 1983), *juan* 6, 131. Translation adapted from James Legge, trans., *The Chinese Classics* (Oxford: Clarendon, 1893; repr. Taipei: SMC, 1991), 1:250.
3. On the catastrophe of the Cultural Revolution for the Confucius temples, see Yazi 亞子 and Liangzi 良子, *Kongfu da jienan* 孔府大劫難 (Hong Kong: Tiandi tushu gongsi, 1992).
4. Chak Chi-shing 翟志成, "Qishi niandai dalu pi Kong yundong zai pingjia" 七十年代大陸批孔運動再評價, in *Dangdai xinruxue shilun* 當代新儒學史論 (Taipei: Asian Culture Press, 1993), 413–488; Kam Louie, *Critiques of Confucius in Contemporary China* (Hong Kong: Chinese University Press, 1980).

5. *Renmin ribao* 人民日報 [*People's Daily*], editorial, February 2, 1974, in Zhonggong yanjiu zazhishe bianweihui 中共研究雜誌社編委會, ed., "Ba pi Lin pi Kong de douzheng jinxing daodi" 把批林批孔的鬥爭進行到底, *Zhonggong "pi Kong" ziliao xuanji* 中共「批孔」資料選輯 (Taipei: Zhonggong yanjiu zazhishe, 1974), 639.
6. Hu Shi 胡適, "Wu Yu wenlu xu" 吳虞文錄序 (June 16, 1921), in *Hu Shi wencun* 胡適文存 (Taipei: Far East, 1953), vol. 1, *juan* 4, 797.
7. Chen Duxiu 陳獨秀, "Zailun Kongjiao wenti" 再論孔教問題 (January 1, 1917), in *Duxiu wencun* 獨秀文存 (Shanghai Yadong Library 上海亞東圖書館, 1922; repr., Hefei: Anhui Renmin chubanshe, 1987), 1:94.
8. Tse-tsung Chow, "The Anti-Confucian Movement in Early Republican China," in *The Confucian Persuasion*, ed. Arthur F. Wright (Stanford, Calif.: Stanford University Press, 1960), 288–312.
9. Zhu Xi, *Mengzi jizhu* 孟子集注, in *Sishu zhangju jizhu*, *juan* 11, 336, utilized and changed to pinyin in D. C. Lau, trans., *Mencius* (London: Penguin, 1970), 169.
10. Quoted in Pang Zhonglu 龐鍾璐, *Wenmiao sidian kao* 文廟祀典考 (1877; repr., Taipei: Zhongguo liyue xuehui, 1977), *juan* 1, 12b.
11. Kong Zhencong 孔貞叢, ed., *Queli zhi* 闕里志, *juan* 10, 40b. Published in the Wanli reign of the Ming dynasty (1573–1620).
12. Tuo Tuo 脫脫, *Songshi* 宋史 (Taipei: Dingwen shuju, 1978), *juan* 351, 11101.
13. Yuan Jue 袁桷, *Qingrong jushi ji* 清容居士集, in *Sibu congkan chubian, suoben* 四部叢刊初編・縮本 (Taipei: Commercial Press, 1965), vols. 295–297, *juan* 35, 516. Yuan Shizu 元世祖 (Kublai Kahn) issued this edict in 1261, and similar orders were later repeatedly made. See Anonymous 佚名, *Miaoxue dianli* 廟學典禮, ed. Wang Ting 王頲 (Hangzhou: Zhejiang guji chubanshe, 1992), *juan* 1, 12; *juan* 2, 41–42.
14. Zhu Guozhen 朱國禎, *Yong chuang xiaopin* 湧幢小品, in *Biji xiaoshuo daguan* 筆記小說大觀 (Taipei: Xinxing shuju, 1984), vol. 22.7, *juan* 19, 3a.
15. Zhang Dai 張岱, "Kongmiao kuai" 孔廟檜, in *Tao'an mengyi* 陶菴夢憶, in *Meihua wenxue mingzhu congkan* 美化文學名著叢刊, ed. Zhu Jianmang 朱劍芒 (Shanghai: Shijie shuju, 1947), 9; Jiang Weiqiao 蔣維喬, *Qufu jiyou* 曲阜紀遊, in *Xin youji huikan xubian* 新遊記彙刊續編, ed. Yao Zhuxuan 姚祝萱 (Shanghai: Chung Hwa, 1925), vol. 1, *juan* 7, 20.
16. Lu Xun 魯迅, "Zai xiandai Zhongguo de Kongfuzi" 在現代中國的孔夫子 (April 29, 1935), in *Qiejieting zawen erji* 且介亭雜文二集, in *Lu Xun quanji* 魯迅全集 (Taipei: Tangshan chubanshe, 1989), 8:102.
17. Liang Qichao 梁啟超, "Bianfa tongyi" 變法通議, in *Yinbingshi wenji* 飲冰室文集 (Taipei: Chung Hwa, 1970), vol. 1, *juan* 1, 49.
18. Wang Shouren (Wang Yangming) 王守仁, "Yong liangzhi sishou shi zhusheng" 詠良知四首示諸生, in *Wang Yangming quanji* 王陽明全集, ed. Wu Guang 吳光 (Shanghai: Shanghai guji chubanshe, 1992), vol. 1, *juan* 20, 790.

19. See Huang Chin-shing, "Knowledge and Belief: Confucian Canonization and the Confucian Conception of Orthodoxy" 學術與信仰：論孔廟從祀制與儒家道統意識, in *Entering the Master's Sanctuary: Power, Belief and Legitimacy in Traditional China* 優入聖域：權力、信仰與正當性 (Taipei: Asian Culture Press, 1994), 217–311; or (Beijing: Zhonghua, 2010), 185–260. First published in *New History* 新史學 5, no. 2 (June 1994): 1–82.
20. Zhu Xi, *Lunyu jizhu*, juan 1, 57; Legge, *Chinese Classics*, 1:150.

Conclusion

A version of this chapter was first published in Japanese as "Reflections on My Study of Confucianism as a Religion," in the *Journal of East Asian Cultural Interaction Studies* 東アジア文化交渉研究：東アジア文化交渉学の新しい展望, supp. vol. 8 (February 2012): 27–40; and in Chinese in Huang Chin-shing, *From Virtue to Morality: The Transformation of Moral Consciousness during the Late Qing and Early Republic Era* 從理學到倫理學：清末民初道德意識的轉化 (Taipei: Asian Culture Press, 2013), 234–264.

1. Gu Jiegang 顧頡剛, "Zi xu" 自序, in *Gushi bian* 古史辨, ed. Gu Jiegang, in *Minguo congshu* 民國叢書 (Pushe 樸社, 1926; repr., Shanghai: Shanghai shudian, 1992), series 4, no. 65, 1:31.
2. Pang Zhonglu 龐鍾璐, *Wenmiao sidian kao* 文廟祀典考 (1877; repr., Taipei: Zhongguo liyue xuehui, 1977).
3. Bryan S. Turner, *Religion and Social Theory* (London: Sage, 1991), 15–16.
4. Émile Durkheim, *The Elementary Forms of Religious Life*, trans. Karen E. Fields (New York: Free Press, 1995), chap. 1.
5. William James, *The Varieties of Religious Experience* (New York: Penguin, 1982), 26. See also 27–29 for James's declaration that all definitional approaches to religious studies were in vain and so the focus of his research was on personal religion, not institutional religion. More recent research still struggles with efforts to create definitions of religion. For instance, even though Charles Taylor (b. 1931) acknowledges the difficulty of definitions, he proposes a distinction between transcendent and immanent religions. See Taylor, *A Secular Age* (Cambridge, Mass.: Belknap Press of Harvard University Press, 2007), 15.
6. Max Weber, *The Sociology of Religion*, trans. Ephraim Fischoff (Boston: Beacon, 1964), 1.
7. Max Weber, *The Methodology of the Social Sciences*, trans. and ed. Edward A. Shils and Henry A. Finch (Taipei: Rainbow-Bridge, 1971), 115.
8. Weber, *Methodology*, 116.

9. Talal Asad, *Genealogies of Religion: Discipline and Reasons of Power in Christianity and Islam* (Baltimore, Md.: Johns Hopkins University Press, 1993), 29.
10. Ludwig Wittgenstein, *Philosophical Investigations*, trans. G. E. M. Anscombe (New York: Macmillan, 1968), 32.
11. Aydan Turanli, "Nietzsche and the Later Wittgenstein: An Offense to the Quest for Another World," *Journal of Nietzsche Studies* 26 (Autumn 2003): 55–63.
12. Friedrich Nietzsche, *On the Genealogy of Morals*, trans. Walter Kaufmann and R. J. Hollingdale (New York: Vintage, 1967), 80.
13. For example, see Friedrich Engels's criticism of Ludwig Feuerbach's conceptions. Engels, *Ludwig Feuerbach and the End of Classical German Philosophy* (London: ElecBook, 1886), 32–33.
14. Chen Huanzhang 陳煥章, *Kongjiao lun* 孔教論, in *Minguo congshu* (Kongjiaohui 孔教會, 1913; repr., Shanghai: Shanghai shudian, 1992), series 4, no. 2, 2–3, 93; Chen Duxiu 陳獨秀, "Bo Kang Youwei zhi zongtong zongli shu" 駁康有為致總統總理書 (October 1, 1916), in *Duxiu wencun* 獨秀文存 (Shanghai Yadong tushuguan 上海亞東圖書館, 1922; repr., Hefei: Anhui Renmin chubanshe, 1987), 1:69; Cai Yuanpei 蔡元培, "Zai xinjiaoziyouhui zhi yanshuo" 在信教自由會之演說 (January 1917), in *Cai Yuanpei wenji* 蔡元培文集, ed. Gao Pingshu 高平叔 (Taipei: Jinxiu chuban shiye gufen youxian gongsi, 1995), *juan* 5, "Zhexue" 哲學, 299.
15. Kang Youwei 康有為, "Kongjiaohui xu er" 孔教會序二 (October 7, 1912), in *Kang Nanhai zhengshi wenxuan (1898–1927)* 康南海政史文選, ed. Shen Maojun 沈茂駿 (Guangzhou: Guangdong Higher Education Press, 1993), 115–116; Liang Qichao 梁啟超, "Baojiao fei suoyi zun Kong lun" 保教非所以尊孔論 (1902), in *Yinbingshi wenji* 飲冰室文集 (Taipei: Chung Hwa, 1970), vol. 2, *juan* 9, 53; Chen Duxiu, "Bo Kang Youwei zhi zongtong zongli shu," 69–70.
16. Liang Qichao, "Baojiao fei suoyi zun Kong lun," 52.
17. *Analects* 11:12 and 7:21, adapted from James Legge, trans., *The Chinese Classics* (Oxford: Clarendon, 1893; repr., Taipei: SMC Publishing Inc., 1991), 1:240–241, 201.
18. Liang Qichao, "Baojiao fei suoyi zun Kong lun," 52.
19. Kang Youwei, "Qing zun Kongsheng wei guojiao li jiaobu jiaohui yi Kongzi jinian er fei yinsi zhe" 請尊孔聖為國教立教部教會以孔子紀年而廢淫祀折 (June 19, 1898), in *Kang Youwei zhenglun ji* 康有為政論集, ed. Tang Zhijun 湯志鈞 (Beijing: Zhonghua, 1981), 1:282.
20. Liang Qichao, "Lun Fojiao yu qunzhi de guanxi" 論佛教與群治的關係 (1902), in *Yinbingshi wenji*, vol. 2, *juan* 10, 45.
21. For an overview, see Jaroslav Pelikan, "Christianity," in *The Encyclopedia of Religion*, ed. Mircea Eliade (New York: Simon & Schuster Macmillan, 1995), 3:348–62.

22. See Huang Chin-shing, "Decoding the Symbols of Confucian Temples: Remarks on the Religiosity of Confucianism" 解開孔廟祭典的符碼——兼論其宗教性, in *Wenhua yu lishi de zhuisuo: Yu Yingshi jiaoshou bazhi shouqing lunwen ji* 文化與歷史的追索：余英時教授八秩壽慶論文集, ed. Hoyt Tillman (Taipei: Linking, 2009), 535–558 [in Chinese]; Huang Chin-shing, "Dentou chūgoku ni okeru kōshibyō no saiten to sono shūkyōsei" 伝統中国における孔子廟の祭典とその宗教性 (trans. Lin Yaqing 林雅清), in *Higashi Ajia no girei to shūkyo* 東アジアの儀礼と宗教, ed. Azuma Juji and Nikaido Yoshihiro (Tokyo: Yushodo, 2008), 139–165 [in Japanese].

23. How many among the masses would first read scriptures and thereupon be convinced to go visit a temple? My guess is that it is quite rare. If one were to ask people going into a Buddhist temple, one would probably find that this assumption is not without substantial evidence.

24. "Zhang Daoling qi shi Zhao Sheng" 張道陵七試趙昇, in *Gujin xiaoshuo* 古今小說, ed. Feng Menglong, in *Guben xiaoshuo congkan* 古本小說叢刊 (Beijing: Zhonghua, 1990), vol. 31, no. 1–4, *juan* 13, 1a.

25. See Huang Chin-shing, "Knowledge and Belief: Confucian Canonization and the Confucian Conception of Orthodoxy" 學術與信仰：論孔廟從祀制與儒家道統意識, in *Entering the Master's Sanctuary: Power, Belief and Legitimacy in Traditional China* 優入聖域：權力、信仰與正當性 (Taipei: Asian Culture Press), 217–311. First published in *New History* 新史學 5, no. 2 (June 1994): 1–82.

26. Chen Huanzhang, *Kongjiao lun*, 27.

27. Regarding the evolution of the Confucius temples in relation to schools, see Huang Chin-shing, "Power and Belief: The Shaping of a National Cult, Worship of the Confucian Temple in Imperial China" 權力與信仰：孔廟祭祀制度的形成, *Continent Magazine* 大陸雜誌 86, no. 5 (May 1993): 8–34. Reginald Johnston, an expert on Chinese matters in the early republic, was among those who did not think of Confucianism as a religion; however, when he witnessed the rituals of sacrificial offerings, he found it difficult to reject the idea that Confucianism was a pagan religion in opposition to Christianity. See Johnston, *Confucianism and Modern China* (New York: D. Appleton-Century Company, 1935), 77.

28. As cited in Chen Yuan 陳垣, "Kaifeng Yisileyejiao kao" 開封一賜樂業教考, in *Chen Yuan shixue lunzhu xuan* 陳垣史學論著選, ed. Wu Ze 吳澤 (Shanghai: Shanghai Renmin chubanshe, 1981), 67–68. See also Xu Ke 徐珂, "Qing hui-huijiao" 青回回教, in *Qing bai leichao* 清稗類鈔 (Qing Petty Matters Anthology) (Taipei: Commercial Press, 1966), *juan* 15, 40. Three Pure Ones (三清) refers to Yuanshi *tianzun* 元始天尊, Lingbao *tianzun* 靈寶天尊, and Daode *tianzun* 道德天尊.

29. Yang Yongchang 楊永昌, "Zhongguo Qingzhensi mingcheng de youlai ji qi yange" 中國清真寺名稱的由來及其沿革, in *Mantan Qingzhensi* 漫談清真寺

(Yinchuan: Ningxia Renmin chubanshe, 1981), 1; Chen Yuan, "Kaifeng Yisileyejiao kao," 77.

30. Xiang Mai 祥邁, *Bianwei lu* 辯偽錄, in *Taisho Shinshu Daizokyo* 大正新修大藏經 (1924–1934; repr., Taipei: Xinwenfeng chuban gongsi, 1983), vol. 52, no. 3, 770c.

31. Cai Meibiao 蔡美彪 et al., eds., *Zhongguo lishi dacidian: Liao Xia Jin Yuan shi juan* 中國歷史大辭典 · 遼夏金元史卷 (Shanghai: Shanghai Lexicographical, 1986), 314, "Diexie" 迭屑; 334, "Mishihe" 彌失訶; 478, "dashiman" 答失蠻. "Dashiman" 達失蠻 is also written as "tashiman" 答失蠻.

32. Tang Peng 湯鵬, "Yuanjiao shang" 原教上, in *Fuqiuzi* 浮邱子 (Changsha: Yuelu shushe, 1987), *juan* 11, 337.

33. José Casanova, "Public Religions Revisited," in *Religion: Beyond a Concept*, ed. Hent de Vries (New York: Fordham University Press, 2008), 101–119. For the relatively recent rise in the West of communal religion focused on the space between the nation and the individual, see José Casanova, *Public Religions in the Modern World* (Chicago: University of Chicago Press, 1994).

34. Qing Shengzu 清聖祖, "Kangxi ershisan nian yuti wanshi shi biao keshi" 康熙二十三年御題萬世師表刻石 (1684), in *Shitou shang de rujia wenxian: Qufu beiwen lu* 石頭上的儒家文獻：曲阜碑文錄, ed. Luo Chenglie 駱承烈 (Jinan: Qilu shushe, 2001), 2:800. That rich source is limited to Qufu, but there are preserved inscriptions for local Confucius temples elsewhere. For example, see Han Yu 韓愈, "Chuzhou Kongzi miao bei" 處州孔子廟碑, in *Han Changli wenji jiaozhu* 韓昌黎文集校注 (Taipei: Huazheng shuju, 1975), 283–284; Liu Zongyuan 柳宗元, "Daozhou Wenxuanwang miao bei" 道州文宣王廟碑, and "Liuzhou Wenxuanwang xin xiu miao bei" 柳州文宣王新修廟碑, in *Liu Zongyuan ji* 柳宗元集 (Taipei: Hanjing wenhua shiye youxian gongsi, 1982), 120–126.

35. Hong Gua 洪适, *Li shi* 隸釋 (Hongshi Huimuzhai 洪氏晦木齋; repr., Beijing: Zhonghua, 1985), *juan* 1, 15a–15b, 18a, 26b.

36. Emperor Wen of Wei 魏文帝, "Huangchu yuannian Lu Kongzi miao bei" 黃初元年魯孔子廟碑, in *Shitou shang de Rujia wenxian: Qufu beiwen lu*, 1:62–64. Chen Shou 陳壽 gives the date of the second year of this reign (221). See Chen Shou, *Sanguo zhi* (Taipei: Dingwen shuju, 1983), *juan* 2, 77–78.

37. Yuan Chengzong 元成宗, "Dade wunian zhongjian zhisheng Wenxuanwang miao bei" 大德五年重建至聖文宣王廟碑 (1301), in *Shitou shang de Rujia wenxian: Qufu beiwen lu*, 1:248.

38. Yuan Renzong 元仁宗, "Zhida sinian baohu Yanmiao jin yue bang bei" 至大四年保護顏廟禁約榜碑 (1311), in *Shitou shang de Rujia wenxian: Qufu beiwen lu*, 1:258.

39. Yuan Wenzong 元文宗, "Qian guan ji Queli miao bei" 遣官祭闕里廟碑 (1329), in *Queli zhi* 闕里志, ed. Kong Zhencong 孔貞叢, *juan* 10, 40b. Published in the Wanli reign of the Ming dynasty (1573–1620).
40. Ming Taizu 明太祖, "Hongwu yuannian Zhu Yuanzhang yu Kong Kejian Kong Xixue duihua bei" 洪武元年朱元璋與孔克堅孔希學對話碑 (1368), in *Shitou shang de Rujia wenxian: Qufu beiwen lu*, 1:349.
41. As cited in Pang Zhonglu, *Wenmiao sidian kao*, *juan* 1, 12b, "Yongzheng yu libu" 雍正諭禮部 (1727).
42. Ming Shenzong 明神宗, "Wanli sishiqi nian Lü Weiqi xiu Kongmiao shu jie" 萬曆四十七年呂維琪修孔廟疏碣 (1619), in *Shitou shang de Rujia wenxian: Qufu beiwen lu*, 2:681. Local officials had raised the concern that an unusual occurrence of natural disasters might be a sign that the Confucius temple lacked enough offerings of dried meat.
43. Ye Sheng 葉盛, *Shui dong riji* 水東日記 (Beijing: Zhonghua, 1980), *juan* 19, 191, "Taizong Wenhuangdi yuzhi chongxiu Kongmiao beiwen" 太宗文皇帝御製重修孔廟碑文 (stele erected in 1417). Compare with Ming Xiaozong 明孝宗, "Hongzhi shiliunian zhongli Yongle shiwunian yuzhi zhongxiu Kongzi miao bei" 弘治十六年重立永樂十五年御製重修孔子廟碑 (1503), in *Shitou shang de Rujia wenxian: Qufu beiwen lu*, 1:443.
44. Yuan Wuzong 元武宗, "Dade shiyinian jiafeng zhizhao bei" 大德十一年加封制詔碑 (1307), in *Shitou shang de Rujia wenxian: Qufu beiwen lu*, 1:250. See also Song Lian 宋濂, *Yuanshi* 元史 (Taipei: Dingwen shuju, 1980), *juan* 22, 484.
45. Kong Jifen 孔繼汾, *Queli wenxian kao* 闕里文獻考 (1762), *juan* 9, 6b.
46. Yuan Huizong 元惠宗, "Houzhiyuan wunian yusi shangli shidian bei" 後至元五年御賜尚醴釋奠碑 (1339), in *Shitou shang de Rujia wenxian: Qufu beiwen lu*, 1:290.
47. Ming Sizong 明思宗, "Shuo zao ye shengmiao" 朔蚤謁聖廟, in "Chongzhen shisannian Wang Jiaren ye sheng bayongshi jie" 崇禎十三年王洤仁謁聖八詠詩碣 (1640), poem 1, in *Shitou shang de Rujia wenxian: Qufu beiwen lu*, 2:705.
48. Zhu Xi 朱熹, *Zhuzi wenji* 朱子文集, ed., Chen Junmin 陳俊民 (Taipei: Defu wenjiao jijinhui, 2000), *juan* 86. For philosophical or ideological purposes in Zhu's prayers to Confucius, see Hoyt Cleveland Tillman, "Zhu Xi's Prayers to the Spirit of Confucius and Claim to the Transmission of the Way," *Philosophy East and West* 54, no. 4 (2004): 489–513.
49. Ming Xianzong 明憲宗, "Chenghua shiernian baochong xiansheng liyue ji bei" 成化十二年褒崇先聖禮樂記碑 (1476), in *Shitou shang de Rujia wenxian: Qufu beiwen lu*, 1:409. Another source in this collection mistakenly provides a date two years earlier.

50. As Song Xiaozong 宋孝宗 said, "Use Buddhism to cultivate the mind, Daoism to nurture life, and Confucianism to govern the world." See Zhi Pan 志磐, *Fozu tongji* 佛祖統紀, in *Taisho Shinshu Daizokyo*, vol. 49, *juan* 47, 430a.
51. See Anonymous, "Yue bao ji huisheng eyan yize shuai shu qi hou" 閱報紀毀聖訛言一則率書其後, *Shen bao* 申報 9022 (May 29, 1898), section 1.
52. Qin Huitian 秦蕙田, *Wuli tongkao* 五禮通考 (Weijingwo 味經窩; repr., Taoyuan: Shenghuan tushu gongsi, 1994), *juan* 117, 1b.
53. Yan Fu 嚴復, "Baojiao yuyi" 保教餘義 (June 7–8, 1898), in *Yan Fu wenji biannian (1)* 嚴復文集編年 (一), in *Yan Fu heji* 嚴復合集, ed. Lin Zaijue 林載爵 (Taipei: C. F. Koo Foundation, 1998), 1:157.
54. Kang Youwei, "Liang Yue Guangrenshantang shengxuehui yuanqi" 兩粵廣仁善堂聖學會緣起 (May 17, 1897), in *Kang Youwei quanji* 康有為全集, ed. Jiang Yihua 姜義華 and Wu Genliang 吳根樑 (Shanghai: Shanghai guji chubanshe, 1990), 2:621.
55. Feng Youlan 馮友蘭, "Sansongtang zixu" 三松堂自序, in *Sansongtang quanji* 三松堂全集 (Zhengzhou: Henan Renmin chubanshe, 1985), 1:44.
56. Chen Que 陳確, "Shengmiao yi" 聖廟議, in *Chen Que ji* 陳確集 (Taipei: Yanjing wenhua chuban gongsi, 1984), *juan* 7, 190.
57. Liang Fa 梁發, "Lun shiren mihuo yu ge shen Fo Pusa zhilei" 論世人迷惑於各神佛菩薩之類, in *Quanshi liangyan* 勸世良言 (Taipei: Taiwan xuesheng shuju, 1965), *juan* 1, 5a–5b. Original held at Harvard University.
58. Liang Qichao, "Bianfa tongyi" 變法通議, in *Yinbingshi wenji*, vol. 1, *juan* 1, 49.
59. Pang Zhonglu, "Yongzheng wu nian chun eryue yu Neige" 雍正五年春二月諭內閣 (1727), in *Wenmiao sidian kao, juan* 1, 11b–12a.
60. As cited in Chen Yuan, "Kongzi dan ganyan" 孔子誕感言, in *Chen Yuan quanji* 陳垣全集, ed. Chen Zhichao 陳智超 (Hefei: Anhui University Press, 2009), 1:49.
61. Compare with Tao Xisheng 陶希聖, "Zitong Wenchangshen zhi shehuishi de jieshuo" 梓潼文昌神之社會史的解說, *Shihuo yuekan* 食貨月刊 2, no. 8 (November 1972): 1–9.
62. Tan Sitong 譚嗣同, *Renxue* 仁學, in *Tan Sitong quanji* 譚嗣同全集, ed. Cai Shangsi 蔡尚思 (Beijing: Zhonghua, 1981), 2:289–374.
63. Liang Shuming 梁漱溟, *Dongxi wenhua ji qi zhexue* 東西文化及其哲學 (Hong Kong: Ziyou xueren she, 1960), 140–141.
64. Zhu Xi, *Lunyu jizhu* 論語集注, in *Sishu zhangju jizhu* 四書章句集注 (Beijing: Zhonghua, 1983), *juan* 6, 131; Legge, *Chinese Classics*, 1:250.
65. Peter van der Veer, "Spirituality in Modern Society," in *Religion: Beyond a Concept*, ed. Hent de Vries (New York: Fordham University Press, 2008), 789–797.

66. Herbert Fingarette, *Confucius: The Secular as Sacred* (New York: Harper & Row, 1972). On language analysis, see J. L. Austin, *How to Do Things with Words* (Cambridge, Mass.: Harvard University Press, 1962).
67. I also found inspiration in the work of John Rawls. One reason he could develop his theory of justice was that he discarded analytical philosophy and avoided being endlessly stuck in clarification of meaning. See John Rawls, *A Theory of Justice* (Cambridge, Mass.: Belknap Press of Harvard University Press, 1971), xi.

Bibliography

Aleni, Guilio 艾儒略. *Zhi fangwai ji jiaoshi* 職方外紀校釋. Ed. Xie Fang 謝方. Beijing: Zhonghua, 1996.

Anonymous 不著撰人. *DaJin jili* 大金集禮. In *Jingyin Wenyuange sikuquanshu* 景印文淵閣四庫全書, vol. 648. Taipei: Commercial Press, 1983–1986.

Anonymous 佚名. *Miaoxue dianli* 廟學典禮. Ed. Wang Ting 王頲. Hangzhou: Zhejiang guji chubanshe, 1992.

Anonymous. *Xinchou jiwen* 辛丑紀聞. In *Zhongguo yeshi jicheng* 中國野史集成. Chengdou: Bashu shushe, 2000.

Anonymous. "Yue bao ji huisheng eyan yize shuai shu qi hou" 閱報紀毀聖訛言一則率書其後. *Shen bao* 申報 9022 (May 29, 1898) 光緒二十四年四月初十日, section 1.

Asad, Talal. *Genealogies of Religion: Discipline and Reasons of Power in Christianity and Islam*. Baltimore, Md.: Johns Hopkins University Press, 1993.

Attwater, Donald, and Catherine Rachel John. *The Penguin Dictionary of Saints*. London: Penguin, 1995.

Augustine. *The City of God*. Trans. Marcus Dods. Chicago: Encyclopaedia Britannica, 1952.

———. *Confessions*. Trans. F. J. Sheed. Indianapolis, Ind.: Hackett, 1993.

Austin, J. L. *How to Do Things with Words*. Cambridge, Mass.: Harvard University Press, 1962.

Bai Juyi 白居易. *Bai Juyi ji jianjiao* 白居易集箋校. Commentary by Zhu Jincheng 朱金城. Shanghai: Shanghai guji chubanshe, 1988.

Ban Gu 班固. *Hanshu* 漢書. Taipei: Dingwen shuju, 1987.

Beijing shifan daxue lishixi zhongguo jindaishi zu 北京師範大學歷史系中國近代史組, ed. *Zhongguo jindai shi ziliao xuanbian* 中國近代史資料選編. Beijing: Zhonghua, 1977.

Beiping gugongbowuyuan wenxianguan 北平故宮博物院文獻館, ed. *Qingdai wenziyu dang* 清代文字獄檔. 1934. Reprint, Taipei: Huawen shuju, 1969.

Berman, Harold J., and John Witte Jr., "Church and State." In *The Encyclopedia of Religion*, ed. Mircea Eliade. New York: Simon & Schuster Macmillan, 1995.

Brown, Peter. *Augustine of Hippo: A Biography*. Berkeley: University of California Press, 1969.

———. *The Cult of the Saints: Its Rise and Function in Latin Christianity*. Chicago: University of Chicago Press, 1981.

———. "The Saint as Exemplar in Late Antiquity." In *Saints and Virtues*, ed. John Stratton Hawley, 3–14. Berkeley: University of California Press, 1987.

———. *Society and the Holy in Late Antiquity*. Berkeley: University of California Press, 1982.

Burckhardt, Jacob. *The Age of Constantine the Great*. Trans. Moses Hadas. Berkeley: University of California Press, 1949.

Butler, Alban. *Butler's Lives of the Saints*. Ed. Michael Walsh. San Francisco: Harper Collins, 1991.

Cai Meibiao 蔡美彪 et al., eds. *Zhongguo lishi dacidian: Liao Xia Jin Yuan shi juan* 中國歷史大辭典·遼夏金元史卷. Shanghai: Shanghai Lexicographical Publishing, 1986.

Cai Yuanpei 蔡元培. *Cai Yuanpei wenji* 蔡元培文集. Ed. Gao Pingshu 高平叔. Taipei: Jinxiu chuban shiye gufen youxian gongsi, 1995.

Calvin, John. *Jidujiao yaoyi* 基督教要義 [Institutes of the Christian Religion]. Ed. J. T. McNeill. Trans. Xu Qingyu 徐慶譽 and Xie Bingde 謝秉德. Hong Kong: Jidujiao fuqiao chubanshe, Jinling shenxueyuan tuoshi bu, 1995.

Campany, Robert Ford. *To Live as Long as Heaven and Earth: A Translation and Study of Ge Hong's Traditions of Divine Transcendents*. Berkeley: University of California Press, 2002.

Cang Xiuliang 倉修良 and Chen Yangguang 陳仰光. "Cong Dunhuang tujing canjuan kan Sui Tang Wudai tujing fazhan" 從敦煌圖經殘卷看隋唐五代圖經發展. *Wenshi* 55 (2001): 117–139.

Cao An 曹安. *Lanyan zhangyu* 讕言長語. In *Baoyantang miji* 寶顏堂祕笈. Ed. Chen Jiru 陳繼儒. Shanghai: Wenming shuju, 1922.

Casanova, José. *Public Religions in the Modern World*. Chicago: University of Chicago Press, 1994.

———. "Public Religions Revisited." In *Religion: Beyond a Concept*, ed. Hent de Vries, 101–119. New York: Fordham University Press, 2008.

Chak Chi-shing 翟志成. *Dangdai xinruxue shilun* 當代新儒學史論. Taipei: Asian Culture Press, 1993.

Chan, Wing-tsit. *Religious Trends in Modern China*. New York: Columbia University Press, 1953.

Chang So-an 張壽安. *Yi Li dai Li* 以禮代理. Taipei: Institute of Modern History, Academia Sinica, 1994.

Cheetham, Nicolas. *A History of the Popes*. New York: Dorset, 1982.

Chen Baochen 陳寶琛. *DaQing Dezong Jinghuangdi (Guangxu) shilu* 大清德宗景(光緒)皇帝實錄. Taipei: Xinwenfeng chuban gongsi, 1978.

Chen Dengyuan 陳登原. *Guoshi jiuwen* 國史舊聞. Taipei: Mingwen shuju, 1984.

Chen Duxiu 陳獨秀. *Chen Duxiu xuanji* 陳獨秀選集. Tianjin: Tianjin Renmin chubanshe, 1990.

———. *Duxiu wencun* 獨秀文存. Shanghai: Shanghai Yadong tushuguan 上海亞東圖書館, 1922. Reprint, Hefei: Anhui Renmin chubanshe, 1987.

Chen Hao 陳鎬. *Queli zhi* 闕里誌. Jinan: Shandong Friendship, 1989.

Chen Hsi-yuan 陳熙遠. "'Zongjiao/Religion': A Keyword in the Cultural History of Modern China" 「宗教」：一個中國近代文化史上的關鍵詞. *New History* 13, no. 4 (December 2002): 37–66.

Chen Huanzhang 陳煥章, ed. *Gaige Qufu lin miao banfa boyi* 改革曲阜林廟辦法駁議. In *Zun Kong congshu* 尊孔叢書. Kowloon: Yiqiang yinshuachang, 1963.

———. *Kongjiao lun* 孔教論. Kongjiaohui 孔教會, 1913. In *Minguo congshu* 民國叢書 4, no. 2. Shanghai: Shanghai shudian, 1992.

Chen Kuo-tung 陳國棟. "Lamenting in the Confucius Temple and Burning of the Confucian Garments: Two Social Gestures of the Licentiates in the Seventeenth Century" 哭廟與焚儒服—明末清初生員層的社會性動作. *New History* 3, no. 1 (March 1992): 69–94.

Chen Pan 陳槃. "A Revision of 'An Explanation of Jung Huang's Annotations in *The Canon of Filial Piety*'" 孝經中黃讖解題改寫本. *Bulletin of the Institute of History and Philology Academia Sinica* 59, no. 4 (December 1988): 891–897.

Chen Qiyou 陳奇猷. Taipei: Heluo tushu chubanshe, 1974.

Chen Que 陳確. *Chen Que ji* 陳確集. Taipei: Yanjing wenhua chuban gongsi, 1984.

Chen Shan 陳善. *Men shi Xinhua* 捫蝨新話. Published by Baoyantang miji 寶顏堂祕笈. In *Congshu jicheng chubian* 叢書集成初編. Shanghai: Commercial Press, 1939.

Chen Shike 陳士珂, ed. *Kongzi jiayu shuzheng* 孔子家語疏證. Taipei: Commercial Press, 1976.

Chen Shou 陳壽. *Sanguo zhi* 三國志. Taipei: Dingwen shuju, 1983.

Chen Yin-ke 陳寅恪. *Tangdai zhengzhi shi shulun gao, shang pian* 唐代政治史述論稿·上篇. In *Chen Yin-ke xiansheng wenji* 陳寅恪先生文集. Taipei: Liren shuju, 1981.

Chen Yuan 陳垣. *Chen Yuan quanji* 陳垣全集. Ed. Chen Zhichao 陳智超. Hefei: Anhui University Press, 2009.

———. *Chen Yuan shixue lunzhe xuan* 陳垣史學論著選. Ed. Wu Ze 吳澤. Shanghai: Shanghai Renmin chubanshe, 1981.

Chen Zhongyu 陳衷瑜, ed. *Linzi benxing shilu* 林子本行實錄. Jinjiang: Shangyang shuyuan, 1939.

Cheng Hao 程顥 and Cheng Yi 程頤. *Er Cheng ji* 二程集. Taipei: Liren shuju, 1982.

Cheng Minzheng 程敏政. *Huangdun wenji* 篁墩文集. In *Jingyin Wenyuange sikuquanshu* 景印文淵閣四庫全書, vol. 1252–1253. Taipei: Commercial Press, 1983–1986.

———. *Huangdun wenji shiyi* 篁墩文集拾遺. In *Jingyin Wenyuange sikuquanshu* 景印文淵閣四庫全書, vol. 1253. Taipei: Commercial Press, 1983–1986.

Cheng Shude 程樹德. *Lunyu jishi* 論語集釋. Beijing: Zhonghua, 1990.

Chow, Kai-wing. *The Rise of Confucian Ritualism in Late Imperial China*. Taipei: SMC, 1996.

Chow, Tse-tsung. "The Anti-Confucian Movement in Early Republican China." In *The Confucian Persuasion*, ed. Arthur F. Wright, 288–312. Stanford, Calif.: Stanford University Press, 1960.

———. *The May Fourth Movement: Intellectual Revolution in Modern China*. Stanford, Calif.: Stanford University Press, 1967.

Daoxuan 道宣. *Guang hong ming ji* 廣弘明集. In *Taisho Shinshu Daizokyo* 大正新修大藏經, vol. 52. 1924–1934. Reprint, Taipei: Xinwenfeng chuban gongsi, 1983.

———. *Ji gujin Fo Dao lunheng* 集古今佛道論衡. In *Taisho Shinshu Daizokyo* 大正新修大藏經, vol. 52. 1924–1934. Reprint, Taipei: Xinwenfeng chuban gongsi, 1983.

de Voragine, Jacobus. *The Golden Legend: Readings on the Saints*. Trans. William Granger Ryan. Princeton, N.J.: Princeton University Press, 1993.

Delehaye, Hippolyte. *The Legends of the Saints*. Trans. Donald Attwater. Dublin: Four Courts Press, 1998.

Delooz, Pierre. "Toward a Sociological Study of Canonized Sainthood." In *Saints and Their Cults: Studies in Religious Sociology, Folklore, and History*, ed. Stephen Wilson, 189–216. Cambridge, N.Y.: Cambridge University Press, 1983.

Deng Qiu 鄧球. *HuangMing yonghua leibian* 皇明詠化類編. Published in Ming dynasty, Longqing era (1567–1572).

Ding Wenjiang 丁文江. *Liang Rengong nianpu changbian chugao* 梁任公年譜長編初稿. Taipei: Shijie shuju, 1972.

Dong Gao 董誥, ed. *Qin ding quan Tang wen* 欽定全唐文. Taipei: Datong shuju, 1979.

Dong Zhongshu 董仲舒. *Chunqiu fanlu* 春秋繁露. Taipei: Shijie shuju, 1975.

Du You 杜佑. *Tongdian* 通典, ed. Wang Wenjin 王文錦. Beijing: Zhonghua, 1988.

Durkheim, Émile. *The Elementary Forms of Religious Life*. Trans. Karen E. Fields. New York: Free Press, 1995.

Eertai 鄂爾泰. *DaQing Shizong Xianhuangdi shilu* 大清世宗憲皇帝實錄. Taipei: Wen Hai, n.d.

Eire, Carlos M. N. *War against the Idols: The Reformation of Worship from Erasmus to Calvin*. Cambridge: Cambridge University Press, 1989.

Eisenman, Robert. *James, the Brother of Jesus: The Key to Unlocking the Secrets of Early Christianity and the Dead Sea Scrolls.* New York: Viking Penguin, 1997.

Eliade, Mircea, ed. *The Encyclopedia of Religion.* New York: Simon & Schuster Macmillan, 1995.

———. *The Sacred and the Profane: The Nature of Religion.* Trans. Willard R. Trask. New York: Harcourt Brace Jovanovich, 1959.

Elie, Paul. "The Patron Saint of Paradox." *New York Times Magazine* (November 8, 1998): 44.

Engels, Frederick. *Ludwig Feuerbach and the End of Classical German Philosophy.* London: ElecBook, 1886.

Erlande-Brandenburg, Alain. *Notre-Dame de Paris.* Trans. John Goodman. New York: Abrams, 1997.

———. *Saint-Denis' Basilica.* Trans. Angela Moyon. Rennes: Ouest-France, 1984.

Fan Ye 范曄. *Hou Hanshu* 後漢書. Taipei: Dingwen shuju, 1983.

Fang Bao 方苞. *Shanding Xunzi* 刪定荀子. In *Wuqiubeizhai Xunzi jicheng* 無求備齋荀子集成, ed. Yan Lingfeng 嚴靈峰, vol. 28. Taipei: Cheng Wen, 1977.

Fang Erjia 方爾加. *Xunzi xinlun* 荀子新論. Beijing: Zhongguo heping chubanshe, 1993.

Fang Xuanling 房玄齡. *Jinshu* 晉書. Taipei: Dingwen shuju, 1987.

Farmer, David Hugh. *The Oxford Dictionary of Saints.* Oxford: Oxford University Press, 1992.

Fei Mi 費密. *Hong dao shu* 弘道書. In *Feishi yishu* 費氏遺書. Yilantang 怡蘭堂, 1919.

Feng Menglong 馮夢龍, ed. *Gujin xiaoshuo* 古今小說. In *Guben xiaoshuo congkan* 古本小說叢刊. Beijing: Zhonghua, 1990.

Feng Qi 馮琦, ed. *Songshi jishi benmo* 宋史紀事本末. Beijing: Zhonghua, 1955.

Feng Youlan 馮友蘭. *Sansongtang quanji* 三松堂全集. Zhengzhou: Henan Renmin chubanshe, 1985.

———. *Sansongtang xueshu wenji* 三松堂學術文集. Beijing: Peking University Press, 1984.

Fingarette, Herbert. *Confucius: The Secular as Sacred.* New York: Harper & Row, 1972.

Finucane, Ronald C. *Miracles and Pilgrims: Popular Beliefs in Medieval England.* Totowa, N.J.: Rowman and Littlefield, 1977.

Freedberg, David. *The Power of Images: Studies in the History and Theory of Response.* Chicago: University of Chicago Press, 1989.

Fu Sinian 傅斯年. *Fu Sinian quanji* 傅斯年全集. Taipei: Linking, 1980.

Fu Weilin 傅維麟. *Mingshu* 明書. Taipei: Huazheng shuju, 1974.

Furen shenxue zhezuo bianyihui 輔仁神學著作編譯會. Ed. *Shenxue cidian* 神學辭典. Taipei: Kuangchi Program Service, 1996.

Ganguly, Meenakshi. "The Road to Sainthood." *Time* (May 17, 1999): 21.

Gao Ming 高明, ed. *Liang-Han Sanguo wenhui* 兩漢三國文彙. Taipei: Zhonghua congshu bianshen weiyuanhui, 1960.

Gao Mingshi 高明士. "Suidai de zhili zuoyue: Suidai liguo zhengce yanjiu zhier" 隋代的制禮作樂——隋代立國政策研究之二. In *Studies on the Sui and Tang Dynasties* 隋唐史論集, ed. Joseph Wong 黃約瑟 and Lau Kin-Ming 劉健明, 15–35. Centre of Asian Studies, University of Hong Kong, 1993.

——. *Zhongguo chuantong zhengzhi yu jiaoyu* 中國傳統政治與教育. Taipei: Wenjin chubanshe, 2003.

Gao Pingshu 高平叔. *Cai Yuanpei nianpu zhangbian* 蔡元培年譜長編. Beijing: People's Education Press, 1998.

Ge Hong 葛洪. *Shenxian zhuan* 神仙傳. In *Daocang jinghua lu* 道藏精華錄, ed. Shouyizi 守一子. Hangzhou: Zhejiang guji chubanshe, 1989.

Geary, Patrick J. *Living with the Dead in the Middle Ages*. Ithaca, N.Y.: Cornell University Press, 1994.

Gibbon, Edward. *The Decline and Fall of the Roman Empire*. Chicago: Encyclopaedia Britannica, 1952.

Giddens, Anthony. *The Constitution of Society: Outline of the Theory of Structuration*. Berkeley: University of California Press, 1986.

Gong Yanxing 宮衍興 and Wang Zhengyu 王政玉. *Kongmiao zhushen kao* 孔廟諸神考. Jinan: Shandong Friendship, 1994.

Gu Jiegang 顧頡剛, ed. *Gushi bian* 古史辨. Pushe 樸社, 1930. Reprint, Taipei: Minglun chubanshe, 1970.

Gu Yanwu 顧炎武. *Yuan chaoben Rizhi lu* 原抄本日知錄. Taipei: Minglun chubanshe, 1971.

Gui E 桂萼. *Gui Wenxiang gong zouyi* 桂文襄公奏議. 1762.

Gui Youguang 歸有光. *Zhenchuan xiansheng ji* 震川先生集. Taipei: Yuanliu chubanshe, 1983.

Guo Qiyong 郭齊勇. "Dangdai xinrujia dui ruxue zongjiaoxing wenti de fansi" 當代新儒家對儒學宗教性問題的反思. *Zhongguo zhexueshi* 1 (1999): 40–61.

Guo Tingxun 過庭訓. *Ben chao fensheng renwu kao* 本朝分省人物考. Taipei: Chengwen chubanshe, 1971.

Guo Zhikun 郭志坤. *Xunxue lungao* 荀學論稿. Shanghai: Joint Publishing, 1990.

Gurevich, Aron. *Medieval Popular Culture: Problems of Belief and Perception*. Trans. János M. Bak and Paul A. Hollingsworth. Cambridge: Cambridge University Press, 1993.

Hallam, Elizabeth. *Saints: Who They Are and How They Help You*. New York: Simon & Schuster, 1994.

Han Fei 韓非. *Han Fei Zi jishi* 韓非子集釋. Ed. Chen Qiyou 陳奇猷. Taipei: Heluo tushu chubanshe, 1974.

Han Hua 韓華. *Minchu Kongjiaohui yu guojiao yundong yanjiu* 民初孔教會與國教運動研究. Beijing: Beijing tushuguan chubanshe, 2007.

Han Yu 韓愈. *Han Changli wenji jiaozhu* 韓昌黎文集校注. Taipei: Huazheng shuju, 1975.
———. *Han Yu quanji jiaozhu* 韓愈全集校注. Ed. Qu Shouyuan 屈守元 and Chang Sichun 常思春. Chengdu: Sichuan daxue chubanshe, 1996.
He Lin 賀麟. *Dangdai Zhongguo zhexue* 當代中國哲學. 1945. Reprint, Chiayi: Xibu chubanshe, 1971.
Hong Gua 洪适. *Li shi* 隸釋. Hongshi Huimuzhai 洪氏晦木齋. Beijing: Zhonghua Book Company, 1985.
———. *Lixu* 隸續. Hongshi Huimuzhai 洪氏晦木齋. Beijing: Zhonghua Book Company, 1985.
Hong Liangji 洪亮吉. *Chunqiu Zuozhuan gu* 春秋左傳詁. Beijing: Zhonghua, 1987.
Hong Mai 洪邁. *Rongzhai suibi* 容齋隨筆. Shanghai: Shanghai guji chubanshe, 1978.
———, ed. *Yijian zhi* 夷堅志. Taipei: Mingwen shuju, 1982.
Hsiao Ch'i-ch'ing 蕭啟慶. *Yuanchao shi xinlun* 元朝史新論. Taipei: Asian Culture Press, 1999.
Hsing I-tien 邢義田. "Handai Kongzi jian Laozi huaxiang de goucheng ji qi zai shehui, sixiangshi shang de yiyi" 漢代孔子見老子畫像的構成及其在社會、思想史上的意義. Unpublished.
Hu Juren 胡居仁. *Ju ye lu* 居業錄. In *Congshu jicheng xinbian* 叢書集成新編, Zhexue lei 哲學類, vol. 23. Taipei: Xinwenfeng chuban gongsi, 1985.
Hu Shi 胡適. *Hu Shi wencun* 胡適文存. Taipei: Far East, 1953.
———. *Zhongguo zhexue shi dagang, juan shang* 中國哲學史大綱·卷上. Taipei: Liren shuju, 1982.
Hu Yin 胡寅. *Chongzheng bian* 崇正辯. Beijing: Zhonghua, 1993.
Hu Yitang 胡亦堂 and Xie Yuanzhong 謝元鍾, eds. *Linchuan xian zhi* 臨川縣志. Taipei: Chengwen chubanshe, 1989.
Hu Zi 胡仔. *Kongzi biannian* 孔子編年. In *Jingyin Wenyuange sikuquanshu*, 景印文淵閣四庫全書, vol. 446. Taipei: Commercial Press, 1983–1986.
Huang Chang-chien 黃彰健, ed. *Ming shilu* 明實錄. Taipei: Institute of History and Philology, Academia Sinica, 1966.
———. *Wuxu bianfa shi yanjiu* 戊戌變法史研究. Taipei: Institute of History and Philology, Academia Sinica, 1970.
Huang Chin-shing 黃進興. "Decoding the Symbols of Confucian Temples: Remarks on the Religiosity of Confucianism" 解開孔廟祭典的符碼——兼論其宗教性. In *Wenhua yu lishi de zhuisuo: Yu Yingshi jiaoshou bazhi shouqing lunwen ji* 文化與歷史的追索:余英時教授八秩壽慶論文集, ed. Hoyt Tillman, 535–558. Taipei: Linking, 2009.
———. *Entering the Master's Sanctuary: Power, Belief and Legitimacy in Traditional China* 優入聖域:權力、信仰與正當性. Taipei: Asian Culture Press, 1994; Beijing: Zhonghua, 2010.

——. *From Virtue to Morality: The Transformation of Moral Consciousness during the Late Qing and Early Republic Era* 從理學到倫理學：清末民初道德意識的轉化. Taipei: Asian Culture Press, 2013; Beijing: Zhonghua, 2014.

——. "Hsün-tzu: The Confucian Temple's Absentee" 荀子：孔廟從祀的缺席者. In *Sifenxi lunxue ji: qingzhu Li Yuan-Tseh xiansheng qishi shouchen* 四分溪論學集：慶祝李遠哲先生七十壽辰, ed. Liu Ts'ui-jung 劉翠溶, 477–502. Taipei: Asian Culture Press, 2006.

——. "On Iconoclasm and the Cult of 'Sage-Master'" 毀像與聖師祭. *Continent Magazine* 99, no. 5 (November 1999): 1–8.

——. "On the Secular Character of Confucianism: Discussion from Li Fu's Article 'Yuan Jiao'" 論儒教的俗世性格：從李紱的〈原教〉談起. *Journal of Intellectual History* 1 (September 2013): 59–84.

——. *Sages and Saints: Collected Essays on History and Religions* 聖賢與聖徒：歷史與宗教論文集. Taipei: Asian Culture Press, 2001, 2004; Beijing: Peking University Press, 2005.

Huang Ko-wu 黃克武. "The Debate of the Confucian State Religion during Early Republican China (1912–1917)" 民國初年孔教問題之爭論. *Bulletin of Historical Research, National Taiwan Normal University* 12 (1984): 197–223.

Huang Shengmin 黃聖旻. "Wang Xianqian 'Xunzi jijie' yan jiu" 王先謙〈荀子集解〉研究. Master's thesis, National Cheng Kung University, 1997.

Huang Xiaofeng 黃曉峰 and Qian Guanyu 錢冠宇. "Zhu Yuqi tan Qingdai biansai jigong bei yu guojia rentong" 朱玉麒談清代邊塞紀功碑與國家認同. *Dongfang zaobao* 東方早報 (*Shanghai Oriental Morning Daily*), *Shanghai shuping* 上海書評 (*Shanghai Review of Books*), July 12, 2015.

Huang Zongxi 黃宗羲. *Song Yuan xuean* 宋元學案. Beijing: Zhonghua, 1986.

Huang Zunxian 黃遵憲. *Huang Zunxian quanji* 黃遵憲全集. Ed. Chen Zheng 陳錚. Beijing: Zhonghua, 2005.

Huizinga, Johan. *The Autumn of the Middle Ages*. Trans. Rodney J. Payton and Ulrich Mammitzsch. Chicago: University of Chicago Press, 1996.

James, William. *The Varieties of Religious Experience*. New York: Penguin, 1982.

Jao Tsung-i 饒宗頤. "Sanjiao lun yu Song Jin xueshu" 三教論與宋金學術. *Dongxi wenhua* 11 (May 1968): 24–32.

Jiang Weiqiao 蔣維喬. "Qufu jiyou" 曲阜紀遊. In *Xin youji huikan xubian* 新遊記彙刊續編, vol. 1, *juan* 7, ed. Yao Zhuxuan 姚祝萱. Shanghai: Chung Hwa, 1925.

Jiao Hong 焦竑. *Yutang congyu* 玉堂叢語. Beijing: Zhonghua, 1981.

Jiao Xun 焦循. *Mengzi zhengyi* 孟子正義. Beijing: Zhonghua, 1987.

Jin Shen 金申. *Fojiao diaosu mingpin tulu* 佛教雕塑名品圖錄. Beijing: Beijing gongyi meishu chubanshe, 1995.

——. *Zhongguo lidai jinian Foxiang tudian* 中國歷代紀年佛像圖典. Beijing: Cultural Relics Publishing House, 1994.

Jin Zheng 金諍. *Keju zhidu yu Zhongguo wenhua* 科舉制度與中國文化. Shanghai: Shanghai Renmin chubanshe, 1990.

Johnston, Reginald F. *Confucianism and Modern China*. New York: D. Appleton-Century Company, 1935.

Jones, A. H. M. *The Later Roman Empire, 284–602: A Social, Economic, and Administrative Survey*. Norman: University of Oklahoma Press, 1964.

Kam, Louie. *Critiques of Confucius in Contemporary China*. Hong Kong: Chinese University Press, 1980.

Kaneko, Shuichi 金子修一. "Toudai no daishi, chūshi, shoushi ni tsuite" 唐代の大祀・中祀・小祀について. *Kouchi daigaku gakujutsu kenkyūhoukoku, Jimbunkagaku* 25, no. 2 (1976): 13–19.

Kang Youwei 康有為. *Kang Nanhai zhengshi wenxuan (1898–1927)* 康南海政史文選. Ed. Shen Maojun 沈茂駿. Guangzhou: Guangdong Higher Education Press, 1993.

———. *Kang Nanhai zi bian nianpu* 康南海自編年譜. Beijing: Zhonghua, 1992.

———. *Kang Youwei quanji* 康有為全集. Ed. Jiang Yihua 姜義華 and Wu Genliang 吳根樑. Shanghai: Shanghai guji chubanshe, 1990.

———. *Kang Youwei zaoqi yigao shuping* 康有為早期遺稿述評. Ed. Huang Mingtong 黃明同 and Wu Xizhao 吳熙釗. Guangzhou: Sun Yat-sen University Press, 1988.

———. *Kang Youwei zhenglun ji* 康有為政論集. Ed. Tang Zhijun 湯志鈞. Beijing: Zhonghua, 1981.

———. *Kongzi gaizhi kao* 孔子改制考. Beijing: Zhonghua, 1988.

———. *Wanmu caotang koushuo* 萬木草堂口說. In *Kang Youwei xueshu zhuzuo xuan* 康有為學術著作選, ed. Lou Yulie 樓宇烈. Beijing: Zhonghua, 1988.

Kant, Immanuel. *Religion within the Limits of Reason Alone*. Trans. Theodore M. Greene and Hoyt H. Hudson. New York: Harper & Row, 1960.

Kaplan, Abraham. *The Conduct of Inquiry: Methodology for Behavioral Science*. San Francisco: Chandler, 1964.

Kemp, Eric Waldram. *Canonization and Authority in the Western Church*. London: Oxford University Press, 1948.

Kenny, Anthony. *Aquinas on Mind*. London: Routledge, 1994.

Kieckhefer, Richard. "Imitators of Christ: Sainthood in the Christian Tradition." In *Sainthood: Its Manifestations in World Religions*, ed. Richard Kieckhefer and George D. Bond, 1–42. Berkeley: University of California Press, 1988.

Kitzinger, Ernst. *Byzantine Art in the Making: Main Lines of Stylistic Development in Mediterranean Art, 3rd–7th Century*. Cambridge, Mass.: Harvard University Press, 1980.

———. *Early Medieval Art in the British Museum*. London: British Museum, 1963.

Knoblock, John, trans. *Xunzi: A Translation and Study of the Complete Works*. Stanford, Calif.: Stanford University Press, 1988.

Koerner, Brendan. "Saint Makers." *U.S. News and World Report* (January 11, 1999): 54.

Kong Chuan 孔傳. *Dongjia zaji* 東家雜記. In *Jingyin Wenyuange sikuquanshu* 景印文淵閣四庫全書, vol. 446. Taipei: Commercial Press, 1983–1986. Also appears in *Congshu jicheng chubian* 叢書集成初編, vol. 3315. Shanghai: Commercial Press, 1939.

Kong Demao 孔德懋. *Kongfu neizhai yishi: Kongzi houyi de huiyi* 孔府內宅軼事：孔子後裔的回憶. Tianjin: Tianjin Renmin chubanshe, 1982.

Kong Jifen 孔繼汾. *Queli wenxian kao* 闕里文獻考. 1762. In *Ru Cang* 儒藏. Chengdou: Sichuan daxue chubanshe, 2005.

Kong Yingda 孔穎達. *Chunqiu Zuochuan Zhengyi* 春秋左傳正義. *Shisanjing zhushu* edition 十三經注疏本. Taipei: Yiwen yinshuguan, 2001.

Kong Yuan-cuo 孔元措. *Kongshi zuting guangji* 孔氏祖庭廣記. Published by Linlang mishi congshu 琳琅秘室叢書. In *Congshu jicheng chubian* 叢書集成初編, vol. 3316–3317. Reprint, Shanghai: Commercial Press, 1939.

Kong Zang 孔臧. *Lian cong zi* 連叢子. In *Jingyin Wenyuange sikuquanshu* 景印文淵閣四庫全書, vol. 695. Taipei: Commercial Press, 1983–1986.

Kong Zhencong 孔貞叢, ed. *Queli zhi* 闕里志. Taipei: Institute of History and Philology, Academia Sinica. Published in the Wanli reign of the Ming dynasty (1573–1620).

Kongfu dangan xuanbian 孔府檔案選編. Beijing: Zhonghua, 1982.

Lau, D. C., trans. *Mencius*. London: Penguin, 1970.

Lao Naixuan 勞乃宣. *Tongxiang Lao xiansheng (Naixuan) yigao* 桐鄉勞先生（乃宣）遺稿. Tongxiang Lushi 桐鄉盧氏, 1927.) In *Jindai Zhongguo shiliao congkan* 近代中國史料叢刊 36, no. 357. Taipei: Wenhai chubanshe, 1969.

Legge, James, trans. *The Chinese Classics*. Oxford: Clarendon, 1893. Reprint, Taipei: SMC, 1991.

Lei Wen 雷聞. *Jiaomiao zhiwai: Sui Tang guojia jisi yu zongjiao* 郊廟之外：隋唐國家祭祀與宗教. Beijing: Joint Publishing, 2009.

Levenson, Joseph R. *Confucian China and its Modern Fate*. Berkeley: University of California Press, 1965.

Li Daoyuan 酈道元, Yang Shoujing 楊守敬, and Xiong Huizhen 熊會貞. *Shuijing zhushu* 水經注疏. Nanjing: Jiangsu guji chubanshe, 1989.

Li Dazhao 李大釗. *Li Dazhao quanji* 李大釗全集. Ed. Zhu Wentong 朱文通. Shijiazhuang: Hebei jiaoyu chubanshe, 1999.

Li Dongyang 李東陽. *DaMing huidian* 大明會典. Ed. Shen Shixing 申時行. Taipei: Xinwenfeng chuban gongsi, 1976.

———. *Ming huidian* 明會典. Ed. Shen Shixing. Beijing: Zhonghua, 1989.

Li Guan 黎貫. "Lun kongzi sidian shu" 論孔子祀典疏. In *Guangdong wenzheng* 廣東文徵, ed. Jiang Maosen 江茂森. Hong Kong: Chu Hai College, 1973.

Li Linfu 李林甫. *Tang liudian* 唐六典. Beijing: Zhonghua, 1992.

Li Qiao 李喬. *Zhongguo hangyeshen chongbai* 中國行業神崇拜. Beijing: Zhongguo huaqiao chuban gongsi, 1990.

Li Xinchuan 李心傳. *Jianyan yilai jinian yaolu* 建炎以來繫年要錄. Commercial Press. In *Guoxue jiben congshuben*. Beijing: Zhonghua, 1988.

Li Yuangang 李元綱. *Shengmen shiye tu* 聖門事業圖. Song text in *Baichuan xuehai* 百川學海. Available at Chinese Text Project, https://ctext.org.

Li Zhi 李贄. *Cang shu* 藏書. Taipei: Xuesheng shuju, 1974.

———. *Fen shu / Xu fen shu* 焚書／續焚書. Taipei: Hanjing wenhua gongsi, 1984.

Li Zhizao 李之藻. *Pangong liyue shu* 頖宮禮樂疏. In *Jingyin Wenyuange sikuquanshu* 景印文淵閣四庫全書, vol. 651. Taipei: Commercial Press, 1983–1986.

Liang Fa 梁發. *Quanshi liangyan* 勸世良言. Taipei: Taiwan xuesheng shuju, 1965. Original held at Harvard University.

Liang Qichao 梁啟超. *Qingdai xueshu gailun* 清代學術概論. Beijing: Dongfang chubanshe, 1996.

———. *Yinbingshi heji* 飲冰室合集. Shanghai: Chung Hwa, 1936.

———. *Yinbingshi wenji* 飲冰室文集. Taipei: Chung Hwa, 1970.

Liang Shuming 梁漱溟. *Dongfang xueshu gaiguan* 東方學術概觀. Bashu shushe, 1986. Reprint, Hong Kong: Chung Hwa, 1988.

———. *Dongxi wenhua ji qi zhexue* 東西文化及其哲學. Hong Kong: Ziyou xueren she, 1960.

———. *Liang Shuming quanji* 梁漱溟全集. Ed. Zhongguo wenhua shuyuan xueshu weiyuanhui 中國文化書院學術委員會. Jinan: Shandong People's Publishing House, 1992.

———. *Zhongguo wenhua yaoyi* 中國文化要義. Taipei: Cheng Chung Bookstore, 1969.

Liang Yuansheng 梁元生. *Xuanni fuhai dao nanzhou: Rujia sixiang yu zaoqi xinjiapo huaren shehui shiliao huibian* 宣尼浮海到南洲：儒家思想與早期新加坡華人社會史料彙編. Hong Kong: Chinese University Press, 1995.

Liao Ping 廖平. *Guxue kao* 古學考. Taipei: Taiwan Kaiming shudian, 1969.

Liebeschuetz, J. H. W. G. *Continuity and Change in Roman Religion*. Oxford: Oxford University Press, 1979.

Lin Guoping 林國平. *Lin Zhao'en yu sanyijiao* 林兆恩與三一教. Fuzhou: Fujian Renmin chubanshe, 1992.

Lin Keguang 林克光. *Gexin pai juren Kang Youwei* 革新派巨人康有為. Beijing: China Renmin University Press, 1998.

Lin Zhao'en 林兆恩. *Linzi quanji* 林子全集. (Published in Ming dynasty, Chongzhen era, 1628–1644). In *Sikuquanshu cunmu congshu, zibu* 四庫全書存目叢書・子部, vol. 91–92. Tainan: Zhuangyan wenhua shiye youxian gongsi, 1995.

Ling Tingkan 凌廷堪. *Jiaoli tang wenji* 校禮堂文集. In *Xuxiu sikuquanshu* 續修四庫全書, vol. 1480. Shanghai: Shanghai guji chubanshe, 1995.

Linghu Defen 令狐德棻. *Zhoushu* 周書. Taipei: Dingwen shuju, 1980.

Liu Shipei 劉師培. *Liu Shenshu yishu buyi* 劉申叔遺書補遺. Ed. Wan Shiguo 萬仕國. Yangzhou: Guangling shushe, 2008.

———. *Liu Shipei lunxue lunzheng* 劉師培論學論政. Ed. Li Miaogen 李妙根. Shanghai: Fudan University Press, 1990.

Liu Xu 劉昫. *Jiu Tangshu* 舊唐書. Taipei: Dingwen shuju, 1981.

Liu Yiqing 劉義慶. *Shi shuo xin yu jiaojian* 世說新語校箋. Commentary by Liu Xiaobiao 劉孝標 and Yang Yong 楊勇. Taipei: Minglun chubanshe, 1970.

Liu Yuxi 劉禹錫. *Liu Yuxi ji* 劉禹錫集. Shanghai: Shanghai Renmin chubanshe, 1975.

Liu Zhen 劉珍. *Dongguan Han ji jiaozhu* 東觀漢記校注. Ed. Wu Shuping 吳樹平. Zhengzhou: Zhongzhou guji chubanshe, 1987.

Liu Zongyuan 柳宗元. *Liu Zongyuan ji* 柳宗元集. Taipei: Hanjing wenhua shiye youxian gongsi, 1982.

Lowden, John. *Early Christian and Byzantine Art*. London: Phaidon, 1998.

Lü Buwei 呂不韋. *Lüshi chunqiu jiaoshi* 呂氏春秋校釋. Ed. Chen Qiyou 陳奇猷. Taipei: Huazheng shuju, 1985.

Lü Kun 呂坤. *Shenyin yu* 呻吟語. Taipei: Hanjing wenhua shiye gongsi, 1981.

Lü Simian 呂思勉. *Du shi zhaji* 讀史札記. Taipei: Muduo chubanshe, 1983.

Lu Xun 魯迅. *Lu Xun quanji* 魯迅全集. Taipei: Tangshan chubanshe, 1989.

———. *Zhongguo xiaoshuo shilue* 中國小說史略. Beijing: Dongfang chubanshe, 1996.

Lü Yuanshan 呂元善. *Shengmen zhi* 聖門志. In *Congshu jicheng chubian* 叢書集成初編, vol. 3318–3321. Shanghai: Commercial Press, 1939.

Lu Zengxiang 陸增祥, ed. *Baqiongshi jinshi buzheng* 八瓊室金石補正. (Wuxing: Liushi xigulou 劉氏希古樓, 1924.) In *Shike shiliao xinbian* 石刻史料新編. Taipei: Xinwenfeng chuban gongsi, 1977.

Luo Qinshun 羅欽順. *Kun zhi ji* 困知記. In *Congshu jicheng xinbian* 叢書集成新編, Zhexue lei 哲學類, vol. 23. Taipei: Xinwenfeng chuban gongsi, 1985.

Luo Xianglin 羅香林. "Tangdai sanjiao jianglun kao" 唐代三教講論考. *Journal of Oriental Studies* 1, no. 1 (January 1954): 85–97.

Luther, Martin. "The Freedom of a Christian." In *Luther: Selected Political Writings*, ed. J. M. Porter, 25–35. Philadelphia: Fortress, 1974.

Ma Duanlin 馬端臨. *Wenxian tongkao* 文獻通考. Shanghai: Commercial Press, 1936. In *Wanyou wenku shitongben* 萬有文庫十通本. Beijing: Zhonghua, 1986.

Ma Fu 馬浮. "Shaoxingxian zhongxiu wenmiao ji" 紹興縣重修文廟記. *Huaguo* 1, no. 4 (1923): 1.

Ma Jigao 馬積高. *Xunxue yuanliu* 荀學源流. Shanghai: Shanghai guji chubanshe, 2000.

Ma Qi 馬齊 and Zhang Tingyu 張廷玉, eds. *DaQing Shengzu Renhuangdi (Kangxi) shilu* 大清聖祖仁 (康熙) 皇帝實錄. Taipei: Xinwenfeng chuban gongsi, 1978.

MacCulloch, J. A., and Vincent A. Smith. "Relics." In *Encyclopedia of Religion and Ethics*, ed. James Hastings, 10:650–662. New York: Charles Scribner's Sons; and Edinburgh: T. & T. Clark, 1924–1927.

MacMullen, Ramsay. *Christianizing the Roman Empire (A.D. 100–400)*. New Haven, Conn.: Yale University Press, 1984.

Mao Qiling 毛奇齡. "Bianding Jiajing daliyi" 辨定嘉靖大禮議. In *Longwei mishu* 龍威秘書, ed. Ma Junliang 馬駿良. N.P., n.d.

Mathews, Thomas F. *The Clash of Gods: A Reinterpretation of Early Christian Art*. Princeton, N.J.: Princeton University Press, 1993.

McBrien, Richard P. *Catholicism*. San Francisco: Harper Collins, 1994.

Michalski, Sergiusz. *The Reformation and the Visual Arts: The Protestant Image Question in Western and Eastern Europe*. London: Routledge, 1993.

Miller, James. "The Opium of the People." In *Chinese Religions in Contemporary Societies*, ed. James Miller. Santa Barbara, Calif.: ABC-Clio, 2006.

Ming Taizu 明太祖. *Ming Taizu wenji* 明太祖文集. Ed. Yao Shiguan 姚士觀 and Shen Fu 沈鈇. In *Jingyin Wenyuange sikuquanshu* 景印文淵閣四庫全書, vol. 1223. Taipei: Commercial Press, 1983–1986.

Miyakawa Hisayuki 宮川尚志. "Jukyō no shūkyō teki seikaku" 儒教の宗教的性格. *Shūkyō kenkyū* 38, no. 1 (January 1960): 1–24.

Mou Zhongjian 牟鍾鑒. *Zhongguo zongjiao yu wenhua* 中國宗教與文化. Taipei: Tangshan chubanshe, 1995.

Mou Zongsan 牟宗三. *Xinti yu xingti* 心體與性體. Taipei: Zhengzhong shuju, 1996.

———. *Xunxue dalue* 荀學大略. Taipei: Xuesheng shuju, 1990.

———. *Zhongguo zhexue de tezhi* 中國哲學的特質. In *Mou Zongsan xiansheng quanji* 牟宗三先生全集. Taipei: Cultural Foundation of the United Daily News Group, 2003.

———. Xu Fuguan 徐復觀, Zhang Junmai 張君勱, and Tang Junyi 唐君毅. "Wei Zhongguo wenhua jinggao shijie renshi xuanyan" 為中國文化敬告世界人士宣言. *Huanghuagang zazhi* 9 (May 2004): 85; 10 (August 2004): 106–116; 11 (November 2004): 72–83. First published simultaneously in *Minzhu pinglun* (January 1, 1958) and *Zaisheng* (January 1, 1958).

Murray, Sister Charles. "Art and the Early Church." In *Art, Archaeology, and Architecture of Early Christianity*, ed. Paul Corby Finney, 303–345. New York: Garland, 1993.

Nietzsche, Friedrich. *On the Genealogy of Morals*. Trans. Walter Kaufmann and R. J. Hollingdale. New York: Vintage, 1967.

Nolan, Mary Lee, and Sidney Nolan. *Christian Pilgrimage in Modern Western Europe*. Chapel Hill: University of North Carolina Press, 1989.

Okamatsu Santaro 岡松參太郎. *Linshi Taiwan jiuguan diaochahui diyi bu diaocha disan huibaogaoshu, Taiwan sifa* 臨時臺灣舊慣調查會第一部調查第三回報告書・臺灣私法.

Trans. Chen Jintian 陳金田. Nantou: Taiwan sheng wenxian weiyuanhui, 1990.

Ostrogorsky, George. *History of the Byzantine State*. Trans. Joan Hussey. New Brunswick, N.J.: Rutgers University Press, 1957.

Ouyang Xiu 歐陽修. *Ouyang Wenzhonggong ji* 歐陽文忠公集. In *Guoxue jiben congshu*. Taipei: Commercial Press, 1967.

———. *Ouyang Xiu quanji* 歐陽修全集. Taipei: Shijie shuju, 1961. Reprint, Taipei: Huazheng shuju, 1975.

Ouyang Xiu 歐陽修 and Song Qi 宋祁. *Xin Tangshu* 新唐書. Taipei: Dingwen shuju, 1981.

Pan Jingruo 潘鏡若, ed. *Sanjiao kaimi guizheng yanyi* 三教開迷歸正演義. In *Guben xiaoshuo jicheng* 古本小說集成. Shanghai: Shanghai guji chubanshe, 1990.

Pan Xiang 潘相, ed. *Qufu xianzhi* 曲阜縣志. 1774. Taipei: Taiwan Xuesheng shuju, 1968.

Pang Zhonglu 龐鍾璐. *Wenmiao sidian kao* 文廟祀典考. 1877. Taipei: Zhongguo liyue xuehui, 1977.

Pelikan, Jaroslav. "Christianity." In *The Encyclopedia of Religion*, ed. Mircea Eliade. New York: Simon & Schuster Macmillan, 1995.

———. *Imago Dei: The Byzantine Apologia for Icons*. Princeton, N.J.: Princeton University Press, 1990.

———. *Mary through the Centuries: Her Place in the History of Culture*. New Haven, Conn.: Yale University Press, 1996.

Pi Xirui 皮錫瑞. *Jingxue tonglun* 經學通論. (Sixian shuju, 1875.) In *Xuxiu sikuquanshu* 續修四庫全書, vol. 180. Shanghai: Shanghai guji chubanshe, 1995.

Qian Daxin 錢大昕. *Qianyantang ji* 潛言堂集. Shanghai: Shanghai guji chubanshe, 1986.

Qian Mu 錢穆. "Shiyou zayi" 師友雜憶 (Recollections of Teachers and Friends). *China Monthly* 2, no. 5 (May 1980): 53–59.

———. *Zhongguo xueshu sixiang shi luncong* 中國學術思想史論叢. Taipei: Dongda tushu gongsi, 1980.

Qin Huitian 秦蕙田. *Wuli tongkao* 五禮通考. Weijingwo 味經窩. Reprint, Taoyuan: Shenghuan tushu gongsi, 1994.

Qing Gaozong 清高宗. *Yuzhi wenji, chuji* 御製文集·初集. Ed. Yu Minzhong 于敏中. In *Jingyin Wenyuange sikuquanshu* 景印文淵閣四庫全書, vol. 1301. Taipei: Commercial Press, 1983–1986.

Qing Shengzu 清聖祖. *Shengzu Renhuangdi yuzhiwen dier ji* 聖祖仁皇帝御製文第二集. Ed. Zhang Yushu 張玉書 and Yunlu 允祿. In *Jingyin Wenyuange sikuquanshu* 景印文淵閣四庫全書, vol. 1298. Taipei: Commercial Press, 1983–1986.

Qing Shizong 清世宗. *Shizong Xianhuangdi yuzhi wenji* 世宗憲皇帝御製文集. In *Jingyin Wenyuange sikuquanshu* 景印文淵閣四庫全書, vol. 1300. Taipei: Commercial Press, 1983–1986.

———. *Yongzheng zhupi yuzhi* 雍正硃批諭旨. Ed. E'ertai 鄂爾泰. Taipei: Wenhai chubanshe, 1965.

Qiu Jun 丘濬. *Daxue yanyi bu* 大學衍義補. In *Jingyin Wenyuange sikuquanshu* 景印文淵閣四庫全書, vol. 712–713. Taipei: Commercial Press, 1983–1986.

Qu Jiusi 瞿九思. *Kongmiao liyue kao* 孔廟禮樂考. Published in the Wanli reign of the Ming dynasty (1573–1620).

Rawls, John. *A Theory of Justice*. Cambridge, Mass.: Belknap Press of Harvard University Press, 1971.

Ren Jiyu 任繼愈. *Daocang tiyao* 道藏提要. Beijing: China Social Sciences Press, 1995.

———. *Zhongguo Daojiao shi* 中國道教史. Shanghai: Shanghai Renmin chubanshe, 1990.

Ricci, Matteo 利瑪竇. *Tianzhu shiyi* 天主實義. Published in the Ming dynasty, Chongzhen era (1628–1644).

Rothkrug, Lionel. "Popular Religion and Holy Shrines." In *Religion and the People, 800–1700*, ed. James Obelkevich, 20–86. Chapel Hill: University of North Carolina Press, 1979.

Russell, Bertrand. *The Problem of China*. London: Allen and Unwin, 1966.

———. *Why I Am Not a Christian*. London: Routledge, 2004.

Sengyou 僧祐. *Hong ming ji* 弘明集. In *Taisho Shinshu Daizokyo* 大正新修大藏經, vol. 52. 1924–1934. Reprint, Taipei: Xinwenfeng chuban gongsi, 1983.

Shao Changheng 邵長蘅. *Qingmen lugao* 青門簏槀. In *Changzhou xianzhe yishu* 常州先哲遺書, ed. Sheng Xuanhuai 盛宣懷. In *Yuanke jingyin congshu jicheng sanbian* 原刻景印叢書集成三編. Taipei: Yiwen yinshuguan, 1960.

Shen Cuifen 沈粹芬, ed. *Qing wen hui* 清文匯. Beijing: Beijing chubanshe, 1996.

Shen Defu 沈德符. *Wanli yehuo bian* 萬曆野獲編. Beijing: Zhonghua, 1980.

Shen Yue 沈約. *Songshu* 宋書. Taipei: Dingwen shuju, 1980.

Shi Jie 石介. *Culai Shi xiansheng wenji* 徂徠石先生文集. Beijing: Zhonghua, 1984.

Shi Zhecun 施蟄存. *Shuijing zhu bei lu* 水經注碑錄. Tianjin: Tianjin guji chubanshe, 1987.

Shigematsu Toshiaki 重松俊章. "Shina sankyo shi jo no jakkan no mondai" 支那三教史上の若干の問題. *Shien* 21 (1939): 143–152.

Shitou shang de Rujia wenxian: Qufu beiwen lu 石頭上的儒家文獻：曲阜碑文錄. Ed. Luo Chenglie 駱承烈. Jinan: Qilu shushe, 2001.

Sima Qian 司馬遷. *Records of the Grand Historian*. Trans. Burton Watson. New York: Columbia University Press, 1993.

———. *Shiji* 史記 [Records of the Grand Historian]. Beijing: Zhonghua, 1982.

Smith, Wilfred Cantwell. *The Meaning and End of Religion*. Minneapolis, Minn.: Fortress, 1991.

Song Lian 宋濂. *Song Lian quanji* 宋濂全集. Hangzhou: Zhejiang guji chubanshe, 1999.

———. *Songxueshi quanji* 宋學士全集. In *Congshu jicheng chubian* 叢書集成初編, vol. 2110–2133. Shanghai: Commercial Press, 1939.

———. *Yuanshi* 元史. Taipei: Dingwen shuju, 1980.

Song Na 宋訥. *Xi yin wengao* 西隱文稿. Taipei: Wenhai chubanshe, 1970.

Song Shou 宋綬 and Song Minqiu 宋敏求. *Song dazhaoling ji* 宋大詔令集. Ed. Si Yizu 司義祖. Beijing: Zhonghua, 1962.

Song Shu 宋恕. *Song Shu ji* 宋恕集. Ed. Hu Zhusheng 胡珠生. Beijing: Zhonghua, 1993.

Stouck, Mary-Ann, ed. *Medieval Saints: A Reader*. Peterborough: Broadview, 1998.

Su Shi 蘇軾. *Su Shi wenji* 蘇軾文集. Ed. Kong Fanli 孔凡禮. Beijing: Zhonghua shuju, 1992.

Su Yu 蘇輿, ed. *Yi jiao congbian* 翼教叢編. Taipei: Institute of Chinese Literature and Philosophy, Academia Sinica, 2005.

Sun Chengze 孫承澤. *Chunmingmeng yulu* 春明夢餘錄. Hong Kong: Longmen shuju, 1965.

———. *Tianfu Guangji* 天府廣記. Beijing: Tianjing chubanshe, 1962.

Sun Fu 孫復. *Sun Mingfu xiaoji* 孫明復小集. In *Jingyin Wenyuange sikuquanshu* 景印文淵閣四庫全書, vol. 1090. Taipei: Commercial Press, 1983–1986.

Sun Xidan 孫希旦. *Liji jijie* 禮記集解. Ed. Shen Xiaohuan 沈嘯寰 and Wang Xingxian 王星賢. Beijing: Zhonghua, 1989.

Sun Yirang 孫詒讓, Wang Wenjin 王文錦, and Chen Yuxia 陳玉霞, eds. *Zhouli zhengyi* 周禮正義. Beijing: Zhonghua, 1987.

Taisho Shinshu Daizokyo 大正新修大藏經 (*Taishozo* series). 1924–1934. Reprint, Taipei: Xinwenfeng chuban gongsi, 1983.

Takezoe Koko 竹添光鴻. *Saden Kaisen* (*Zuozhuan huijian*) 左傳會箋. Tokyo: Seisei shohku 井井書屋, 1903. Reprint, Taipei: Guangwen shuju, 1968.

Tan Sitong 譚嗣同. *Tan Sitong quanji* 譚嗣同全集. Ed. Cai Shangsi 蔡尚思. Beijing: Zhonghua, 1981.

Tang Peng 湯鵬. *Fuqiuzi* 浮邱子. Zhangsha: Yuelu shushe, 1987.

Tang Yongtong 湯用彤. *Han Wei liang Jin Nanbeichao Fojiao shi* 漢魏兩晉南北朝佛教史. Beijing: Zhonghua, 1955.

Tang Zhen 唐甄. *Qian shu* 潛書. Beijing: Zhonghua, 1984.

Tang Zhijun 湯志鈞, ed. *Zhang Taiyan nianpu changbian* 章太炎年譜長編. Beijing: Zhonghua, 1979.

Tao Xisheng 陶希聖. "Wumiao zhi zhengzhi shehui de yanbian" 武廟之政治社會的演變. *Shihuo yuekan* 2, no. 5 (August 1972): 1–19.

———. "Zitong Wenchangshen zhi shehuishi de jieshuo" 梓潼文昌神之社會史的解說. *Shihuo yuekan* 2, no. 8 (November 1972): 1–9.

Tao Zongyi 陶宗儀. *Nancun chuo geng lu* 南村輟耕錄. Beijing: Zhonghua, 1980.

Taylor, Charles. *A Secular Age*. Cambridge, Mass.: Belknap Press of Harvard University Press, 2007.

Taylor, Rodney L. "The Sage as Saint." In *Sainthood: Its Manifestations in World Religions*, ed. Richard Kieckhefer and George D. Bond, 218–242. Berkeley: University of California Press, 1988.

Thomas, Keith. *Religion and the Decline of Magic: Studies in Popular Beliefs in Sixteenth- and Seventeenth-Century England*. New York: Charles Scribner's Sons, 1971.

Thurston, H. "Saints and Martyrs." In *Encyclopaedia of Religion and Ethics*, ed. James Hastings, 11:51–59. New York: Charles Scribner's Sons; and Edinburgh: T. & T. Clark, 1924–1927.

Tillich, Paul. *Dynamics of Faith*. New York: Harper & Row, 1957.

Tillman, Hoyt Cleveland. "A New Direction in Confucian Scholarship: Approaches to Examining the Differences between Neo-Confucianism and Tao-hsueh." *Philosophy East and West* 42, no. 3 (1992): 455–474.

———. "The Uses of Neo-Confucianism, Revisited: A Reply to Professor de Bary." *Philosophy East and West* 44, no. 1 (1994): 135–142.

———. "Zhu Xi's Prayers to the Spirit of Confucius and Claim to the Transmission of the Way." *Philosophy East and West* 54, no. 4 (2004): 489–513.

Troeltsch, Ernst. *The Social Teaching of the Christian Churches*. Trans. Olive Wyon. Louisville, Ky.: Westminster/John Knox Press, 1992.

Tu Cheng-sheng 杜正勝. "Xingti, Jingqi yu hunpo: zhongguo chuantong dui 'ren' renshi de xingcheng" 形體、精氣與魂魄：中國傳統對「人」認識的形成. *New History* 2, no. 3 (September 1991): 1–65.

Tu, Weiming. *Centrality and Commonality: An Essay on Confucian Religiousness*. 1976. Rev. ed. Albany: State University of New York Press, 1989.

———. *Lun ruxue de zongjiaoxing: dui Zhongyong de xiandai quanshi* 論儒學的宗教性：對《中庸》的現代詮釋. Trans. Duan Dezhi 段德智. Wuchang: Wuhan University Press, 1999.

Tu, Weiming, and Mary Evelyn, eds. *Confucian Spirituality*. New York: Crossroad, 2003.

Tuo Tuo 脫脫. *Jinshi* 金史. Taipei: Dingwen shuju, 1980.

———. *Liaoshi* 遼史. Taipei: Dingwen shuju, 1980.

———. *Songshi* 宋史. Taipei: Dingwen shuju, 1978.

Turanli, Aydan. "Nietzsche and the Later Wittgenstein: An Offense to the Quest for Another World." *Journal of Nietzsche Studies* 26 (Autumn 2003): 55–63.

Turner, Bryan S. *Religion and Social Theory*. London: Sage, 1991.

Turner, Victor, and Edith Turner. *Image and Pilgrimage in Christian Culture: Anthropological Perspectives*. New York: Columbia University Press, 1978.

van der Veer, Peter. "Spirituality in Modern Society." In *Religion: Beyond a Concept*, ed. Hent de Vries, 789–797. New York: Fordham University Press, 2008.

Vauchez, André. "The Saint." In *The Medieval World*, ed. Jacques Le Goff, trans. Lydia G. Cochrane. London: Collins & Brown, 1990.

———. *Sainthood in the Later Middle Ages.* Trans. Jean Birrell. Cambridge: Cambridge University Press, 1997.

von Stietencron, Heinrich. "Hindu Religious Traditions and the Concept of 'Religion': Consequences of Cross-Cultural Research." The 4th Gonda Lecture (1996). *International Institute for Asian Studies Newsletter* 11 (1997): 18.

Wang Anshi 王安石. *Linchuan xiansheng wenji* 臨川先生文集. Taipei: Huazheng shuju, 1975.

Wang Chong 王充. *Lunheng jijie* 論衡集解. Ed. Liu Pansui 劉盼遂. Taipei: Shijie shuju, 1990.

Wang Dang 王讜. *Tang yulin jiaozheng* 唐語林校證. Ed. Zhou Xunchu 周勛初. Beijing: Zhonghua, 1987.

Wang Fan-sen 王汎森. "The Religious Transformation of Confucianism in Late Ming and Early Ch'ing Thought" 明末清初儒學的宗教化———以許三禮的告天之學為例. *New History* 9, no. 2 (June 1998): 89–123.

———. "The T'ai-ku School: Sectarian Confucianism in Nineteenth-Century China" 道咸年間民間性儒家學派———太谷學派研究的回顧. *New History* 5, no. 4 (December 1994): 141–162.

Wang Jing 王涇. *DaTang jiaosi lu* 大唐郊祀錄. (Published by Qian Xizuo 錢熙祚, Qian Peirang 錢培讓, and Qian Peijie 錢培杰 in Qing Daoguang era, 1821–1850). In *Baibu congshu jicheng, Zhihai congshu* 百部叢書集成·指海叢書, vol. 7. Taipei: Yiwen yinshuguan, 1966.

Wang Ming 王明. *Baopuzi neipian jiaoshi* 抱朴子內篇校釋. Beijing: Zhonghua, 1988.

———. *Taipingjing hejiao* 太平經合校. Beijing: Zhonghua, 1960.

Wang Pu 王溥. *Tang huiyao* 唐會要. Kyoto: Chubun Shuppansha, 1978.

———. *Wudai huiyao* 五代會要. Taipei: Jiusi chubanshe, 1978.

Wang Qi 王圻. *Xu wenxian tongkao* 續文獻通考. 1603. Held by the Institute of History and Philology, Academia Sinica, Taipei.

Wang Qinruo 王欽若, ed. *Cefu yuangui* 冊府元龜. Taipei: Chung Hwa, 1972.

Wang Shizhen 王世貞. *Yanzhou shanren sibu gao* 弇州山人四部稿. Taipei: Weiwen tushu gongsi, 1976. Published by Shijingtang 世經堂 in the Wanli reign of the Ming dynasty (1573–1620).

Wang Shouren (Wang Yangming) 王守仁. *Wang Yangming quanji* 王陽明全集. Ed. Wu Guang 吳光. Shanghai: Shanghai guji chubanshe, 1992.

Wang Su 王肅, ed. *Kongzi jiayu* 孔子家語. In *Jingyin Wenyuange sikuquanshu* 景印文淵閣四庫全書, vol. 695. Taipei: Commercial Press, 1983–1986.

Wang Xianqian 王先謙. *Hou Hanshu jijie* 後漢書集解. Taipei: Yiwen yinshuguan, 1951.

———. *Xunzi jijie* 荀子集解. Beijing: Zhonghua, 1988.

Wang Xisun 汪喜孫. *Wang Xisun zhuzuoji* 汪喜孫著作集. Ed. Yang Jinlong 楊晉龍. Taipei: Institute of Chinese Literature and Philosophy, Academia Sinica, 2003.

Wang Yi 王褘. *Wang Zhongwengong ji* 王忠文公集. In *Congshu jicheng chubian* 叢書集成初編, vol. 2421–2428. Shanghai: Commercial Press, 1939.
Wang Zhong 汪中. *Wang Zhong ji* 汪中集. Taipei: Institute of Chinese Literature and Philosophy, Academia Sinica, 2000.
Weber, Max. *Economy and Society: An Outline of Interpretive Sociology*. Ed. Guenther Roth and Claus Wittich. Berkeley: University of California Press, 1978.
——. *The Methodology of the Social Sciences*. Trans. and ed. Edward A. Shils and Henry A. Finch. Taipei: Rainbow-Bridge, 1971.
——. *The Protestant Ethic and the Spirit of Capitalism*. Trans. Talcott Parsons. New York: Charles Scribner's Sons, 1958.
——. *The Religion of China: Confucianism and Taoism*. Trans. Hans H. Gerth. New York: Macmillan, 1964.
——. *The Sociology of Religion*. Trans. Ephraim Fischoff. Boston: Beacon, 1964.
Wei Liaoweng 魏了翁. *Heshan wenji* 鶴山文集. In *Jingyin Wenyuange sikuquanshu* 景印文淵閣四庫全書, vol. 1172–1173. Taipei: Commercial Press, 1983–1986.
Wei Shou 魏收. *Weishu* 魏書. Taipei: Dingwen shuju, 1980.
Wei Yuan 魏源. *Wei Yuan quanji* 魏源全集. Ed. Wei Yuan quanji bianweihui 魏源全集編委會. Changsha: Yuelu shushe, 2004.
Wei Zheng 魏徵. *Suishu* 隋書. Taipei: Dingwen shuju, 1980.
Weinstein, Donald, and Rudolph Bell. *Saints and Society: The Two Worlds of Western Christendom, 1000–1700*. Chicago: University of Chicago Press, 1982.
Wen Yanbo 文彥博. *Lugong wenji* 潞公文集. In *Sikuquanshu zhenben, liuji* 四庫全書珍本·六集, vol. 245–246. Taipei: Commercial Press, 1976.
Wen Yiduo 聞一多. *Wen Yiduo quanji* 聞一多全集. Beijing: SDX Joint Publishing, 1982.
Wilson, Thomas A., ed. *On Sacred Grounds: Culture, Society, Politics, and the Formation of the Cult of Confucius*. Cambridge, Mass.: Harvard University Press, 2002.
Wittgenstein, Ludwig. *Philosophical Investigations*. Trans. G. E. M. Anscombe. New York: Macmillan, 1968.
Woodward, Kenneth L. *Making Saints: How the Catholic Church Determines Who Becomes a Saint, Who Doesn't, and Why*. New York: Simon & Schuster, 1996.
Wu Yu 吳虞. *Wu Yu wenlu* 吳虞文錄. Yadong tushuguan 亞東圖書館, 1927. In *Minguo congshu* 民國叢書 2, no. 96. Reprint, Shanghai: Shanghai shudian, 1992.
Wu Yun 吳雲, ed. *Tang Taizong ji* 唐太宗集. Xian: Shaanxi Renmin chubanshe, 1986.
Xia Jingqu 夏敬渠. *Yesou pu yan* 野叟曝言. Taipei: Shijie shuju, 1962.
Xiang Mai 祥邁. *Bianwei lu* 辯偽錄. In *Taisho Shinshu Daizokyo* 大正新修大藏經, vol. 52. 1924–1934. Reprint, Taipei: Xinwenfeng chuban gongsi, 1983.
Xiao Song 蕭嵩. *DaTang Kaiyuan li* 大唐開元禮. In *Jingyin Wenyuange sikuquanshu* 景印文淵閣四庫全書, vol. 646. Taipei: Commercial Press, 1983–1986.
Xiao Zixian 蕭子顯. *Nan Qi shu* 南齊書. Taipei: Dingwen shuju, 1980.

Xinbian lianxiang soushenguangji 新編連相搜神廣記. (Published in Yuan dynasty.) In *Huitu sanjiao yuanliu soushen daquan* 繪圖三教源流搜神大全. Shanghai: Shanghai guji chubanshe, 1990.

Xing Bing 邢昺. *Xiaojing zhushu* 孝經注疏. *Shisanjing zhushu* edition 十三經注疏本.

Xiong Cilu 熊賜履. *Xuetong* 學統. In *Congshu jicheng xinbian* 叢書集成新編, Shidi lei 史地類, vols. 99–100. Taipei: Xinwenfeng chuban gongsi, 1985.

Xiong He 熊鉌. *Xiong Wuxuan xiansheng wenji* 熊勿軒先生文集. Shanghai: Commercial Press, 1936.

Xiong Shili 熊十力. *Dujing shiyao* 讀經示要. Nanfang yinshuguan, 1945. In *Minguo congshu* 民國叢書 5, no. 1. Shanghai: Shanghai shudian, 1992.

Xu Gan 徐幹. *Zhong Lun* 中論. In *Zhongguo zixue mingzhu jicheng, zhenben chubian* 中國子學名著集成・珍本初編. Rujia zibu 儒家子部, vol. 30. Taipei: Zhongguo zixue mingzhu jicheng bianyin jijinhui, 1978. Published by Cheng Rong 程榮, Han Wei congshu ben 漢魏叢書本, Ming dynasty.

Xu Jie 徐階. *Shijingtang ji* 世經堂集. 1681.

Xu Ke 徐珂. *Qing bai leichao* 清稗類鈔. Taipei: Commercial Press, 1966.

Xu Song 徐松, ed. *Song huiyao jigao* 宋會要輯稿. Beiping: Guoli Beiping tushuguan, 1936.

Xu Song 許嵩. *Jiankang shilu* 建康實錄. Beijing: Zhonghua, 1986.

Xu Xuemo 徐學謨. *Shimiao shi yulu* 世廟識餘錄. Taipei: Guofeng chubanshe, 1965.

Xu Yikui 徐一夔. *DaMing jili* 大明集禮. In *Jingyin Wenyuange sikuquanshu* 景印文淵閣四庫全書, vol. 650. Taipei: Commercial Press, 1983–1986.

Xue Juzheng 薛居正. *Jiu Wudai shi* 舊五代史. Taipei: Dingwen shuju, 1980.

Xue Xuan 薛瑄. *Xue Xuan quanji* 薛瑄全集. Taiyuan: Shanxi Renmin chubanshe, 1990.

Yan Fu 嚴復. *Yan Fu heji* 嚴復合集. Ed. Lin Zaijue 林載爵. Taipei: C. F. Koo Foundation, 1998.

——. *Yan Jidao wenchao* 嚴幾道文鈔. Shanghai Guohua shuju, 1922. Reprint, Taipei: Shijie shuju, 1971.

Yan Kejun 嚴可均, ed. *Quan shanggu sandai Qin Han sanguo liuchao wen* 全上古三代秦漢三國六朝文. Taipei: Hongye shuju, 1975.

——. *Tieqiao mangao* 鐵橋漫稿. In *Congshu jicheng xubian* 叢書集成續編, Wenxue lei 文學類, vol. 158. Taipei: Xinwenfeng chuban gongsi, 1989.

Yan Qinghuang 顏清湟. "1899–1911 nian xinjiapo he malaiya de Kongjiao fuxing yundong" 1899–1911 年新加坡和馬來亞的孔教復興運動. In *Guowai zhongguo jindaishi yanjiu* 國外中國近代史研究, 8:215–246. Beijing: China Social Sciences Press, 1985.

Yan Ruoqu 閻若璩. *Shangshu guwen shuzheng* 尚書古文疏證. In *Jingyin Wenyuange sikuquanshu* 景印文淵閣四庫全書, vol. 66. Taipei: Commercial Press, 1983–1986.

Yang, C. K. *Religion in Chinese Society: A Study of Contemporary Social Functions of Religion and Some of Their Historical Factors.* Berkeley: University of California Press, 1961.

Yang Hsien-yi and Gladys Yang, trans. *Records of the Historian.* Shanghai: Commercial Press, 1974.

Yang Qiyuan 楊起元. *Taishi Yang Fusuo xiansheng zhengxue bian* 太史楊復所先生證學編. She Yongning 佘永寧, 1617. In *Sikuquanshu cunmu congshu, zibu* 四庫全書存目叢書•子部, vol. 90. Tainan: Zhuangyan wenhua gongsi, 1995.

Yang Xiong 揚雄. *Fayan zhu* 法言注. Beijing: Zhonghua, 1992.

Yang Xuanzhi 楊衒之. *Luoyang qielanji xiaozhu* 洛陽伽藍記校注. Ed. Fan Xiangyong 范祥雍. Taipei: Huazheng shuju, 1980.

Yang Yongchang 楊永昌. *Mantan Qingzhensi* 漫談清真寺. Yinchuan: Ningxia Renmin chubanshe, 1981.

Yazi 亞子 and Liangzi 良子. *Kongfu da jienan* 孔府大劫難. Hong Kong: Tiandi tushu gongsi, 1992.

Ye Sheng 葉盛. *Shui dong riji* 水東日記. Beijing: Zhonghua, 1980.

Ye Shi 葉適. *Ye Shi ji* 葉適集. Beijing: Zhonghua, 1983.

Yelü Chucai 耶律楚材. *Zhanran jushi wenji* 湛然居士文集. (Written in Yuan dynasty, collected by Wuxi sunshi xiaolutian 無錫孫氏小綠天, printed by Shanghai Hanfenlou 涵芬樓.) In *Sibu congkan chubian, ji bu* 四部叢刊初編•集部, vol. 223. Shanghai: Shanghai shudian, 1989.

Yongrong 永瑢 and Ji Yun 紀昀. *Qin ding sikuquanshu zongmu tiyao* 欽定四庫全書總目提要. In *Jingyin Wenyuange sikuquanshu* 景印文淵閣四庫全書, vol. 1–5. Taipei: Commercial Press, 1983–1986.

———. *Siku quanshu zongmu tiyao* 四庫全書總目提要. Wuyingdian 武英殿 edition. Taipei: Commercial Press, 1983.

Young, Allen John (林樂知). "Xiao bian mingjiao lun" 消變明教論. In *Zhongguo sixiang baoku* 中國思想寶庫. Beijing: Zhongguo guangbo dianshi chubanshe, 1990.

Yu, Anthony C. *State and Religion in China.* Chicago: Open Court, 2005.

Yu Jiaxi 余嘉錫. *Yu Jiaxi lunxue zazhe* 余嘉錫論學雜著. Beijing: Zhonghua, 2007.

Yu Yingshi (Yü, Ying-shih) 余英時. "'O Soul, Come Back!' A Study in the Changing Conception of the Soul and Afterlife in Pre-Buddhist China." *Harvard Journal of Asiatic Studies* 47, no. 2 (December 1987): 363–395.

———. *Qing huai zhongguo—Yu Yingshi zixuanji* 情懷中國—余英時自選集. Hong Kong: Cosmos Books, 2010.

———. *You ji fengchui shuishang lin: Qian Mu yu jindai Zhongguo xueshu* 猶記風吹水上鱗：錢穆與近代中國學術. Taipei: San Min, 1991.

———. *Zhongguo sixiang chuantong de xiandai quanshi* 中國思想傳統的現代詮釋. Taipei: Linking, 1987.

———. *Zhongguo zhishi jieceng shilun: Gudai pian* 中國知識階層史論・古代篇. Taipei: Linking, 1980.

Yu Yue 俞樾. *Chunzaitang zawen* 春在堂襍文. In *Chunzaitang quanshu* 春在堂全書. Taipei: Zhongguo wenxian chubanshe, 1968.

Yu Zhengxie 俞正燮. *Guisi cungao* 癸巳存稿. Taipei: Commercial Press, 1971.

Yuan Jue 袁桷. *Qingrong jushi ji* 清容居士集. In *Sibu congkan chubian, suoben* 四部叢刊初編・縮本, vol. 295–297. Taipei: Commercial Press, 1965.

Yuan Zheng 袁征. "Cong Kongmiao zhidu kan Songdai ruxue de bianhua" 從孔廟制度看宋代儒學的變化. In *Songshi yanjiu lunwenji* 宋史研究論文集, ed. Deng Guangming 鄧廣銘 and Wang Yunhai 王雲海, 490–509. Kaifeng: Henan daxue chubanshe, 1993.

Yuwen Maozhao 宇文懋昭. *Qinding zhongding daJin guozhi* 欽定重訂大金國志. Ed. Ji Yun 紀昀. In *Jingyin Wenyuange sikuquanshu* 景印文淵閣四庫全書, vol. 383. Taipei: Commercial Press, 1983–1986.

Zhang Cong 張璁. *Luoshan zoushu* 羅山奏疏. 1577. In *Sikuquanshu cunmu congshu, shibu* 四庫全書存目叢書・史部, vol. 57. Baolunlou 寶綸樓, 1609. Reprint, Tainan: Zhuangyan wenhua shiye gongsi, 1996.

———. *Yudui lu* 諭對錄. In *Sikuquanshu cunmu congshu, shibu* 四庫全書存目叢書・史部, vol. 57. Baolunlou 寶綸樓, 1609. Reprint, Tainan: Zhuangyan wenhua shiye gongsi, 1996.

Zhang Dai 張岱. *Tao'an mengyi* 陶菴夢憶. In *Meihua wenxue mingzhu congkan* 美化文學名著叢刊. Ed. Zhu Jianmang 朱劍芒. Shanghai: Shijie shuju, 1947.

Zhang Dongsun 張東蓀. "Yu zhi Kongjiao guan" 余之孔教觀. In *Minguo jingshi wenbian* 民國經世文編. Shanghai: Jingshi wenshe, 1914. In *Jindai Zhongguo shiliao congkan* 50, no. 492–498, *juan* 28. Reprint, Taipei: Wenhai chubanshe, 1970.

Zhang Jiuling 張九齡. *Qujiang ji* 曲江集. Guangzhou: Guangdong Renmin chubanshe, 1986.

Zhang Lei 張耒. *Zhang Lei ji* 張耒集. Beijing: Zhonghua, 1990.

Zhang Taiyan 章太炎. *Zhang Taiyan quanji* 章太炎全集. Shanghai: Shanghai Renmin chubanshe, 1985.

———. *Zhang Taiyan zhenglun xuanji* 章太炎政論選集. Ed. Tang Zhijun 湯志鈞. Beijing: Zhonghua, 1977.

Zhang Tingyu 張廷玉. *Mingshi* 明史. Taipei: Dingwen shuju, 1980.

Zhang Weibo 張衛波. *Minguo chuqi zun Kong sichao yanjiu* 民國初期尊孔思潮研究. Beijing: Renmin jiaoju chubanshe, 2006.

Zhang Xiaoxiang 張孝祥. *Yuhu jushi wenji* 于湖居士文集. Ed. Xu Peng 徐鵬. Shanghai: Shanghai guji chubanshe, 1980.

Zhang Xuecheng 章學誠. *Wen shi tongyi jiaozhu* 文史通義校注. Taipei: Hanjing wenhua gongsi, 1986.

Zhang Zhijiang 張治江 and Li Fangyuan 李芳圓, eds. *Jidujiao wenhua* 基督教文化. Changchun: Changchun chubanshe, 1992.

Zhang Zuoyao 張作耀. *Dazai Kongzi* 大哉孔子. Hong Kong: Peace, 1991.

Zhao Bingwen 趙秉文. *Fu shui ji* 滏水集. In *Jingyin Wenyuange sikuquanshu* 景印文淵閣四庫全書, vol. 1190. Taipei: Commercial Press, 1983–1986.

Zhao Erxun 趙爾巽. *Qingshi gao* 清史稿. Ed. Qi Gong 啟功. Beijing: Zhonghua, 1994.

Zhao Yi 趙翼. *Gai yu congkao* 陔餘叢考. Taipei: Shijie shuju, 1960.

"Zhengling" 政令. In *Wushiwu nian dongzi di sishisi qi* 五十五年冬字第四十四期 44 (November 24, 1966). In *Taiwan sheng zhengfu gongbao* 臺灣省政府公報 (Nantou: Taiwan Provincial Government), 2.

Zhipan 志磐. *Fozu tongji* 佛祖統紀. In *Taisho Shinshu Daizokyo* 大正新修大藏經, vol. 49. 1924–1934. Reprint, Taipei: Xinwenfeng chuban gongsi, 1983.

Zhiqian 支謙, trans. *Fo shuo taizi ruiying benqi jing* 佛說太子瑞應本起經. In *Taisho Shinshu Daizokyo* 大正新修大藏經, vol. 3. 1924–1934. Reprint, Taipei: Xinwenfeng chuban gongsi, 1983.

Zhong Zhaopeng 鍾肇鵬. "Yi ruxue dai zongjiao" 以儒學代宗教. In *Feng Youlan xueji* 馮友蘭學記, ed. Wang Zhongjiang 王中江 and Gao Xiuchang 高秀昌, 82–90. Beijing: Joint Publishing, 1995.

Zhonggong yanjiu zazhishe bianweihui 中共研究雜誌社編委會, ed. *Zhonggong "pi Kong" ziliao xuanji* 中共「批孔」資料選輯. Taipei: Zhonggong yanjiu zazhishe, 1974.

Zhongguoshi xuehui 中國史學會 and Jian Bozan 翦伯贊, eds. *Wuxu bianfa* 戊戌變法. Shanghai: Shenzhou guoguang she, 1955.

Zhou Mi 周密. *Qidong yeyu* 齊東野語. Ed. Zhang Maopeng 張茂鵬. In *Jingyin Wenyuange sikuquanshu* 景印文淵閣四庫全書, vol. 865. Taipei: Commercial Press, 1983–1986.

Zhou Yutong 周予同. *Zhou Yutong jingxueshi lunzhu xuanji* 周予同經學史論著選集. Ed. Zhu Weizheng 朱維錚. Shanghai: Shanghai Renmin chubanshe, 1983.

Zhu Guozhen 朱國禎. *Yong chuang xiaopin* 湧幢小品. In *Biji xiaoshuo daguan* 筆記小說大觀, vol. 22, no. 7. Taipei: Xinxing shuju, 1984.

Zhu Jincheng 朱金城. *Bai Juyi ji jianjiao* 白居易集箋校. Shanghai: Shanghai guji chubanshe, 1988.

Zhu Silan 朱絲欄, ed. *Jiajing sidain kao* 嘉靖祀典考. Taipei: Institute of History and Philology, Academia Sinica, n.d.

Zhu Xi 朱熹. *Sishu zhangju jizhu* 四書章句集注. Beijing: Zhonghua, 1983.

——. *Zhuzi daquan* 朱子大全. (Published in Ming dynasty by Mr. Hu 胡氏.) In *Sibu beiyao, zibu* 四部備要·子部. Taipei: Taiwan Chung Hwa, 1965.

——. *Zhuzi wenji* 朱子文集. Ed. Chen Junmin 陳俊民. Taipei: Defu wenjiao jijinhui, 2000.

———. *Zhuzi yulei* 朱子語類. Ed. Li Jingde 黎靖德. Beijing: Zhonghua, 1986.

Zhu Yi 朱溢. "Tang zhi BeiSong shiqi de dasi, zhongsi he xiaosi" 唐至北宋時期的大祀、中祀和小祀. *Tsing Hua Journal of Chinese Studies* (*Hsinchu*) new series 39, no. 2 (2009): 287–324.

Zhu Yizun 朱彝尊. *Jingyi kao* 經義考. Taipei: Institute of Chinese Literature and Philosophy, Academia Sinica, 1997.

———. *Pushuting ji* 曝書亭集. Taipei: Shijie shuju, 1964.

Zhuang Chao 莊綽. *Jile bian* 雞肋編, ed. Xiao Luyang 蕭魯陽. Beijing: Zhonghua, 1983.

Index

Page numbers in *italics* refer to tables and figures.

Aleni, Guilio, 108
Analects (*Lunyu*), 61, 100, 111, 136, 140, 198, 215, 227; vernacular translation of, 177. *See also* Confucius
Antireligion League, 192
Antireligious Declaration, 193
Austin, John Langshaw, 227

Bao Jiao. *See* Protect the Cult
bayiwu. *See* Confucian rites, dances and vessels
beijiao (divine blocks), 178
Biyong (Royal Academy), 11, 69; in comparison to temple in Qufu, 8
Biyong (rites). *See* Confucian rites
Book of Documents (*Shangshu*), 10, 160
Book of Rites (*Liji*), 28, 111
Buddha (Gautama), 114, 123, 55, 66, 69, 70, 73, 153, 155, 158, 219
Buddhism, 48, 77, 78, 80, 175, 216, 217; anti-Buddhism, 74–75, 79;

bodhisattvas (*Fo pusa*), 80, 173, 218, 223; conflict with Daoism, 70–72; Huang-Lao (Yellow Emperor and Laozi) worship, 65–66, 67; iconography and relics, use of, 109, 114; integration with Daoism, 66–67, 70; introduction to China, 66; syncretism. *See* Three Religions

Cai Yuanpei, 62, 63, 183, 190–191, 192; on *Kongjiao* being read as a noun, 193, 215
Cao Cao, 69
Cao Yuanyong, 45, 203, 221
Catholicism, 101, 109, 118; iconoclasm, 116–117: influence in China, 187; and Reformation, 118, 119; relics, veneration of, 109–110; saints. *See* sainthood; Virgin Mary, 95, 118
Chan, Wing-tsit, 171, 194
Chen Baozhen, 182–183

[323]

Chen Duxiu, 62, 190, 200; abolition of Confucius temples and rites, 1, 86, 167, 191, 200; on *jiao* as teaching or education, 63, 193, 215

Chen Huanzhang, 59, 61, 184, 196; calling Confucius temples churches, 218; on *jiao* as religion, 63, 193, 215,

Cheng Minzheng, 102, 131, 159

Cheng Xu, 20, 140

Cheng Yi, 126, 138; critical evaluation of Xunzi and Yang Xiong, 157, 159

Chronicle of the Three Kingdoms (*Sanguo zhi*), 29

chuan Dao zhi shi (transmitting the Way). *See* Confucian enshrinement, criteria and standards

chuan jing zhi shi (transmitting the classics). *See* Confucian enshrinement, criteria and standards

ci xiansheng wen (Reporting to Confucius on the Discharge of Local Service), 223. *See* Confucian rites, rite of report

city god (*chenghuang*), 140

classics mat (*jingyan* [lectures for the emperor]), 19

Collected Debates on the Great Rites Controversy (*Dali jiyi*), 127. *See also* Great Rites Controversy

Confucian enshrinement (*congsizhi*), 3, 13, 43, 90, 150, 209; Confucian sages vs. Catholic saints, 89; correlative worship (*peixiang*), 14, 48, 50, 90, 96–97; criteria and standards, 93, 98, 209–210; criteria, court meeting (*tingyi*), 13, 18, 92–93; criteria, shift from emphasis on transmitting classics to the Way, 131; fluctuations, 15, 16–17, 44, 131; hierarchy, 15. *See also* correlative and subordinate worship; relationship with state education and imperial exams, 19, 50; restoration and reinstatement of, 27, 150–151, 211; social composition (of the enshrined), 100–103, *104*, 107; subordinate worship (*congsi*), 14, 15, 90, 96; placement in two galleries, 15; scholars (*xianru*), 15, 96; worthies (*xianxian*), 15, 96

Confucian rites, 19, 39, 46, 53; abolition of sacrifices, 222; assuming office, prior to, 23, 27, 46–48, 121–122, 223. *See also* Confucian rites, rite of report; Biyong (rite), 26, 27; cult of ritual propriety or teaching of rituals (*lijiao*), 62, 227; dances and vessels, 32, 43, 44, 129, 130–131, 132, 137, 138, 207, 208; decline of, 189, 206; exclusivity, 53–54, 55, 56, 107; father and son, principle of, 18, 128–129, 131, 133–134, 137–138; icons and iconoclasm, 39, 112, 113–114; icons, destroying and reduction of, 115–116; indifference, modern, 199, 200; *ku miao* (weep ritually), 19, 51, 109; rite of investiture (*shihe*), 50, 122; rite of libations (*shidian*), 28, 29–30 (merging with Biyong), 40; rite of report (*jigao*), 51–52, 223; sacrifices by (or on behalf of) the emperor, 9, 10–11, 23–24, 51; full sacrifice of an ox, sheep, and pig (*tailao*), 6, 23, 27, 29; sanctity of the body, 111; systemizing of, ix, 13, 27, 32–37, 51–52; veneration of Confucius (*ji Kong*), 10, 206

Confucianism: anti-Confucian movement, 1, 62, 183, 200. *See also Kongjiao*, countermovement against; denial of religiosity, 80, 194, 216–217; depoliticization, importance of, xi, 207–208; disenchantment, modern,

171; distinction from private religions, 172, 173–174; exclusivity, 79, 107–108, 173, 177 (on overcoming exclusivity), 181, 203–204, 223; exegesis, and, 63, 193, 196, 215, 217; as exterior religion, 77; *jingshi jimin* (manage the affairs of state and aid the people), 199; mass appeal, lack of, 174, 184, 205, 223; religiosity, ix, x, 54, 58, 62, 63–64, 85, 175, 195–196, 219. See also *Kongjiao*; secularization of, 188, 190, 192, 194–196, 216; as state cult, 60–61. See *Kongjiao*; state ideology and, 13, 68–69; Three Religions, as one of the, 53, 58–59, 217. See also Three Religions

Confucius (Kongzi 孔子), 61, 96, 178, 194; birthday as official holy day, 226; comparison to Socrates and religious leaders, 184, 188, 204, 205, 216; disciples, 15, 96, 159; posthumous title(s), 7, 30, 37, 39, 40, 43, 46, 130; removal of, 17, 43, 44, 115–116, 129, 131–133, 137, 145, 146; as prophetic figure or "king without title," 25, 68, 136; as religious founder, 216; as secular scholar, 185, 188–189, 215

Confucius cult, 59–60, 173–176, 181, 183, 195; abolition of unauthorized shrines, 178, 180; Christian influence, 177–179, 182–183; Church for Assisting the Sage, 177; Confucius society (*Kongshe*), 189; countermovement against, 61–62, 64, 185–187, 189–191; Cult of Confucius Association (*Kongjiao Hui*), 59, 61, 184, 190; failure as a movement, 184–185; as state religion, 179, 220

Confucius society (*Kongshe*), 189

Confucius temple(s) (*Kongzi miao*), 16 (illustration), 33, 47, 177, 202; abandonment, modern, 204; bribing for entry, 54, 204; destruction and reinstatement, 11–12; destruction of sculptures, 132; education function. See temple schools; exclusion of women, 53, 101, 180, 181; from family shrine to state temple, 4, 8, 22–23, 69; proliferation of, 11–12, 91–92, 202; reforms, 17, 132–133, 140–141, 146–147, 178; reform of 1530, 17, 42–43, 115, 125, 127, 134–139, 160–161; symbiotic relation with state power, 19, 20, 57, 202, 203, 221; as symbol (political legitimacy), 12, 13, 20; temple custodian, 26, 28, 30; temples of other religions, in comparison with, 80, 174, 204

Confucius temple, at Qufu (previously known as Queli), 8–9, *9* (figure); pilgrimages to, 23, 24, 28–29, 45, 46, 47, 54, 90, 140, 173–174, 222–223

correlative worship. See Confucian enshrinement

Cult of the Three Unified (*sanjiao heyi*), 81–83. See also Three Religions

dances (eight-row and six-row). See Confucian rites, dances and vessels

Dao (Way), 25, 41, 42, 47, 60, 66, 98, 140, 142, 144, 210

daotong (transmission and succession of the Way), 13, 125, 147, 209, 220

Daoism, 65, 66–67, 70, 71, 73, 80, 81, 217. See also Buddhism, integration with Daoism; Buddhism, conflict with Daoism; and Three Religions

Daoxue (School of the Way), 97, 256–258n37

Dashimans (Islamic mullahs), 78–79, 219, 294n

Debates on Ancient History (*Gushi bian*), 212
descendants (of Confucius). *See* Kong clan
Diexie (Jesus), 78, 219
Doctrine of the Mean (*Zhongyong*), 63, 139, 193, 215
Dong Zhongshu, 25
Du Xun (*Reading Xunzi*), 155–156
Du You, 51
Duke of Tai of Qi, 37–38
Duke of Yansheng, 141, 142, 190, 211. *See also* Kong Kejian, Kong Qingrong, and Xu Xixue
Duke of Zhou, 10, 72–73, 81, 155, 162, 238n55, 238n62; competition with Confucius as main ritual devotional figure, 33–36, 146–147; Temple for Rites to the, 113
Durkheim, Émile, 64, 213

Eastern Jin, 11–12; syncretism, beginnings of, 81
Eastern Jin emperor Xiaowu, 31; Second Confucius temple, construction of, 91; debate on ritual propriety, convened, 29, 32
Eastern Han emperor An, 14, 90
Eastern Han emperor Huan, 8, 25, 65–67
Eastern Han emperor Guangwu, 28, 31–32
Eastern Han emperor Ming, 10, 14, 26, 29, 48, 50, 66, 90, 237n33
Eastern Han emperor Zhang, 14, 29, 90
Eliade, Mircea, vii

Fei Mi, 147, 271–272n98
Feng Menglong, 80, 217
Feng Youlan, 87, 177, 188–189, 192, 224
fengsi jun (bestow an official title on Confucius's descendant), 6

Fingarette, Herbert, 227–228
Five Religions (*wuda zongjiao* [Buddhism, Daoism, Confucianism, Christianity, and Islam]), 219
Fu Qiu Shi (Tang Peng), 219
Fu Sinian (Fu Ssu-nien), 194
fusheng (third sage), 156

Gan Bao, 83
gao xiansheng wen (Reporting to Confucius), 121, 220, 223. *See* Confucian rites, before assuming office and rite of report
Ge Hong, 71, 73
Great Rites Controversy (*daliyi*), 43, 126–128, 266n11
Gu Jiegang, 185, 194, 212
Guan Yin, 226
Guan Yu, 224, 225, 226
Gujin xiaoshuo. *See* *Tales Old and New*
Guoxue. *See* National University
Guozijian. *See* National University
Gushi bian. *See* *Debates on Ancient History*

Han emperor Gaozu, 6, 24, 121
Han emperor Cheng, 7
Han emperor Wu, 68, 154
Han Fei, 24, 158
Han Yu, 37–38, 101, 152, 153, 154, 157, 158, 161; on Mencius as superior thinker to Xunzi; and Yang Xiong, 155–156
Heaven and Earth. *See* Qian Kun
homogeneity of *qi* (*qilei*), 120
Hu Juren, 161
Hu Shih, 62, 166, 192, 200
Huang Zunxian, 185, 187; call for the separation of church and state, 187–188
Huo Tao, 168

James, William, 213, 291n5
Jesuits, 182; modeling Confucian church after, 177
jigao (rite of report). *See* Confucian rites, rite of report
ji Kong. *See* Confucian rites, veneration of Confucius
ji Kong wen (Dedication to the Veneration of Confucius). *See* Confucian rites, veneration of Confucius
Ji Yun, 82, 164
Jianxu, 76
Jiajing Emperor. *See* Ming emperor Shizong
Jiang Shang, 33
jiao (teaching; religion), 188, 193, 215
jiaoyu (education). See *jiao*
jiaozhu (religion's founding masters), 74
Jinsi, 33
jisi (continuing the dynastic line). *See* Great Rites Controversy
jitong (continuing the imperial order). *See* Great Rites Controversy
Judaism, viii, 80, 229n3

Kang Youwei, 224; attribution of Christianity as pillar of the West, 60, 63, 182–183, 215; on Confucianism compared with other religions, 173, 174, 175; on Confucius as religious founder, 171, 216, 246n12; on exclusivity of Confucianism, 54; exile, 59; as founder of Confucius religion or state cult, 174. *See also* Confucius cult; Liang Qichao, falling out with. *See* Liang Qichao, defection from Kang Youwei; as the Martin Luther of the Confucius cult, 61, 175; on Mencius, 163, 169–170, 179; reforming Confucianism, 59–60, 86, 171, 279n4; ruined reputation, 60; sacred learning society, establishing, 176; writing Confucius veneration into constitution of the republic, 57
Kangxi Emperor, 21, 52, 148, 220, 271n95; augmenting temple rites, 45; calligraphy "teaching exemplar for ten thousand generations" (*wanshi shibiao*), 107, 220
keji (overcoming oneself), 197
King Pu, 138
Kong clan, 30–31, 201, 202, 208, 222; as cultural symbol, 10; descendants (*shengyi*), 4, 7, 49 (stone rubbing), 201, 221; hereditary titles, 24; major lineage (*dazong*), 7; minor lineage (*xiaozong*), 7
Kong Ji, 7
Kong Jifen, 22
Kong Kejian. 8, 141–142
Kongli. *See* Kong village
Kong Qingrong, 211
Kong Qiu, 70, 72,
Kong village (*Kongli*), 4, 6, 23
Kong Xian, 11, 30
Kong Yingda, 112
Kong Zan, 28
Kongzi. *See* Confucius
Kongjiao. *See* Confucius cult
Kongzi miao. *See* Confucius temple(s)
Kublai Khan, 79, 173
Kuixing, 123, 174, 181, 205–206, 225
Külüg Khan, 222

Lao Naixuan, 190
Laozi, 55, 56 (painting), 57, 65, 67, 70, 76, 153, 155, 181; incarnation as Buddha, 71–73, 74; Tang rulers as descendants of, 81

Laozi huahu jing (*Classic of Laozi's Transformation of Barbarians*), 72
Levenson, Joseph R., 198
li (principle), 148
li (ritual propriety), 86, 227
Li Ciming, 164
Li Daoyuan, 113
Li Dazhao, 193
Li Gong, 100, 151, 210, 277n79
Li Guan, 132, 135, 137, 146
Li Shu, 38, 144
Li Ting, 114
Li Wengang, 158
Li Zhi, 162
Lian Xixian, 79
Liang Fa, 225
Liang Qichao: anti-Xunzi discourse, 165–166 ; Christianity as anachronistic force, 63, 194, 215; Confucius as secular leader, 215–216; defection from Kang Youwei, 61, 171, 186–187, 282n44; early advocate of protect the cult movement, 60–61; on popular religion and worship, 123, 174, 205, 225; on saving the nation, 186, 188
Liang Shuming, 192, 195, 197, 227; castigating Kang Youwei, 283n1
Liao Ping, 25
Lidai diwang miao. See Temple of Kings and Emperors
lijiao. See Confucian rites, teaching of rituals
Lin Biao, 200
Lin Tingkan, 163
Lingyin Monastery, 199
Liu Shipei, 185
Liu Xin, 35
liuyiwu. See Confucian rites, dances and vessels
lixue (School of Principle), 114

Lord Guan (Yu), 226
Lu Ban, 108, 178, 181, 226
Lu Guimeng, 160
Lu Jiuyuan, 98
Lu Na, 32
Lu Xun, 123, 184, 194, 204–205
Lü Kun, 147–148
Lü Wang, 70
Luo Changyuan, 47
Luo Qinshun, 161
Luo Zu, 226

Ma Yuan, 55, 83. See also Three Religions, *Portrait of the Cult of the Three Unified*
Mao Qiling, 127
martial temple (*Wu miao*), 37–38, 52, 145, 224, 230n2
Mei Fu, 7
memorial tablets (*muzhu*), 114
Mencius (Mengzi), 116, 134, 200; as correlate, 42, 142, 152, 154; thinking in contrast with Xunzi, 152, 155–156, 160, 163, 166, 168–169, 170, 210; Cheng-Zhu interpretation, 157–158
Mencius, 154; Ming Taizu's interpretation, 42, 142
miao xue ji. See Record of the Temple Schools
Ming emperor Chengzu (Yongle), 120, 222
Ming emperor Shizong (Jiajing), 17, 44, 125, 134–135, 145, 205, 222; vetoing enshrinement of Xue Xuan, 18, 93
Ming emperor Sizong, 223
Ming emperor Wuzong, 19, 126, 222
Ming Taizu, 41, 81, 130, 221; addressing Kong Kejian about his duty, 8, 141–142; using scholars to pacify the people, 20

mingfen, 138
Minglun dadian (*Great Statutes of Ming Ethics*), 127
Mishihe (Messiah), 78, 219
Möngke Khan, 78, 219
Mou Zhongjian, 195
Mou Zongsan, 87, 167, 195–196
Mouzi, 70
Mozi, 6, 24, 71, 152
music (*yue*), 227

National University, 26, 29, 30, 33, 44, 50, 113–114, 122, 140; opening up to public, recommendation to, 19, 54, 204
New Confucians, 87, 168, 196, 197, 198, 227
Nietzsche, Friedrich, 214
Northern Wei emperor Xiaowen, 12, 31, 52–53
Northern Zhou emperor Wu, 75

Ouyang Xiu, 40, 131, 267n21

Pan Ni, 114
Pang Zhonglu, 164
Pei Kan: on preeminence of relation between father and son, 18, 133
Pi Xirui, 35
Prince Liu De of Hejian, 103
Protect the Cult (*Bao Jiao*), 59, 61
Puyuan debates, 126, 131, 138

Qian Daxin, 164
Qian Kun (Heaven and Earth), 220
Qian Tang, 42, 140, 142
Qin emperor Shihuang, 6, 24
Qin Huitian, 122, 144–145, 172–173, 223
Qing emperor Qianlong (Gaozong), 15, 45, 52, 226

Qing emperor Shengzu. *See* Kangxi Emperor
Qing emperor Shizong. *See* Yongzheng Emperor
Qingzhen temples, 80, 218
Qisheng ci. *See* Shrine of Giving Birth to the Sage
Qisheng wang ci, 134
Qiu Jun, 114, 130
qizhi (physical constitution), 164
Qu Jiusi, 15, 143, 267n28
Queli. *See* Confucius temple, at Qufu
Qufu. *See* Confucius temple, at Qufu

Record of the Rebuilding of Qingzhen Temples, 80
Record of the Temple Schools (*miao xue ji*), 121
religious syncretism. *See* Three Religions
ren (humaneness), 38, 86, 163, 197, 227; New Confucians and valuation over *li* (ritual or propriety), 198, 226, 227
renxue (The Learning of Ren [humanness]), 226
Ricci, Matteo, 58
rites, imperial system of: hierarchy and categories, 28, 37; integration of Confucian system, 52; *Rites of Zhou* (*Zhouli*), 28, 147; use of ritual vessels, 43
Royal Academy. *See* Biyong
rujia (Confucian, Confucianism), 59, 195
Rujiao (Confucius religion). *See Kongjiao*

sage (*shengxian*), 89, 218; ten philosophers (*shizhe*), 15, 96. *See also* Confucian enshrinement
sage's temples (*sheng miao*), 218. *See also* Confucius temples

INDEX [329]

Sanguo zhi. See Chronicle of the Three
  Kingdoms
saint (*shengtu*), 89. See also sainthood
sainthood, 90–91, 93–94; criteria and
  standards for canonization, 98–100;
  differentiation of *sancti* and *beati*, 95;
  Jesus's twelve apostles, 96; social
  composition, 105, *106*, 107, 223
Shangshu. See Book of Documents
Shen Buhai, 158, 166
Shen Defu, 137
Shen Li, 18
Shuyu (Duke of Tang's grandson), 33
Shengmen shiye tu (Genealogical Diagram
  of the Sage's School), 158
Shengrong halls, 80, 218
scholar-officials (*shi*), 162, 210, 222, 223
shi (political power), 148, 203–204
Shi Chen, 27
shidian. See Confucian rites, rite of
  libations
shihe. See Confucian rites, rite of
  investiture
Shrine of Giving Birth to the Sage
  (*Qisheng ci*), 17, 43, 131, 267n28
Shrine to the Five Worthies
  (*Wuxiantang*), 155
Shuliang He (Father Kong), 95, 128,
  129, 132
Shuijing zhu, 113
sipei (four distinguished disciples), 15, 96
Si River, 22
Sima Guang, 126
Sima Qian, 154, 169; on Confucius, 23,
  25, 96; eyewitness to Confucius
  temple, 6, 23
Song emperor Gaozong, 47
Song Yingzong, 138
Song Lian, 115, 133, 141, 146, 159,
  270n71
Song Shu, 176–177

stele (and inscriptions), 25–26, 27, 46, 67,
  68, 101, 115, 121, 220; Dismounting
  stele, 5, 45
Su Shi, 114, 160
subordinate worship. See Confucian
  enshrinement
Sun Chuo, 81
Sun Fu, 83

Taigong Wang, 144–145
tailao. See Confucian rites, full sacrifice
  of an ox, sheep, and pig
Taishang Laojun, 80, 217
Taixue. See National University
Tales Old and New (*Gujin xiaoshuo*), 80,
  217
Tan Sitong, 165, 174, 226
Tang emperor Gaozong, 34
Tang emperor Taizong, 12, 30, 34, 50,
  92, 96, 202, 252n102
Tang emperor Xuanzong, 14, 36, 37, 81,
  90, 136, 232n47
Tang Junyi, 195
Tang Zhen, 77
Tao Dalin, 14
Temple Hall of Great Completion
  (*Dacheng dian*), 39, 80, 131, 218;
  renamed *Qisheng ci* (Shrine of Giving
  Birth to the Sage), 43, 131–132. See
  also Confucian temples; Shrine of
  Giving Birth to the Sage
Temple of Kings and Emperors (*Lidai
  diwang miao*), 143
Temple of the King of Military
  Accomplishment (*Wuchengwang miao*),
  144
temple schools, 40, 120, 123, 173, 177,
  218; development (merging of
  Confucius temple and academies), 11,
  12, 30
Temür Khan, 21, 221

Three Dynasties (*sandai*), 219
Three Religions (*sanjiao* [Buddhism, Confucianism, and Daoism]), 55, 58–59, 66–67, 69–69, 73–74, 78, 81–82, 84, 218, 223; analogies describing, 78; debates and disputes among, 70–72, 75–76, 84; persecution and regulation of, 74–75; *Portrait of the Cult of the Three Unified*, by Ma Yuan (Song) (*Sanjiao tu*), 55, 57, 83; portrayal in literary texts, 79–80, 82, 83; Ting Yun-peng's painting of Confucius, Laozi, and Buddhist arhat (Ming), 56
Three Teachings. *See* Three Religions
Three Unified (*Sanyi jiao*), 81–82. *See* Three Religions
tianming (Heaven's mandate), 221
tingyi. *See* Confucian enshriment, court meeting
tongtian zhu (the pillar to the Heavens), 207
Tu Weiming, 196

Wang Anshi (King of Shu or Shu-wang), 17, 40, 156, 157–158, 233n53
Wang Chong, 25
Wang Fu, 72
Wang Jian, 32
Wang Mang. 7, 30, 130, 157, 158
Wang Pang, 233n53
Wang Shizhen, 92, 93, 116
Wang Tung, 158
Wang Xisun, 164
Wang Yangming, 82, 163, 206, 256–257n37; enshrinement of, 13–14
Wang Yi, 159
Wang Zhong, 154, 162, 164
wanshi shibiao (exemplar of teachers for ten thousand generations). *See* Kangxi Emperor

Weber, Max, 85, 88, 120, 213–214
Wei emperor Wen, 11, 30, 67, 69, 91, 113, 221
Wenchang, 123, 174, 205, 225
Wenchang shrine, 205
Wenchang temple, 224
wenmiao (temple of culture), 38, 127–128, 204, 224. *See also* Confucius temple
Wenmiao sidian kao (*A Study of Confucian Temple Rites and Rituals*), 212
Wen Yanbo, 47
Wei Yuan, 52
Wittgenstein, Ludwig: family resemblance, ix, 120, 214, 264n158
Wu Chen, 130, 146
Wu Cheng, 17, 233n54
Wu Pei, 181
Wu Yu, 62, 166, 200
Wuchengwang miao. *See* Temple of the King of Military Accomplishment
Wuxiantang. *See* Shrine to the Five Worthies

Xiang jiao (icon religion), 114. *See also* Buddhism
xianru (Confucian scholars). *See* Confucian enshrinement, subordinate worship
xiansheng (first sage), 144, 146
xianshi (master, referring to Confucius), 146
xianxian (Confucian worthies). *See* Confucian enshrinement, subordinate worship
xianxue (prominent learning), 6, 12
Xiao He, 108
Xiaojing (*Classic of Filial Piety*), 81, 97, 111; vernacular translation of, 177
Xie Youwei, 192
xinxue (New School), 97
Xiong He, 13, 131, 146, 158, 167, 271n97

Xiong Shili, 192
xiucai (scholar), 78, 219
Xu Fuguan, 195
Xu Gan, 155
Xu Jie, 132–133, 134
Xu Xixue, 141, 142
Xuanyuan. See Yellow Emperor
xue gong (the palace of learning), 218. See also temple schools
Xue ji (Records of Academies and Temple Schools), 220
Xue Xuan, 18, 93, 98, 168, 233n62
Xun Kuang. See Xunzi
Xun Qing. See Xunzi
Xunzi, 149, 151, 152, 153; from decline to expulsion as correlate, 157–160; on human nature, 153–154, 157, 158, 159, 161, 163, 164, 169; in juxtaposition with Mencius, 155–156, 163, 210; modern reinstatement as correlate, 168–170, 210–211; New Text attacks, 165, 166; Qing revival of, 161–165; teacher of Li Si, 160–161, 165
Xunzi, 111, 154–155, 161–162

Yan Fu, 173, 186, 223
Yan Kejun, 163–164
Yan Ruoqu, 163
Yan Yuan (Confucius's disciple), 29, 72, 114, 253n128, 289n2
Yan Yuan (Qing scholar), 100, 151, 210, 277n79
Yan Hui, 2, 14, 17, 34, 36, 43, 50, 128, 156, 224, 249–50n61
Yanzi, 2, 90, 114, 152
Yang Jing, 154
Yang Shen, 134
Yang Xiong, 152, 155, 157–159
Yao Chen, 163–164
yasheng (second sage), 156

Ye Dehui, 123, 177, 178, 185
ye xiansheng wen (On Paying a Visit to Confucius), 223. See also Confucian rites, before assuming office and rite of report
Yellow Emperor, 65, 108, 146, 269–270n70
Yelü Chucai, 77
Yesou puyan (Humble Words of a Rustic Elder), 79
yi xi (barbarian custom), 115
yiduan (heterodoxies), 164
yili (moral principles), 164
Yisileye halls, 80, 218
Yongzheng Emperor (Shizong), 17, 20, 45, 59, 82, 205, 221, 226; lambasting Ming emperor Shizong, 44
Yu Ying-shih, 196
Yu Yue, 169
Yuan Dao (Seeking the Origin of the Way), 155
Yuan emperor Chengzong. See Temür Khan
Yuan emperor Xianzong. See Möngke Khan
Yuan emperor Shizu. See Kublai Khan
Yuan emperor Wuzong. See Külüg Khan
Yuan Shikai, 62, 151, 178, 191, 201
Yue (Guangdong), 123, 205, 225
Yuhuang halls, 80, 218
Yushitai (Censorate), 179

Zeng Sen, 17, 18, 128, 134
Zhang Cong, 128–129, 130, 133, 135
Zhang Dai, 46, 54, 174, 204
Zhang Dehui, 79
Zhang Dongsun, 190
Zhang Jiugong, 159–160
Zhang Taiyan, 61, 64, 107–108, 166, 185, 277n78

Zhang Xiaoxiang, 48
Zhang Xun, 60, 189, 201
Zhang Zai, 158
Zhao Bingwen, 170
Zhao Meng, 116, 201
Zhao Qi, 154
Zheng Kongzi sidian shenji (Extensive Record of the Corrected Sacrifice to Confucius), 135, 136, 139
Zheng Kongzi sidian shuo (Explanation of the Corrected Sacrifice to Confucius), 135
Zheng Xuan, 28, 33
zhisheng (the supreme sage), 34
zhitong (the tradition of legitimate governance), 125
zhiyong (apply and use tradition), 63, 194, 215
Zhonglun, 155
Zhongni. See Confucius
Zhongyong. See *Doctrine of the Mean*
Zhipan (monk), 55, 83
Zhiqian, 73
Zhou Huanshu, 177
Zhou Shuangxi, 48, 121–122

Zhou Yutong, 189
Zhouli. See *Rites of Zhou*.
Zhu Guozhen, 54, 173–174, 204
Zhu Lang, 115
Zhu Lu yitong (Similarities and Differences Between Chu and Lu), 164
Zhu Xi, 3, 48, 114, 120, 157–158, 210, 223, 256n37
Zhu Yuanzhang, 221. See also Ming Taizu
zi zun fu bei (revering the son and humbling the father). See Confucian rites, principle of father and son
Zigong, 22
Zilu, 114, 179, 224, 281n31
Zisi, 24, 128, 134, 153, 159
Zitong miao (temples), 205, 224
Ziyu, 224
Zizhang, 224, 226
zongjiao (religion): negative connotation, 191–192, 217; religious toleration, 81. See also *jiao*
zongmiao (royal clan temple), 19

GPSR Authorized Representative: Easy Access System Europe, Mustamäe tee
50, 10621 Tallinn, Estonia, gpsr.requests@easproject.com

www.ingramcontent.com/pod-product-compliance
Lightning Source LLC
Chambersburg PA
CBHW021933290426
44108CB00012B/819